Presentation and Analysis
of Financial Management
Information

2ND edition

By Jay D. Kenton

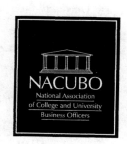

NACUBO
National Association
of College and University
Business Officers

National Association of
College and University Business Officers

Washington, DC

www.nacubo.org

Printed in the United States of America
ISBN 1-56972-021-5

TABLE OF CONTENTS

EXHIBITS

ACKNOWLEDGMENTS

I would like to recognize the many contributions without which this manuscript would not have been completed. Many individuals assisted with this endeavor by providing information, reviewing drafts, or providing exhibits and other materials.

I would like to begin by thanking Ron Smith, vice president for finance at Berea College for providing the framework and introductory materials for this manuscript. Ron's work formed the foundation upon which the balance of this text was built.

I would also like to recognize Tom Anderes, Mike Green, and Gary Rogers of the Oregon University System (OUS) for allowing me to use the OUS financial reports in this text. Similarly, I would also like to thank Randy Livingston, vice president of business affairs and CFO at Stanford University, and Timothy Shad, vice president for finance at Grand Valley State University, for allowing me to use their annual financial reports as appendices to this text. A special appreciation goes to Ed Poppell, vice president at University of Florida for permitting me to use the many management reports from their Web site; the University of Florida maintains one of the most comprehensive Web sites containing financial management information that I have encountered.

I would like to thank the staff of Portland State University's (PSU) Office of Institutional Research and Planning for providing many exhibits. This office, directed by Kathi Ketcheson, and staffed by David Burgess, Jolliet Storing, and Lina Lu was most helpful throughout the process of writing this text. Other individuals who deserve recognition at PSU, include George Persteiner, vice president of finance and administration; Brian Chase, director of facilities; Dee Wendler, director of business affairs; Pat Soto, bursar; John Fowler, director of campus public safety; Judy Ngai, senior financial analyst; Alan Kolibaba, financial analyst; and Tom Palm, faculty emeritus. The contributions and assistance provided by this group of colleagues was critical to the development of this material.

I would also like to express my gratitude to Michael Carbine, editor extraordinaire for his patience and persistence in helping make my unrefined drafts into something useable. I also want to recognize two individuals who reviewed drafts of this text. Gina Kranitz, president of Paradise Valley Community College, and Charles Tegan, comptroller at Clemson University, offered valuable insights and comments that substantially improved my draft materials.

Finally, I would like to acknowledge and thank both Donna Klinger and Elissa Fitzgerald of the National Association of College and University Business Officers (NACUBO) for the assistance they provided throughout the development of this manuscript. Without the contributions of these many individuals this work would not have been completed.

Jay Kenton
June 2002

PREFACE

To many individuals, a college or university's financial statements or annual reports are the most identifiable type of management report; with the increasing complexity of college and university operations, a need for additional and various types of management reports has developed. Governing boards are not just interested in financial information but in information on enrollment projections, endowment management, student recruitment and retention, and myriad other topics. Increased concern over the cost of higher education has prompted colleges and universities to provide additional information on the relationship of the cost of higher education to services and programs provided. Similarly, increasing competition for students, faculty, and resources have necessitated that universities and colleges manage their affairs more effectively. These trends coupled with improved information processing capabilities has provided the stimulus for many colleges and universities to better understand and analyze financial management information as a strategic resource for the enterprise.

Presentation and Analysis of Financial Management Information, now updated in a second edition, was written to assist financial and other managers of colleges and universities in identifying and responding to the needs of individuals and groups requesting management information. *Presentation and Analysis of Financial Management Information* focuses on effective communication in institutional management, specifically in colleges and universities. A productive management report is informative, succinct, and relevant. This book attempts to facilitate the communication process through management reports.

It is important to view communication in a holistic context. Communication is more than just collecting and recording data; for communication to be effective, data must be analyzed and interpreted. Interpretation is the basis for management reporting and presentation. Strategic considerations, or the ways that information can be used to facilitate decision making, should dictate how information is arrayed and the order in which it is presented. Comparing standard information against similar information from peer institutions and other examples of contrasting information against benchmark data are provided to facilitate the understanding and meaningfulness of information being presented. The approach used in this book is based on strategic considerations, not on the random compilation of data into report formats.

In addition to guidance on report preparation and data analysis, *Presentation and Analysis of Financial Management Information* provides guidance on effective presentation techniques, on how to analyze and present information, and on how to assess the adequacy of existing reports and reporting practices. Model report formats are presented to facilitate this process.

CHAPTER 1
THE NATURE AND ROLE OF FINANCIAL MANAGEMENT INFORMATION

According to Jody Blazek, author of *Financial Planning for Nonprofit Organizations*, financial management is "the administration of financial affairs through planning, budgeting, recording, reporting, and analyzing an entity's flow of funds. It can also mean safeguarding the resources or properties owned by the organization, using the funds for the purposes to which they were dedicated, accumulating necessary information concerning work performed, and submitting whatever reports are required by funders and governmental authorities" (1996, p. 3). Thus, the term encompasses a broad range of activities and purposes.

Throughout this book, financial management information will include basic financial information as well as productivity reports that are not necessarily measured in monetary terms. The latter constitute units of production which create value or costs for the institution, since they represent methods by which colleges and universities attract and retain faculty, students, financial resources, and political support. As a result, it is important to report these types of value- and cost-adding activities in addition to basic financial information.

CHARACTERISTICS OF USEFUL MANAGEMENT INFORMATION

James A. Hyatt writes, "a key characteristic of good management information is the ability to communicate in a clear and concise manner. Such communication should seek to inform and facilitate decision-making. Unfortunately, many financial managers and other administrators lack or fail to exercise good communication skills" (1989, p. xiii). Management information should also facilitate a deeper understanding of the enterprise and the opportunities, challenges, and risks inherent in its operations. Many of those engaged in college and university finance may lack exposure to, experience with, and a fundamental understanding of the scope and complexity of the activities of the faculty as well as with their attitudes, beliefs, and values. While colleges and universities engage primarily in instructional, research, and service activities, many secondary, or auxiliary, activities are important as well. Thus, financial management information should inform readers about both the primary and secondary activities of the institution.

This book discusses the analysis and presentation of financial management information from the perspective of college and university administrators. Executive administrators and board members are accountable to a number of stakeholders and constituents, all requiring financial information with different degrees of complexity. Similarly, other college and university administrators are accountable to a diverse clientele, including faculty, students, parents, legislative leaders, board members, and the general public. The analysis and presentation of financial information should take into account the perspective of these stakeholders, as well as the reasons why the information is being analyzed and presented.

PURPOSES OF FINANCIAL MANAGEMENT INFORMATION

The goal of managerial financial reporting is to evaluate and measure institutional, financial, and managerial performance. In addition, and perhaps most importantly, financial management information is used to enhance the effectiveness of institutional decision-making and to facilitate goal setting, thereby enabling the institution to excel in achieving its mission(s). Beyond these basic purposes, financial management information and reporting also are used to help the institution:

- maintain control of institutional finances and other institutional services;
- define accountability for specific initiatives and responsibilities;
- maintain compliance with established standards and regulations; and
- enhance communications regarding important initiatives, objectives, and goals of the institution.

CONSIDERATIONS IN FINANCIAL MANAGEMENT INFORMATION REPORTING

Factors to be considered in financial management information reporting include the types of information being reported, time frames for reporting, and the recipients of these reports and their levels of sophistication.

Types of financial management information reported:

- Sources of funding
- Uses of funding
- Reports of financial condition at given points in time
- Ratios of costs to benefits, or costs/revenues per unit
- Measures of achievement or performance for a specified period of time
- Comparisons with other peer institutions regarding pricing, costs, performance, productivity, etc.
- Status reports regarding condition of facilities, use of facilities, inventory levels, contingent liabilities, and other factors that can affect an institution's competitiveness, reputation, financial planning, or other management concerns.

Time frames for financial management reporting:

- A single or a multiple month(s)/year(s) of historical information—some information may be needed based on fiscal year, calendar year, or project year, if different (e.g., grants and contracts, construction projects, etc.)
- Forecasts of future resource: availability and requirements
- A combination of past and future periods

Recipients of financial management information:

- Internal users (Note: Board members typically are considered to be internal users)
- External users

Recipients' level of sophistication and knowledge of the enterprise:

- High degree of sophistication and extensive knowledge about the enterprise
- Moderate degree of sophistication and a general understanding of the enterprise
- Low degree of sophistication and little or no knowledge of the enterprise

SOURCES OF FINANCIAL MANAGEMENT INFORMATION

Financial management information is typically stored in an electronic format as part of an institution's management information system. Some financial management information may need to be collected manually, however, much information is readily accessible in electronic format. Some systems, especially the newer generations of information systems, are more user-friendly than older

generation systems. Some systems require technical experts to extract information, while others provide non-sophisticated users with the capability of easily downloading or extracting information for subsequent manipulation and reporting. The type of system used by an institution can either facilitate or inhibit the presentation and analysis of financial management information. Obviously, systems requiring specialized staff may result in more costly and more limited information. This should be a consideration when deciding to purchase and/or upgrade a financial management information system.

User needs also should be an important consideration when purchasing and/or upgrading financial management information systems. User needs will drive decisions regarding the chart of accounts, data definitions, and transaction processing requirements. Most financial information systems function with fund, organization, program, account (or object), activity, and location features in the chart of accounts. Similarly, data need to be defined in such a way as to ensure consistent treatment of similar transactions and to ensure that financial controls can be maintained. Implementation processes must ensure that transaction processing requirements are easily understood, are efficient, and will provide the source data that users need to obtain meaningful financial management reports. In many ways, these decisions are just as important as the type of software to use for financial management reporting, because even the best software may fail to meet management reporting needs if these factors are not adequately addressed in the formulative stage of any implementation.

To make decisions concerning costs associated with upgrading computer systems, managers need information about the age and current capability of the present inventory of systems. Accrediting bodies request information so they can determine whether the institution has the capacity to offer quality programs given the faculty-student ratio, availability of funds for research and service, and other issues. When making upgrade decisions, ask if the system contains the essential data elements for critical management reporting, since the cost of not having this critical information should be considered in this decision.

Financial management information is derived from the following systems or records:

- Financial information systems
  - General ledger/balance sheet (real accounts)
    - Assets
    - Liabilities
    - Net assets, also referred to as reserves and previously referred to as fund balances
  - Operating ledger/operating statements (nominal accounts)

- Budgets (also sometimes available from unique budget information systems)
  - Revenues
  - Expenses
  - Encumbrances
- Human resource information systems
  - Job/position information
  - Employee records and information
  - Payroll information
  - Benefits/perquisites information
  - Leave information
- Student information systems
  - Student demographic information, course registration and transcript information, etc.
  - Course information, offerings, instructors, location, etc.
  - Degrees granted—level, type, number
  - Student types—levels, sex, age, number, residency, etc.
  - Admissions data—applications/matriculation information
  - Fees assessed and collected, including accounts receivable amounts
- Financial aid administrative systems
  - Aid awarded by type and amount
  - Aid disbursed by type and amount
  - Applicant/recipient information
- Development systems
  - Donations by type/amount
  - Pledges receivable
  - Donor information
- Facility information
  - Building attributes—age, composition, number, type, square feet, etc.
  - Type of space—by use and function
  - Maintenance records
- Other:
  - Investments
  - Equipment records
  - Inventory records
  - Debt records

NEED FOR FINANCIAL MANAGEMENT INFORMATION

Financial management information should be presented and analyzed in such a way that it can be used as:

1. a management tool to evaluate performance and establish institutional goals;
2. a communication tool; and
3. a tool to inform and facilitate decision-making.

As a management tool, financial management information can be used to measure the progress of an institution, college, program, or project. For example, if the institution's strategic plan assigns a high priority to launching an aggressive capital development program, the institution must be able to show that progress has been made in building its net assets if it wants to position the institution's credit rating in the most favorable light for rating agencies. For this example, a two-year schedule is set to build the net assets by 5 percent per year. In this situation, higher education administrators must be able to develop a reporting model that provides timely information on those areas of the institution in which thresholds have not been met.

A second example is measuring expenses and matching them with revenues generated by particular programs. The criteria for measuring the expenses may be determined by the institution's executive management, or by legislative mandate, or it may be specified by donors. But regardless of source of the mandate, results must be measured and reported in a manner that addresses the objectives of the analysis. In addition, it may be important to measure a program's performance in relation to expectations, including generating information on whether resources were allocated to the program properly, if the resources were sufficient for program operation, and whether the program met its expected goals.

Financial management information can also be used as a ***communication tool*** to set goals or expectations or describe the impact of particular management decisions to those inside and outside the institution. For example, if a strategic plan includes acquiring a new administrative computing system for campus operations, a budget and time schedule must be established that fits within the project plan and available resources. The time schedule and budget must first be communicated to all pertinent campus administrators in order to define the necessary action steps and create an understanding of the level of resources available for the project. During the life of the project, progress on system implementation should be communicated on a timely and frequent basis. Part of this includes reporting on the amount of financial resources expended versus the anticipated budget.

Finally, financial information can be presented to ***inform and facilitate decision-making.*** For example, assume that a board of trustees is trying to determine how best to distribute salary increments to the faculty population. Information can be developed and presented to contrast current salaries to salaries being paid at peer institutions. In this case, a comparison by discipline and rank at the comparator institutions would provide meaningful information to facilitate reaching a decision.

DESIRABLE QUALITIES OF FINANCIAL MANAGEMENT INFORMATION

Financial management information must be *clear, concise, and meaningful.* For many, the problem is not a lack of information, but too much information. It is difficult to sift through reams of data looking for the few nuggets of truly meaningful and valuable information. Many executives work under severe time constraints, so it is imperative that information be summarized and presented in a concise and cogent manner.

To be useful for decision making and other management purposes, financial management information should contain certain characteristics. These characteristics, discussed below, take on added importance in light of the growing demands for accountability by governmental agencies, governing boards, and the general public, and the fact that these demands are altering the content of, and the way college and university administrators and their institutions present, financial management information.

The information provided must be *audience-appropriate,* i.e., it should be understandable to the receiver. To do this, consider the audience and whether it is able to evaluate the complexities of the information. It also must be *relevant.* The information must answer the question being asked or address the point being made. Providing superfluous or irrelevant information increases the probability that the audience will miss the point, and this will likely result in greater confusion and lack of action. The information should be presented in as *brief* a format as possible. But the presentation should not be so brief as to sacrifice audience understanding. At the executive level, it is often desirable to provide a brief summary of the information accompanied by the full, detailed report so the manager can examine the details as necessary. Also, when preparing reports, remember that graphs, charts, and diagrams often make a point more effectively and more efficiently than text.

The information also should be *complete.* Present the negatives along with the positives to avoid leading the audience to false conclusions or misrepresenting the information being conveyed. These elements combine to determine the *usefulness* of information. Too frequently, a large amount of effort and resources is put into providing information that is thrown away or sits on a shelf with no consideration. The information must be *accurate* and

timely if it is to be useful in making decisions. If the information is to be used in making comparisons with prior time periods or other institutions, it must be *consistent,* i.e., prepared using the same method and reflecting the same sets of assumptions throughout. If information needed to make meaningful comparisons is unavailable, the provider of the information should include caveats and other cautions about using the information to make accurate comparisons.

Many states mandate that public agencies maintain records that can be readily accessed by the public. In this case, *accessibility* is important. But this must be balanced with confidentiality in certain situations. Some types of information may be in the public domain and can therefore be openly shared and reported. Other information, however, will be considered private or confidential with limits on its uses and release. For example, the Family Education Rights and Privacy Act of 1974 (FERPA) precludes the release of certain information pertaining to students. In other cases, donors may wish to remain anonymous for various reasons. Such issues must be considered in preparing and presenting financial management information, especially if the target audience is external to the institution. This becomes a critical issue given the fact that the Internet enables large amounts of information to be accessible via Web sites and other accessible forms. It is not uncommon to find volumes of data about an institution's finances and activities posted on its Web site. Take care to ensure that the confidentiality of this and other appropriate information is protected by developing safeguards against inappropriate release of confidential information.

RECIPIENTS OF FINANCIAL MANAGEMENT INFORMATION

Financial management information is used by internal and/or external audiences. Internal users include institutional managers (administrators, college business officers, etc.), faculty, staff, students, and governing boards. These users typically are interested in using the information as a managerial tool. The information is used to make decisions regarding critical projects or events, set goals, measure a project's progress, benchmark an activity's performance, or determine the adequacy of a resource commitment.

External constituents include people or organizations affiliated with, but not an integral part of, the day-to-day operations of the institution. Examples include state and federal governmental agencies and legislative bodies; rating agencies; investment bankers; bond counsel; external investors; donors; alumni; taxpayers; vendors; business partners; accrediting agencies; and other institutions and organizations. Information provided to external audiences typically presents explanations and fulfills the need for accountability; in some cases, it is used to create an understanding of an institution's programs, projects, or other institutional initiatives that are important to the external users.

SUMMARY

Financial management information is used for many purposes within an organization including maintaining financial control; defining accountability and responsibility; maintaining compliance with established standards and regulations; and enhancing communications regarding important initiatives. Financial management information should be presented and analyzed in such a way that it can be used as a management tool to evaluate perform-ance, to aid communication, and to inform and facilitate decision-making. To be useful, presenters of financial management information should consider the types of information to present, time frames for reporting, and the recipients of this information and their level of sophistication. Financial management information should have the following attributes: clear, concise, meaningful, audience appropriate, relevant, brief, complete, useful, accurate, timely, consistent, and accessible.

The next chapter will discuss the importance of monitoring and reporting financial management information, including the reasons why this reporting is essential to effective management of higher education institutions.

CHAPTER 2
IMPORTANCE OF MONITORING AND REPORTING

Most financial management reports are used to help college and university managers make decisions, set goals, and evaluate the performance of the entity being analyzed. At the executive level, reporting requirements assume a multitude of purposes and forms. Internally, reports are used to measure the institution's performance as well as provide managerial control information, such as budget to actual analyses. Externally, reports are used to evaluate the effectiveness of the institution and its capacity for sustaining future actions. External entities interested in college and university financial management reports include bond and credit rating agencies, donors, legislative committees, accrediting bodies, and parents of prospective students.

In addition to generating traditional financial and management information, higher education is now changing the emphasis of how it reports and markets its product, and is reporting economic and social impact statistics as well. Several national issues are responsible for this shift, including:

- public and governmental attitudes that the cost of education is too high;

- competition among institutions for students;

- comparisons to other institutions, such as in benchmarking studies and in publications, including *U.S. News and World Report's* rankings on institutional quality;

- performance funding initiatives prompted by state legislators;

- growing awareness of higher education's impact on the economy;

- increasing government reporting and compliance issues;

- national and international competition for faculty and research funding; and

- increasing pressure for philanthropic and other private sources of financial support.

These changes are reflected in the strategic plans and goals of institutions. Greater emphasis is being placed on distance learning (including technology-based instruction), the diversity of the student and faculty population, the price and quality of programs being offered, and external research and fund raising. Reports are being generated for such external constituents as legislative committees, public constituents, and governmental agencies, and these reports need to address the resources and expenditures devoted to efforts tied to access and diversity, as well as the relationship of higher education to economic development. Internally, more effort will be directed at evaluating the cost and demand of programs and success at generating alternative forms of financial support for the institution.

COST AND ACCOUNTABILITY PRESSURES AND DEMANDS

Over the past few years, the public has become increasingly critical of the cost of higher education, with the perception that the price is too high compared to the quality of service being rendered. Many question the use of graduate assistants and less expensive part-time faculty while full-time faculty spend increasing amounts of time out of the classroom performing research or other activities. Critics are taking a closer look at the value of institutional programs based upon their reputation and in comparison to price. Additionally, state and federal governments are providing proportionately smaller subsidies for programs while at the same time asking why the cost of education is rising at a rate faster than the Consumer Price Index. This has generated increased accountability and reporting requirements to ensure proper control of costs and program direction. Ironically, the National Commission on the Cost of Higher Education identified increased external regulatory and compliance reporting requirements as one of the major cost drivers in higher education.

Care must be exercised when discussing the costs of higher education with people outside of the higher education community. Colleges and universities have many different types of costs, making it important to be clear about the type of cost being analyzed. Typically, these discussions focus on instructional costs, yet in many institutions there is a tendency to overstate an institution's instructional costs and understate its research, public service, or administrative costs. (Note: In this context, we are referring to costs that are not externally funded via grants and contracts. Typically, this confusion results from discussions of costs that are funded by Education and General budgets).

Unless required by external sponsors, few higher education managers are willing to ask faculty to regularly report on the time they spend on instruction, research, service, or administrative projects. Instead, most of these costs remain buried in instructional budgets, because either there is no designated funding to cover such costs, or it is administratively efficient and politically expedient to do so.

State and federal lawmakers have increased the number of reporting requirements to ensure accountability and defend their expenditures for public colleges and universities. Currently, student tuition is increasing at a rate much higher than inflation due to reductions in state funding allocations and endowment earnings. This has led to the perception that the value gained from postsecondary education is falling short of the costs associated with that education. As state governments decrease the percentage of resources available for higher education, legislators have been demanding more data and information to justify current and future levels of public support. One result is the growing use of performance funding programs by many states. In addition, legislators are increasingly interested in faculty workload analyses, program reviews, and privatization of as many services as possible.

Federal and state policymakers are contributing to the call for accountability and are requiring additional reporting from higher education institutions. One example is the Taxpayer Relief Act of 1997, which requires that institutions report student payment and grant information to the IRS in order to comply with the Hope Scholarship and Lifetime Learning tax credits that were made available as a part of this act. Although many of the reporting requirements associated with this act were later scaled back, this is an example of a law that could have required a significant reporting burden for the provider thereby making administrative systems even more complex. This type of requirement has prompted colleges and universities to make major investments in their administrative systems in order to comply with these reporting requirements. As a result, college and university administrators must quantify the time and resources being allocated to support these additional demands.

Another recent requirement, the Cost Disclosure Statement by the Cost Accounting Standards Board (CASB), illustrates the government's shift toward greater accountability. Others include the Single Audit requirements as well as various certifications and specific program audits from federal agencies.

The growing emphasis on accountability means that college and university administrators must increasingly justify and defend the institution's expenditures as an effective and efficient means of realizing the mission of the institution. The objective is to provide complete and accurate information on the factors driving up the cost of higher education, including the true costs, such as the cost of renovation and updating old buildings to accommodate modern and/or more efficient technology and to ensure the safety of students, faculty, and staff working in those buildings. Deferred maintenance costs are staggering at many institutions and must be monitored and addressed where feasible. New reporting requirements promulgated by the Governmental Accounting Standards Board (GASB) will require public institutions to record depreciation on the historical costs of fixed assets thereby forcing institutions to recognize these costs in their financial records. (Note: Private colleges and universities subject to the Financial Accounting Standards Board [FASB] have been required to recognize depreciation for more than a decade). These changing standards may prompt states and governing boards to address this situation, as these costs will now be measured and reported in a consistent and systematic manner (see chapter 3 for a discussion of the GASB reporting requirements).

Other cost drivers include faculty salaries, employee medical benefits, utility price increases, and the cost of providing and maintaining current technologies on the campus. Institutions compete nationally for faculty, and many organizations track and report faculty salaries by institution type, discipline, and rank. The College and University Professional Association for Human Resources (CUPA-HR), Oklahoma State University, and the University of Delaware all compile national faculty salary information. Many institutions benchmark themselves against these national indicators and use these benchmarks formally in collective bargaining agreements as the basis for salary distributions, or in support of legislative or other requests for supplemental funding to recruit and retain faculty.

Increases in the cost of medical benefits also contribute to escalating expenses and have been used to justify tuition increases as a way to offset these costs. Similarly, recent deregulation and other changes in the utilities markets have led to significant increases in the price of electricity, natural gas, and other utilities. This has prompted some campuses to adopt energy surcharges that are assessed to students. Finally, adopting and maintaining current technology is a major cost driver for colleges and universities, and these costs have been escalating at rates well above inflation. Most universities view technology investments as essential to being able to provide state-of-the-art instructional services, as well as a means for reducing administrative costs. Accordingly, many institutions now assess technology surcharges to students as a means of recovering some, or all, of these added costs. But customers view these surcharges as tuition increases. Thus, college and university administrators should emphasize the future benefits to society of the investment in education, including the overall public good of an educated citizenry.

ADDRESSING THE VALUE OF HIGHER EDUCATION

Recently, emphasis has been placed on the value of the college degree rather than on the broader benefits to be derived from higher education itself, arguing for the necessity of a college degree to enhance the lifetime earning potential of the individual. The Tax Relief Act of 1998 refers to private value and access to postsecondary education in justifying the Hope Scholarship and Lifetime Learning tax credits. As a result, policy makers tend to emphasize individual economic value rather than overall public considerations. Following that emphasis, college and university administrators have tried to make a case for individual improvement as compared to the price of education in justifying the cost of education and in seeking funding support from state legislative committees.

In presenting information to these legislative bodies, it is important to distinguish between the cost of education and the price. Although there is the perception that the price of higher education is high, the actual costs are much higher. Instruction, traditionally funded by tuition payments, is subsidized with state appropriation dollars in public institutions or endowment earnings or other forms of support in private institutions. Additionally, it is subsidized even further through research activity, gifts, and other institutional funds (Institute for Higher Education Policy, 1998).

Higher education administrators should continue to emphasize the value of an education to those obtaining a college degree. Their messages should include information supporting the benefits that accrue to the public when students attend college and receive a degree. Examples of this benefit include (1) a workforce that is employable, thereby reducing welfare expenditures; (2) higher salaries earned by college graduates, which translate into greater tax payments by these individuals; (3) the extent to which a university contributes to and often drives the economy of the community and the state in which it is located; and (4) the amount and value of the knowledge created through university-sponsored research.

COMPETITION FOR STUDENTS AND FACULTY

Higher education is changing the ways in which it provides instruction. Two examples are technology based instruction and the proliferation of proprietary educational institutions, such as ITT and the University of Phoenix. Distributed education has taken on an entirely new meaning for higher education institutions. The ability to deliver online coursework or distance education means that nontraditional students can now access this education and use it to obtain needed certification and knowledge for career advancement. While Internet-based instruction has created a unique marketing opportunity for colleges and universities, it has also increased the competition for nontraditional students. Those engaged in higher education must evaluate the cost and effectiveness of alternative methods of delivering their services and be able to articulate the benefits to faculty and students.

GLOBAL ECONOMIC ISSUES

In addition to becoming more service-oriented, our economy has become global in its nature and scope. Higher education institutions now compete for research dollars within a global market. Programs or services are offered with an eye toward global marketability. Economic downturns in other parts of the world have a discernable impact on the U.S. economy as well as the budgets of colleges and universities.

Globalization increases the diversity of institutions, in terms of programs and student body, faculty, and staff, and this necessitates a deeper understanding of different cultures and societies. Due to new technology, programs can be delivered to any location in the world, at any time, and from any place. This means that institutions must now compete on a much broader scale than they have at any time in the past, and the reporting of diversity statistics and efforts becomes an important mechanism to demonstrate progress in this area.

PERFORMANCE AND MANAGERIAL CONTROL

Performance measurement and managerial controls are also important financial management information considerations. Performance measurement reports can be used internally to provide leadership with information to evaluate decisions regarding all aspects of institutional operations and programming. Financial measurement provides a yardstick for gauging resource consumption during the fiscal year and efforts to adhere to budgets. In addition, financial and performance measurement are important to external constituents such as rating agencies, donors, alumni, and governmental regulatory agencies. Good reporting and evaluation techniques are necessary tools for helping external partners gain confidence in the university's operations. Finally, other universities use financial and demographic information to benchmark their own activities and operations.

INTERNAL REPORTING

College and university administrators use internal reports to evaluate the results of past decisions or support decisions currently being made. For example, the results of student enrollment by program compared to the actual cost of education associated with those individual programs, would provide some sense of performance. A comparison of programs with high resource consumption and low demand may be a "red flag" indicating the need for evaluation. Political and access considerations may enter into the decision to make adjustments, but it is important that college and university administrators assure that their reasons for supporting a program are well founded and that they are able to articulate those reasons.

Budget and managerial control are also important reporting objectives. Comparing expenditures to budgeted amounts and previous year balances for the same period produces indicators of efficiency levels within a campus unit. For the most part, information of this nature would be presented at a summary level. A more detailed report may be necessary for specific managerial evaluation or for other reasons. Other subjects of internal reporting include financial reports, capital improvement plans, debt capacity and debt management reports, and other ad hoc reports addressing specific issues on campus.

It is important that planning documentation and reporting be provided at the executive level to allow for the proper allocation of resources. Included in the formula that should be used when assessing the viability of resource allocation are the consideration of new programs, capital expenditures, new administrative systems, and major one-time expenses. Managers will be analyzing their current resources for answers to the following key strategic questions:

- What changes have occurred in sources of revenue and patterns of expenses?
- Of those who enroll in each program each year, how many students finish and how long do they take?
- How have enrollments by program shifted over time?
- Where do students come from, and what is their background?
- What do assessment results say about the effectiveness of each program?
- How are the institution's facility and financial resources changing in amount and condition?

(Source: NACUBO, 1994).

EXTERNAL REPORTING

External reports provide data and information that illustrate or demonstrate performance effectiveness or the results of operations. The detail and complexity of these reports or presentations are driven by the purpose of the report. Information to donors, for example, could include a summary of investment income earned on their donation and the specific identification of expenses funded with this income. For rating agencies, the presentation would include greater detail regarding the financial condition of the institution, including financial ratios and trend analysis.

Information provided in external reports is intended primarily to explain the condition and traits of the institution to interested parties. Areas of interest would include instructional and research programs, enrollment statistics and student profile information, human resource base (like faculty and staff full-time equivalencies), institutional recognition awards, and the state of the physical plant. It is important to provide whatever information is necessary to communicate the key messages or otherwise to present the institution in the best possible light. Therefore, it is critical to evaluate the audience and provide the graphic and visual structure necessary to get important points across to the reader.

BENCHMARKING

Benchmarking is used to identify and achieve best practices within an industry as well as across industries. Higher education has incorporated benchmarking into business process improvement programs to measure the success of these efforts. Benchmarking can be used as a way to gauge:

- performance and efficiency at the present time;
- improvement from the identified base or previous measurement;
- identification of performance in relation to goals; and
- performance in relation to peers.

While benchmarking can be a beneficial exercise, the process can entail significant resources. Also, benchmarking is more likely to be of benefit if it is used to identify and adopt methods for radical shifts in business that result in large differentials in processing time and/or costs.

The approach to benchmarking should take a less elaborate form and a more tactical direction (*Harvard Management Update*, 1999). This article suggests seven guides to follow in the benchmarking process:

1. Determine what you are seeking and how use of benchmark will help you obtain this goal. Look for practices that can spark fresh ideas and determine where they fit into the overall arsenal of learning tools.

2. Benchmark institutions roughly at your own level. There are advantages to comparing yourself to institutions with common concerns that are of relatively the same size and level of complexity.

3. Study the entire system you are benchmarking, not just one technique.

4. Ensure that those involved are committed to the process and pay attention to it on a regular basis.

5. Adapt what you see rather than copying it. Institutions are rarely identical, so review and identify the critical variable that can be applied to your institution.

6. Use the benchmarking process to measure subjective qualities. It can be more of a creative process than a scientific approach.

7. Remember why you entered into the benchmarking exercise to begin with. It is easy to get wrapped up in the measurement process and never implement improvements.

SUMMARY

Financial management reporting is important in helping institutions make decisions, set goals, and evaluate the performance of the enterprise. It can also help the institution market its products and services and respond to cost and accountability pressures and demands. It is important that financial management reports be presented in such a way to demonstrate higher education's value to society; position the institution to compete effectively for students and faculty; address global economic issues; and ensure effective institutional performance and managerial control. To be effective, some financial management information will be designed for internal use, whereas other reports will be directed at external audiences. Wherever possible, institutional financial management information should be benchmarked against other institutional or industry information as a point of reference and comparison.

In the next chapter we will turn our attention to accounting issues and a discussion of the financial statements of colleges and universities. This chapter will also offer some suggestions on how to analyze information contained within these statements and will discuss related fiscal policies and reporting issues.

CHAPTER 3
FINANCIAL MANAGEMENT INFORMATION

Much of the financial management information contained in financial management reports will entail accounting information of one type or another. Thus, an understanding of basic accounting principles can be very useful in presenting and analyzing financial management information. The American Institute of Certified Public Accountants (AICPA) defines accounting as "the art of recording, classifying, and summarizing, in a significant manner and in terms of money, transactions and events that are, in part at least, of financial character, and interpreting the results thereof" (AICPA, 1941, pg. 9). Other organizations have expanded this definition to suggest that an accounting system records and summarizes the financial activities of the organization in a manner that:

- "lends itself to revealing clearly and fully the organization's financial position, sources, and amounts of revenue, and the nature and extent of expenditures, including per unit cost, where feasible; and

- complies with all legal and technical requirements of governmental and other authoritative organizations" (United Way of America, 1989, pg. 9).

BASIS OF ACCOUNTING

In order to ensure that the limits and restrictions placed on the use of resources available to colleges or universities are observed, accounts are maintained in accordance with the principles of fund accounting. Resources for various purposes are classified for accounting and reporting purposes into funds that are in accordance with specified activities or objectives. This is done in ways that meet the regulations, restrictions, or limitations imposed by donors or sponsoring agencies outside the university, or in accordance with directives issued by the governing trustees or board. Fund accounting is based on generally accepted accounting principles (GAAP) as determined by the National Association of College and University Business Officers (NACUBO), the American Institute of Certified Public Accountants (AICPA), and either the Financial Accounting Standards Board (FASB) for private institutions or the Governmental Accounting Standards Board (GASB) for public institutions.

Although fund accounting continues to be used for the underlying accounting records in most colleges and universities, both FASB and GASB have promulgated rules that have had (in the case of FASB institutions) and will have (in the case of most GASB institutions), a profound impact on the presentation of college and university financial statements. This new format deviates greatly from the multi-column fund formats used in the past, and presents financial information in one unified single-column format that merges all funds into one accounting presentation. While the impact of these changes on fund accounting principles is yet to be determined, the preparation of financial statements in the newly required GASB formats will require reconciliation with the books maintained in the old fund accounting format. These GASB changes are so new that many public college and university financial administrators have yet to prepare financial statements using these new formats, and additional changes are likely as more institutions convert to the new format.

The implementation of GASB's Statements 34 and 35 will have a profound impact on the presentation of public college and university financial statements. The two GASB pronouncements require that the proprietary fund statement of net assets and statement of revenues, expenses, and changes in net assets be presented using the economic resources measurement and the accrual basis of accounting. The economic resources measurement focus essentially means full accrual accounting, including required depreciation of capital assets. The "basis of accounting" - refers to when revenues, expenses, and the related assets and liabilities are recognized in the accounts and reported in the financial statements. The accrual basis stipulates that:

- revenues should be recognized in the accounting period in which they are earned and become measurable; and

- expenses should be recognized in the period incurred, if measurable.

COLLEGE AND UNIVERSITY FINANCIAL STATEMENTS

Currently, there are three different financial statement reporting requirements depending on the type of institution: FASB for private institutions, the fund accounting/

AICPA model for public institutions, and the GASB 34/35 model for public institutions that have already implemented it. GASB Statement 34 requires this new unified format for public institutions for fiscal years beginning on or after June 15, 2001 (phased in through 2003 depending upon the size of the institution, with the largest institutions transitioning first). Exhibit 3.1 contrasts the fund accounting/AICPA reporting model (old GASB), the new GASB 34/35 reporting model, and the FASB reporting model. In addition, for a more detailed comparison of these reports, refer to statements prepared using the fund accounting/AICPA model in Appendix A (Oregon University System), the new GASB statements in Appendix B (Grand Valley State University's Annual Report), and the FASB reporting model in Appendix C (Stanford University's Annual Report).

EXHIBIT 3.1: FINANCIAL STATEMENT REPORTING MODEL COMPARISON

Fund Accounting/AICPA Model	GASB 34/35 Model	FASB Model
No introductory material required	Management's Discussion and Analysis	No introductory material required
Balance Sheet	Statement of Net Assets	Statement of Financial Position
Statement of Current Funds Revenues, Expenditures, and Other Changes	Statement of Revenues, Expenses, and Changes in Net Assets	Statement of Activities
Statement of Changes in Fund Balances	Not required	Not required
Statement of Cash Flows (not applicable)	Statement of Cash Flows (required)	Statement of Cash Flows (required)
Notes to the Financial Statements	Notes to the Financial Statements	Notes to the Financial Statements

The new GASB standards require a Management's Discussion and Analysis (MD&A) section, along with a Statement of Net Assets (similar to a balance sheet); a Statement of Revenues, Expenses, and Changes in Net Assets (a combination of the old statement of changes in fund balances and the statement of current funds revenues, expenditures, and other changes); and a Cash Flow Statement (mostly unchanged). The following section discusses pertinent changes and other issues associated with each section/statement.

Management's Discussion and Analysis (MD&A). A new section called Management's Discussion and Analysis will precede the financial statements. This is technically classified as part of the Required Supplementary Information (RSI) section, and is an objective analysis of the government's financial position based on currently known information. The goal is to have the MD&A written in easy-to-understand language, supplemented by charts, tables, and graphs that will help the average reader understand the true financial condition of the entity. GASB 34 requires that the MD&A include the following.

1. A discussion of the financial statements

2. A comparison of current to prior-year financial statements

3. An analysis of the overall financial position that helps users determine whether the financial position has improved or deteriorated

4. An analysis of significant changes in net assets

5. A description of significant long-term liabilities and debt activities

6. A discussion of infrastructure assets (if the modified approach is utilized)

7. A statement of currently known facts, decisions, or conditions that are likely to influence the financial position of the entity

Many believe that the MD&A will be the most widely read portion of a public institution's financial reports; its contents must be of high quality and should contain the key messages regarding the college or university's financial condition that management wants delivered to the report's readers.

Statement of Net Assets. Assets and liabilities should be presented in classified format to distinguish between current and long-term assets and liabilities. In addition, institutions may use either the net assets format in which assets less liabilities equal net assets, or a statement of net assets format in which assets equal liabilities plus net assets. Net assets are to be displayed in three broad components: (1) invested in capital assets, net of related debt; (2) unrestricted; and (3) restricted (distinguishing between major categories of restrictions and whether they are expendable or nonexpendable). Nonexpendable net assets are those required to be retained in perpetuity, i.e., true endowments.

Statement of Revenues, Expenses, and Changes in Net Assets. This is the operating statement for proprietary funds, enterprise funds, and other business-type activities. Revenues are to be reported by major source and should identify revenues used as security for revenue bonds. Revenues and expenses are to be presented in order to distinguish between operating and non-operating revenues and expenses, complete with separate subtotals for each. Non-operating revenues and expenses should be reported after operating income; thus, many public institutions will show operating losses since appropriation funding will be displayed as non-operating income lower in the presentation. Similarly, revenues from capital contributions and additions to the principal of permanent and term endowments, special and extraordinary items, and transfers (i.e., refunds of state appropriations) should be reported separately, after non-operating revenues and expenses. This change also affects the revenue recognition principles governing capital contributions, additions to permanent and term endowments, and other non-exchange revenues that are the subject of GASB Statement 34.

Statement of Cash Flows. This statement helps to judge the ability of the institution to meet its obligations and determine if the institution needs external financing. This statement classifies cash flows from operating activities, non-capital financing activities, capital and related financing activities, and investing activities. Accrual data must be converted into cash basis activities. The direct reporting method is prescribed for GASB institutions; however, a reconciliation (indirect method) of this conversion must be presented at the bottom of the statement. Cash inflows are reported by major source and outflows by payment type.

The objective of these financial statements is the full and adequate disclosure of all pertinent financial information. When analyzing the financial statements of a college or university, interested external parties want to be able to evaluate the efficiency and effectiveness of the institution's operations and determine the extent to which fiscal and other compliance responsibilities have been met. However, due to differences in operating objectives and organizational characteristics, the relationships and ratios used for analytical purposes differ significantly between various types of institutions.

All the basic financial statements—statement of net assets [statement of financial position (FASB) or balance sheet (old GASB)]; statement of revenues, expenses and changes in net assets [statement of activities (FASB) or statement of changes in fund balances and statement of current funds revenues, expenditures, and other changes (old GASB)]; and statement of cash flows—are interrelated. The amounts shown on the statement of net assets reflect the results of operation reported in statement of revenues, expenses, and changes in net assets. The statement of cash flows reconciles the cash balances (as reported on the statement of net assets) at the beginning of the fiscal period with the cash balances at the end of the fiscal period. In addition, the financial statements should be accompanied by notes that provide further details about the financial statements, including a summary of significant accounting policies. Financial statements and Comprehensive Annual Financial Reports (CAFR) may also include an opinion issued by an independent auditor and operating statistics.

Each of these statements will now be discussed in more detail. Note: the following discussion will be modeled around the new GASB 34/35 statements.

STATEMENT OF NET ASSETS

According to Thomas McLaughlin (1995), the statement of net assets (also know as the Statement of Financial Position for FASB institutions; or Balance Sheet for GASB institutions that have not transitioned to the new reporting model) is a window on the fiscal heart of a nonprofit organization. The statement of net assets is a statement of financial position or status of resources as of a reporting date. It reports the assets remaining at the end of the fiscal period (the reporting date), showing any related liabilities or claims against these assets and the resulting net assets (also referred to as reserves or fund balances) of the institution. Assets and liabilities are usually listed in order of liquidity (ease of conversion to cash) or maturity (due dates), with current amounts listed first. The term "net assets" is synonymous with the more commonly used terms: fund balance, equity, or reserves.

Assets are things owned, which may be liquid in the sense of being cash or easily convertible to cash; or may be fixed, physical entities that are not easily sold for cash. Assets reflect probable future economic benefits obtained or controlled by an institution as a result of past transactions or events. They include all items of value to an institution and typically include: (1) cash, (2) investments, (3) accounts, notes, and pledges receivable, (4) inventory, (5) prepaid expenses, (6) equipment, (7) buildings, (8) land, (9) improvements other than buildings (sometimes referred to as IOTBs) such as sidewalks and parking lots, and (10) infrastructure such as roads and utility tunnels. They constitute a measure of past expenditures, while liquid assets are a measure of current capacity to act. More liquid assets increases the current spending capacity. Exhibit 3.2 *(page 16)* shows a report summarizing the types of fixed assets and their values over the last seven years.

ANALYZING THE STATEMENT OF NET ASSETS

In analyzing assets, pay particular attention to cash balances, asking whether they are sufficient, excessive, or inadequate. Observe the trends in cash balances from year to year to see if they are increasing or decreasing. Consider the organization's major cash flows, including the timing of receipts and disbursements. If balances are excessive, one could conclude that investment income could be increased by putting excess cash into short-term investments. If balances are insufficient, the institution may need to borrow cash to meet short-term obligations, thereby increasing interest expenses. Consider the relationship between cash and other short-term investments, and determine whether the amounts appear to be proportionate with past amounts. Examine the operating statements to determine whether investment income and interest expense is

EXHIBIT 3.2: STATEMENT OF FIXED ASSETS

STATEMENT OF FIXED ASSETS *(amounts expressed in thousands)*	Year Ending 6/30/94	Year Ending 6/30/95	Year Ending 6/30/96	Year Ending 6/30/97	Year Ending 6/30/98	Year Ending 6/30/99	Year Ending 6/30/00
Land	$6,853	$6,853	$6,853	$7,734	$7,741	$7,877	$9,044
Buildings	$531,059	$574,749	$624,680	$690,959	$759,721	$802,799	$842,730
Buildings and Improvements in Progress	$75,708	$96,023	$106,466	$96,687	$74,886	$67,190	$88,415
Machinery, Equipment and Computer	$339,427	$356,071	$373,455	$387,021	$404,434	$430,278	$422,160
Land Improvements	$31,051	$31,287	$31,287	$31,287	$31,292	$31,683	$40,754
Leased Property Under Capital Lease	$2,880	$5,880	$5,880	$5,880	$3,000	$3,000	$3,000
Library Books	$108,391	$116,756	$125,973	$134,381	$146,484	$157,535	$170,597
Other	$2,069	$1,979	$3,433	$4,238	$4,921	$5,703	$6,081
Total	$1,097,438	$1,189,598	$1,278,027	$1,358,187	$1,432,479	$1,506,065	$1,582,781

Source: University of Florida Web site

rising or falling. Find out whether the institution is using internal or external investment counsel, if a single or multiple manager investment strategy is being used, and which criteria are being used by the institution to evaluate the effectiveness of one investment strategy/manager over another.

It is also important to review the relationship between gross receivables and their estimated net realizable values as reported on the statement of net assets. Compare amounts to prior years and analyze net to gross proportions, asking whether the proportions are increasing or decreasing. Evaluate delinquency rates by monitoring bad debts and rates of uncollectibility, and make adjustments in allowances for bad debt in accordance with delinquency factors. This type of analysis can be best accomplished by reviewing accounts receivable aging reports, paying particular attention to older outstanding debts. Also, review the status of receivables to determine the amounts of debts assigned to independent collection agencies and the amounts written off as uncollectible. (See chapter 5 for a more detailed discussion of account receivable aging reports.)

Liabilities reflect probable future sacrifices of economic benefits arising from present obligations of an institution. Liabilities are amounts owed to external parties and/or employees and typically include accounts payable, notes and bonds payable, leases payable, accrued amounts for compensated absences and other accrued liabilities, deferred revenues, and deposits. Long-term debt levels and changes in short-term debt are the most commonly reviewed statistics regarding liabilities. Interest rates, maturity dates and information regarding refunding or other activities that affect debt are also frequently disclosed. Liabilities vary in respect to their maturity or due dates, and current amounts carry more weight in the analysis than liabilities due at a later date. An increase in current liabilities shows a reduced capacity for immediate action. When reviewing the statement of net assets for a community college or an institution that is part of a system of higher education, bonded indebtedness is frequently aggregated at the system level where the legal authority to borrow monies resides. Thus, these institutions may not have bonded indebtedness as it is aggregated on the system's books.

Excess of total assets over total liabilities equates to the net assets or fund balances of an institution. Net assets are typically subdivided into invested in capital assets, unrestricted, and restricted (expendable and nonexpendable) amounts. These subdivisions indicate the relative flexibility associated with these amounts. The results of operations are reflected as revenues and expenses and these amounts also translate into increases or decreases in fixed and liquid assets and liabilities. Revenues become assets; liquid assets are used for expenditures, and expenditures may result in liabilities and fixed assets.

The most intuitively intelligible concern for business officers is with the yearly and cumulative surplus or deficit position (change in net assets) of the institution. A surplus means more money has been received in a fiscal period (net assets increased), or overall, than was spent. A fiscal period surplus usually results in an increase in liquid assets, a decrease in liabilities, or both. A deficit produces opposite results (net assets decrease). Surpluses and deficits can be analyzed in respect to size (e.g., percentage of expenses), continuity (e.g., collective years of surpluses or deficits), and impact on the institution's net asset balances, which are almost invariably positive.

Solvency refers to the capacity of an institution to pay its bills eventually, as measured by its assets relative to its liabilities. An institution is solvent if its assets exceed its liabilities. While most institutions are solvent; insolvency is an important management consideration and a major concern for creditors. For purposes of financial assessments, the question is whether the institution is becoming more or less solvent.

Liquidity is a characteristic of assets that is often confused with solvency. Liquidity refers to the degree to which assets are usable as or can be converted to cash. Cash is an asset that is totally liquid; it can be spent immediately. Some assets, mostly short-term investments, may be converted relatively quickly to cash, while other assets cannot be converted quickly. Liquidity measures the relative capacity of an institution to spend its assets. Degrees of liquidity are a concern for two reasons. First, financial difficulties can be seen relatively early from declining liquidity. Second, a lack of liquidity increases costs for an institution. For example, when an institution's assets are not sufficient to pay its bills, the basic choices are to borrow money or to liquidate assets. Both options entail costs such as interest charges for borrowing, and losses from the necessity of quickly liquidating an asset.

Institutions should be concerned with their ability to be flexible and adapt quickly to new situations and operating environments. Financial flexibility varies inversely with the degree to which institutions are constrained. If most of the finances, particularly revenues and expenses, are limited in amount or cannot be changed, then the institution is less able to respond to new situations. As with solvency and liquidity, flexibility is a relative notion. Flexibility is usually looked at in respect to legal constraints, but political or financial constraints can also create problems in this respect.

STATEMENT OF REVENUES, EXPENSES, AND CHANGES IN NET ASSETS

This statement, referred to as Statement of Activities by FASB and Current Funds Revenues, Expenditures, and Other Changes by GASB institutions that have not transitioned to the new reporting model, is used to report both operating and nonoperating revenues and expenses for the year. GASB 34/35 requires that operating and non-operating revenues be separately reported. Operating revenues are typically displayed in the following categories:

- Student tuition and fees (net of scholarship allowances)
- Government grants and contracts (separate federal from state and/or local if necessary)
- Non-government grants
- Sales and services of educational activities
- Auxiliary enterprise revenues
- Other revenues

These operating revenues are then contrasted against operating expenses that can either be displayed by functional groupings (instruction, research, public service, academic support, student services, institutional support, operation and maintenance of plant, depreciation expense, student aid expenses, auxiliary activities, and loan administrative and collection costs) or by objects of expense (compensation, scholarships and fellowships, utilities, services and supplies, and depreciation).

The net operating income (loss) is then displayed prior to itemizing non-operating revenues and expenses. Most GASB institutions will show operating losses because they derive non-operating support from state appropriations. After this subtotal, non-operating revenues and expenses will then be displayed in a combined format that typically shows expenses in brackets. Non-operating revenues and expenses typically include:

- state appropriations;
- gifts and pledges (net of allowances for uncollectible pledges);
- investment income;
- interest on capital assets related debt; and
- other non-operating revenues or expenses.

Following the non-operating income and expense section, other revenues, expenses, gains, and losses are displayed. This section usually contains information about capital improvement projects, including capital appropriations, capital grants, capital gifts, and the gain or loss on disposal of capital assets, unless this is treated as an operating activity. Also, additions to permanent endowments are typically reflected here. The bottom line of this statement reflects the net increase or decrease in net assets for the year. This increase of decrease is then added to the net assets at the beginning of the year to derive the net assets at the end of the year.

ANALYZING THE STATEMENT OF REVENUES, EXPENSES, AND CHANGES IN NET ASSETS

In analyzing revenue information, it is important to monitor trends over time, and to ask the following questions:

1. Is the reliance on tuition income increasing or decreasing?

2. What are the sources of revenues and their proportions of total revenues? Are these proportions changing?

3. Is the institution relying more heavily on a source of revenue that could be subject to significant fluctuation in the near term?

4. Are total revenues increasing or decreasing?

5. Are individual revenues increasing or decreasing?

When analyzing expenses, many of the same questions that were asked in the revenue section apply here. For example, when considering trend information, ask whether expenses by category are increasing or decreasing. Also, determine what proportion of the total expenses each category comprises this year as opposed to the last few years. Calculate whether total expenses are increasing or decreasing, and if total expenses are increasing or decreasing at the same rate, or whether it is at a greater or lesser rate than the increase or decrease in revenues.

In judging the operational efficiency of a college or university, begin by examining the relationship between total revenues and total expenses or outflows. Although a college or university may be justified in operating with an excess of expenses over revenue for a certain year or short time span, it cannot operate that way for very long. It is imperative that revenues, including contributions and other forms of non-operating revenues, cover expenses over a period of several years. Any annual excess of revenues over expenses should also not be excessive because that would represent a generational inequity bias against presently enrolled students. In short, an efficiently operated institution uses its current revenues to meets its current expenses. But at the same time, it improves the quality of its services by increasing expenses when revenues significantly exceed expenses. As one anonymous source puts it, colleges and universities will raise all that they can raise and spend all they can raise.

Revenues, along with assets, are the source of monies for financial action. Revenues are most frequently examined in respect to restrictions, dependence, and variability. Limitations may be placed on revenue rates, rate increases, or uses. Dependence on particular revenue sources provides evidence of potential vulnerability. Variability of revenues is seen by looking at elasticity, delinquency, and one-time revenues. Leslie and Brinkman (1987) have studied the elasticity of demand for higher education based on tuition pricing in a longitudinal study spanning many years. What they found is that tuition can be increased at the rate of general inflation with little or no loss of enrollment; however, for every $100 increase in annual tuition in excess of inflation, enrollment declines by approximately 0.7 percent.

In analyzing the expenses of a college or university, it is important to determine the percentages of expenses associated with general administration and overhead, distinguished from such items as instruction, research, and service. It is also important to relate instruction and other student-oriented expenses with tuition and fee income to determine the portion of total student costs being covered by user charges.

Expenses of a particular type create expectations. Besides the total amount of expenses, particularly relative to total revenues, the two most common concerns are (1) fixed expenses, which are legally uncontrollable, and (2) rates of expense change. Another concern is fully measuring future costs that may not be budgeted and may represent huge future expenses. Unfunded public employee fringe benefits, which include pensions and accumulated paid sick and vacation leaves, may not be fully recorded as expenses on an institution's books. These items, combined with other institutional cost increases (i.e., utilities, technology, deferred maintenance, etc.), can become problematic if not monitored and controlled. Reduced expenditures on capital items and their maintenance are often the first sign of a declining financial condition.

The amount and nature of non-operating inflows are also important factors in judging the probability of continuance. An institution that consistently realizes significant resource inflows into endowment and plant funds shows a constituency committed toward improving and enlarging its programs. Similarly, consistent or increasing support from state or other government funders does much to underpin an institution's finances.

The bottom line in the statement of revenues, expenses, and changes in net assets represents the net change to the net assets of the college or university. Most readers of this statement will focus on this bottom line, much like they would when reading a financial statement for a for-profit organization. It is important to know whether the organization has lived within its means, i.e., were revenues sufficient to cover expenses such that the net assets of the university increased? If not, was the reduction in net assets planned, or was it the result of an unforeseen set of events?

The answers to these questions should be addressed in the MD&A section of the report.

STATEMENT OF CASH FLOWS

The FASB and GASB rules now require the preparation and presentation of this statement in the audited financial reports of all colleges and universities. The primary purpose of the statement of cash flows is to provide relevant information about an institution's activities in generating cash through operations, its financing activities, and its expenditures for operations, to repay debt, and to maintain or expand operating capacity. This statement provides information about the relationship between inflow and outflow of resources during a period by presenting cash-related activities during the fiscal year, thereby reconciling the beginning and end-of-the-year cash balances contained in the statement of net assets. The statement provides important information that supplements information provided in the statement of revenues, expenses, and changes in net assets. In particular, it adjusts out the effects of accrual accounting, removes the effects of certain non-cash activities (for example depreciation), and discloses cash generated or used by operating activities, investing activities, and financing activities.

The statement of cash flows provides information for GASB institutions (with the two financing sections combined for FASB institutions) about: (1) how an organization obtains and spends cash or other liquid resources, (2) how it finances operations through borrowing and repayment of same, and (3) other factors that may affect liquidity. This statement is typically divided into four sections:

- *Cash flows from operating activities,* including all transactions and other events that are not encompassed by capital cash flows, investing activities, or financing activities.

- *Cash flows from non-capital financing activities,* including state appropriations, gifts and grants for other than capital purposes, and other non-operating revenues and expenses.

- *Cash flows from capital and related financing activities,* including resources obtained from creditors and repayments of amounts borrowed or otherwise settling the obligations; permanently restricted and temporarily restricted cash receipts from donors of property, plant, or equipment; and those not immediately available for operations, such as from term endowments and gifts subject to life interest.

- *Cash flows from investing activities,* including acquisition and disposal of debt or equity instruments, issuance and collection of non-student loans, and acquisition of property, plant, and equipment and other productive assets held for or used in the production of goods and services by the institution.

The bottom line in the statement of cash flows is the net increase or decrease in cash for the year. This amount is combined with the beginning of the year cash balance to determine the end of the year cash balance. Both the beginning and end of the year cash balances should agree with cash amounts reported on the statement of net assets.

NOTES TO THE FINANCIAL STATEMENTS

A summary of significant accounting policies and notes should accompany the financial statements. The notes provide important supplementary information about amounts reported in the financial statements and other matters of financial consequence.

Notes to the financial statements are an integral part of the financial statements and must be included for the financial statements to be complete.

ANALYZING COLLEGE AND UNIVERSITY FINANCES

Colleges and universities realize a significant amount of their resource inflows from user-based charges in the form of tuition and fees. Therefore, in analyzing the finances of these institutions, some procedures from the for-profit entity analysis are employed in addition to other procedures used to evaluate the financial data of purely non-profit entities.

Given the direct relationship between ownership and control in the for-profit sector, boards of directors are expected to act in the best interests of the stockholder constituents. But this relationship does not necessarily exist in the nonprofit sector. Legislative bodies and boards controlling colleges and universities have a propensity to enlarge and expand organizational activities, sometimes without appropriate regard for the affordability of the proposed programs. Furthermore, colleges and universities are not required to make a profit, and can continue to operate as long as their constituencies support them.

There is also a natural inclination for internal managers to expand the operations of the enterprise to justify greater salary benefits. This inclination, coupled with similar expectations on the part of governing boards, means that constituents must be prepared to pay more attention to entity operations than is necessary in for-profit organizations.

In evaluating the effectiveness of a college's or university's operations, it is important to know something about the non-financial activities of the entity, such as number of degrees, numbers of credit hours, full-time equivalent faculty employed, etc. These data help external users determine the extent and quality of educational services being rendered. Operational effectiveness also is a requirement if the institution is to continue to exist into the foreseeable future. In addition to the financial ratios discussed later in this chapter, demand statistics such as the relationship between admissions and applications can be important factors in making this judgment. An institution with significantly more qualified applicants than it is able to admit clearly shows a heavy demand for its services that should help sustain it in the event of economic adversity.

One of the most important features in judging effectiveness of college or university operations is reflected in the form of accreditation and other recognition granted to the institution. Various disciplines or schools of a typical college or university are periodically subjected to accreditation evaluations. Agencies performing these evaluations use much of the financial and other data to arrive at overall judgments about the institution's operational effectiveness.

RECOMMENDED FISCAL POLICIES

The National Advisory Council on State and Local Budgeting (NACSLB) and the Government Finance Officers Association (GFOA) recommend that institutions adopt the following policies regarding revenue, expense, reserve, and debt management:

REVENUE POLICIES

Understanding the institutional revenue streams in terms of the mix, trends, and magnitude is essential to prudent planning. Most of these policies seek stability to avoid potential service disruptions caused by revenue shortfalls. At a minimum, institutions should have policies that address (1) revenue diversification, (2) fees and charges, (3) use of one-time revenues, and (4) use of unpredictable revenues.

Revenue Diversification. An institution should adopt a policy(s) that encourages a diversity of revenue sources in order to improve the ability to handle fluctuations in individual sources. (NACSLB Practice 4.6)

Discussion: Tracking revenue dependency can help institutions plan for situations where primary sources of support are changing. Institutions should seek to diversify revenues to the maximum extent possible to avoid becoming overly dependent on a single, or a few, primary sources of revenue that could be subject to significant fluctuations over time. If levels or sources of support are changing, plans should be made to correct adverse trends or to seek other forms of support. Obviously, decreases in primary revenue sources lead to offsetting reductions in expenses, which can have a debilitating effect on the institution. Revenue diversity can be monitored by reviewing trends in primary revenue sources and their relative contribution rates to the total revenues of the institution. Usually, institutions will set goals to increase private giving, funded research, or other

nontraditional sources to increase both the diversity and quantity of funding. Thus, actual revenues can be tracked against predetermined goals to monitor progress in this regard.

Since change is a given in today's operating environment, institutions must pay greater attention to revenue diversification. State and federal appropriation funding levels are no longer guaranteed, and endowment earnings, a primary source of support for many private institutions, have become less than reliable. Thus, it is becoming increasingly important for college and university business officers to actively seek diversification in revenue streams. Analyzing current revenue streams and attempting to achieve greater diversity within these streams is a very important and worthwhile goal.

Fees and Charges. An institution should adopt policy(s) that identify the manner in which fees and charges are set and the extent to which they cover the cost of the service provided. (NACSLB Practice 4.2)

Discussion: Institutions should establish policies regarding the level and extent of institutional fees and charges. Items to be considered in establishing such policies include:

- *Competitiveness*—institutions may wish to determine the level of competition in the marketplace and set rates at a competitive level.

- *Cost recovery*—institutions should consider the costs of delivering the service in relationship to the price charged for the service. In the absence of any specific subsidies or other support, full costs (both direct and indirect) should be recovered.

- *Policy implications*—public institutions need to comply with board directives, public policy requirements, legislative mandates, or other external constraints in setting fees and charges.

- *Access*—tuition discounting or other forms of financial aid for meritorious or needy students are factors that must also be considered in setting prices for services as revenues forgone in the form of fee remissions or institutional scholarships will need to be made up by charging others higher prices or by relying on other forms of support.

An example of a comparison of tuition pricing among competitor institutions is shown in Exhibit 3.3.

Use of One-Time Revenues. An institution should adopt a policy(s) discouraging the use of one-time revenues for ongoing expenses. (NACSLB Practice 4.4)

Discussion: Although it is always tempting to use one-time revenues as a means for offsetting short-term financial challenges, this is not a prudent practice and could lead to problems. In reviewing financial reports, attention should

EXHIBIT 3.3: TUITION AND REQUIRED FEE COMPARISON WITH COMPETITOR INSTITUTIONS

Tuition and Required Fee Comparison with Competitor Institutions
(Note: Semester hours converted to quarter hours where necessary to facilitate comparability)

Undergraduate Tuition	Homestate University	Downstate Rival University	Sister City- University	Private Convenience University	Private Continuing Educ. Univ.	Private Religious Institution	Local Community College
Resident							
Per Year (full-time)	$3,468	$3,810	$3,530	$11,700	$10,806	$17,568	$1,800
Per Credit Hour (based on 45 cr./yr.)	$77	$85	$78	$260	$240	$390	$40
Non-Resident							
Per Year (full-time)	$11,661	$13,197	$10,564	$11,700	$10,806	$17,568	$6,390
Per Credit Hour (based on 45 cr./yr.)	$259	$293	$235	$260	$240	$390	$142
Graduate Tuition							
Resident							
Per Year	$6,293	$6,750	$5,494	$11,628	$9,987	n/a	n/a
Per Credit Hour (based on 36 cr./yr.)	$175	$188	$153	$323	$277		
Non-Resident							
Per Year	$10,766	$11,409	$13,390	$11,628	$9,987	n/a	n/a
Per Credit Hour (based on 36 cr./yr.)	$299	$317	$372	$323	$277		

Source: Portland State University Budget Office

be paid to one-time revenues and their use to ensure that continuing expenses are not funded using one-time revenue sources.

Use of Unpredictable Revenues. An institution should adopt a policy(s) on the collection and use of major revenue sources it considers unpredictable. (NACSLB Practice 4.4a)

Discussion: Just as they pay close attention to the use of one-time revenues, decision-makers should scrutinize the use of unpredictable revenues, given that their future may be in doubt. In such instances where unpredictable revenues are available, significant allowances for uncollectible amounts should be established to protect the institution from becoming overly dependent on such an unreliable source of income.

DEBT, RESERVE, AND EXPENDITURE POLICIES

Institutions should have policies in place addressing debt capacity, reserve requirements, and expense policies in order to ensure financial viability in both the short- and long-run. The expenses of institutions define its ongoing commitments. Prudent expense planning and accountability will help ensure fiscal stability. At a minimum, institutions should have policies that address (1) debt, capacity, issuance, and management; (2) reserve or stabilization accounts, and (3) operating expense/capital expenditure accountability.

Debt Capacity, Issuance, and Management. An institution should adopt a policy(s) that specifies appropriate uses for debt and identifies the maximum amount of debt and debt service that should be outstanding at any time. (NACSLB Practice 4.3, 4.3a, GFOA Recommend Practices pp. 90–92)

Discussion: As mentioned in the ratio discussion below, debt levels should be monitored to ensure that debt service payments do not exceed certain predetermined amounts relative to operating income or expendable net assets. Similarly, institutions should adopt policies to ensure that total outstanding debt does not exceed capital asset equity. These policies help to ensure that an institution does not become over-leveraged in debt, thereby guaranteeing creditors that debts will be repaid and that institutions continue to meet current and long-term obligations.

Reserve or Stabilization Accounts. An institution should adopt a policy(s) to maintain a prudent level of financial resources to protect against the need to reduce service levels or raise taxes and fees due to temporary revenue shortfalls or unpredicted one-time expenditures. (NACSLB Practice 4.1)

Discussion: Most college and university business officers recommend maintaining unrestricted net assets minimally at 10 percent to 15 percent of total expenses. Maintaining reserves at this level provides a certain assurance that institutions will have funds in reserve to protect against revenue shortfalls or unforeseen expenditures. Considerations in determining the appropriate level of reserves to maintain include (a) prevailing economic conditions and climate, (b) stability of major revenue sources, (c) cash flow requirements, (d) expense flexibility and controllability, and (e) other associated factors.

Operating Expense/Capital Expenditure Accountability. An institution should adopt a policy(s) to compare actual expenses to budget periodically (e.g., quarterly) and decide on actions to bring the budget into balance, if necessary. (NACSLB Practice 7.2)

Discussion: Although most institutions do not publish budget to actual amounts in their financial statements, these statements should be provided to board members and other management to ensure that budgets are monitored, and that managerial performance is evaluated.

RATIO ANALYSIS

According to KPMG and L.F. Rothschild, Unterberg and Towbin, "in simplest terms a ratio is the relationship between two numbers. The ratio's utility lies in its ability to impart greater knowledge to the reader than is discernible from the numbers standing alone. A single ratio must, in turn, be related to something else, so that the same type of ratio viewed over time provides substantially greater information than one ratio for one time period. By comparing a ratio for one institution with the same ratio for other similar institutions, the reader gains another useful perspective. Comparing an institution's actual ratio with anticipated or budgeted ratios (sometimes called goal ratios) provides another view of performance" (1991, pg. 2).

Ratios can be extremely useful to readers and internal management when they analyze financial performance and status information, provided the user understands that ratios have certain strengths and weaknesses. Ratios are excellent tools for facilitating communication and understanding large amounts of complicated and detailed financial information. However, no single ratio or set of ratios will ever provide all the answers to all the questions one might ask. Their strength, however, lies in developing at least tentative answers to some basic questions, and serving as an indicator of the need for further analysis.

ASSESSMENT OF OVERALL FINANCIAL CONDITION RATIOS

Readers of financial reports are interested in determining the financial condition of the institution. The most common means of evaluating an institution's financial condition is the statement of net assets, which shows the assets, liabilities, and net assets at a point in time. In this regard, four statement of net assets financial ratios are used to assess the financial condition of an entity:

- *Current ratio*—current assets to current liabilities
- *Primary reserve ratio*—expendable net assets to total expenses
- *Return on net assets ratio*—change in net assets to total net assets
- *Viability ratio*—expendable net assets to long-term debt

CURRENT RATIO

The current ratio is probably the most widely recognized measure of liquidity. This simple calculation matches short-term assets of an institution with the liabilities that it expects to face during the same period. The formula is expressed as:

$$\frac{\text{Current Assets}}{\text{Current Liabilities}}$$

Conventional wisdom holds that this ratio should be at least 2:1; that is, for every dollar of liability coming due there should be at least two dollars of assets available to pay them. Generally, the higher the ratio the better; however, there is a point where one may begin to question the wisdom of holding a significant amount of short-term assets when a higher return could be achieved by investing these excess assets in longer-term investments. Looking at the Grand Valley State University Statement of Net Assets presented in Appendix B, the current ratio presented in Exhibit 3.4 can be derived.

EXHIBIT 3.4: CURRENT RATIO

Current Ratio: Current Assets to Current Liabilities
(Dollars in thousands)

	6/30/2001	6/30/2000
Current Assets	$89,254	$67,807
Current Liabilities	$46,084	$33,951
Current Ratio	1.94	2.00

Comment: A current ratio of 1.94 indicates that the institution has nearly two times more in current assets than current liabilities (nearly equal to the recommended 2:1 ratio). Although slightly less than the recommended level, a current ratio of 1.94:1 is indicative of a liquid financial position.

PRIMARY RESERVE RATIO

The formula for the primary reserve ratio is:

$$\frac{\text{Expendable Net Assets}}{\text{Total Expenses}}$$

This ratio measures the financial strength of the institution by comparing assets that an institution can quickly access and spend to satisfy its debt obligations. The ratio also describes the institution's ability to support its current operations from all available expendable resources without considering revenues generated from operations. Prudent financial management suggests that an institution keep reserves (net assets) as a safeguard against unforeseen events. It is important to monitor this ratio over time to determine if reserve levels are keeping pace with institutional growth. Unrestricted and restricted expendable net assets should increase at least in proportion to the rate of growth in expenses. Failure to keep pace with expense growth will provide less margin for adversity as the institution grows. A negative trend over time indicates a weakening financial condition.

The denominator is composed of operating expenses as reported in the Statement of Revenues, Expenses, and Changes in Net Assets. Exhibit 3.5 presents the calculation of this ratio using the information from the financial statements contained in Appendix B.

EXHIBIT 3.5: PRIMARY RESERVE RATIO

(Dollars in thousands)	6/30/2001	6/30/2000
Unrestricted Net Assets	$60,385	$49,137
Restricted Expendable Net Assets	$43,238	$36,218
Subtotal	$103,623	$85,355
Operating Expenses	$169,411	$145,764
	61.17%	58.56%

Comment: A ratio of more than 61 percent, up from 58 percent in the previous year is indicative of sound financial management.

RETURN ON NET ASSETS RATIO

The formula for this ratio is expressed as:

$$\frac{\text{Change in Net Assets}}{\text{Total Net Assets}}$$

This ratio determines whether the institution is financially better off than in previous years by measuring economic return. A decline in this ratio from one year to the next is not necessarily bad, since it could reflect the institution's strategy created to fulfill its mission more effectively. Alternatively, an improving trend in this ratio is indicative of increasing net assets that will strengthen the institution's financial future. Using the information contained in Appendix B, this ratio is calculated in Exhibit 3.6.

EXHIBIT 3.6: RETURN ON NET ASSETS RATIO

(Dollars in thousands)	6/30/2001	6/30/2000
Increase in Net Assets	$38,607	$46,386
Net Assets at Beginning	$288,711	$242,325
Return on Net Assets	13.37%	19.14%

Comment: The decline in the ratio could be caused by myriad factors, including institutional strategy, changes in financial markets, changes in state funding, etc. Nevertheless, a positive return on net assets indicates that the institution is better off than it was at the beginning of the period, especially since the return is growing faster than the rate of inflation as measured by either the Consumer Price Index (CPI) or the Higher Education Price Index (HEPI).

VIABILITY RATIO

The formula for this ratio is expressed as:

$$\frac{\text{Expendable Net Assets}}{\text{Long-term Debt}}$$

The ratio of expendable net assets to long-term debt indicates the relative liquidity of the institution. It is a fundamental indicator of financial strength in that it reflects the availability of sufficient cash, or other convertible assets, to settle its obligations as of the date of the Statement of Net Assets. There is no absolute threshold that will indicate the institution's financial viability, since long-term debt will not need to be paid off at once. Nevertheless, attention should be paid to the trends in this indicator, and further investigation may be warranted if the ratio declines. The information contained in the Grand Valley State University statement of net assets presented in Appendix B can be used to calculate the viability ratio. This calculation is contained in Exhibit 3.7.

EXHIBIT 3.7: VIABILITY RATIO
Viability Ratio: Expendable Net Assets to Long-Term Debt

(Dollars in thousands)	6/30/2001	6/30/2000
Unrestricted Net Assets	$60,385	$49,137
Restricted Expendable Net Assets	$43,238	$36,218
Subtotal	$103,623	$85,355
Long-Term Debt	$81,457	$48,579
Viability Ratio	1.27	1.76

Comment: There is no right level for this ratio. Most analyses will be institutional specific. However, a decline in the ratio from 1.76:1 to 1.27:1 indicates that institutional debt is growing at a rate faster than the growth in expendable net assets. If this trend continues, the institution's ability to respond to adverse conditions from internal resources diminishes, as does its ability to attract capital from external sources, thereby threatening its flexibility to fund new objectives.

EVALUATION OF FINANCIAL PERFORMANCE— OPERATING STATEMENT RATIOS

To evaluate the financial performance of a higher education institution, one must evaluate the financial activities as reported in the Statement of Revenues, Expenditures, and Changes in Net Assets. This statement reflects financial activities including those monies used to support instruction, research, public service, academic support, student services, operation and maintenance of plant, institutional support, student aid, and auxiliary enterprises. Three primary operating statement ratios are used here to evaluate financial performance:

- *Net operating ratio*—net operating revenues/(expenses) to total operating revenues
- *Contribution ratios*—subcategories of operating revenue to operating expenses
- *Demand ratios*—subcategories of expenditure to total revenues

NET OPERATING RATIO

This ratio measures the net operating revenues (expenses) and contrasts that to the total operating revenues. Obviously, any positive result indicates that the operating revenues were greater than the operating expenses for the year. Alternatively, negative ratios indicate an operating deficit, which may not be indicative of greater problems unless: (1) non-operating revenues are insufficient to cover the operating deficits, or (2) operating expenses grow at rates faster than operating revenues in successive years. This ratio has a direct relationship to the size of unrestricted net assets. In all cases, the formula for this ratio is:

$$\frac{\text{Net Operating Revenues (Expenses)}}{\text{Total Operating Revenues}}$$

Exhibit 3.8 presents the calculation of this ratio for each of the last two years using information presented in the Grand Valley State University financial statements contained in Appendix B.

EXHIBIT 3.8: NET OPERATING RATIO
(Dollars in thousands)

	6/30/2001	6/30/2000
Net Operating Revenues (Expenses)	($52,662)	($43,629)
Operating Revenues	$116,749	$102,135
Net Operating Ratio	(0.45)	(0.43)

Comment: Due to the new GASB formats, most public institutions will show operating losses as state appropriation funding will be classified as non-operating revenue, and will therefore be presented below the operating income/(expense) subtotal in the Statement of Revenues, Expenses, and Changes in Net Assets. The decline in the ratio from the prior year indicates that operating expenses are increasing at a faster rate than operating revenues. If this trend continues, it could eventually create problems for this organization.

CONTRIBUTION RATIOS

Operating revenues and operating expenses are very important for most colleges and universities. Further analysis of these revenues by source are referred to as contribution ratios. The contribution is expressed as a percentage of total operating expenses. By measuring revenues as a contribution to total operating expenses, institutions can ensure that, over time, revenues are keeping pace with expenses. Some institutions prefer to measure specific revenue sources as a percentage of total revenues. But this can be misleading, since expenses may be rising at rates greater or less than revenues. This ratio can be used to analyze the relationship between total (or subcategories of) operating expenses and (a) student tuition and fees; (b) federal government grants and contracts; (c) state government grants and contracts; (d) local government grants and contracts; (e) state appropriations; and (f) investment income. Many institutions strive for diversification in revenue streams, thereby insulating themselves from fluctuations in one or more of their primary funding sources. In all cases, the formula for this ratio is:

$$\frac{\text{Revenue Subcategory}}{\text{Total Operating Expenses}}$$

Exhibit 3.9 presents the calculation of the contribution ratio of net student tuition and required fees to operating expenses for the last two years. This information is taken from the Grand Valley State University financial statements in Appendix B.

EXHIBIT 3.9: CONTRIBUTION RATIO OF STUDENT TUITION AND FEES TO OPERATING EXPENSES
(Dollars in thousands)

	6/30/2001	6/30/2000
Student Tuition and Fees (net)	$69,456	$61,881
Operating Expenses	$169,411	$145,764
Contribution Ratio	41.00%	42.45%

Comment: Student tuition and fees as a percentage of operating expenses has declined from 42.45 percent to

41.00 percent over the last two years. Thus, growth in student tuition and fees has not kept pace with the growth in operating expenses. If this trend continues, the institution will need to (1) develop other sources of operating or non-operating revenues to cover operating expense growth; (2) reduce its operating expenses; or (3) reduce its unrestricted net assets, which could eventually become problematic.

DEMAND RATIOS

Demand ratios derive from the eight functional categories of educational and general expenses, and are expressed as a percentage of operating revenues. Demand ratios are useful in trend analysis to determine when a particular category of expense is consuming a growing or dwindling share of total operating revenues available. These ratios are also valuable for inter-institutional comparisons where differences in demand ratios among similar institutions may yield areas worthy of further investigation. This ratio is used to analyze the relationship of specific functional expenses (i.e., instruction, research, public service, academic support, student services, operation and maintenance of the plant, institutional support, and student financial aid) to total operating revenues. In all cases, the formula for this ratio is:

$$\frac{\text{Functional Operating Expense Category}}{\text{Total Operating Revenues}}$$

Exhibit 3.10 presents the calculation of two discrete demand ratios: (1) instructional expense to total operating revenues; and (2) research expenses to operating revenues. This information is taken from the Grand Valley State University financial statements contained in Appendix B and is displayed in Exhibit 3.3 (Note: Only one year displayed due to availability of information).

EXHIBIT 3.10 DEMAND RATIOS: INSTRUCTION AND RESEARCH EXPENSES TO OPERATING REVENUES

Instructional Expense to Operating Revenues	6/30/2001
Instructional Expense	$69,767,112
Operating Revenue	$116,748,504
Demand Ratio	59.76%

Research Expense to Operating Revenues	
Research Expense	$1,794,503
Operating Revenue	$116,748,504
Demand Ratio	1.54%

Comment: These ratios indicate how much of the operating revenues are being consumed by the expense category being analyzed. In this case, we see that instructional expenses consume nearly 60 percent of the operating revenues, whereas research consumes only 1.54 percent of operating revenues. Monitoring trends in these ratios would be important in determining whether the expenses are growing at the same or different rates as operating revenues.

EVALUATION OF CREDITWORTHINESS: CREDITWORTHINESS RATIOS

Creditors are especially interested in evaluating the creditworthiness of a college or university. When institutions try to secure external financing for capital and other projects, they must be able to demonstrate their ability to repay their current and future debts. Creditors tend to focus on the future, looking at the historical trends for indications that an institution will be able to meet its future obligations. Ultimately, creditworthiness is a matter of judgment, although analyses of the institution's finances and other student demand factors provide the basis for making that judgment.

Three primary financial and two student demand ratios are used to determine an institution's creditworthiness:

Financial Ratios:
- Viability ratio (discussed on page 23)
- Debt burden ratio
- Debt coverage ratio

Student Demand Ratios:
- Student matriculants to completed applications
- Opening fall student FTE enrollment this year compared to opening fall student FTE enrollment in the base year

FINANCIAL RATIOS: VIABILITY RATIO

The viability ratio (see discussion on page 23) measures one of the most basic determinants of clear financial health: the availability of expendable net assets to cover debt should the institution need to settle its obligations as of the date of the statement of net assets.

FINANCIAL RATIOS: DEBT BURDEN RATIO

This ratio examines the institution's dependence on debt as a source of financing its mission and the relative cost of debt to overall expenses. It compares the current level of debt service (principal and interest payments) with the institution's operating expenses. The formula for this ratio is expressed as:

$$\frac{\text{Debt Service}}{\text{Operating Expenses}}$$

The numerator (debt service) includes the required principle and interest payments, plus any other additions to reserves or renewal and replacement funds that may be required under an indenture. The denominator include all operating expenses. Obviously, the higher the ratio, the fewer resources are available for general operating purposes. Therefore, a low ratio, or a declining trend in ratios, indicates that debt service has sufficient coverage. Exhibit 3.11 presents the calculation of the ratio of debt service to operating expenses for the last two years. This information is taken from the Grand Valley State University financial statements and notes to the financial statements (see Appendix B).

EXHIBIT 3.11: DEBT BURDEN RATIO

Dollars in thousands	6/30/2001	6/30/2000
Debt Service	$4,670	$3,382
Operating Expenses	$169,411	$145,764
Debt Burden Ratio	2.76%	2.32%

Comment: Debt service accounts for only 2–3 percent of the operating expenses each year. Since debt service is a legal claim on resources, the higher the ratio the fewer resources available for other operating needs. Investment bankers have identified an upper threshold for this ratio at 7 percent, meaning that current principal and interest expenses should not be greater than 7 percent of operating expenses. While 7 percent is a generally accepted threshold, it will not necessarily preclude an institution from obtaining additional external financing. However, institutions with higher thresholds will likely face greater scrutiny from rating agencies and creditors.

FINANCIAL RATIOS: DEBT COVERAGE RATIO

The formula for this ratio is as follows:

$$\frac{\text{Adjusted Change in Unrestricted Net Assets}}{\text{Debt Service}}$$

This ratio measures the excess income available to cover annual debt service payments. This is important because it gives creditors a level of comfort that the institution has a net income stream available to meet its debt burden should economic conditions change. A high ratio is a positive factor in credit analyses, while a low ratio or declining trend is cause for some concern regarding the institution's ability to sustain its operations.

The numerator includes the change in unrestricted net assets plus interest expense and depreciation expense because this is a significant non-cash expense. The debt coverage ratio for Grand Valley State University is presented in Exhibit 3.12. Once again, only one year is presented as the detailed information needed to calculate this ratio is unavailable from the information presented in Appendix B.

EXHIBIT 3.12: DEBT COVERAGE RATIO

(Dollars in thousands)	6/30/2001
Change in Unrestricted Net Assets:	
Unrestricted Net Assets @ 6/30/01	$60,385
Less: Unrestricted Net Assets @ 6/30/00	$49,137
Change in Unrestricted Net Assets	$11,248
Add: Interest Expense	$3,923
Depreciation Expense	$9,340
Adjusted Change in Net Assets	$24,511
Debt Service	$4,670
Debt Coverage Ratio	5.25

Comment: A ratio of 5.25 is indicative of significant other funds that could be used to cover debt payments if needed. While the trend in this ratio is unavailable from the information presented, it would be an important consideration in determining whether the institution's ability to meet debt service payments is declining or increasing.

STUDENT DEMAND RATIOS

In addition to the financial ratios discussed above, creditors, underwriters, or raters sometimes use two non-financial ratios to measure the ability of an institution to meet its future debt service obligations. These two indicators use enrollment-related information to measure application demand to matriculated students and fall full-time equivalency (FTE) enrollment compared to some base year enrollment benchmark. These two ratios are important because the primary purpose of higher education institutions is to serve students. As a result, measuring the demand for these services can be an indicator of prospective financial viability.

DEBT POLICIES

The Government Finance Officers Association (GFOA, 2001) states that the foundation of any well-managed debt program is a comprehensive debt policy. A debt policy sets parameters for issuing debt and managing the debt portfolio and provides guidance to decision-makers. A debt policy should recognize a long-term commitment to full and timely repayment of all debt as a basic intrinsic requirement when dealing with capital markets. Adherence to a debt policy helps ensure that an institution maintains a sound debt position and that its credit capacity and rating is protected. A debt policy enhances the quality of decisions, rationalizes the decision-making process, identifies objectives for staff to implement, and demonstrates a commitment to long-term financial planning objectives. The existence of a debt policy is viewed positively by the rating agencies.

According to GFOA, a debt policy should include the following:

- The purposes for which debt may be issued
- Legal debt limitations or limitations established by policy, including limitations on the pledge of the issuer's general credit
- Use of moral obligation pledges
- Types of debt permitted to be issued and criteria for issuance of

    1. short-term and long-term debt,
    2. general obligation and revenue debt,
    3. fixed and variable rate debt,
    4. lease-backed debt,
    5. special obligation debt such as assessment district debt,
    6. conduit issues, and
    7. taxable debt.

- Structural features that may be considered, such as:

    1. Maturity of the debt
    2. Setting the maturities of the debt equal to, or less than the useful life of the asset being financed
    3. Use of zero coupon bonds, capital appreciation bonds, deep discount bonds, or premium bonds where practical
    4. Debt service structure (level debt service payments, level principal payments, or other repayment structure defined by law or other policies)
    5. Redemption provisions where possible (mandatory and optional call features)
    6. Use of credit enhancement
    7. Use of senior lien and junior lien obligations
    8. Use of derivative products

- Credit objectives, such as:

    1. Maintenance of specific credit ratings
    2. Adherence to benchmark direct and overall debt ratios and other affordability targets

- Authorized methods of sale, such as:

    1. Competitive sale
    2. Negotiated sale
    3. Private placement

- Method of selecting outside finance professionals
- Policy on refunding of debt
- Primary and secondary market disclosure practices
- Compliance with federal tax law provisions, such as arbitrage requirements
- Integration of capital-planning and debt-financing activities
- Investment of bond proceeds where otherwise not covered by explicit written law or written investment policy

If it is to be an effective management tool, the debt policy must be compatible with the college or university's goals pertaining to its capital program and budget, financial plan, and operating budget. A debt policy also balances the establishment of limits on the debt program while providing sufficient flexibility to respond to unforeseen circumstances and new opportunities. Finally, a debt policy should be formally adopted by the institution's governing or legislative body, and it should be continuously monitored to ensure that the institution is in compliance with the debt policy.

SERVICE EFFORTS AND ACCOMPLISHMENTS REPORTING

In 1987, GASB issued its Concepts and Statement No. 1, *Objectives of Financial Reporting* (May 1987), which initiated research into ways to improve the ability of public entity financial reports to present information useful in monitoring and assessing the "results of operations" of governmental entities. The GASB was seeking ways to provide information that could be used to assess not only how much and what an entity spends, but also what its constituents are getting in return for the use of the public funds, and how efficiently and effectively these funds are being used. This research responded to criticisms that the financial reports of governmental entities do not provide complete information to management, elected officials, and the public about the "results of operations" of the entity or its programs.

Because educators have debated the role of higher education for many years, the GASB used the Carnegie Commission definition of the purpose of higher education:

- the provision of opportunities for intellectual, aesthetic, ethical, and skill development of individual students, and the provision of campus environments which can constructively assist students in their more general development growth;

- the advancement of human capability in society at large;

- the enlargement of educational justice for the post-secondary age group;

- the transmission and advancement of learning and wisdom; and

- the critical evaluation of society—through individual thought and persuasion—for the sake of society's self renewal.

(Source: Carnegie Commission on Higher Education, 1973)

This report noted that individual institutions would relate to some of these purposes more than others, depending on their respective missions. It is this variety of missions (multiple missions) that makes assessing Service Efforts and Accomplishments (SEA) and accountability difficult. Nevertheless, GASB suggested that the following types of indicators and information be used to evaluate colleges and universities:

- *Input Measures*—number of faculty and level of instructional expenses

- *Output Measures*—number of degrees, certificates awarded, student credit hours generated, and full-time equivalent (FTE) students served

- *Outcomes Measures*—test scores on standardized exams, accomplishment of selected student goals, alumni ratings, retention and graduation rates, employment and graduate study rates, and employer satisfaction with graduates

- *Efficiency Measures*—instructional expensess/credit hours, and FTE students/FTE faculty

- *Explanatory Data*—role and mission statement, governmental funding (total and per student FTE), average class size, and other faculty, enrollment, entering test scores/GPA, listing of degree programs, etc.

In addition, GASB recommended that the following four types of comparative data also be considered:

1. Comparisons with prior periods

2. Comparisons with other institutions, including benchmark institutions

3. Comparisons with national and local norms

4. Comparisons with established targets or goals

Although many colleges and universities have yet to report these data in their financial reports, this information is useful when considering the kinds of management financial information that should be presented and analyzed.

FASB's Business Reporting Research Project

The Financial Accounting Standards Board (FASB) has also been conducting a research project considering the types of information (in addition to financial statements) that entities are providing financial statement readers and the means for delivering it. An important portion of the research was done by FASB's constituents—preparers, users, auditors, and academics. Working group activities, now completed, included:

- "Identifying present practices in eight industries for the voluntary disclosure of various types of information such as operating data and performance measures, forward-looking information, background about the company, and information about intangible assets that have not been recognized in the financial statements

- Considering ways to coordinate GAAP and SEC disclosure requirements so as to eliminate redundancies and to gather all of the information about a particular topic in one place

- Studying present systems for delivery of information electronically and considering the implications of technology for business reporting in the future."

(Source: FASB Web site: www.fasb.org/project/busreport.shtml)

The findings of the working groups have been considered and approved by the project steering committee. The findings have been published in a three-volume research report that is available, at no cost, on this aforementioned Web site.

One part of the Business Reporting Research Project is being updated in 2002 to incorporate changes since 1999 in how Web sites communicate with investors and others interested in business reporting information.

Summary

This chapter has attempted to give the reader a better understanding of the basic financial statements used by colleges and universities. In addition, some suggestions regarding the analysis of these statements and related fiscal policies and procedures were discussed.

In the next chapter we will turn our attention to evaluation and reporting issues associated with academic performance, including teaching, mentoring, and curricular activities; assessment of academic quality; research, scholarship, and other creative activities; community outreach and service activities; and library operations.

CHAPTER 4
INDICATORS OF ACADEMIC PERFORMANCE

Understanding, monitoring, and analyzing academic performance indicators is critical to the effective management of higher education institutions. Academic performance indicators represent the core mission and function of the enterprise and are therefore, a very important component of financial management reporting. It is through these academic services of instruction, research, public service, and community outreach that an institution is able to attract and retain faculty, students, financial resources, and political support. It also constitutes the foundation for measuring and reporting institutional quality.

While colleges and universities are engaged in myriad activities, three primary functions are at their core: instruction, public service, and research or scholarship. Some institutions emphasize one or more of these activities over another. Nevertheless, most colleges and universities have multiple missions addressing these three primary activities. Multiple missions also exist within the component units within a given institution. For example, there will likely be different expressions of the mission depending on the level within the university being examined. The following levels are typically present in most institutions:

• Institutional

• School/college within the institution

• Academic department within each school/college

• Individual faculty member within each department

In a sense, while these levels are inter-related, the results of an analysis of academic performance can vary depending upon the level being analyzed. Thus, one of the challenges facing college and university administrators is being able to successfully manage multiple missions with often conflicting and multiple objectives. Accordingly, one of the challenges of presenting and analyzing financial management information within an institution is to understand and attempt to address this concept of multiple missions, especially when preparing reports for internal consumption. Managing multiple missions requires that priorities be established, and communication and financial management information plays a role in this process.

Another factor related to the notion of multiple missions is the level at which reports are drawn. For example,

an analysis of credit hour or research production can be reported at the institutional, school/college, department, or individual faculty member level. Many recommend that central administration reporting remain at the department, school/college, or institutional level. But when a dean, director, or department chairperson wishes to report at the individual faculty member level, that responsibility should remain with the dean, director, or department chair and, generally, not with a central office. Thus, the political aspects of information reporting should be a factor for consideration in any decision to prepare and issue reports on academic achievements, since reporting can be viewed as a form of pejorative scrutiny and an unwanted intrusion into departmental or faculty governance.

Many involved in the presentation and analysis of college and university financial reporting understand that much of the purpose of reporting financial management information is to drive decision-making, communicate priorities and goals, and evaluate outcomes. Decisions that will change the activities of the institution will likely impact the activities of the faculty and, thus an understanding of faculty cultures and their reaction to change initiatives is also important. College and university administrators must be sensitive to the cultural aspects of the faculty, since this will impact on the success in managing and reporting academic activities. A more detailed discussion of faculty perceptions, attitudes, activities, and motivations can be found in Appendix D.

REPORTING ACADEMIC ACCOMPLISHMENTS

A standardized reporting format should be developed that contains agreed upon definitions for use in presenting academic accomplishments. These reports should use criteria that are useful for communicating priorities, making decisions, setting goals, and monitoring performance. For example, the following five measures could be used in making resource allocation decisions and evaluating whether allocations have achieved their intended purpose:

1. Teaching, Mentoring, and Curricular Activities

2. Assessments of Academic Quality

3. Research, Scholarship and Other Creative Activities

4. Community Outreach and Service

5. Library Operations

This list is not all-inclusive, nor is it presented in order of priority. Academic units must be given the flexibility to develop and use other measures as appropriate, since participation and involvement in any change effort will reduce resistance to the initiative. Appendix F contains a theoretical model for evaluating institutional academic productivity and includes a discussion of some of the issues associated with such models. These issues must be addressed if an institution hopes to be successful in reporting and evaluating academic productivity.

REPORTING ON TEACHING, MENTORING, AND CURRICULAR ACTIVITIES

Student credit hour/FTE expectations should be established for each school or college. By setting these expectations at the school or college level, one department may produce significantly more credit hours than another, so

long as a school or college generates the aggregate total credit hours necessary to achieve the benchmark. It may be desirable to further categorize the expectations by lower division, upper division, master's, and doctoral levels. Credit hour attribution agreements and adjustments will need to be made in cases where courses are cross-listed or joint programs are offered through more than one unit.

Credit hour benchmarks should be set using historical credit hour production as adjusted for current initiatives, institutional priorities, and resource levels to ensure that the goals are reasonable and attainable. Exhibit 4.1 is an example of a report of student credit hour production by student level at the institution, school/college, and department levels.

Most higher education systems are driven by formulaic funding algorithms that are influenced largely by student credit hours, commonly converted to student full-time equivalents (FTEs) and/or headcounts. FTE is calculated by taking the total credit hours (usually by level—undergraduate, master's, and doctorate) and dividing this number by a full-time equivalency factor representing the average carrying load for a full-time student each year. For example, for an institution on a quarter calendar, undergraduate students must amass 180 credit hours in most programs to graduate. If students typically take four years to amass 180 credit hour, this means that an average student must take 45 credits per year (180/45 – 4 years). Thus, total undergraduate credit hours per year would be divided by 45 to derive the number of FTE credit hours produced each year. Similarly, one could divide the total number of credit hours taken each quarter by 15 to derive quarterly FTE production. Thus, the production of credit hours becomes the coin of the budget realm, and is a significant factor that must be monitored on a systematic basis.

Many state institutions derive roughly one-half of the operating budget needs from this basis. Many states with systems containing multiple community colleges and other institutions of higher education use funding formulas largely driven by student credit hour generation to allocate funds among the institutions. Furthermore, many institutions use this same student credit hour basis

EXHIBIT 4.1: THREE-TERM CREDIT HOURS BY SCHOOL/COLLEGE, DEPARTMENT, AND STUDENT LEVEL

3-Term Student Credit Hours by School/College and Department by Student Level				
All Campuses*2000 - 2001 (4th Week)				
	Annual			
	UG	GR	PHD	Total
Institutional Unit TOTAL	410,052	109,752	9,319	529,123
College of Liberal Arts & Sciences	243,271	29,477	2,880	275,628
Liberal Arts & Sciences	20	--	--	20
General Arts & Letters	465	4	--	469
Anthropology	5,892	439	--	6,331
Applied Linguistics	5,021	2,318	61	7,400
Biology	14,217	2,562	154	16,933
Black Studies	4,016	54	--	4,070
Center for Science Education	2,157	103	--	2,260
Chemistry	10,974	933	462	12,369
Chicano & Latino Studies	1,333	12	--	1,345
Child & Family Studies	638	1	--	639
Communication	21,111	3,518	34	24,663
Economics	7,842	632	16	8,490
English	22,673	4,044	36	26,753
Environmental Programs	2,027	998	222	3,247
Foreign Languages & Literatures	25,883	3,771	96	29,750
Geography	6,090	1,189	96	7,375
Geology	4,789	771	33	5,593
History	16,748	1,108	5	17,861
International Studies	1,922	6	--	1,928
Mathematical Sciences	27,266	2,705	345	30,316
Philosophy	7,658	1,222	44	8,924
Physics	6,589	460	464	7,513
Psychology	23,167	1,508	703	25,378
Sociology	18,272	998	109	19,379
Women's Studies	6,501	121	--	6,622
School of Business Administration	49,725	11,802	166	61,693
Accounting	12,541	1,773	23	14,337
Administration	19,892	2,577	30	22,499
Finance	4,186	1,558	12	5,756

(table continued on page 31)

to internally allocate funding to participating academic units within the campus. Some institutions even use this as a means of allocating faculty FTE among departments. Thus, the generation of student credit hours must be closely planned and monitored.

Credits hours can be measured on an institutional, school or college, department, or individual faculty level, and most analysis is appropriate at the department, school/college, and institution level. Note, however, that instructional productivity can vary significantly by program and level. Similarly, analyzing costs on a per-credit-hour basis will differ immensely from department to department and by school or college. Class sizes can be constrained by the type of pedagogy employed, facilities, equipment, lab, or workstation capacities and other issues. Faculty salaries vary significantly between disciplines and are also affected by faculty age, sex, rank, teaching/research, and service balance (many times referred to as workload), institutional mission, budget, and the operating cultures of the faculty as well as strength of shared governance, etc. Pedagogies differ since some classes rely solely on lectures, with class sizes ranging from a dozen or more students to hundreds of students; others involve extensive laboratory or individual one-on-one instruction. Generally, graduate class sizes will be smaller than undergraduate courses, etc. Exhibit 4.2 (pages 32–33) presents an example of three-term enrollments by school/college, department, and course level over the last five years. This information, combined with faculty FTE information (see Exhibit 6.1 in chapter 6), can be very useful in analyzing productivity at the unit level.

Related to student credit hours are the numbers of students served by each program. Students can either be majors or they can be taking elective or general education courses needed to meet academic requirements or personal interests. Majors are of the most concern, since they require

advising and receive other direct services from the department. Thus, many institutions monitor the number of students per faculty member or majors per faculty member. It's also important to separate full-time, tenure-track faculty from full-time, fixed term and part-time or adjunct faculty. Part-time faculty typically do not provide advising, nor do they perform research and other public services; thus, unbalanced full-time to part-time faculty ratios can

EXHIBIT 4.1: THREE-TERM CREDIT HOURS BY SCHOOL/COLLEGE, DEPARTMENT, AND STUDENT LEVEL (continued from page 30)

Management	7,627	4,844	73	12,544
Marketing	5,479	1,050	28	6,557
Graduate School of Education	**6,350**	**31,169**	**1,554**	**39,073**
Curriculum & Instruction	3,597	16,278	674	20,549
Ed Policy, Foundation & Admin. Studies	1,815	6,534	737	9,086
Special Ed & Counseling Ed	938	8,357	143	9,438
College of Engineering & Computer Science	**24,469**	**9,642**	**894**	**35,005**
Systems Engineering	967	281	10	1,258
Civil Engineering	5,752	1,799	60	7,611
Computer Science	10,192	3,735	246	14,173
Electrical & Computer Engineering	3,495	1,958	377	5,830
Engineering Management	1,230	1,329	187	2,746
Mechanical Engineering	2,833	540	14	3,387
School of Fine & Performing Arts	**33,035**	**3,467**	**7**	**36,509**
Architecture	2,864	88	--	2,952
Art	16,111	1,156	3	17,270
Music	8,932	1,771	1	10,704
Theater Arts	5,128	452	3	5,583
Graduate School of Social Work	**548**	**12,121**	**762**	**13,431**
College of Urban & Public Affairs	**34,359**	**10,437**	**1,956**	**46,752**
School of Community Health	12,576	1,531	116	14,223
Physical Education	5,452	500	41	5,993
Public Health Ed./Public Health St.	7,124	1,031	75	8,230
School of Government	16,439	5,710	627	22,776
Administration of Justice	7,760	357	34	8,151
Political Science	7,824	544	92	8,460
Public Administration	855	4,809	501	6,165
School of Urban Studies & Planning	5,344	3,196	1,213	9,753
Special Programs	**1,205**	**1,594**	**1,094**	**3,893**
Correspondence Courses	34	--	--	34
Interdisciplinary Courses	937	1,356	263	2,556
Military Science	132	15	--	147
National Student Exchange	72	--	--	72
Systems Science Ph.D.	30	223	831	1,084
Undergraduate Studies	**17,090**	**43**	**6**	**17,139**
University Honors	2,040	43	6	2,089
University Studies	15,050	--	--	15,050

* Includes main campus, Continuing Education, and other self-support programs.

Source: Portland State University Office of Institutional Research and Planning

(continued on page 37)

EXHIBIT 4.2: THREE-TERM ENROLLMENT BY SCHOOL/ COLLEGE, DEPARTMENT, AND COURSE LEVEL: 1996–2001 *(excerpt)*

Department/Course Level	1996-97		1997-98		1998-99		1999-00		2000-01	
	FTE	%	FTE	%	FTE	%	FTE	%	FTE	%
INSTITUTIONAL TOTAL	10,049	100	10,203	100	10,520	100	11,132	100	11,972	100
Lower Division	3,430	34.13	3,496	34.26	3,660	34.79	3,758	33.76	4,062	33.93
Upper Division	4,246	42.25	4,273	41.88	4,539	43.15	4,734	42.53	5,062	42.28
Graduate	2,374	23.62	2,434	23.86	2,321	22.06	2,640	23.71	2,848	23.79
COLLEGE of LIBERAL ARTS & SCIENCES	5,583	55.56	5,461	53.52	5,570	52.95	5,722	51.4	6,085	50.83
Lower Division	2,281	22.7	2,272	22.27	2,322	22.07	2,253	20.24	2,389	19.96
Upper Division	2,681	26.68	2,574	25.22	2,645	25.14	2,827	25.4	2,984	24.93
Graduate	620	6.17	615	6.03	603	5.73	641	5.76	712	5.95
Arts & Sciences	--	--	--	--	--	--	11	0.1	11	0.09
Lower Division	--	--	--	--	--	--	--	--	--	--
Upper Division	--	--	--	--	--	--	11	0.1	11	0.09
Graduate	--	--	--	--	--	--	0	0	0	0
Anthropology	131	1.3	139	1.36	175	1.67	157	1.41	143	1.19
Lower Division	56	0.56	56	0.55	65	0.62	59	0.53	52	0.44
Upper Division	65	0.65	74	0.73	100	0.95	87	0.78	79	0.66
Graduate	9	0.09	9	0.09	11	0.1	12	0.11	12	0.1
Applied Linguistics	93	0.93	117	1.14	140	1.33	155	1.39	171	1.43
Lower Division	21	0.21	29	0.28	45	0.43	69	0.62	67	0.56
Upper Division	44	0.44	53	0.52	56	0.54	53	0.47	58	0.48
Graduate	28	0.28	35	0.34	38	0.36	33	0.3	46	0.39
Biology	427	4.24	354	3.47	374	3.56	350	3.14	393	3.28
Lower Division	155	1.54	131	1.29	136	1.29	133	1.19	140	1.17
Upper Division	221	2.2	183	1.79	197	1.87	172	1.54	199	1.67
Graduate	50	0.5	40	0.39	41	0.39	45	0.4	53	0.45
Black Studies	88	0.87	71	0.69	89	0.84	72	0.65	91	0.76
Lower Division	27	0.27	18	0.18	22	0.21	14	0.13	16	0.13
Upper Division	57	0.57	51	0.5	64	0.61	54	0.49	72	0.6
Graduate	3	0.03	2	0.01	3	0.03	3	0.03	3	0.03
Center for Science Education	34	0.33	68	0.67	70	0.66	67	0.6	49	0.41
Lower Division	20	0.2	41	0.4	27	0.26	25	0.22	19	0.16
Upper Division	12	0.12	26	0.25	37	0.35	38	0.35	26	0.22
Graduate	1	0.01	1	0.01	6	0.05	3	0.03	3	0.03
Chemistry	286	2.85	266	2.61	248	2.36	267	2.4	287	2.4
Lower Division	143	1.43	133	1.3	129	1.22	135	1.21	141	1.18
Upper Division	116	1.15	107	1.05	93	0.88	102	0.92	113	0.94
Graduate	27	0.27	26	0.26	27	0.26	30	0.27	33	0.28
Chicano & Latino Studies	--	--	5	0.05	14	0.14	17	0.15	26	0.22
Lower Division	--	--	4	0.04	9	0.08	7	0.06	4	0.03
Upper Division	--	--	1	0.01	6	0.06	11	0.1	22	0.19
Economics	205	2.04	228	2.23	209	1.99	221	1.99	192	1.61
Lower Division	93	0.92	110	1.08	108	1.03	128	1.15	122	1.02
Upper Division	92	0.91	98	0.96	82	0.78	75	0.68	54	0.45
Graduate	20	0.2	20	0.19	19	0.18	18	0.16	16	0.14
English	595	5.92	561	5.49	542	5.16	574	5.16	591	4.94
Lower Division	157	1.56	166	1.63	151	1.43	141	1.27	168	1.4
Upper Division	328	3.27	285	2.79	291	2.77	320	2.88	322	2.69
Graduate	109	1.09	109	1.07	100	0.95	112	1.01	101	0.84
Environmental Programs	37	0.37	47	0.46	52	0.5	65	0.58	80	0.67
Lower Division	13	0.13	22	0.21	18	0.17	18	0.17	23	0.19
Upper Division	13	0.13	10	0.1	19	0.18	14	0.13	22	0.18
Graduate	11	0.11	15	0.15	15	0.15	32	0.29	35	0.29

(table continued on page 33)

EXHIBIT 4.2: THREE-TERM ENROLLMENT BY SCHOOL/
COLLEGE, DEPARTMENT, AND COURSE LEVEL: 1996–2001 *(continued from page 32)*

Department/Course Level	1996-97		1997-98		1998-99		1999-00		2000-01	
	FTE	%	FTE	%	FTE	%	FTE	%	FTE	%
SCHOOL of BUSINESS ADMINISTRATION	1,110	11.04	1,157	11.34	1,223	11.63	1,281	11.5	1,373	11.47
Lower Division	169	1.68	179	1.76	210	1.99	226	2.03	234	1.95
Upper Division	672	6.69	716	7.02	747	7.1	809	7.26	885	7.39
Graduate	269	2.68	262	2.57	267	2.54	246	2.21	255	2.13
Accounting	146	1.45	136	1.34	121	1.15	124	1.11	122	1.02
Lower Division	12	0.12	--	--	--	--	--	--	--	--
Upper Division	110	1.09	113	1.11	100	0.95	104	0.94	106	0.89
Graduate	24	0.24	23	0.23	22	0.2	19	0.17	17	0.14
Business Administration	500	4.97	564	5.53	617	5.87	655	5.89	719	6
Lower Division	147	1.46	176	1.73	202	1.92	216	1.94	219	1.83
Upper Division	265	2.64	297	2.91	332	3.15	360	3.24	410	3.42
Graduate	88	0.87	91	0.89	84	0.79	80	0.72	90	0.75
Finance	130	1.29	120	1.17	126	1.2	127	1.14	136	1.13
Lower Division	6	0.06	--	--	6	0.05	7	0.07	11	0.1
Upper Division	76	0.75	78	0.76	82	0.78	87	0.78	83	0.69
Graduate	48	0.48	42	0.41	39	0.37	33	0.3	41	0.35
Management	219	2.18	232	2.27	237	2.25	245	2.2	245	2.05
Lower Division	4	0.04	3	0.03	2	0.02	3	0.03	3	0.03
Upper Division	130	1.3	141	1.38	135	1.29	153	1.37	164	1.37
Graduate	85	0.84	88	0.86	99	0.94	89	0.8	78	0.65
Marketing	115	1.15	105	1.03	122	1.16	129	1.16	151	1.26
Lower Division	--	--	--	--	--	--	--	--	--	--
Upper Division	91	0.91	88	0.86	99	0.94	105	0.94	122	1.02
Graduate	24	0.24	18	0.17	23	0.22	24	0.22	29	0.24
GRADUATE SCHOOL OF EDUCATION	571	5.68	616	6.04	609	5.79	773	6.94	903	7.54
Lower Division	--	--	--	--	0	0	18	0.16	13	0.11
Upper Division	56	0.55	61	0.6	75	0.71	85	0.77	106	0.89
Graduate	515	5.13	555	5.44	534	5.08	669	6.01	784	6.55
Curriculum & Instruction	280	2.79	290	2.84	283	2.69	428	3.85	436	3.64
Lower Division	--	--	--	--	0	0	10	0.09	10	0.08
Upper Division	30	0.3	33	0.33	38	0.36	50	0.45	53	0.44
Graduate	251	2.5	257	2.52	245	2.32	369	3.31	373	3.12
Ed. Policy, Foundations & Admin. Studies	106	1.05	145	1.42	156	1.48	125	1.12	217	1.81
Lower Division							9	0.08	3	0.03
Upper Division	14	0.14	19	0.19	27	0.26	24	0.21	38	0.32
Graduate	91	0.91	126	1.23	129	1.23	102	0.91	176	1.47
Special Ed. & Counselor Ed.	185	1.84	181	1.78	170	1.62	211	1.89	250	2.09
Lower Division	--	--	--	--	--	--	--	--	--	--
Upper Division	12	0.12	9	0.09	10	0.09	12	0.11	15	0.13
Graduate	173	1.72	172	1.69	161	1.53	199	1.79	235	1.96

*3-term FTE is defined as the sum of Fall, Winter, and Spring student credit hours divided by: 45 for undergraduate students, 36 for non-doctoral graduate students, and 27 for doctoral students. Lower, Upper, and Graduate divisions are determined by course level, and FTE within each division is calculated strictly by student level using the formula above.

*Excerpt of full report; numbers do not total to 100.

Source: Portland State University–Office of Institutional Research and Planning

EXHIBIT 4.3: ENROLLMENT BY MAJOR/PROGRAM AND STUDENT LEVEL

Fall 2001, 4th Week Major/Program	Undergraduate				Graduate				TOTAL
	Admit	Non-Admit	PB	Total UG	Admit	Non-Admit	PB	Total GR	
INSTITUTIONAL TOTAL	**11,348**	**1,362**	**891**	**13,601**	**3,351**	**1,181**	**487**	**5,019**	**18,620**
College of Liberal Arts & Sciences	**4,701**	**58**	**214**	**4,973**	**774**	**33**	**23**	**830**	**5,803**
Anthropology	128	--	7	135	20	--	--	20	155
Applied Linguistics	44	1	16	61	72	1	1	74	135
Applied Linguistics	40	1	5	46	1	1	--	2	48
Teaching English as a Second Language (C)	4	--	9	13	--	--	1	1	14
Teaching English to Speakers of Other Languages	--	--	2	2	71	--	--	71	73
Biology	446	7	36	489	36	1	3	40	529
Black Studies (C)	1	--	--	1	--	--	--	--	1
Chemistry	116	1	10	127	13	1	--	14	141
Chicano/Latino Studies (C)	1	--	1	2	--	--	--	--	2
Conflict Resolutions	--	--	--	--	54	--	--	54	54
Child & Family Studies	144	2	1	147	--	--	--	--	147
Economics	69	2	3	74	7	2	1	10	84
English	430	4	13	447	86	6	1	93	540
Environmental Management	--	--	--	--	12	--	--	12	12
Environmental Science Ph.D.	5	--	--	5	73	--	--	73	78
Environmental Studies	99	2	9	110	--	1	--	1	111
Foreign Languages & Literatures	205	2	19	226	44	3	2	49	275
General Studies: Arts & Letters	332	7	4	343	--	1	--	1	344
General Studies: Science	150	3	11	164	18	3	--	21	185
General Studies: Social Science	325	1	3	329	7	--	4	11	340
General Studies: Option II	20	--	--	20	--	--	--	--	20
Geography	80	1	5	86	30	3	1	34	120
Geology	52	1	12	65	19	--	--	19	84
History	257	5	7	269	45	--	2	47	316
International Studies	134	5	3	142	--	--	--	--	142
Mathematical Sciences	101	3	6	110	48	2	2	52	162
Philosophy	50	--	--	50	--	2	1	3	53
Physics	47	--	7	54	11	1	--	12	66
Pre-Professional Programs	55	--	6	61	--	--	1	1	62
Allied Health (P)*	5	--	--	5	--	--	--	--	5
Dental Hygiene (P)	3	--	--	3	--	--	--	--	3
Dentistry/Medicine (P)**	22	--	4	26	--	--		--	26
Law (P)	6	--	--	6	--	--	--	--	6
Nursing (P)	9	--	--	9	--	--	--	--	9
Pharmacy (P)	4	--	--	4	--	--	--	--	4
Teacher Education	6	--	2	8	--	--	1	1	9
Psychology	695	6	11	712	23	2	2	27	739
Sociology	305	2	6	313	25	--	--	25	338
Speech Communication	365	3	16	384	85	4	--	89	473
General Speech Communication	309	3	--	312	33	4	--	37	349
Speech & Hearing Sciences	56	--	16	72	52	--	--	52	124
Women's Studies	40	--	--	40	--	--	--	--	40
Women's Studies (C)	1	--	2	3	--	--	1	1	4
Writing	1	--	--	1	46	--	1	47	48
Writing Minor	3	--	--	3	--	--	--	--	3
School of Business Administration	**2,394**	**31**	**149**	**2,574**	**350**	**3**	**7**	**360**	**2,934**
Accounting***	372	2	95	469	--	1	2	3	472
Business Administration****	492	12	7	511	286	1	4	291	802
Business Education	--	--	--	--	1	--	--	1	1
Finance	271	4	10	285	60	1	--	61	346
International Studies Business Administration Minor	5	--	--	5	--	--	--	--	5
Management*****	692	4	31	727	3	--	--	3	730
Marketing	562	9	6	577	--	--	1	1	578

(table continued on page 35)

EXHIBIT 4.3: ENROLLMENT BY MAJOR/PROGRAM AND STUDENT LEVEL (continued from page 34)

Fall 2001, 4th Week Major/Program	Undergraduate				Graduate				TOTAL
	Admit	Non-Admit	PB	Total UG	Admit	Non-Admit	PB	Total GR	
Graduate School of Education	17	1	1	19	913	1	150	1,064	1,083
Curriculum & Instruction	15	--	1	16	468	--	21	489	505
Ed Policy, Foundations & Admin. Studies	--	--	--	--	147	--	116	263	263
Special Ed & Counseling Ed	2	1	--	3	298	1	13	312	315
College of Engineering & Computer Science	1,170	36	121	1,327	340	23	15	378	1,705
Civil Engineering	128	--	16	144	25	--	--	25	169
Computer Engineering	186	3	6	195	--	1	--	1	196
Computer Science	477	23	68	568	90	13	8	111	679
Electrical & Computer Engineering	209	7	17	233	131	7	3	141	374
Engineering Management	--	--	1	1	59	--	4	63	64
Manufacturing Engineering	--	--	1	1	2	--	--	2	3
Mechanical Engineering	170	3	12	185	27	2	--	29	214
System Engineering	--	--	--	--	6	--	--	6	6
School of Fine & Performing Arts	1,177	36	79	1,292	61	3	8	72	1,364
Architecture	172	9	15	196	--	3	--	3	199
Art	626	20	47	693	11	--	5	16	709
Art History	38	1	1	40	--	--	--	--	40
Music	243	4	14	261	43	--	3	46	307
Theater Arts	98	2	2	102	7	--	--	7	109
Graduate School of Social Work	--	--	--	--	379	--	1	380	380
College of Urban & Public Affairs	662	12	11	685	435	5	13	453	1,138
School of Community Health	273	5	6	284	23	2	3	28	312
Community Development	63	1	3	67	--	--	--	--	67
Health Studies	210	4	3	217	23	2	3	28	245
School of Government	378	6	4	388	261	2	1	264	652
Administration of Justice	212	1	3	216	11	1	--	12	228
Political Science	165	4	1	170	16	1	1	18	188
Public Administration******	1	1	--	2	234	--	--	234	236
School of Urban Studies & Planning*******	11	1	1	13	151	1	9	161	174
Other Programs	--	--	2	2	89	--	--	89	91
International Programs (C)	--	--	2	2	--	--	--	--	2
Systems Science Ph.D.	--	--	--	--	89	--	--	89	89
Undeclared or Unknown	1,227	1,188	314	2,729	10	1,113	270	1,393	4,122

*Includes the following pre-professional programs: Chiropractic, Naturopathic Medicine, Nuclear Medicine Technology, Occupational Therapy, Optometry, Physical Therapy, Physician Assistant, and Podiatry.

**Includes the following pre-professional programs: Dentistry, Medical Technology, Medicine, Osteopathy, and Veterinary Medicine.

***Includes post-baccalaureate certificate in Accounting
****Includes the following interdepartmental majors: Business Administration, General Business, International Business (MBA), Supply & Logistics, and International Business Studies Certificate.

*****Includes Human Resource Management, General Management, Information Systems, International Studies Management, and Supply and Logistics Management
******Includes Master of Public Administration, and Public Administration & Policy Ph.D.

*******Includes undergraduate major in Community Development, Master of Urban & Regional Planning, Master of Urban Studies, Ph.D. in Urban Studies, Certificate in Gerontology, and Urban Studies & Planning Minor.

KEY: C=Certificate, I=Interest Area (Non-Degree), P=Pre-Professional Program.

Source: Portland State University–Office of Institutional Research and Planning

EXHIBIT 4.4: UNDUPLICATED HEADCOUNT ENROLLMENT: 2000–01

	Summer Session Only			Academic Year (Fall, Winter, or Spring)			Total (Summer, Fall, Winter, Spring)		
	Credit	Audit	Total	Credit	Audit	Total	Credit	Audit	Total
Main Campus									
Main Campus Only	3,138	176	3,314	20,385	45	20,430	23,523	221	23,744
Main Campus & Challenge Program	--	--	--	47	--	47	47	--	47
Main Campus & Continuing Education	57	--	57	1,652	--	1,652	1,709	--	1,709
Main Campus & ESL	--	--	--	66	--	66	66	--	66
Main Campus & International Programs	1	--	1	102	--	102	103	--	103
Main Campus & Other Combinations of Above	--	--	--	6	--	6	6	--	6
Total	3,196	176	3,372	22,258	45	22,303	25,454	221	25,675
Branch Campuses and Operations									
Challenge Program Only	--	--	--	869	--	869	869	--	869
Continuing Education Only	3,417	5	3,422	4,723	10	4,733	8,140	15	8,155
ESL Only	2	21	23	73	90	163	75	111	186
International Programs Only	86	--	86	126	--	126	212	--	212
Combinations of Above	--	--	--	--	--	--	--	--	--
Total Non-Home U.	3,505	26	3,531	5,791	100	5,891	9,296	126	9,422
TOTAL	6,701	202	6,903	28,049	145	28,194	34,750	347	35,097

Note: Challenge Program courses are college credit courses offered to high school students at high schools in the university's area

Source: Portland State University–Office of Institutional Research and Planning

EXHIBIT 4.5: DEGREES CONFERRED BY TYPE AND PROGRAM

Program Area	BA/BS	Masters	Doctorate	TOTAL	% Total
INSTITUTIONAL TOTAL	2,194	1,199	38	3,431	100.00%
Percent of Total Degrees	64%	35%	1%	100%	
College of Liberal Arts & Sciences	1,333	205	7	1,545	45.03%
Arts & Letters	427	120	0	547	15.94%
Science	211	37	7	255	7.43%
Social Science	670	48	0	718	20.93%
International Studies	25	0	0	25	0.73%
School of Business Administration	465	151	0	616	17.95%
Graduate School of Education	0	448	5	453	13.20%
College of Engineering & Computer Science	118	108	5	231	6.73%
School of Fine & Performing Arts	135	33	0	168	4.90%

Source: Portland State University–Office of Institutional Research and Planning

EXHIBIT 4.6: DEGREES GRANTED BY SCHOOL AND COLLEGE: 1996–2001

School/College	1996-97	1997-98	1998-99	1999-00	2000-01	Change From Preceding Year	% Change 1999-2001
INSTITUTIONAL TOTAL	2,901	3,006	3,129	3,271	3,431	160	5.1
College of Liberal Arts & Sciences	1,330	1,404	1,349	1,449	1,545	96	7.1
Arts & Letters	445	421	451	468	547	79	17.5
Science	240	287	243	289	255	-34	-14
Social Science	595	644	616	657	718	61	9.9
General Studies – Option II	19	19	6	--	--	--	--
International Studies	31	33	33	35	25	-10	-30.3
School of Business Administration	536	533	637	629	616	-13	-2
Graduate School of Education	323	275	287	320	453	133	46.3
College of Engineering & Computer Science	240	252	266	261	231	-30	-11.3
School of Fine & Performing Arts	104	115	158	147	168	21	13.3
Graduate School of Social Work	122	131	138	204	123	-81	-58.7
College of Urban & Public Affairs	240	285	292	253	290	37	12.7
Special Programs	6	11	2	8	5	-3	-150
Systems Science Ph.D.	6	11	2	8	5	-3	-150

Source: Portland State University–Office of Institutional Research and Planning

(continued from page 31)

indicate an area in need of attention. Exhibit 4.3 (pages 34–35) presents an example of a report of enrollment by declared major/program and student level. This chart will be very useful for department chairs/heads and deans in allocating faculty resources, planning for advising, deciding curricular and course section offerings, and other activities.

Knowing the total headcount of all students can also be useful for institutional planning and resource allocation decisions. Exhibit 4.4 (page 36) shows an example of a report of the total enrollment for an institution by academic quarter. This exhibit can inform decision-makers about needed support services such as parking, general advising, food services, housing demand/needs, etc. It can also be useful in estimating and projecting revenues assessed on a headcount basis, or for estimating expenses (such as mailings to go to all students), projecting computer laboratory needs, determining the need for dial-in lines, and other student headcount driven expenditures.

An estimate of the number of degrees to be granted each academic year, or the average time necessary to complete a degree, could also be used as a criterion for evaluating the effectiveness of the schools or colleges in relation to established benchmark, standards, or priorities. This criterion could be weighted for type of degree as appropriate. Attaching rewards for improvements in these outcome measures would bring a focus to curriculum planning and other activities. An example of a report of degree production at an institution is presented in Exhibit 4.5 (page 36).

Calculating the institutional costs of producing degrees is a very difficult undertaking. This is due partially to the fact that it takes multiple years for a student to earn a degree, plus the fact that many of the credits required for a degree results from classes taught outside the student's major area of study. Therefore, any attempt to measure instructional costs per degree result, at best, in surrogate measures of the cost. Nevertheless, it is interesting to track the costs per degree simply by dividing the total instructional costs by the number of degrees produced by department. The trends in this indicator would be the most important output, and would serve to indicate if the production of degrees is rising faster or slower than the department's instructional costs.

Exhibit 4.6 *(page 37)* presents an example of a report of degree production by school or college and program for the last five years. Looking at data arrayed longitudinally can help the reader understand if the numbers are increasing or decreasing. Again, this can be used for planning purposes, such as projecting the number of faculty needed in each department, estimating demand for courses, and calculating space needs.

ASSESSING ACADEMIC QUALITY

Most accrediting agencies now require some form of assessment to evaluate academic quality generally, or quality of specific school/college or program performance. Focus groups and interviews are effective ways of collecting information for use in undertaking quality assessments, especially in the area of "community outreach." Quality assurance should be a part of every unit, and should extend to programs and majors.

Examples of the elements identified for consideration in a quality assessment are:

- whether graduates find employment consistent with their expectations;

- employers' evaluations of graduates;

- surveys of graduates to determine if their expected goals were achieved;

- pass rates on professional exams (CPA, etc.);

- persistence (retention rate), adjusted for students who have goals other than graduating from the institution, and for areas where there is a high attrition rate nationally;

EXHIBIT 4.7: SPONSORED RESEARCH EXPENDITURES BY DEPARTMENT: 1994–2001

Grants and Contracts - Funded Research Expenditures
Current Restricted Fund Activities
(Based on Expenditures)

	1994-95	1995-96	1996-97	1997-98	1998-99	1999-2000	2000-01	% Change 99-00 to 00-01
College of Liberal Arts & Sciences								
Dean's Office	$71,642	$518,039	$782,168	$441,848	$957,561	$738,004	$572,035	-22.49%
Anthropology	$24,025	$20,500	$4,430	$10,702	$1,756	$35,197	$28,883	-17.94%
Biology	$190,312	$203,227	$177,647	$195,072	$490,101	$930,826	$938,740	0.85%
Science Educ. Center	$400,727	$292,168	$580,024	$683,725	$836,126	$775,805	$600,989	-22.53%
Chemistry	$117,663	$536,271	$642,392	$405,842	$410,211	$466,830	$413,064	-11.52%
Child and Family Studies	$0	$0	$0	$400,291	$634,031	$993,708	$1,097,178	10.41%
Economics	$3,945	$2,313	$11,856	$722	$1,663	$35,995	$80,454	123.51%
Environmental Sciences	$15,309	$61,880	$68,077	$172,519	$153,927	$246,769	$470,613	90.71%
English	$0	$1,397	$2,970	$1,216	$292	$1,018	$482	-52.65%
Foreign Language	$0	$36	$49,443	$27,930	$8,790	$52,693	$54,911	4.21%
Geology	$173,429	$87,138	$239,108	$208,548	$421,368	$445,739	$598,268	34.22%
Geography	$120,086	$68,073	$167,275	$78,881	$86,522	$121,880	$109,293	-10.33%
International Studies	$0	$0	$0	$851	$255	$0	$25,501	Not Available
Linguistics	$34,635	$25,260	$0	$0	$503,536	$558,392	$670,251	20.03%
History	$0	$0	$25,906	$118,629	$138,396	$159,495	$132,115	-17.17%
Mathematics	$407,517	$167,941	$131,962	$254,825	$226,012	$1,026,391	$1,210,385	17.93%
Philosophy	$0	$0	$0	$43,840	$89,478	($656)	$0	-100.00%
Physics	$143,139	$517,566	$474,560	$567,617	$412,089	$406,772	$277,777	-31.71%
Psychology	$46,442	$71,788	$8,945	$9,802	$25,725	$115,256	$151,736	31.65%
Sociology	$448	$0	$718	$364	$3,320	$8,589	$55,764	549.25%
Speech Communication	$154,668	$12,235	$22,257	$8,338	$21,208	$545	$19,840	3540.37%
Women's Studies	$0	$0	$5,574	$4,462	$8,910	$4,527	$506	-88.82%
Totals	**$1,903,987**	**$2,585,831**	**$3,395,311**	**$3,636,024**	**$5,431,277**	**$7,123,775**	**$7,508,785**	**5.40%**

Source: Portland State University–Budget Office

- surveys of current students to assess satisfaction, opinion of current services, perceptions of the institution or its programs and departments; and

- other qualitative information such as course and instructor evaluations.

Although most quality assessments rely on qualitative information, this information is still useful when presenting and analyzing financial management information, especially when monitoring trends or making comparisons with peer institutions.

ASSESSING RESEARCH, SCHOLARSHIP, AND OTHER CREATIVE ACTIVITIES

Points to be considered when assessing funded research include the source of funding (some sources being more prestigious than others), the application of research funds (do they benefit the institution by providing support for graduate assistants, faculty, equipment, etc.), and research outcomes related to institutional goals (such as integration

with the curriculum). While not all research and other creative activities result in outside funding or publication, they may contribute to the scholarship goals of the individual, department, or unit. Thus, institutions may wish to develop other mechanisms to track unfunded research.

Exhibit 4.7 *(page 38)* presents an example of a report displaying the amount of funded research, by department, in the College of Liberal Arts and Sciences for the period 1994–2001.

Publications, presentations, and performances should also be assessed using such evaluative criteria as (a) whether a publication is refereed or otherwise evaluated before publication; (b) the significance or application in the field of knowledge (some people use Science Citation Index, and Social Science Citation Index to determine how frequently a publication is cited in other publications); and (c) awards or other forms of special recognition.

Disclosures of intellectual property developed can also be used as evidence of research accomplishments, as can

(continued on page 41)

EXHIBIT 4.8: LIBRARY BUILDING USE (HEADCOUNT): 1996–2001

Millar Library	1996-97	1997-98	1998-99	1999-00	2000-01	5-Year Average
	750,293	712,749	742,749	746,356	755,306	741,491

Source: Portland State University–Office of Institutional Research and Planning

EXHIBIT 4.9: LIBRARY BUILDING USE: 1996–2001

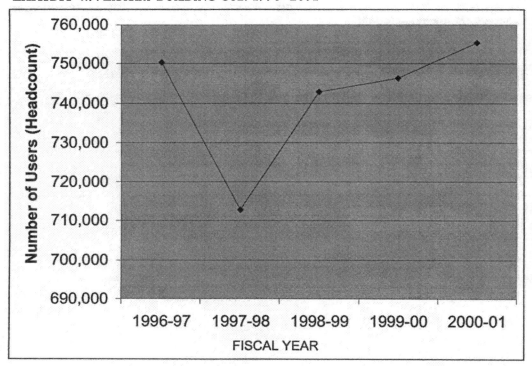

EXHIBIT 4.10: INVENTORY OF LIBRARY HOLDINGS; AND LIBRARY INVENTORY PER STUDENT FTE: 1996–2001

Inventory	1996-97	1997-98	1998-99	1999-00	2000-01	5-Year Average
Volumes Held	1,091,196	1,145,539	1,247,885	1,278,573	1,242,337	1,201,106
Net Volumes Added	27,981	25,905	104,576**	32,003	48,357	26,849
Periodical Subscriptions	5,516	5,372	5,545	4,685	5,191	5,262
Other Serials	5,085	4,224	4,784	5,545	3,781	4,684
A/V Materials	102,654	102,778	105,927	127,965	44,081****	96,681
Government Documents	477,622	489,345	397,549	401,426	405,516	434,292
Microforms	2,289,386	2,366,730	2,427,690	2,323,418	2,341,538	2,349,752
Maps***	55,635	68,043	58,360	59,267	60,561	60,373
Other	11,968	20,097	14,212	18,409	29,118*****	18,761
Library Inventory Per FTE Student*						
Volumes Held	103	107	114	110	101	107
Volumes Added	3	2	--	3	4	2
Periodical Subscriptions	1	1	1	0	0	0
Other Serials	0	0	0	0	0	0
A/V Materials	10	10	10	11	4	9
Government Documents	45	46	36	35	33	39
Microforms	217	221	222	200	191	210
Maps***	5	6	5	5	5	5
Other	1	2	1	2	2	2

* Fall Term 4th Week Full Time Equivalent. Student FTE is calculated as follows: SCH/15 for all undergraduate students, SCH/12 for graduate (Masters', Postbac. Graduate, and Non-Admitted Graduate) students, and SCH/9 for doctoral students.

** This figure consists of 101,839 cataloged government documents added that were previously uncataloged and 2,737 volumes as gifts as part of a archive records entered into database.

*** Includes pamphlets, tests, archives, and manuscripts.

**** All slides, filmstrips, motion pictures withdrawn from collection from 07/01/00.

***** Including pictures/prints, CD-Roms, and computer software.

Source: Portland State University–Office of Institutional Research and Planning

EXHIBIT 4.11: LIBRARY CIRCULATION TRANSACTIONS: 1996–2001

Type of Circulation Transaction	1996-97	1997-98	1998-99	1999-00	2000-01	5-Year Average
General	163,003	148,388	142,753	125,022	128,984	141,630
Other**	60,200	58,163	54,553	35,006	36,613	48,907
TOTAL	223,203	206,551	197,306	160,028	165,597	190,537
Circulation Transactions Per FTE Student*						
General	15.4	13.9	13.1	10.8	10.5	12.7
Other**	5.7	5.4	5	3	3	4.4
TOTAL	21.2	19.3	18	13.8	13.5	17.2

** Includes Reserve and Restricted Books.

*** Fall Term 4th Week Full Time Equivalent. Full-Time Equivalent Enrollment (FTE) is calculated as follows: SCH/15 for all undergraduate students, SCH/12 for graduate (Masters', Postbac. Graduate, and Non-Admitted Graduate) students, SCH/9 for doctoral students.

Source: Portland State University Office of Institutional Research and Planning

(continued from page 39)

other scholarly contributions, which are defined in promotion and tenure guidelines, faculty handbooks, and other similar productions. It is useful to establish some benchmarks, first at the institutional level, and then at the school or college level, based on historical data, national averages, or other standards. But the school or college must be given the flexibility to allow for departmental differences so long as aggregate (institutional) standards are met.

EVALUATING PUBLIC SERVICE AND COMMUNITY OUTREACH

Financial analyses should include consideration of such things as community partnerships, student involvement through activities such as internships and capstone projects, public events (including both those that are part of academic programs such as those found in the arts, and those that are independent of academic programs, such as athletic events), and other forms of community service as identified in promotion and tenure documents. Among the criteria that can be used for evaluating quality in this area are (a) the duration of such partnerships, (b) community assessments of program impact, (c) evaluations from advisory groups, and (d) the generation of gifts and other forms of support in connection with such efforts.

EVALUATING LIBRARY OPERATIONS

A library is an important asset for many institutions both in terms of its value to the campus community for research and instructional endeavors, and for its value to the larger community as an information and public service resource. Institutional libraries are judged in two ways: (1) by their use, as measured by number of users and in terms of circulation, and (2) by the numbers and types of volumes they contain. Given today's technology, it may also be desirable to keep track of the number of databases that can be accessed, the number of inter-library loan transactions, and other statistics indicative of technology access and transactions. Web site hits could be counted, as could other electronically tracked statistics. Such data are useful in preparing for accreditation visits, when negotiating indirect cost (Facilities and Administrative) reimbursement rates, and for press releases and other forms of information for funding agencies.

Evaluation criteria used for institutional libraries include the following:

• Library funding as percentage of the total Education and General Fund (E&G) budget

• Collection size and growth rate

• Staff size and distribution

• Cost of materials and inflation trends

• Need for capital investment (e.g., new technology)

• Comments received during accreditation reviews

• User surveys

• Other statistics (e.g., volumes added, usage, etc.)

• Performance measures (e.g., items orders per staff, turn-around time, etc.)

The following exhibits provide examples of the type of library data that most institutions report, as well as the formats that can be used. Exhibits 4.8 and 4.9 *(page 39)* address library use.

Exhibit 4.9 displays this same information but in a graphic format.

Another important measure for library reporting is the inventory of holdings. Exhibit 4.10 *(page 40)* presents an example of a library inventory of holdings report by type and numbers and expressed as a per-student FTE amount. The size of an institution's library holdings is an indicator of the quality of both the institution and its library.

Another report produced for libraries is a count of circulation transactions and circulation transactions per student FTE. This type of report is used mainly for planning and budgeting purposes. Exhibit 4.11 *(page 41)* shows an example of such a report.

Note that the report indicates that transactions have actually declined in recent years. This is due to the introduction and availability of many materials via the Internet, thus minimizing the number of circulation transactions. Although this trend is discernible in Exhibit 4.11, presenting this information in a graphic format, as shown in Exhibit 4.12, makes the same point in a more prominent manner.

SUMMARY

This chapter has addressed evaluation and reporting criteria for academic issues, including teaching, mentoring and curricular activities; assessment of academic quality; research, scholarship and other creative activities; community outreach and service; and library operations. In the next chapter we will turn our attention to evaluation and reporting criteria for noninstructional units.

EXHIBIT 4.12: LIBRARY CIRCULATION TRANSACTIONS: 1996–2001

Type of Circulation Transaction						
	1996-97	1997-98	1998-99	1999-2000	2000-01	5-Year Average
General	163,003	148,388	142,753	125,022	128,984	141,630
Other**	60,200	58,163	54,553	35,006	36,613	48,907
TOTAL	223,203	206,551	197,306	160,028	165,597	190,537
Circulation Transactions Per FTE Student***						
General	15.4	13.9	13.1	10.8	10.5	12.7
Other**	5.7	5.4	5	3	3	4.4
TOTAL	21.2	19.3	18	13.8	13.5	17.2

** Includes Reserve and Restricted Books.

*** Fall Term 4th Week Full Time Equivalent. Full-Time Equivalent Enrollment (FTE) is calculated as follows: SCH/15 for all undergraduate students, SCH/12 for graduate (Masters', Postbac. Graduate, and Non-Admitted Graduate) students, SCH/9 for doctoral students.

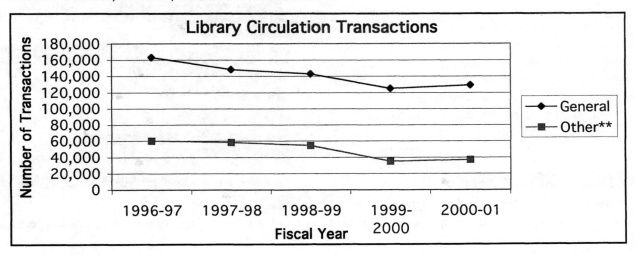

Chapter 5
Evaluation and Reporting Criteria for Non-Instructional Units

Nonacademic units are an important component of any institution and should be managed as such, since their contributions can have a significant influence on the accomplishment of the institution's mission. In many ways, academic support functions, student services, plant operation and maintenance, institutional support, and auxiliary enterprises and service department operations form the infrastructure that facilitates and supports the primary instruction, research, public service, and administrative activities of the institution. Preparing and analyzing financial management information for these activities is critical if they are to be effectively managed.

As is the case with academic units, evaluation and reporting criteria for noninstructional areas should be used for making decisions, communicating priorities, setting goals, and monitoring performance. Noninstructional units include (1) academic support (graduate studies, research and sponsored projects administration, computing, and other support functions), (2) student services (student affairs, admissions, financial aid, etc.), (3) operations and maintenance of the physical plant (architectural services, building maintenance, grounds maintenance, janitorial, etc.), and (4) institutional support (administration generally, president's office, provost's office, finance and administration offices, and development functions). In addition, there are (5) auxiliary enterprises and service departments (housing, food services, student union operation, student health services, parking operation, print shops, telecommunications, etc.) that provide services to both internal and external users.

At a very basic level, three primary actions can be used in the management of these activities:

1. Increasing activities that add value.

2. Decreasing activities that do not add value.

3. Ensuring that certain items that are important and necessary to the institution's infrastructure (such as facility maintenance) are given some consideration. They may be ignored if the focus is simply on value-adding activities or other outcome measures.

To add value, a service or function must be viewed as positive from an external perspective. That is, the value must be perceived not by the unit providing the service but by the external customer or user, allowing for the fact that there are both internal (other faculty and staff) and external (students and public) customers and users of the services being rendered. Many institutions do this formally by applying one or more of the following activities: (1) management personnel evaluations; (2) some type of peer review using one or more external experts to compare and contrast funding, service priorities, or other factors of interest; or (3) survey data collected from the customer base. Other institutions do this informally through (4) conversations; (5) monitoring budgets and other performance data; and (6) other informal systems. To add value, the service or function must contribute to the mission of the institution or one of its component units. That is, the service or function must generally contribute to instruction, research, or public service and community involvement as expressed in the broadest sense.

An institution's fiduciary obligation to manage its activities, maintain the facilities, and otherwise protect the institution from risk may be jeopardized when an institution focuses simply on value-adding activities. Thus, reports should be prepared that present information on general management effectiveness, levels of deferred maintenance, and risk management activities. Reports can be prepared displaying levels of deferred maintenance in each facility, maintenance costs per square foot, and other measures of institutional investment in facilities each year. Risk can come in many forms, including tort liabilities, property damages, financial exposure, legal exposure, security and safety issues, and other challenges that can generate costly issues for the institution.

When analyzing noninstructional activities, it is helpful to consider the categories used by the National Association of College and University Business Officers (NACUBO) in its benchmarking study in the 1990s. While many of these benchmark indicators do not involve financial management directly, they do relate to customer satisfaction, use, and other factors that can contribute both positively and negatively to revenues and cost factors associated with noninstructional operations. In many cases, illustrative examples or reports have been provided to give the reader a better sense of the type of reports being used to present and analyze information in this regard. These noninstructional functions are discussed in this chapter in groupings sorted by the following functional or program categories: (1) academic support, (2) student services, (3) plant operation and maintenance; (4) institutional support, and (5) auxiliary enterprises. This is not an all-inclusive list. Rather, it serves as a guide to suggested reporting criteria.

ACADEMIC SUPPORT FUNCTIONS

GRADUATE STUDIES

This function oversees the institution's graduate programs by setting policies for graduate assistantships, monitoring student progress, and working with academic units to ensure program quality. Key evaluation and reporting criteria include:

- number of graduate students and degrees;
- number of graduate assistants employed; and
- results from user satisfaction surveys.

RESEARCH AND SPONSORED PROJECTS SUPPORT

This area includes the pre-award cycle and the post-award cycle. The pre-award function includes all activities that lead to the award of a sponsored project, grant, or contract. Sponsored projects include federal, state, local, or privately funded grants and contracts. The post-award cycle includes coordinating, managing, reviewing, and reporting to external sponsors about the use of sponsored project monies on campus. In order to make decisions, set goals, and monitor the performance of this unit, the following items should be monitored, analyzed, and reported:

- Numbers of proposals coordinated each year
- Proportion of proposals submitted to awards received
- User satisfaction with pre-award services
- User satisfaction with post-award services
- Audit issues—disallowances or other findings and issues
- Amounts refunded to grantors
- Number of late reports
- Indirect cost recoveries and the usage of these funds to reward or provide incentives for additional activities

COMPUTING SUPPORT

This area supports academic and administrative activities by providing the technology infrastructure that has become essential for institutional operations. Computing support can take many forms, including (a) help desk functions for faculty, students, and administrative users;

(b) networking, telecommunications, operations, and other infrastructure; and (c) academic and research support areas that directly assist faculty in converting classes to Web formats, computational support, and other support services directly linked to these activities. Due to the many different administrative structures and preferences, it can be difficult to identify computing costs across an institution and then compare those costs to other institutions. Many institutions have distributed computing costs in a decentralized environment, whereas others have chosen to centralize services to the extent feasible. Regardless of the approach taken, areas to be evaluated and measured include:

- instructional support, as measured by the number of courses offered via the Internet or other electronic or distance delivery mechanisms, number of instructional classrooms supported, numbers of student computer labs, student accounts, etc. or other means;
- research support, as measured by access to research databases, high speed network connectivity, and other data collection and analysis mechanisms supported by this unit;
- public service activities, as measured by services facilitated by this unit;
- numbers of accounts maintained, including remote access;
- user satisfaction with services as measured using customer satisfaction surveys;
- cost of services, either measured in the aggregate, or on per student FTE or per faculty FTE bases, including comparisons with peer institutions;
- currency of technology on campus;
- ratio of support staff to faculty/administrators; and
- network or system downtime.

STUDENT SERVICES

ADMISSIONS AND RECORDS

This function is responsible for engaging in promotional activities to develop the size and quality of the applicant pool, as well as selecting from the applicant pool those prospective students who meet or exceed the institution's academic and non-academic requirements. This function is also responsible for all processes relating to student registration and record maintenance. Evaluation criteria include:

- number or percentage of students that progress to the next step in the process: from prospective student pool

(continued on page 46)

EXHIBIT 5.1: SOURCES OF NEW STUDENTS BY STUDENT LEVEL

Fall 2001

Source	FR	SO	JR	SR	PB Non-grad	NU	Total UG	PB Grad	GM	GD	NG	Total Grad	Grand Total
TOTAL NEW STUDENTS	1,419	654	798	157	281	798	4,107	149	674	45	483	1,351	5,458
New From High Schools	1,164	9	1	1	--	--	1,175	--	1	--	--	1	1,176
Oregon	860	5	--	--	--	--	865	--	--	--	--	--	865
Other States	226	4	1	--	--	--	231	--	--	--	--	--	231
Foreign	31	--	--	1	--	--	32	--	1	--	--	1	33
GED	47	--	--	--	--	--	47	--	--	--	--	--	47
New From Oregon Community Colleges	80	338	470	33	44	--	965	6	36	1	--	43	1,008
Blue Mountain	--	1	4	--	--	--	5	--	--	--	--	--	5
Central Oregon	1	5	6	1	2	--	15	--	--	--	--	--	15
Chemeketa	5	25	30	1	--	--	61	--	6	--	--	6	67
Clackamas	8	29	61	4	--	--	102	--	1	--	--	1	103
Clatsop	--	1	10	--	1	--	12	--	1	--	--	1	13
Lane	4	24	14	--	--	--	42	--	4	1	--	5	47
Linn-Benton	1	5	7	--	2	--	15	--	1	--	--	1	16
Mt. Hood	14	68	75	12	--	--	169	1	2	--	--	3	172
Portland	45	169	255	14	39	--	522	5	21	--	--	26	548
Rogue	--	3	1	--	--	--	4	--	--	--	--	--	4
Southwestern Oregon	2	3	3	1	--	--	9	--	--	--	--	--	9
Treasure Valley	--	--	--	--	--	--	--	--	--	--	--	--	--
Umpqua	--	5	4	--	--	--	9	--	--	--	--	--	9
New From OUS Institutions	40	64	53	35	37	--	229	26	91	2	--	119	348
Eastern Oregon University	1	2	2	2	--	--	7	--	8	--	--	8	15
Oregon Health Science University	--	--	--	--	1	--	1	1	2	--	--	3	4
Oregon Institute of Technology	1	--	--	1	--	--	2	1	2	--	--	3	5
Oregon State University	12	18	16	10	15	--	71	11	26	--	--	37	108
Southern Oregon University	8	16	8	4	3	--	39	2	7	--	--	9	48
University of Oregon	13	18	21	14	13	--	79	6	35	2	--	43	122
Western Oregon University	5	10	6	4	5	--	30	5	11	--	--	16	46
New Admits From PSU	1	--	--	--	21	--	22	25	128	1	--	154	176
New From Other Oregon Colleges	10	31	25	12	25	--	103	16	57	4	--	77	180
New From Colleges Outside Oregon	77	200	237	62	133	--	709	42	262	23	--	327	1,036
New From Foreign Colleges	2	7	7	8	16	--	40	23	72	10	--	105	145
New Admits – Source Unknown	45	5	5	6	5	--	66	11	27	4	--	42	108
New Non-Admitted	--	--	--	--	--	798	798	--	--	--	483	483	1,281

Source: Portland State University–Office of Institutional Research and Planning

(continued from page 44)

to applicants, to admits, to matriculations by market segment:

1. freshmen and transfer students (in-district, in-state, nonresident, and international)

2. Graduate students

3. Post-baccalaureate, and non-degree seeking students

4. Full-time and part-time students

5. Under-represented populations

- turnaround time between application and admission decisions;

- timeliness of statement, grades, and other post-admission correspondence;

- ratio of applicants and enrollments to prospects each term;

- average turnaround time to process transcript requests;

- number of successful appeals each year;

- quality and timeliness of registration schedule production;

- turnaround time to complete enrollment verification requests;

- accuracy and timeliness of registration data tables maintenance, including articulation tables and Web student information;

- efficiency and efficacy of classroom scheduling;

- accuracy and quantity of degree audits performed; and

- user satisfaction surveys.

Reporting on the sources of new students can be an effective way to understand the effectiveness of marketing programs in certain geographical areas as well as knowing the sources of demand for students. This information can be used to negotiate articulation or co-admissions agreements with other educational providers or to target admissions and marketing efforts in future years. Exhibit 5.1 *(page 45)* presents an example of a report on the sources of students by student level.

Exhibit 5.2 illustrates a report that further elaborates on the characteristics of the incoming freshmen class, including type, fee status, gender, carrying load, ethnic origin, and full-time/part-time status. Many institutions track freshmen in cohorts to determine retention and graduation rates, and to evaluate the effectiveness of their recruiting strategies and programs.

EXHIBIT 5.2: NEW FRESHMAN PROFILE

New Freshman Profile FALL 2001					
Total Enrollment	**1,293**		**Fee Status**		
Student Type			Enrolled for 9 or More Credits		
			Resident	986	76.30%
GED	53	4.10%	Non-Resident	176	13.60%
Directly from HS	1,016	78.60%	Staff	6	0.50%
With College Credits	94	7.30%	Graduate Assistant	--	0.00%
1 to 11 Transfer Hrs	30	2.30%			
12 to 29 Transfer Hrs	100	7.70%	Enrolled for 8 or Fewer Credits		
			Part-time Fee Policy	124	9.60%
Gender			Staff	1	0.10%
			Graduate Assistant	--	0.00%
Men	599	46.30%			
Women	694	53.70%			
			Full-Time/Part-Time		
Average Carrying Load	12.7				
			Full-Time*	1,055	81.60%
Ethnic Origin			Part-Time**	238	18.40%
White, Non-Hispanic	801	61.90%	**Average Age**	19.3	
Declined to Respond/Other	102	7.90%			
International Student	25	1.90%	GED	23.6	
Asian/Pacific Islander	219	16.90%	Directly from HS	18.9	
Black, Non-Hispanic	44	3.40%	With College Credits	18.6	
Hispanic	60	4.60%	1 to 11 Transfer Hrs	20	
Native American	22	1.70%	12 to 29 Transfer Hrs	21.5	
Multiple Ethnicity	20	1.50%			
* Full-time = undergraduates enrolled for 12 or more credits.					
** Part-time = undergraduates enrolled for 11 or fewer credits.					

Source: Portland State University–Office of Institutional Research and Planning

Tracking the profile of all current students by gender, age, ethnic origin, fee status, level, and full-time/part-time status can prove useful in making enrollment management decisions, financial projections, and other resource need determinations based on the number and types of students. Exhibit 5.3 shows an example of a report that presents student profile information.

Tracking credit hour enrollments can also be useful for institution, school/college, and departmental planning purposes. Data can be used to evaluate performance against goals, make financial projections, and determine short-term and long-term need for faculty. Knowing the number and type of students by level can be used for enrollment (continued on page 50)

EXHIBIT 5.3: STUDENT PROFILE

STUDENT PROFILE FALL 2000					
Total Enrollment	**17,241**		**Fee Status**		
Gender			Enrolled for 9 or More Credits		
Men	7,463	43.30%	Resident	8,465	49.10%
Women	9,778	56.70%	Non-Resident	1,118	6.50%
			Staff	41	0.20%
Average Age	**28.1**		Graduate Assistant	496	2.90%
Undergraduate	25.8		Enrolled for 8 or Fewer Credits		
Graduate	34.4		Part-time Fee Policy	6,963	40.40%
			Staff	157	0.90%
Ethnic Origin			Graduate Assistant	1	0.00%
White, Non-Hispanic	11,641	67.50%			
Declined to Respond/Other	1,681	9.80%	**Student Level**		
International Student	961	5.60%	Undergraduate	12,598	73.10%
Asian/Pacific Islander	1,489	8.60%	Graduate	4,643	26.90%
Black, Non-Hispanic	486	2.80%			
Hispanic	644	3.70%	**Full-Time/Part-Time**		
Native American	189	1.10%	Full-Time*	9,415	54.60%
Multiple Ethnicity	150	0.90%	Part-Time**	7,826	45.40%
* Full-time = undergraduates enrolled for 12 or more credits; graduates enrolled for 9 or more credits.					
** Part-time = undergraduates enrolled for 11 or fewer credits; graduates enrolled for 8 or fewer credits.					

Source: Portland State University–Office of Institutional Research and Planning

EXHIBIT 5.4: ENROLLMENT BY STUDENT LEVEL AND GENDER

Fall 2001	FR	SO	JR	SR	PB Non-grad	NU	Total UG	PB Grad	GM	GD	NG	Total Grad	Grand Total
TOTAL HEADCOUNT	**2,230**	**2,095**	**3,196**	**3,827**	**891**	**1,362**	**13,601**	**487**	**2,969**	**382**	**1,181**	**5,019**	**18,620**
Male	1,064	891	1,343	1,753	397	752	6,200	227	1,141	197	511	2,076	8,276
Female	1,166	1,204	1,853	2,074	494	610	7,401	260	1,828	185	670	2,943	10,344
Full-Time*	1,718	1,511	2,222	2,477	312	25	8,265	111	1,527	198	3	1,839	10,104
Male	819	648	919	1,123	147	6	3,662	63	514	100	--	677	4,339
Female	899	863	1,303	1,354	165	19	4,603	48	1,013	98	3	1,162	5,765
Part-Time**	512	584	974	1,350	579	1,337	5,336	376	1,442	184	1,178	3,180	8,516
Male	245	243	424	630	250	746	2,538	164	627	97	511	1,399	3,937
Female	267	341	550	720	329	591	2,798	212	815	87	667	1,781	4,579
* Full-time = undergraduates with 12 or more hours; graduates with 9 or more hours.													

Source: Portland State University–Office of Institutional Research and Planning

EXHIBIT 5.5: ENROLLMENT BY DECLARED MAJOR/PROGRAM AND STUDENT LEVEL

Fall 2001, 4th Week Major/Program	Undergraduate				Graduate				TOTAL
	Admit	Non-Admit	PB	Total UG	Admit	Non-Admit	PB	Total GR	
INSTITUTIONAL TOTAL	**11,348**	**1,362**	**891**	**13,601**	**3,351**	**1,181**	**487**	**5,019**	**18,620**
College of Liberal Arts & Sciences	**4,701**	**58**	**214**	**4,973**	**774**	**33**	**23**	**830**	**5,803**
Anthropology	128	--	7	135	20	--	--	20	155
Applied Linguistics	44	1	16	61	72	1	1	74	135
Applied Linguistics	40	1	5	46	1	1	--	2	48
Teaching English as a Second Language (C)	4	--	9	13	--	--	1	1	14
Teaching English to Speakers of Other Languages	--	--	2	2	71	--	--	71	73
Biology	446	7	36	489	36	1	3	40	529
Black Studies (C)	1	--	--	1	--	--	--	--	1
Chemistry	116	1	10	127	13	1	--	14	141
Chicano/Latino Studies (C)	1	--	1	2	--	--	--	--	2
Conflict Resolutions	--	--	--	--	54	--	--	54	54
Child & Family Studies	144	2	1	147	--	--	--	--	147
Economics	69	2	3	74	7	2	1	10	84
English	430	4	13	447	86	6	1	93	540
Environmental Management	--	--	--	--	12	--	--	12	12
Environmental Science Ph.D.	5	--	--	5	73	--	--	73	78
Environmental Studies	99	2	9	110	--	1	--	1	111
Foreign Languages & Literatures	205	2	19	226	44	3	2	49	275
General Studies: Arts & Letters	332	7	4	343	--	1	--	1	344
General Studies: Science	150	3	11	164	18	3	--	21	185
General Studies: Social Science	325	1	3	329	7	--	4	11	340
General Studies: Option II	20	--	--	20	--	--	--	--	20
Geography	80	1	5	86	30	3	1	34	120
Geology	52	1	12	65	19	--	--	19	84
History	257	5	7	269	45	--	2	47	316
International Studies	134	5	3	142	--	--	--	--	142
Mathematical Sciences	101	3	6	110	48	2	2	52	162
Philosophy	50	--	--	50	--	2	1	3	53
Physics	47	--	7	54	11	1	--	12	66
Pre-Professional Programs	55	--	6	61	--	--	1	1	62
Allied Health (P)*	5	--	--	5	--	--	--	--	5
Dental Hygiene (P)	3	--	--	3	--	--	--	--	3
Dentistry/Medicine (P)**	22	--	4	26	--	--	--	--	26
Law (P)	6	--	--	6	--	--	--	--	6
Nursing (P)	9	--	--	9	--	--	--	--	9
Pharmacy (P)	4	--	--	4	--	--	--	--	4
Teacher Education	6	--	2	8	--	--	1	1	9
Psychology	695	6	11	712	23	2	2	27	739
Sociology	305	2	6	313	25	--	--	25	338
Speech Communication	365	3	16	384	85	4	--	89	473
General Speech Communication	309	3	--	312	33	4	--	37	349
Speech & Hearing Sciences	56	--	16	72	52	--	--	52	124
Women's Studies	40	--	--	40	--	--	--	--	40
Women's Studies (C)	1	--	2	3	--	--	1	1	4
Writing	1	--	--	1	46	--	1	47	48
Writing Minor	3	--	--	3	--	--	--	--	3
School of Business Administration	**2,394**	**31**	**149**	**2,574**	**350**	**3**	**7**	**360**	**2,934**
Accounting***	372	2	95	469	--	1	2	3	472
Business Administration****	492	12	7	511	286	1	4	291	802
Business Education	--	--	--	--	1	--	--	1	1
Finance	271	4	10	285	60	1	--	61	346
International Studies Business Administration Minor	5	--	--	5	--	--	--	--	5
Management*****	692	4	31	727	3	--	--	3	730
Marketing	562	9	6	577	--	--	1	1	578

(table continued on page 49)

EXHIBIT 5.5: ENROLLMENT BY DECLARED MAJOR/PROGRAM AND STUDENT LEVEL *(continued from page 48)*

Fall 2001, 4th Week

Major/Program	Undergraduate				Graduate				TOTAL
	Admit	Non-Admit	PB	Total UG	Admit	Non-Admit	PB	Total GR	
Graduate School of Education	17	1	1	19	913	1	150	1,064	1,083
Curriculum & Instruction	15	--	1	16	468	--	21	489	505
Ed Policy, Funda. & Admin. Studies	--	--	--	--	147	--	116	263	263
Special Ed & Counseling Ed	2	1	--	3	298	1	13	312	315
College of Engineering & Computer Science	1,170	36	121	1,327	340	23	15	378	1,705
Civil Engineering	128	--	16	144	25	--	--	25	169
Computer Engineering	186	3	6	195	--	1	--	1	196
Computer Science	477	23	68	568	90	13	8	111	679
Electrical & Computer Engineering	209	7	17	233	131	7	3	141	374
Engineering Management	--	--	1	1	59	--	4	63	64
Manufacturing Engineering	--	--	1	1	2	--	--	2	3
Mechanical Engineering	170	3	12	185	27	2	--	29	214
System Engineering	--	--	--	--	6	--	--	6	6
School of Fine & Performing Arts	1,177	36	79	1,292	61	3	8	72	1,364
Architecture	172	9	15	196	--	3	--	3	199
Art	626	20	47	693	11	--	5	16	709
Art History	38	1	1	40	--	--	--	--	40
Music	243	4	14	261	43	--	3	46	307
Theater Arts	98	2	2	102	7	--	--	7	109
Graduate School of Social Work	--	--	--	--	379	--	1	380	380
College of Urban & Public Affairs	662	12	11	685	435	5	13	453	1,138
School of Community Health	273	5	6	284	23	2	3	28	312
Community Development	63	1	3	67	--	--	--	--	67
Health Studies	210	4	3	217	23	2	3	28	245
School of Government	378	6	4	388	261	2	1	264	652
Administration of Justice	212	1	3	216	11	1	--	12	228
Political Science	165	4	1	170	16	1	1	18	188
Public Administration******	1	1	--	2	234	--	--	234	236
School of Urban Studies & Planning*******	11	1	1	13	151	1	9	161	174
Other Programs	--	--	2	2	89	--	--	89	91
International Programs (C)	--	--	2	2	--	--	--	--	2
Systems Science Ph.D.	--	--	--	--	89	--	--	89	89
Undeclared or Unknown	1,227	1,188	314	2,729	10	1,113	270	1,393	4,122

*Includes the following pre-professional programs: Chiropractic, Naturopathic Medicine, Nuclear Medicine Technology, Occupational Therapy, Optometry, Physical Therapy, Physician Assistant, and Podiatry.

**Includes the following pre-professional programs: Dentistry, Medical Technology, Medicine, Osteopathy, and Veterinary Medicine.

***Includes postbaccalaureate certificate in Accounting

****Includes the following interdepartmental majors: Business Administration, General Business, International Business (MBA), Supply & Logistics ,and International Business Studies Certificate.

*****Includes Human Resource Management, General Management, Information Systems, International Studies Management, and Supply and Logistics Management

******Includes Master of Public Administration, and Public Administration & Policy Ph.D.
*******Includes undergraduate major in Community Development, Master of Urban & Regional Planning, Master of Urban Studies, Ph.D. in Urban Studies, Certificate in Gerontology, and Urban Studies & Planning Minor.

KEY: C=Certificate, I=Interest Area (Non-Degree), P=Pre-Professional Program.

Source: Portland State University–Office of Institutional Research and Planning

(continued from page 47)

planning purposes, since current freshmen enrollments are good predictors of next year's sophomore class, current sophomores predict next year's junior class, etc. Exhibit 5.4 *(page 47)* is an example of this type of enrollment management report by student level, gender, and full-time/part-time enrollment status.

Enrollment by declared major and program further elaborates enrollment management information and can be used by department chairpersons for enrollment planning and faculty assignment purposes. Exhibit 5.5 *(pages 48–49)* shows a report of enrollment by declared major/program and student level.

It is also important to know the headcount enrollments served by the institution over the years. This information is useful when talking with legislators and funding agents, and for other purposes. Exhibit 5.6 *(page 51)* is an example of an enrollment report that can be used to monitor enrollment trends since the university was established.

As noted in chapter 4, student credit hours and enrollments represent the coin of the realm in higher education. College and university administrators must understand enrollment mix, trends, and other information concerning enrollment characteristics, since they can have a profound impact on the finances of the institution. Projecting likely future enrollment and monitoring enrollment trends can provide many early warning indications prior to actual revenue fluctuations.

ADVISING

This function primarily provides academic advising services for students. Evaluation criteria for advising functions include:

- frequency and number of student contracts, both by student and in the aggregate;

- advisor to student ratios, including comparison with student to advisor ratios at comparator institutions;

- customer satisfaction surveys;

- number of students on academic probation or suspension;

- retention rates;

- partnerships with internal and external entities to meet mission of the unit; and

- overall institutional GPA.

Student advising is important to overall student success and retention. Assisting students in being successful can generate positive outcomes for the institution, since these students will be satisfied customers who are more likely to support the institution in the form of gifts. In addition, retaining current students means that less money and time must be spent on recruiting new students each year.

CAREER CENTER

This function is responsible for assisting students and alumni in developing, evaluating, and implementing career and employment decisions and plans. This involves career counseling and advising, providing career information resources, preparing students to interact successfully with prospective employers, and facilitating access to part-time jobs, internships, and full-time career positions. Evaluation and reporting criteria for this function include:

- overall placement rates;

- ratio of career counselors per student or per graduate, including comparisons to peer institutions;

- number of employers who participate in career fairs and campus interviews;

- number of partnerships with academic units and support services to enhance student access to career center programs and resources; and

- user satisfaction with career planning and placement services.

FINANCIAL AID

This operation is responsible for selecting from a pool of qualified applicants those students who meet the institution's guidelines for receiving financial assistance. Excluded from this area are the processes of non-need based award recipient selection that occurs outside of financial aid (e.g., merit-based institutional award selection that may be performed by departments and athletic scholarship selection that usually falls within the purview of the athletic department). This operation must follow numerous federal and donor directives with strict audit and other requirements. Evaluation and reporting criteria for this function include:

- turnaround time from receipt of aid application to award of aid;

- number and/or percentage of students that progress to the next step in the process: from inquiries, to applicants, to awards, to recipients;

- user satisfaction with office services;

- student to staff ratios;

- amount of aid disbursed by type;

- default rates;

- tracking the increase in regulations and compliance costs, including training costs;

- number or percentage of students who receive aid packages on time;

- audit disallowances or repayments due to processing errors; and

- expediency in getting awards out in a timely manner each spring as this can be a major factor in student decisions.

EXHIBIT 5.6: END OF TERM ENROLLMENT: 1946–2001

Academic Year	Fall Term	Winter Term	Spring Term	Academic Year	Fall Term	Winter Term	Spring Term
1946-47	1,411	1,521	1,398	1974-75	14,934	13,519	13,005
1947-48	1,468	1,527	1,470	1975-76	15,389	14,342	13,375
1948-49	1,232	1,387	1,340	1976-77	15,296	14,107	13,462
1949-50	1,624	1,638	1,414	1977-78	15,980	14,507	13,636
1950-51	1,349	1,100	957	1978-79	16,062	14,586	13,900
1951-52	1,025	940	845	1979-80	16,964	15,219	14,183
1952-53	1,357	1,336	1,122	1980-81	16,875	15,064	14,009
1953-54	1,629	1,622	1,513	1981-82	15,572	13,951	13,087
1954-55	2,370	2,267	2,093	1982-83	14,546	13,282	12,444
1955-56	2,800	2,532	2,245	1983-84	14,559	13,464	12,642
1956-57	2,999	2,795	2,543	1984-85	14,448	13,397	12,566
1957-58	3,200	3,105	2,784	1985-86	14,832	13,878	13,180
1958-59	3,717	3,477	3,144	1986-87	15,713	14,554	13,757
1959-60	4,008	3,650	3,296	1987-88	15,777	14,771	14,076
1960-61	4,552	4,248	3,932	1988-89	16,192	15,011	14,127
1961-62	5,285	4,907	4,427	1989-90	15,037	14,046	13,256
1962-63	5,788	5,532	5,047	1990-91	14,977	14,100	13,248
1963-64	6,723	6,338	5,776	1991-92	14,544	13,769	13,207
1964-65	7,587	7,117	6,622	1992-93	14,953	14,176	13,203
1965-66	9,125	8,232	7,388	1993-94	14,519	13,769	12,835
1966-67	8,776	8,176	7,630	1994-95	14,443	13,692	12,817
1967-68	9,557	8,895	8,428	1995-96	14,342	13,866	12,946
1968-69	10,422	9,644	9,266	1996-97	14,785	14,042	13,035
1969-70	11,146	10,654	10,252	1997-98	14,828	14,018	13,311
1970-71	11,354	11,044	10,438	1998-99	15,160	14,529	13,857
1971-72	14,701	13,691	12,555	1999-00	16,062	15,292	14,568
1972-73	13,591	13,038	12,111	2000-01	17,239	16,795	16,061
1973-74	13,201	12,410	11,937				

NOTE: End of term enrollment averages about 1% greater than enrollment at the end of the 4th week of classes, the cut-off for all other enrollment data in the Fact Book and Statistical Portrait. These figures are used for long-term analyses because 4th week enrollments are unavailable prior to 1967-68. Students auditing all of their courses are included beginning end of fall term 1991.

Source: Portland State University–Office of Institutional Research and Planning

Exhibit 5.7 (page 52) shows a typical report of financial aid disbursed by program type, numbers of recipients, recipient ethnicity, average aid disbursed per recipient, and applicant to recipient percentages for the last five years. Monitoring trends in aid disbursement can be useful for planning purposes, since the amounts disbursed can be correlated with costs of attendance and other factors. The number and types of recipients is useful for enrollment management purposes.

Another example of a report of aid disbursed by type and program is illustrated in Exhibit 5.8 (pages 53–54). This report, while similar to the previous exhibit, provides further elaboration of the type of aid disbursed and the number of recipients per program.

Student financial aid is becoming increasingly important in attracting and retaining meritorious students as well as preserving access to higher education opportunities. For many institutions, certain types of financial aid programs are self-funded, so the costs of these programs must be contrasted to the benefits provided in terms of other revenues generated resulting from students coming to the campus, diversity issues, institutional reputation, and other issues.

STUDENT AFFAIRS

This unit is responsible for coordinating student campus activities to ensure that the quality of student life is kept at a satisfactory level. In addition, this unit handles student conduct code violations, and otherwise provides advice to student leadership on the role and function of the student senate, allocation of student fees, and other related activities. Useful evaluation and reporting criteria for this function include:

• number of student contacts per year;

(continued on page 53)

EXHIBIT 5.7: FINANCIAL AID AWARDED BY PROGRAM TYPE AND ETHNICITY

1996-97 to 2000-2001						
Expenditures by Program Type*	1996-97	1997-98	1998-99	1999-2000	2000-01	% Change
Grants	$6,806,186	$7,459,605	$8,649,351	$9,896,252	$11,663,818	17.86%
Loans	39,374,920	46,186,022	52,790,240	60,496,307	64,362,494	6.39%
Work Study	1,522,101	1,431,423	1,958,457	2,003,871	2,676,492	33.57%
Scholarships**	2,473,890	3,376,295	4,252,429	2,344,911	2,197,902	-6.27%
Athletic Scholarships***	1,249,564	1,347,869	1,445,789	1,687,098	1,896,471	12.41%
Tuition Remission**	5,887,983	6,262,682	6,095,887	4,291,644	3,276,163	-23.66%
Total	$57,314,644	$66,063,896	$75,192,153	$80,720,083	$86,073,340	6.63%
Applicants	14,767	15,560	15,427	17,004	17,678	3.96%
Recipients by Ethnicity						
Asian/Pacific Islander	839	864	1,012	902	894	-0.89%
Black	308	324	373	334	396	18.56%
Hispanic	351	370	447	393	461	17.30%
Native American	134	140	158	147	162	10.20%
White	4,973	5,318	6,143	6,271	6,617	5.52%
Unknown	812	786	994	940	1,030	9.57%
Total	7,417	7,802	9,127	8,987	9,560	6.38%
Ave. Aid per Recipient	$7,727	$8,468	$8,238	$8,982	$9,003	0.24%
Ratio of Recipients to Applicants	50.23%	50.14%	59.16%	52.85%	54.08%	

*Dollars awarded to enrolled admitted students. In some instances (particularly in the case of loans) students may choose to accept a lesser amount than awarded.

**The figures show only funds that are awarded as direct payments through financial aid funds, due to the new SCT Banner financial aid system in 1999-2000.

***In 1999-2000 athletic aid included $1,134,054 fee remission. In 2000-01 athletic aid was funded by scholarships.

continued from page 51

- user satisfaction with student affairs services; and
- numbers of student conduct code issues.

STUDENT COUNSELING

The activity is responsible for providing professional guidance services to students who are having difficulties adjusting academically or socially to campus life. Criteria that can be used for decision making, setting goals, and monitoring performance in this area include:

- utilization of counseling services as a percentage of enrolled students;
- user satisfaction with counseling services; and
- counselors per 1,000 students.

PLANT OPERATION AND MAINTENANCE

FACILITIES

This department is responsible for ensuring the maintenance and smooth operation of all campus buildings and grounds. The facilities function includes all trades, custodial staff, grounds staff, maintenance staff, architects, and planners. Evaluation and reporting criteria for this unit include:

- quality of custodial services, based on surveys;
- amount of deferred maintenance per building at given points in time;
- user satisfaction with facility services;
- operating costs—total and costs per square foot, also comparisons of this information with comparable institutions;

(continued on page 55)

EXHIBIT 5.8: SUMMARY OF STUDENT AID BY TYPE 1998–1999

	NUMBER OF RECIPIENTS	AMOUNT DISBURSED
Custodial Funds	7,447	$7,736,485
Employment		
College Work Study Program	1,620	$1,904,062
Other Personnel Services	5,617	$8,375,129
Total	7,237	$10,279,191
Grants		
Pell	7,571	$14,549,374
Fl Student Grant	3,249	$3,196,544
Lottery Trust Grant	0	$0
SEOG	2,847	$2,930,080
Athletic	1,196	$2,684,870
Turner Grant	3,328	$5,981,195
Metta Heathcote	150	$107,752
SSRS Grant	262	$492,186
Misc. Grants	98	$59,371
Total	18,701	$30,001,372
Loans		
Subsidized Stafford Loans	15,976	$63,345,387
Unsubsidized Stafford Loans	13,628	$50,973,685
Perkins Loan	1,841	$4,006,220
PLUS	1,117	$5,352,597
Short Term Loan	918	$593,504
UF College Awarded	371	$816,017

(table continued on page 54)

EXHIBIT 5.8: SUMMARY OF STUDENT AID BY TYPE 1998–1999 *(continued from page 53)*

	NUMBER OF RECIPIENTS	AMOUNT DISBURSED
Private Loans	439	$2,724,768
Dentistry	80	$227,720
Medical	0	$0
Stud Aid for Education	83	$161,413
SLS	0	$0
Vet. Med.	28	$68,731
UF Long Term	3	$10,365
Arthur L Wallace Loan	31	$73,747
Master Teachers Fellow	0	$0
HEAL	0	$0
OCC Physical Therapy Loan	4	$16,000
Miscellaneous Loans	9	$12,827
Total	34,528	$128,382,981
Scholarships		
Brecht	19	$18,500
Challenger Memorial	0	$0
Chappie James Teach	45	$67,500
Dental/Disadvantaged	5	$23,344
Fl Academic Scholars	9,564	$22,597,384
Fl Merit Scholarships	4,365	$5,641,214
FL Grad Scholars	0	$0
Fl Top Scholars	119	$170,810
Fl Teachers	26	$156,000
General & Special	259	$314,203
Grad Tuition Scholarships	352	$535,657
In-state Matriculation Waivers	6,955	$9,106,849
Medical/Disadvantaged	11	$28,769
Misc. Scholarships	14	$26,000
Misc Tuition Waiver	373	$365,346
National Merit	785	$2,180,171
National Merit Stipend	638	$560,350
National Science Scholars	0	$0
O/S Matriculation Waivers	2,036	$11,587,784
Other State Scholarships	385	$714,490
Paul Douglas Teachers	0	$0
Pres. Academic-Minority	560	$1,082,922
Pres. Achievement-Minority	25	$50,000
UF College Awarded	4,089	$8,283,315
Univ. Academic Scholarship	207	$328,701
Virgil Hawkins	30	$498,531
Vocational Gold Seal	816	$1,079,497
Total	31,678	$65,417,337
Florida Prepaid Tuition	5,404	$10,499,156
GRAND TOTAL	104,995	$252,316,522

Source: University of Florida Web site.

continued from page 53

- inventory of buildings and total assignable square feet;
- space utilization analyses;
- construction cost per square foot;
- utility consumption;
- status reports on approved capital projects; and
- capital budgets by sources of funding.

Exhibit 5.9 below illustrates a report on facility operating costs per square foot, and contrasts this information to peer institutions. This constitutes useful benchmarking information and can indicate areas that need improvement or are functioning at more efficient rates than their peers.

Exhibit 5.10 *(page 56)* is an example of a report that displays investment in facilities, including the date of construction/acquisition, square footage, cost, and cost per square foot. In addition, the amount of investment in improvements other than buildings and equipment is reported.

As noted earlier, the amount of deferred maintenance present in college and university facilities represents a major financial challenge that must be confronted in the coming years. Institutions spend a great deal of time and energy documenting the levels of deferred maintenance in order to track these levels from year to year, and to make the case to funding agencies and boards for supplemental funding to address this problem. Exhibit 5.11 *(page 57)* is an example of a chart displaying the level of the deferred maintenance problems by building at an institution. It was

developed for a presentation to a governing board. This graphic representation clearly shows the severity of the problem, given that many of the education and general fund buildings at this institution have more than 30 percent of their value in deferred maintenance.

Space utilization information is used to prepare facility and administration (F&A) rate calculations, and is helpful for planning and facility management purposes. Exhibit 5.12 *(pages 57–59)* is an example of a report that lists space assignments by departments as well as the classification of their use.

Facilities management has assumed a far more important role given the fact that colleges and universities need large physical plants to sustain their operations. Much of this space is highly specialized and extremely expensive to construct and operate. As facilities age, many colleges and universities have deferred maintenance and diverted funding to other purposes. The tendency to defer maintenance has resulted in the accumulation of a very serious backlog of maintenance and repairs needs. Many building also need renovation if they are to support the latest technology applications and pedagogy. In addition, given the rising costs of utilities, especially electricity and natural gas, the operation of these facilities is consuming an increasing portion of institutional operating budgets. Institutions must develop systems to monitor and track these items, and begin to formulate strategies to reduce both deferred maintenance backlog and operating costs.

(continued on page 61)

EXHIBIT 5.9: FACILITY OPERATING COST PER SQUARE FOOT COMPARED TO PEER INSTITUTIONS: 1999 – 2000

Operating Costs Per Gross Square Foot by Institution
1999-2000 Data

Institution	Total Costs	Admin. Costs	Custodial Costs	Grnds. Cost	Maint. Costs	Utility Costs	Environ. Costs	Waste Costs	Other Costs
Institution #1	$2.85	$0.29	$1.05	$0.08	$1.12	$0.26	$0.00	$0.03	$0.02
Institution #2	$3.26	$0.38	$1.15	$0.02	$1.59	$0.00	$0.00	$0.03	$0.09
Institution #3	$3.24	$0.54	$1.17	$0.07	$1.05	$0.14	$0.00	$0.05	$0.22
Institution #4	$4.23	$0.52	$0.92	$0.23	$1.69	$0.02	$0.13	$0.03	$0.69
Institution #5	$2.58	$0.29	$0.98	$0.05	$0.99	$0.20	$0.07	$0.00	$0.00
Institution #6	$3.83	$0.50	$1.61	$0.12	$1.53	$0.00	$0.00	$0.07	$0.00
Institution #7	$3.23	$0.27	$1.07	$0.10	$1.32	$0.21	$0.00	$0.11	$0.15
Baseline University	$2.68	$0.55	$0.64	$0.12	$0.69	$0.28	$0.14	$0.05	$0.21
Average Cost of Comparators	$3.32	$0.40	$1.14	$0.10	$1.33	$0.12	$0.03	$0.05	$0.17
Difference Baseline vs. Comparators	($0.64)	$0.15	($0.50)	$0.02	($0.64)	$0.16	$0.11	$0.00	$0.04

Source: The Association of Higher Education Facilities Officers–1999–00 Comparative Costs and Staffing Report for Educational Facilities

EXHIBIT 5.10: INVESTMENT IN FACILITIES: JUNE 2001

	Date of Construction or Acquisition	Approximate Acreage or Square Footage	Investment*	Investment per Square Foot
LAND				
Campus		36.5	$14,361,561	
Off Campus		2.645	$14,440	
TOTAL LAND		**39.145**	**$14,376,001**	
BUILDINGS				
Lincoln Hall	1949	135,052	$3,630,993	$27
Cramer Hall	1956	239,564	$6,544,572	$27
Extended Studies Building	1956	30,000	$557,973	$19
Smith Memorial Center	1957	222,391	$9,416,617	$42
Neuberger Hall	1961	222,515	$4,977,279	$22
Harder House	1961	5,045	$30,812	$6
Systems Science	1963	4,770	$18,764	$4
Honors Program	1962	7,128	$26,426	$4
Science Building I	1965	91,164	$2,723,604	$30
Peter W. Stott Center	1965	153,492	$3,129,901	$20
Parking Structure I	1965	315,937	$1,280,474	$4
Heating Plant	1965	4,237	$569,740	$134
Campus and Grounds Building	1965	10,025	$26,392	$3
Millar Library	1966	194,783	$12,273,866	$63
East Hall	1966	23,042	$251,130	$11
Recycling Center	1967	634	$10,200	$16
Shattuck Hall	1969	67,940	$1,574,563	$23
Parkway Building	1969	40,500	$1,245,378	$31
Blackstone Apartments	1969	40,655	$1,262,031	$31
Montgomery Building	1969	43,320	$1,339,439	$31
Maryanne Building	1969	13,320	$424,293	$32
Stratford Building	1969	22,950	$698,664	$30
St. Helens Building	1969	36,280	$1,137,257	$31
King Albert Building	1969	31,950	$1,028,959	$32
Birmingham Building	1969	9,480	$304,097	$32
Adeline Building	1969	11,190	$418,508	$37
President's Residence	1969	8,002	$69,766	$9
Parking Structure II	1971	110,877	$1,425,770	$13
Campus Security	1971	2,288	$23,518	$10
University Services Building	1970	59,067	$1,042,569	$18
Harrison Building	1972	1,960	$14,540	$7
Gordon Child Dev. Center	1972	15,692	$392,184	$25
Science Building II	1973	213,333	$10,654,945	$50
The Ondine	1976	214,031	$2,624,522	$12
Parking Structure III	1979	234,256	$3,231,671	$14
School of Education	1980	53,293	$3,694,222	$69
Center for Adv. Technology	1985	70,453	$4,480,411	$64
West Hall	1986	195,900	$8,232,635	$42
Business Administration	1987	52,270	$5,638,385	$108
George C. Hoffmann Hall	1995	9,744	$1,882,875	$193
Sixth Avenue Building	1996	19,812	$620,000	$31
Fourth Avenue Building	1996	204,599	$20,634,085	$101
Urban Center Building	1998	143,319	$23,701,009	$165
University Center Building	1999	180,594	$5,101,228	$28
Simon Benson House	2000	4,163	$1,400,000	$336
TOTAL BUILDINGS		**3,442,941**	**$149,766,267**	**$44**
IMPROVEMENTS OTHER THAN BUILDING			**$9,042,719**	
EQUIPMENT**				
Library Books & Equipment			$50,713,642	
Equipment			$15,754,652	
TOTAL EQUIPMENT			**$66,468,294**	
TOTAL INVESTMENT IN PLANT			**$239,653,281**	

Source: Portland State University–Office of Institutional Research and Planning

EXHIBIT 5.11: PERCENT OF BUILDING VALUATION IN DEFERRED MAINTENANCE

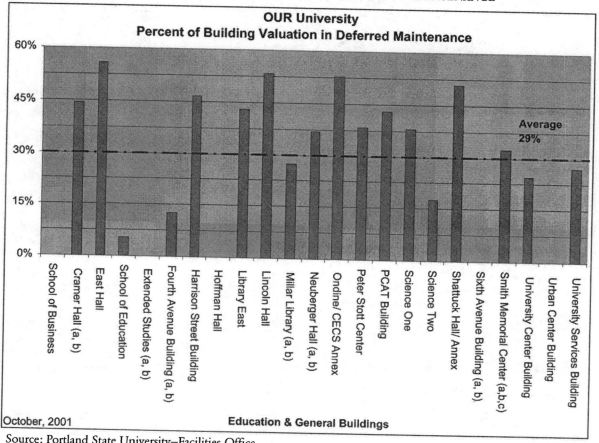

Source: Portland State University—Facilities Office

EXHIBIT 5.12: TYPE OF SPACE BY DEPARTMENT AND BY USAGE *(excerpt)*

BUDGET/COLLEGE/DEPARTMENT	CLASSRM. SQ. FT.	INSTRU. LAB SQ. FT.	RES. LAB SQ. FT.	OFFICE SQ. FT.	LIBRARY SQ. FT.	MEDICAL SQ. FT.	HOUSING SQ. FT.	SUPPORT SQ. FT.	OTHER SQ. FT.	TOTAL SQ. FT.
AUXILIARY										
ADMINISTRATIVE AFFAIRS										
Business Service Division	0	0	0	2,393	0	0	0	0	0	2,393
Campus Concessions	0	0	0	0	0	0	0	0	1,878	1,878
Campus Shop and Bookstore	0	0	0	189	0	0	0	8,465	2,064	10,718
Gator Corner Dining	0	0	0	134	0	0	0	0	16,442	16,576
Gator Dining Service	0	0	0	1,628	0	0	0	188	43,707	45,523
Hub Food Court	0	0	0	0	0	0	0	0	2,984	2,984
Laundry	0	0	0	1,216	0	0	0	20,078	0	21,294
Law Center Cafeteria	0	0	0	102	0	0	0	0	4,112	4,214
O'Connell Center	0	0	0	155	0	0	0	0	5,202	5,357
Parking - Admin. Services	0	0	0	6,184	0	0	0	0	25	6,209
Parking Garage	0	0	0	53	0	0	0	1,255,591	0	1,255,644
Pest Control	0	0	0	606	0	0	0	1,357	245	2,208
Recreational Center Dining	0	0	0	985	0	0	0	0	8,804	9,789
Telecommunications Admin.	0	0	0	1,792	0	0	0	0	0	1,792
University I.D. Cards	0	0	0	729	0	0	0	0	1,122	1,851
University Printing	0	0	0	115	0	0	0	2,934	0	3,049
Total	0	0	0	16,281	0	0	0	1,288,613	86,585	1,391,479

(table continued on page 58)

EXHIBIT 5.12: TYPE OF SPACE BY DEPARTMENT AND BY USAGE *(continued from page 57)*

BUDGET/COLLEGE/DEPARTMENT	CLASSRM. SQ. FT.	INSTRU. LAB SQ. FT.	RES. LAB SQ. FT.	OFFICE SQ. FT.	LIBRARY SQ. FT.	MEDICAL SQ. FT.	HOUSING SQ. FT.	SUPPORT SQ. FT.	OTHER SQ. FT.	TOTAL SQ. FT.
ADVANCEMENT										
U.F. Foundation	0	0	0	19,978	0	0	1,025	5,946	221	27,170
Total	0	0	0	19,978	0	0	1,025	5,946	221	27,170
DESIGN, CONSTRUCTION, AND PLANNING										
Rinker School of Bldg Constr.	0	0	0	0	0	0	0	0	2,540	2,540
Total	0	0	0	0	0	0	0	0	2,540	2,540
FINE ARTS										
Performing Arts Center	0	0	0	2,532	0	0	0	0	29,507	32,039
Total	0	0	0	2,532	0	0	0	0	29,507	32,039
HEALTH AFFAIRS										
Student Health Care Ctr	0	0	0	10,279	196	18,859	0	1,477	2,640	33,451
Total	0	0	0	10,279	196	18,859	0	1,477	2,640	33,451
HEALTH AND HUMAN PERFORMANCE										
Living Well Program	0	0	0	455	0	0	0	0	6,774	7,229
Total	0	0	0	455	0	0	0	0	6,774	7,229
JOURNALISM & COMMUNICATIONS										
Radio Station - WRUF	0	790	0	1,952	0	0	0	0	1,067	3,809
Total	0	790	0	1,952	0	0	0	0	1,067	3,809
NORTHEAST REGIONAL DATA CENTER										
NERDC	0	0	0	16,089	0	0	0	0	0	16,089
Total	0	0	0	16,089	0	0	0	0	0	16,089
STUDENT AFFAIRS										
J. W. Reitz Union	0	0	0	11,872	1,382	0	11,128	5,442	62,357	92,181
Reitz Union Leased Space	0	0	0	0	0	0	0	0	4,314	4,314
Total	0	0	0	11,872	1,382	0	11,128	5,442	66,671	96,495
STUDENT GOVERNMENT										
Student Gov't Activities	0	0	0	5,292	0	0	0	0	205	5,497
Total	0	0	0	5,292	0	0	0	0	205	5,497
UNIVERSITY PRESS OF FLORIDA										
University Press of Florida	0	0	0	4,259	0	0	0	352	0	4,611
Total	0	0	0	4,259	0	0	0	352	0	4,611
TOTAL AUXILIARY	0	790	0	88,989	1,578	18,859	12,153	1,301,830	196,210	1,620,409
CONTRACTS & GRANTS										
EDUCATION										
Baby Gator Child Care	0	0	0	0	0	0	0	0	7,804	7,804
Total	0	0	0	0	0	0	0	0	7,804	7,804
TOTAL CONTRACTS & GRANTS	0	0	0	0	0	0	0	0	7,804	7,804
EDUCATIONAL AND GENERAL										
ACADEMIC AFFAIRS										
Affirmative Action	0	0	0	1,160	0	0	0	0	0	1,160
Chief Information Office	0	0	0	1,913	0	0	0	0	0	1,913
Institutional Research	0	0	0	1,647	0	0	0	245	0	1,892
Office of the Provost	0	0	0	8,211	0	0	0	1,914	0	10,125
U. F. International Center	0	0	0	4,663	0	0	0	0	0	4,663
United Faculty of Florida	0	0	0	485	0	0	0	0	0	485
University Honors Program	0	0	0	1,157	0	0	0	0	0	1,157
Total	0	0	0	19,236	0	0	0	2,159	0	21,395
ADMINISTRATIVE AFFAIRS										
Building Services	0	0	0	2,229	0	0	0	2,793	351	5,373
Campus Mail	0	0	0	90	0	0	0	9,323	0	9,413

(table continued on page 59)

EXHIBIT 5.12: TYPE OF SPACE BY DEPARTMENT AND BY USAGE *(continued from page 58)*

BUDGET/COLLEGE/DEPARTMENT	CLASSRM. SQ. FT.	INSTRU. LAB SQ. FT.	RES. LAB SQ. FT.	OFFICE SQ. FT.	LIBRARY SQ. FT.	MEDICAL SQ. FT.	HOUSING SQ. FT.	SUPPORT SQ. FT.	OTHER SQ. FT.	TOTAL SQ. FT.
CENTERS AND INSTITUTES										
Biotechnology Institute	0	0	1,783	684	0	0	0	0	0	2,467
Ctr For Latin Am. Studies	0	0	452	4,478	1,096	0	0	0	0	6,026
Ctr For Pre-Collegiate Ed/Trng	0	0	0	3,207	0	0	0	0	0	3,207
Ctr Humanities & Soc. Sci.	0	0	0	2,800	0	0	0	0	0	2,800
Ctr I & R Computing Activities	0	10,822	0	5,851	18,004	0	0	0	0	34,677
Harn Art Museum	0	0	0	5,155	820	0	0	0	35,342	41,317
Inst For Advanced Study Comm.	455	665	2,461	2,395	0	0	0	0	0	5,976
Institute of Gerontology	0	0	0	766	0	0	0	0	0	766
Microfabritech	0	0	6,376	473	0	0	0	0	0	6,849
Total	455	11,487	11,072	25,809	19,920	0	0	0	35,342	104,085
CONTINUING EDUCATION										
DOCE - English Language Institute	2,584	0	0	2,883	0	0	0	0	0	5,467
Total	2,584	0	0	2,883	0	0	0	0	0	5,467
EIES										
Aeronomy & Other Atmos Sci	0	0	2,069	457	0	0	0	96	0	2,622
Center for Wetlands	0	0	1,883	2,332	342	0	0	720	0	5,277
Total	0	0	3,952	2,789	342	0	0	816	0	7,899
EDUCATION										
Counselor Education	593	362	840	3,984	0	0	0	0	0	5,779
Dean - Education	9,675	8,028	2,384	16,510	599	0	0	652	1,350	39,198
Educational Leadership	0	0	0	4,200	0	0	0	0	0	4,200
Foundations	0	0	422	4,474	0	0	0	0	0	4,896
Instruction & Curriculum	0	3,232	0	9,063	0	0	0	0	0	12,295
Special Education	0	0	0	4,441	0	0	0	0	0	4,441
Total	10,268	11,622	3,646	42,672	599	0	0	652	1,350	70,809
ENGINEERING										
Biomedical Engineering	0	0	2,219	551	0	0	0	0	0	2,770
Chemical Engineering	0	8,515	18,025	9,285	0	0	0	0	0	35,825
Civil Engineering	859	9,745	19,303	27,906	1,233	0	0	0	238	59,284
Coastal Engineering	0	0	46,680	8,669	1,713	0	0	0	0	57,062
Computer & Information Science	0	4,233	8,080	21,184	0	0	0	0	0	33,497
Dean - Engineering	233	0	6,283	15,880	0	0	0	0	1,044	23,440
Digital Design	0	0	0	1,377	0	0	0	822	0	2,199
Electrical Engineering	219	12,824	32,056	34,209	0	0	0	0	0	79,308
Engineering - Feeds	7,489	431	0	1,884	0	0	0	0	0	9,804
Engineering Sciences	2,071	2,459	17,355	11,672	0	0	0	350	0	33,907
Environmental Engineering	0	3,394	14,482	10,193	0	0	0	0	0	28,069
Erc Aerospace Engineering	0	0	13,138	5,627	490	0	0	0	0	19,255
Industrial & Systems Engineerg	0	3,884	3,117	7,652	0	0	0	0	162	14,815
Materials Science Engineering	0	6,997	51,043	24,016	744	0	0	0	1,030	83,830
Mechanical Engineering	0	5,571	31,615	11,712	386	0	0	0	155	49,439
Nuclear Engineering	0	1,727	15,445	7,273	615	0	0	0	228	25,288
Total	10,871	59,780	278,841	199,090	5,181	0	0	1,172	2,857	557,792
FINE ARTS										
Art	1,299	43,035	0	8,494	0	0	0	0	510	53,338
Dean - Fine Arts	0	0	0	3,385	0	0	0	0	280	3,665
Music	3,036	20,890	0	7,518	0	0	0	0	0	31,444
Performing Arts Center	0	0	0	0	0	0	0	0	1,340	1,340
Theater	1,345	3,955	0	4,296	0	0	0	0	15,149	24,745
University Gallery	0	0	0	975	0	0	0	0	2,830	3,805
Total	5,680	67,880	0	24,668	0	0	0	0	20,109	118,337
TOTAL OFF CAMPUS	14,988	20,471	454,073	164,760	16,067	6,664	261,134	147,513	1,055,528	2,141,198
TOTAL UNIVERSITY	327,246	473,330	1,976,809	2,394,541	425,422	629,314	2,050,626	1,784,250	2,421,126	12,482,664

Source: University of Florida Web site

EXHIBIT 5.13: EDUCATION AND GENERAL FUND BUDGET BY PROGRAM

Program	Unclas. Salaries	Unclas. Pay	Clas. Salaries	Clas. Pay	Student Pay	Grad. Asst. Salaries	Grad Asst /Other Fee Remis	Other Payroll Expense	Services and Supplies	Capital Outlay	Internal Sales Reimbrsmnt	Total Budget	Unclas. FTE	Clas. FTE	Grad. Asst. FTE
Instruction:															
College of Liberal Arts & Sciences	$14,874,512	$41,565	$648,785	$0	$65,788	$564,462	$1,285,600	$5,072,468	$967,729	$89,513	$0	$23,610,422	294.18	23.75	33.31
Undergraduate Studies	$1,432,922	$0	$69,666	$0	$116,688	$139,351	$183,110	$549,311	$351,647	$0	$0	$2,842,695	32.17	2.75	8.24
School of Business Admin.	$4,596,613	$5,000	$75,817	$0	$12,609	$34,544	$241,314	$1,393,671	$1,443,911	$0	$0	$7,803,479	63.35	3.50	2.04
School of Education	$2,581,197	$51,273	$119,611	$0	$6,693	$65,988	$124,173	$928,748	$211,720	$21,327	$0	$4,110,730	51.48	5.00	3.90
College of Engineering & Computer Science	$3,795,040	$5,000	$289,456	$6,640	$42,868	$96,789	$302,900	$1,272,555	$1,590,163	$114,555	($30,667)	$7,478,659	50.17	10.25	5.71
School Fine & Perf. Arts	$2,764,222	$19,292	$197,044	$0	$10,708	$48,666	$174,415	$1,000,572	$491,504	$12,076	$0	$4,725,139	57.98	7.50	2.88
School of Social Work	$1,234,483	$14,955	$147,830	$0	$608	$17,336	$41,750	$468,789	$322,986	$11,000	$0	$2,259,737	22.80	5.75	1.02
College of Urban & Public Affairs	$3,573,372	$5,000	$156,057	$0	$4,563	$92,681	$359,321	$1,183,373	$161,654	$0	$0	$5,536,021	65.30	6.00	5.48
School of Extended Studies	$1,264,666	$2,868,643	$200,100	$0	$54,385	$205,428	$0	$1,124,377	$364,338	$0	$0	$6,081,937	35.80	8.00	12.14
Other Instruction	$349,549	$0	$31,792	$0	$0	$42,327	$35,478	$107,970	$9,141,743	$422,000	$0	$10,130,859	3.02	1.00	2.50
Total, Instruction	$36,466,576	$3,010,728	$1,936,158	$6,640	$314,910	$1,307,572	$2,748,061	$13,101,834	$15,047,394	$670,471	($30,667)	$74,579,677	676.25	73.50	77.22
Research	$486,634	$0	$64,438	$0	$3,398	$15,950	$37,477	$181,739	$1,772,013	$0	$0	$2,561,649	7.39	2.25	0.94
Public Service	$603,704	$0	$54,976	$0	$0	$4,648	$5,913	$219,608	$726,100	$0	$0	$1,614,949	10.69	2.00	0.27
Academic Support	$7,258,399	$184,293	$3,069,259	$0	$1,075,249	$27,350	$492,533	$3,739,796	$2,821,822	$3,307,358	$0	$21,976,059	128.89	102.49	1.62
Student Services	$2,211,140	$11,383	$1,374,199	$0	$113,875	$7,631	$76,784	$1,427,336	$4,373,003	$0	$0	$9,595,351	50.00	54.33	0.45
Operation & Maint. of Plant	$714,705	$0	$1,123,277	$69,580	$51,864	$0	$0	$698,627	$8,086,357	$1,069,106	($105,094)	$11,708,422	13.40	31.80	0.00
Institutional Support	$5,091,115	$16,253	$2,795,082	$95,132	$217,429	$15,440	$37,456	$2,913,683	$5,311,888	$250,000	($1,297,604)	$15,445,874	99.19	87.81	0.91
Budgeted Reserves	$1,768,522	$0	$309,541	$0	$0	$0	$4,217,761	$471,938	$5,355,084	$300,000	$0	$12,422,846	0.00	0.00	0.00
Total, Educational & General Services	$54,600,795	$3,222,657	$10,726,930	$171,352	$1,776,725	$1,378,591	$7,615,985	$22,754,561	$43,493,661	$5,596,935	($1,433,365)	$149,904,827	985.81	354.17	81.41

EXHIBIT 5.14: EDUCATION AND GENERAL FUND BUDGET BY ORGANIZATION

Organization	Unclas. Salaries	Unclas. Pay	Clas. Salaries	Clas. Pay	Student Pay	Grad. Asst. Salaries	Grad Asst /Other Fee Remis	Other Payroll Expense	Services and Supplies	Capital Outlay	Internal Sales Reimbrsmnt	Total Budget	Unclas. FTE	Clas. FTE	Grad. Asst. FTE
Academic Affairs															
College of Liberal Arts & Sciences	$15,385,100	$47,047	$974,846	$0	$72,234	$564,462	$1,285,600	$5,379,662	$1,074,811	$89,513	$0	$24,873,275	302.87	35.00	33.31
Undergraduate Studies	$1,609,214	$0	$69,666	$0	$116,688	$139,351	$183,110	$606,146	$361,647	$0	$0	$3,085,822	35.17	6.00	8.24
School of Social Work	$1,706,500	$14,955	$153,852	$0	$2,342	$17,336	$41,750	$618,937	$363,739	$11,000	$0	$2,930,411	29.96	6.00	1.02
School of Business Admin.	$5,116,128	$5,000	$137,722	$0	$16,601	$34,544	$241,314	$1,593,552	$1,546,338	$21,327	$0	$8,691,199	72.28	6.00	2.04
School of Education	$2,922,761	$73,386	$241,654	$0	$7,325	$93,338	$423,859	$1,101,893	$233,393	$21,327	$0	$5,118,936	56.98	10.00	5.52
College of Engineering & Computer Science	$4,532,252	$5,000	$317,132	$6,640	$48,988	$96,789	$302,900	$1,516,658	$2,994,100	$114,555	($30,667)	9897706.834	61.24		
School of Extended Studies	$1,538,788	$3,030,823	$318,288	$0	$64,585	$205,428	$0	$1,293,040	$530,966	$0	$0	$6,981,918	40.30	12.00	12.14
School Fine & Performing Arts	$3,051,778	$19,292	$252,833	$0	$20,708	$48,666	$174,415	$1,118,973	$505,787	$12,076	$0	$5,211,168	62.98	9.50	2.88
College of Urban & Public Affairs	$4,521,438	$5,000	$320,563	$0	$18,329	$113,279	$359,321	$1,551,417	$262,991	$0	$0	$7,152,338	79.20	11.75	6.69
Library	$1,850,574	$0	$1,219,293	$0	$300,576	$0	$0	$1,162,057	$749,748	$3,258,758	$0	$8,541,006	33.00	44.50	0.00
Office of Academic Affairs	$1,195,027	$0	$105,802	$0	$18,846	$15,440	$78,107	$427,863	$868,433	$422,000	$0	$3,131,518	19.70	3.51	0.91
Graduate Studies & Research	$676,946	$0	$132,011	$0	$20,604	$42,327	$1,271,388	$280,553	$1,621,609	$0	$0	$4,045,438	11.57	5.00	2.50
International Affairs	$473,703	$0	$74,466	$0	$571	$0	$445,933	$176,715	$177,648	$0	$0	$1,349,036	13.47	3.00	0.00
Student Affairs	$1,861,088	$11,383	$1,321,567	$0	$113,304	$7,631	$2,365,400	$1,284,666	$1,157,491	$0	($30,667)	$8,122,530	43.00	52.33	0.45
Total, Academic Affairs	$46,441,297	$3,211,886	$5,639,695	$6,640	$821,701	$1,378,591	$7,173,097	$18,112,132	$12,448,701	$3,929,229	($30,667)	$99,132,302	861.72	212.58	81.41
Total, President	$721,423	$0	$11,166	$0	$15,810	$0	$17,739	$232,274	$365,204	$0	$0	$1,363,616	10.72	0.50	0.00
Total, University Relations	$1,512,824	$0	$69,582	$0	$55,049	$0	$0	$555,129	$1,019,314	$0	$0	$3,211,898	31.82	2.50	0.00
Finance and Administration															
Information Systems	$1,360,776	$0	$1,725,899	$10,000	$768,927	$0	$11,826	$1,134,968	$2,948,458	$48,600	($468,452)	$8,009,454	24.00	42.84	0.00
Business Office	$468,073	$0	$1,354,056	$28,560	$16,201	$0	$0	$739,176	$619,919	$0	$0	$2,757,533	9.00	45.00	0.00
Physical Plant	$751,785	$0	$1,221,128	$69,580	$81,190	$0	$0	$760,079	$7,878,801	$23,000	($126,852)	$10,658,711	14.40	35.80	0.00
Other Finance Adm.	$1,528,833	$10,771	$395,863	$56,572	$17,847	$0	$0	$735,359	$1,491,165	$1,296,106	($257,394)	$5,275,122	33.65	14.95	0.00
Total, Finance and Administration	$4,109,467	$10,771	$4,696,946	$164,712	$884,165	$0	$11,826	$3,369,582	$12,938,343	$1,367,706	($852,698)	$26,700,820	81.05	138.59	0.00
Total, University General	$1,815,784	$0	$309,541	$0	$0	$0	$413,323	$485,444	$16,722,100	$300,000	($550,000)	$19,496,192	0.50	0.00	0.00
Total Education and General Services	$54,600,795	$3,222,657	$10,726,930	$171,352	$1,776,725	$1,378,591	$7,615,985	$22,754,561	$43,493,661	$5,596,935	($1,433,365)	$149,904,827	985.81	354.17	81.41

(continued from page 55)

INSTITUTIONAL SUPPORT AND DEVELOPMENT ACTIVITIES

ACCOUNTS PAYABLE

This function processes, enters, and verifies data for all invoices and cuts the institution's non-payroll checks. The following reporting criteria can be used to make decisions, set goals for, and monitor the performance of an accounts payable unit:

- Amounts paid to vendors sorted by vendor and date
- Time from receipt of invoice to payment
- Accounts payable balances
- Vendor perceptions of the institution as a place where they want to conduct business
- Amount of vendor discounts obtained due to expedient processing and discounts lost due to processing delays

ALUMNI RELATIONS

The Alumni Relations Office is responsible for developing and maintaining a strong relationship between the institution and its alumni, and for instilling in those alumni a sense of pride in their degree and a sense of loyalty to the institution. The alumni function accomplishes these goals by (a) assisting with the maintenance of the alumni/donor database; (b) providing services to alumni to enhance their connectedness to the institution; (c) acting as liaison between the alumni association and the institution; and (d) directing and staffing the all-volunteer alumni board of directors that governs the alumni association.

The purpose of the alumni association is to promote the interests and ideals of the institution and to sponsor and develop institution alumni activities for the interests and benefit of alumni. The following evaluation and reporting criteria can be used for this activity:

- Number of alumni to whom the office provides services
- Number of responses to mailings (such as update cards, new graduate mailings, and requests for information
- Number of alumni on whom Alumni Relations finds information to add to the alumni/donor database (alumni notes, employment information, potential donor information, and other information)
- Awareness in the community of institution alumni
- Percent of alumni making donations

BUDGET OFFICE

This office is responsible for the institutional budget and for monitoring departmental, school, and/or divisional budgets in accordance with the overall goals of the organization. This department also is responsible for reporting any deviations to upper management. Evaluation and reporting criteria for this function include:

- user satisfaction with annual budget process;
- user satisfaction with fiscal planning, analysis, and information; and
- timely budget implementation and transfers after approval.

(continued on page 62)

EXHIBIT 5.15: INCOME PROJECTIONS

Revenue Projection:	Col. 1	Col. 2	Col. 3	Col. 4	Col. 5	Col. 6	Col. 7
			Derived Col. 1/Col.2			Derived Col. 5/Col.3	Derived Col. 6-Col. 4
Education and General Fund Tuition Income	YTD 12-31-00	YTD 6-30-01	12/31/2000 % of Total	2001-02 Budget	YTD 12-31-01	Projected YTD 6-30-02	Projected Variance
Resident Undergraduate	$11,453,240	$19,347,210	59.20%	$21,223,930	$12,742,081	$21,524,365	$300,435
Non-Resident Undergraduate	$4,761,652	$7,852,848	60.64%	$8,614,591	$5,387,650	$8,885,235	$270,644
Part-time Undergraduate	$2,921,009	$4,833,423	60.43%	$4,153,224	$2,583,420	$4,274,811	$121,587
Western Undergraduate Exchange	$243,214	$425,428	57.17%	$466,676	$271,685	$475,229	$8,553
Faculty/Staff Fees	$79,368	$129,310	61.38%	$141,851	$87,561	$142,658	$807
Resident Graduate	$5,046,089	$8,564,784	58.92%	$9,395,057	$5,558,826	$9,435,058	$40,001
Non-Resident Graduate	$1,195,618	$1,895,334	63.08%	$2,079,466	$1,331,666	$2,111,002	$31,536
Part-time Graduate	$3,396,627	$5,876,572	57.80%	$4,695,614	$2,765,825	$4,785,209	$89,595
Total	$29,096,817	$48,924,909	59.47%	$50,770,409	$30,707,721	$51,633,568	$863,159

Source: Portland State University Budget Office

(continued from page 61)

Budgets are the practical fiscal plan of operation for institutions. They are blueprints for executing program plans and serve as control mechanisms to match the anticipated revenue plan. Budgets translate departmental priorities into reality. A complete budget, including budget narrative, can serve as the operational plan for most institutions. Budgets are typically published in formats sorted by program, organization, or fund. Exhibit 5.13 *(page 60)* is an example of an education and general fund budget in program format.

This same information can also be displayed in an organization format. Exhibit 5.14 *(page 60)* is an example of a budget sorted by responsible organization. This information can be used to establish managerial responsibility for different budgets.

The budget office also should develop projections of revenues and expenses, and publish budget to actual reports to help the institution and its component departments manage their affairs within available resources. Exhibit 5.15 *(page 61)* is an example of the types of reports that can be useful in making projections of income or expense.

Budget officers also typically present other analyses of the sources and uses of funds. This is an area where bar and pie charts can be very useful in displaying these relationships graphically. When analyzing college and university revenues, it is helpful to analyze past trends and use this information in making future projections. The following exhibits provide examples that can be used to understand and analyze revenue and expense relationships. Exhibit 5.16 below displays the revenues and expenses over the last 10 years.

EXHIBIT 5.16: REVENUE, EXPENDITURE, AND TRANSFERS FOR THE PAST 10 YEARS

Analysis of Portland State University Revenues, Expenditures, and Transfers 1991–2001

Description

	1991-92	1992-93	1993-94	1994-95	1995-96	1996-97	1997-98	1998-99	1999-2000	2000-01
Revenues:										
Student Tuition and Fees	$32,157,377	$36,203,263	$39,320,922	$43,468,503	$46,973,759	$52,960,568	$54,425,117	$58,720,232	$63,706,466	$68,508,542
Government Appropriations	$42,650,706	$44,294,337	$43,971,461	$44,699,059	$38,904,458	$40,264,299	$46,198,798	$46,905,477	$61,125,151	$66,068,648
Gifts, Grants and Contracts	$202,072	$246,379	$215,615	$5,220	$86,197	$125,539	$67,964	$566,180	$278,280	$199,464
Sales and Services of Educational Depts.	$2,185,535	$1,700,650	$1,498,524	$2,944,091	$4,681,545	$4,599,641	$5,102,501	$4,619,628	$4,943,719	$5,032,248
Auxiliary Enterprise Revenues	$12,372,860	$12,656,792	$13,851,902	$12,995,610	$13,723,728	$14,707,052	$16,248,959	$17,434,765	$21,051,971	$22,401,801
Other Revenues	$566,103	$656,366	$1,075,049	$755,203	($899,114)	$1,718,439	$737,876	$811,493	$521,852	$648,717
Indirect Cost Recoveries	$840,403	$1,049,918	$1,220,458	$1,628,599	$1,925,007	$1,973,871	$2,088,770	$2,545,719	$2,836,247	$3,202,667
Total Revenues	$90,975,056	$96,807,705	$101,153,931	$106,496,285	$105,395,580	$116,349,409	$124,869,985	$131,603,494	$154,463,686	$166,062,087
Expenditures:										
Instruction	$43,475,950	$45,098,982	$45,645,571	$49,017,794	$51,563,428	$55,216,256	$58,956,013	$62,812,364	$65,107,301	$70,009,279
Public Service	$2,468,865	$2,639,009	$2,128,518	$2,391,028	$2,275,882	$2,111,423	$2,365,129	$2,819,242	$4,025,482	$4,123,561
Research	$994,809	$1,382,045	$1,210,807	$1,218,440	$1,286,928	$1,361,702	$1,583,705	$1,657,981	$1,789,815	$2,306,757
Academic Support	$11,329,990	$12,319,855	$13,424,804	$14,281,342	$15,596,924	$16,578,683	$17,676,416	$19,582,281	$20,494,560	$21,226,209
Student Services	$4,218,730	$4,350,936	$4,398,547	$4,800,911	$4,425,639	$4,680,932	$4,909,922	$5,024,174	$5,561,491	$6,031,466
Operation and Maintenance of Plant	$5,969,106	$6,334,745	$5,428,178	$6,175,900	$7,049,943	$6,185,361	$7,659,545	$7,626,422	$9,644,504	$10,185,716
Capital Improvements	$387,140	$345,035	$506,931	$0	$0	$0	$0	$0	$0	$0
Institutional Support	$7,633,318	$7,954,401	$7,950,225	$8,501,223	$11,451,034	$10,164,416	$10,096,770	$10,245,613	$13,620,449	$13,379,931
Student Aid	$35,946	$2,461,562	$2,430,240	$2,802,748	$2,912,250	$3,440,751	$3,259,530	$3,238,144	$3,529,385	$3,917,029
Service Departments	$258,961	($1,159,974)	($551,617)	($298,809)	$53,675	$422,906	$268,823	$430,394	$63,833	$128,183
Auxiliary Program Expenditures	$10,247,682	$10,522,788	$11,291,225	$10,619,841	$12,060,864	$14,001,504	$14,671,242	$15,825,385	$18,490,116	$19,410,171
Other Expenditures	$12,715	$3,854	$3,716	$316,252	$2,695	($598,643)	$865,751	$610	$17	$245
Total Expenditures	$87,033,212	$92,253,238	$93,867,145	$99,826,670	$108,679,262	$113,565,291	$122,312,846	$129,262,610	$142,326,953	$150,718,547
Transfers:										
Mandatory Transfers – Debt Service	($1,942,665)	($3,293,029)	($3,871,961)	($2,515,065)	($3,637,448)	($3,241,727)	($2,513,658)	($3,976,067)	($5,747,985)	($5,636,001)
Non-mandatory Transfers	$277,211	$70,699	$1,140,410	($1,183,103)	($621,438)	($1,652,605)	($1,606,715)	$34,079	($1,115,484)	($640,087)
Total Transfers	($1,665,454)	($3,222,330)	($2,731,551)	($3,698,168)	($4,258,886)	($4,894,332)	($4,120,373)	($3,941,988)	($6,863,469)	($6,276,088)
Excess of Revenues over Expenditures	$2,276,390	$1,332,137	$4,555,235	$2,971,447	($7,542,568)	($2,110,214)	($1,563,234)	($1,601,104)	$5,273,264	$9,067,452
Other Additions (Deductions):										
Refunds to Grantors	$0	$0	$0	$0	$0	$0	$0	$0	$0	$0
Excess of Restricted Receipts over Revenues Applied	$0	$0	$0	$0	$0	$0	$0	$0	$0	$0
Other Adjustments	$495,091	($478,375)	$117,526	$0	$0	$0	$0	$0	$0	
Net Change in Fund Balance	$2,771,481	$853,762	$4,672,761	$2,971,447	($7,542,568)	($2,110,214)	($1,563,234)	($1,601,104)	$5,273,264	$9,067,452
Fund Balance at Beginning of the Year	$2,317,798	$5,089,279	$5,943,041	$10,615,802	$13,587,249	$6,044,681	$3,934,467	$2,371,233	$770,129	$6,043,393
Fund Balance at End of the Year	$5,089,279	$5,943,041	$10,615,802	$13,587,249	$6,044,681	$3,934,467	$2,371,233	$770,129	$6,043,393	$15,110,845

Source: Portland State University Budget Office

In analyzing the two pie charts presented in Exhibits 5.17 and 5.18, we see that the state appropriations funding has diminished from 47 percent of the revenues in 1992–93 to 40 percent in 2000–01. Similarly, we can see that tuition income has risen from 35 percent to 42 percent of the total revenue during this same time. This is due largely to reductions in state appropriations coupled with both tuition increases and increased enrollment over this same period.

Exhibit 5.19 *(page 64)* displays the expenses by object over the last 10 years.

Expenses are reported in NACUBO functional categories by program. This programmatic classification includes instruction, public service, research, academic support, student services, operation and maintenance of the plant, institutional support, and student aid within the educational and general fund category. In addition, service departments, auxiliary enterprises, and other expenses associated with the operation of hospitals or other inde-

pendent operations are also reported as expense categories in both the unrestricted and restricted fund columns. Exhibit 5.20 *(page 64)* breaks out the expenses by function.

Exhibit 5.21 *(page 65)* displays the trends in expenses by function over the last 10 years.

Transfers are usually displayed separately from revenues and expenditures on the face of this statement, and typically are broken down between mandatory and nonmandatory amounts. Transfers resulting from requirements imposed by external entities are referred to as "mandatory transfers." Those resulting from administrative actions are referred to as "voluntary" or "nonmandatory transfers." The basis of a mandatory transfer is a contractual commitment, such as a bond indenture agreement that the institution has made.

When analyzing transfers, it is important to track the proportion of mandatory transfers in relation to total or certain specified revenue amounts, and determine whether

(continued on page 64)

EXHIBIT 5.17: REVENUES BY SOURCE 1991–92

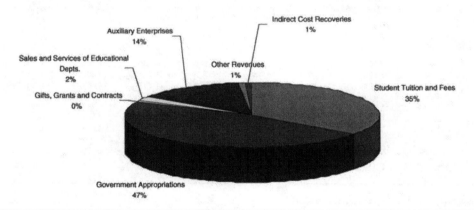

EXHIBIT 5.18: REVENUES BY SOURCE 2000–01

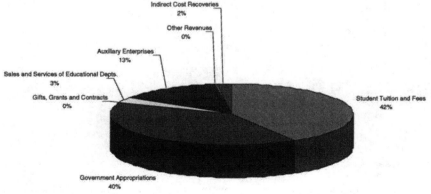

Source: Portland State University—Budget Office

(continued from page 63)

the amount is increasing or decreasing. It is also important to understand why nonmandatory transfers are being made and at whose direction.

COLLECTIONS

This function contacts students with overdue accounts and obtains payments and/or commitments to pay. This function may be performed by internal staff or by external collection agents, or both. Evaluation and reporting criteria for this activity include:

- collection/delinquency rates;
- costs of collection;

- levels of late fees and interest assessed to overdue accounts;
- number of registration holds applied to student accounts due to overdue balances;
- aging of accounts receivable balances; and
- amounts written off each year as uncollectible.

Exhibit 5.22 *(page 66)* is an example of an accounts receivable aging report.

Exhibit 5.23 *(page 67)* is an example of this same information displayed graphically. Aging information can be used for many purposes, including the formulation of debt

EXHIBIT 5.19: EXPENDITURES BY OBJECT 1991–2001

Analysis of Portland State University
Unrestricted Current Fund Expenditures - By Object
1991-2001

Description

	1991-92	1992-93	1993-94	1994-95	1995-96	1996-97	1997-98	1998-99	1999-2000	2000-01
Salaries and Wages	$49,288,428	$51,923,202	$52,630,547	$53,112,360	$57,104,904	$60,736,319	$63,853,769	$68,160,365	$73,133,839	$79,040,808
OPE	$15,963,800	$16,190,050	$16,435,763	$18,369,166	$19,769,720	$21,291,650	$22,245,768	$23,467,098	$28,095,284	$27,816,366
Services and Supplies	$22,296,694	$22,961,017	$23,131,205	$25,313,028	$28,331,485	$28,453,226	$30,084,336	$31,043,636	$36,285,437	$39,772,257
Capital Outlay	$3,807,338	$4,088,591	$4,189,638	$5,408,382	$3,921,267	$3,221,111	$3,990,542	$4,346,768	$3,854,459	$3,794,839
Merchandise for Resale	$1,018,051	$1,358,066	$2,107,631	$3,050,822	$2,946,524	$1,784,644	$1,666,405	$1,493,499	$1,032,258	$834,907
Other	$860,777	$786,292	$734,639	$498,728	$893,753	$1,368,057	$1,505,758	$2,103,088	$2,297,870	$5,037,032
Service Credits	($6,201,878)	($6,626,573)	($6,880,520)	($8,169,048)	($7,188,415)	($6,349,767)	($2,312,556)	($2,472,272)	($2,629,800)	($2,834,271)
Total	$87,033,210	$90,680,645	$92,348,903	$97,583,438	$105,779,238	$110,505,240	$121,034,022	$128,142,182	$142,069,347	$153,461,938

Percentage of the Total

	1991-92	1992-93	1993-94	1994-95	1995-96	1996-97	1997-98	1998-99	1999-2000	2000-01
Salaries and Wages	56.63%	57.26%	56.99%	54.43%	53.98%	54.96%	52.76%	53.19%	51.48%	51.51%
OPE	18.34%	17.85%	17.80%	18.82%	18.69%	19.27%	18.38%	18.31%	19.78%	18.13%
Services and Supplies	25.62%	25.32%	25.05%	25.94%	26.78%	25.75%	24.86%	24.23%	25.54%	25.92%
Capital Outlay	4.37%	4.51%	4.54%	5.54%	3.71%	2.91%	3.30%	3.39%	2.71%	2.47%
Merchandise for Resale	1.17%	1.50%	2.28%	3.13%	2.79%	1.61%	1.38%	1.17%	0.73%	0.54%
Other	0.99%	0.87%	0.80%	0.51%	0.84%	1.24%	1.24%	1.64%	1.62%	3.28%
Service Credits	-7.13%	-7.31%	-7.45%	-8.37%	-6.80%	-5.75%	-1.91%	-1.93%	-1.85%	-1.85%
Total	100.00%	100.00%	100.00%	100.00%	100.00%	100.00%	100.00%	100.00%	100.00%	100.00%

Source: Portland State University Budget Office

EXHIBIT 5.20: Expenditures by Function 2000–01

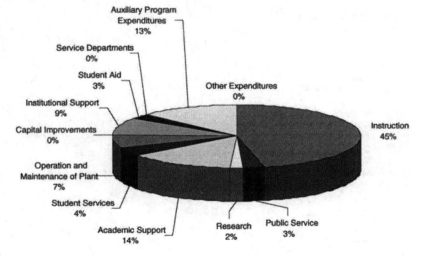

Auxiliary Program Expenditures 13%
Service Departments 0%
Student Aid 3%
Institutional Support 9%
Capital Improvements 0%
Operation and Maintenance of Plant 7%
Student Services 4%
Academic Support 14%
Research 2%
Public Service 3%
Instruction 45%
Other Expenditures 0%

EXHIBIT 5.21: Expenditures by Function 1992–2001

Fiscal Year
(Note: 1- 1992-93; 10 - 2000-01)

Source: Portland State University Budget Office

policies (incentives and sanctions for early or late payments), making bad debt reserve/allowance adjustments, and determining the number of staff needed for the collections function, among other uses.

DEVELOPMENT OFFICE

The central development office is responsible for cultivating, requesting, and stewarding gifts from alumni and other donors in coordination with constituent development officers who are located within the schools and units of the institution. The development function is responsible for raising funds for high-priority institution programs, meeting annual fund-raising goals, and building a donor database of alumni and other donors. Development and gift processing functions can be performed either directly by the institution or in collaboration with an affiliated foundation. For public institutions, the use of affiliated foundations can help to protect the confidentiality of donors, since many public institutions are subject to public records laws that restrict the institution's ability to maintain donor confidentiality. The following are examples of financial management information that could be analyzed and reported for development operations:

- Total dollars raised and pledges committed divided by total fund-raising costs
- Annual growth in total giving to the institution
- Number of prospect contacts and solicitations completed
- Annual growth in the number of donors
- Number of alumni solicited as a percentage of known alumni
- Percentage of alumni who give
- Total donations versus costs of fund raising
- Pledge write-offs

Exhibit 5.24 *(page 67)* graphically displays the total gifts to an institution and its affiliated foundation by type over the last seven years.

Another example of this type of report, with more detail of the gifts by type, is shown in Exhibit 5.25 *(page 68)*.

GENERAL ACCOUNTING

This department is responsible for posting journal entries to the general ledger and subsidiary ledgers, preparing financial reports, and performing other institution-wide accounting functions. Evaluation and reporting criteria include:

- time from end of month until financial reports are distributed;
- satisfactory audit outcomes; and
- user satisfaction with accounting services.

(continued on page 66)

EXHIBIT 5.22: ACCOUNTS RECEIVABLE AGING ANALYSIS

A/R AGING SUMMARY AS OF NOVEMBER 2001				
DUE DATE	NUMBER OF ACCOUNTS	TOTAL DOLLARS	PERCENT OF CURRENT	Average Balance
< 1 Year				
0-30 Days:	3,967	$1,377,573.31	15.72%	$347.26
31-60 Days:	1,421	$665,864.36	7.60%	$468.59
61-90 Days:	1,579	$1,362,744.25	15.55%	$863.04
91-120 Days	1,105	$984,314.93	11.23%	$890.78
121-150 Day	287	$164,096.11	1.87%	$571.76
151-180 Day	307	$564,280.72	6.44%	$1,838.05
181-210 Day	371	$292,371.56	3.34%	$788.06
211-240 Day	231	$191,338.68	2.18%	$828.31
241-270 Day	366	$351,705.13	4.01%	$960.94
271-300 Day	77	$67,364.27	0.77%	$874.86
301-330 Day	159	$162,531.86	1.85%	$1,022.21
Subtotal:	9,870	$6,184,185.18	70.58%	$626.56
1-2 Years				
0-30 Days:	85	$99,803.15	1.14%	$1,174.15
31-60 Days:	63	$82,941.79	0.95%	$1,316.54
61-90 Days:	201	$180,354.73	2.06%	$897.29
91-120 Days	121	$141,280.38	1.61%	$1,167.61
121-150 Day	77	$41,240.25	0.47%	$535.59
151-180 Day	84	$50,526.84	0.58%	$601.51
181-210 Day	64	$51,271.47	0.59%	$801.12
211-240 Day	129	$87,970.63	1.00%	$681.94
241-270 Day	81	$85,948.75	0.98%	$1,061.10
271-300 Day	61	$63,889.30	0.73%	$1,047.37
301-330 Day	73	$87,756.20	1.00%	$1,202.14
Subtotal:	1,039	$972,983.49	11.10%	$936.46
2-3 Years:				
0-90 Days:	151	$166,451.97	1.90%	$1,102.33
91-180 Days	154	$144,005.46	1.64%	$935.10
181-270 Day	106	$163,460.06	1.87%	$1,542.08
Subtotal:	411	$473,917.49	5.41%	$1,153.08
3-4 Years				
0-90 Days:	82	$113,240.89	1.29%	$1,380.99
91-180 Days	76	$137,732.89	1.57%	$1,812.27
181-270 Day	100	$111,699.24	1.27%	$1,116.99
271-360 Day	358	$452,874.57	5.17%	$1,265.01
Subtotal:	616	$815,547.59	9.31%	$1,323.94
4-5 Years				
0-90 Days:	46	$51,554.14	0.59%	$1,120.74
91-180 Days	44	$40,389.99	0.46%	$917.95
181-270 Day	38	$40,263.31	0.46%	$1,059.56
271-360 Day	23	$40,691.24	0.46%	$1,769.18
Subtotal:	151	$172,898.68	1.97%	$1,145.02
> 5 Years:	161	$142,964.98	1.63%	$887.98
Total Current:	12,248	$8,762,497.41	100.00%	$715.42

Source: Portland State University Bursar's Office

(continued from page 65)

HUMAN RESOURCES

This function is responsible for employee recruitment, employee relations, records management, compensation and benefits administration, performance evaluation, training, management development, labor relations, and affirmative action. The following items should be monitored, analyzed, and reported.

- User satisfaction with benefits administration services

- User satisfaction with labor relations activities: bargaining, grievance handling, and other labor-related activities

- User satisfaction with organizational training and development programs

- User satisfaction with employee relations/affirmative action programs

EXHIBIT 5.23: ACCOUNTS RECEIVABLE AGING ANALYSIS

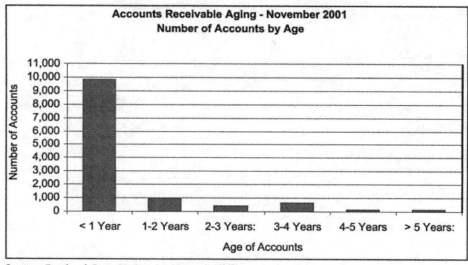

Source: Portland State University Bursar's Office

EXHIBIT 5.24: GIFTS AND PLEDGES 1994–2001

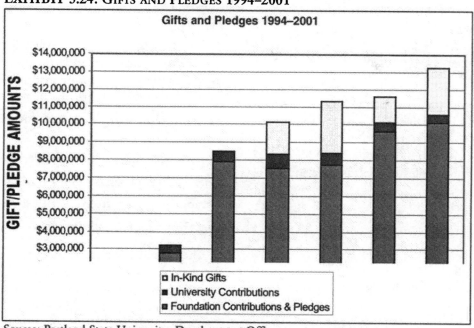

Source: Portland State University–Development Office

- Time elapsed from position vacancy to refill;
- Number of grievances
- Number of involuntary terminations
- Turnover rate
- Vacancy rate
- User satisfaction with recruitment assistance provided by human resource office

Exhibit 5.26 *(page 69)* shows a comparison of salaries at one university to average salaries (by discipline and rank) from a peer group that reports annual salary data to the College and University Professional Association for Human Resources (CUPA-HR). This table shows faculty member's name, department, Department of Education's Classification of Instructional Program (CIP) code, rank, rank date, years in rank, current salary, comparator salary averages by discipline (as categorized by CIP code) and rank, and current salary as a percentage of the comparator salary averages. The report provides the basis for disproportionate salary increases to ensure equity by discipline and rank across an institution. It also serves as a measure to ensure that campus salaries remain competitive with

(continued on page 68)

EXHIBIT 5.25: PRIVATE SUPPORT TO THE UNIVERSITY OF FLORIDA: 1993–2001

PRIVATE SUPPORT TO THE UNIVERSITY OF FLORIDA	1993-94	1994-95	1995-96	1996-97	1997-98	1998-99	1999-2000	2000-2001
Alumni	$13,601,319	$14,580,635	$15,854,923	$25,170,391	$31,560,096	$41,437,569	$43,373,213	$43,164,763
Nonalumni Parents	$186,824	$137,352	$296,524	$334,602	$3,743,471	$967,605	$1,655,902	$942,961
Other Individuals	$15,110,243	$24,415,330	$20,378,943	$19,546,740	$27,173,732	$19,117,675	$28,363,726	$30,890,453
Foundations	$7,683,666	$8,664,258	$14,093,466	$14,085,729	$9,945,364	$19,111,892	$41,895,111	$25,454,771
Corporations	$18,846,232	$13,983,914	$21,619,939	$24,404,136	$43,699,800	$41,414,740	$38,772,969	$23,967,577
Other	$15,667,341	$10,734,732	$8,916,363	$7,606,797	$6,669,151	$13,339,694	$9,539,495	$18,524,277
Total Support	$71,095,625	$72,516,221	$81,160,158	$91,148,395	$122,791,614	$135,389,175	$163,600,416	$142,944,802

Source: University of Florida Web site

(continued from page 67)

national, regional, or other markets based on the selection of comparator or aspirant institutions.

The human resources office also typically manages employee benefit programs, including both retirement and health and dental insurance programs for employees. From time to time it is important to compare program costs to other similar universities or colleges. Exhibits 5.27 and 5.28 *(page 70)* are examples of reports that are useful for comparison purposes.

MAIL SERVICES

This office is responsible for collecting, processing, and distributing in a timely manner all mail throughout the institution, including internal mail, U.S. mail, and overnight delivery mail. Evaluation and reporting criteria for this function include:

- turnaround time to have mail delivered internally; and
- user satisfaction with other mail services.

PAYROLL

This department is responsible for collecting and processing payroll data, coordinating direct deposit arrangements, preparing and distributing employee paychecks, and ensuring the accuracy of payroll charges to accounts. Evaluation and reporting criteria for this function include:

- percentage of employees utilizing direct deposit of paychecks;
- user satisfaction with payroll services; and
- number of manual checks (due to missed pay deadlines).

SECURITY

This department is responsible for ensuring the safety and security of the institution's staff, students, and faculty as well as the security of the institution's property. Evaluation and reporting criteria for this activity include:

- number and type of serious incidents on campus per year;
- user satisfaction with security services;
- perceptions of safety while on campus;
- amount of losses from theft each year; and
- security response calls by type.

The federal government now requires colleges and universities to report crimes on and near the campus in order to inform the public of these activities. Exhibit 5.29 *(page 71)* is an example of a crime statistics report.

PURCHASING

This office is responsible for coordinating the purchasing process, including working with users to understand and articulate the needs of the institution; negotiating with vendors to obtain the best possible price, terms, and conditions; and placing orders with vendors. Evaluation and reporting criteria for this activity include:

- total volume of purchases processed each year;
- average time involved in the purchasing process—time required from requisition to receipt;
- user satisfaction with purchasing services provided;
- vendor satisfaction with institution purchasing processes;

EXHIBIT 5.26: PORTLAND STATE UNIVERSITY FACULTY SALARY COMPARISONS BY DISCIPLINE AND RANK

Name	Department	CIP Code	CIP Description	RANK	RANK DATE	YEARS IN RANK	JUL/SEP 2001 9-MO Equiv Salary Rate	CUPA Average Salary Rate	Salary Rate as a % of CUPA Average
	SYS Systems Science	300000	Multi/Interdisciplinary Studies	Prof	09/16/71	30	$84,933	$81,422	104.3%
	SYS Systems Science	300000	Multi/Interdisciplinary Studies	Prof	09/16/80	21	$75,942	$81,422	93.3%
	SYS Systems Science	300000	Multi/Interdisciplinary Studies	Assc	09/16/93	8	$66,852	$59,024	113.3%
	SYS Systems Science	300000	Multi/Interdisciplinary Studies	Assc	09/16/00	1	$63,000	$59,024	106.7%
	IAF Int'l Affairs Office	50000	Area, Ethnic and Cultural Studies	Asst	08/14/96	5	$44,937	$45,701	98.3%
	ANT Anthropology	450200	Anthropology	Prof	09/16/91	10	$62,154	$76,582	81.2%
	ANT Anthropology	450200	Anthropology	Prof	09/16/97	4	$57,249	$76,582	74.8%
	ANT Anthropology	450200	Anthropology	Assc	09/16/00	1	$44,028	$54,938	80.1%
	ANT Anthropology	450200	Anthropology	Asst	09/01/96	5	$40,302	$43,915	91.8%
	ANT Anthropology	450200	Anthropology	Asst	09/16/95	6	$39,888	$43,915	90.8%
	BIO Biology	260100	Biology, General	Prof	03/16/98	4	$95,886	$78,674	121.9%
	BIO Biology	260100	Biology, General	Prof	09/16/83	18	$86,670	$78,674	110.2%
	BIO Biology	260100	Biology, General	Prof	09/16/76	25	$74,628	$78,674	94.9%
	BIO Biology	260100	Biology, General	Prof	09/16/80	21	$84,123	$78,674	106.9%
	BIO Biology	260100	Biology, General	Assc	01/01/95	7	$49,014	$57,070	85.9%
	BIO Biology	260100	Biology, General	Asst	01/01/99	3	$56,466	$47,238	119.5%
	BIO Biology	260100	Biology, General	Asst	09/01/01	-	$44,514	$47,238	94.2%
	BIO Biology	260100	Biology, General	Asst	09/16/00	1	$44,001	$47,238	93.1%
	BIO Biology	260100	Biology, General	Asst	12/16/97	4	$43,191	$47,238	91.4%
	BST Black Studies Prgm	50000	Area, Ethnic and Cultural Studies	Prof	07/01/90	11	$59,931	$83,178	72.1%
	BST Black Studies Prgm	50000	Area, Ethnic and Cultural Studies	Asst	09/16/97	4	$44,766	$45,701	98.0%
	BST Black Studies Prgm	50000	Area, Ethnic and Cultural Studies	Asst	07/01/01	-	$43,002	$45,701	94.1%
	SEC Science Ed Center	300000	Multi/Interdisciplinary Studies	Asst	09/16/95	6	$42,030	$43,621	96.4%
	SEC Science Ed Center	300000	Multi/Interdisciplinary Studies	Asst	09/16/94	7	$42,192	$43,621	96.7%
	CHE Chemistry	400500	Chemistry	Prof	09/16/81	20	$95,436	$85,737	111.3%
	CHE Chemistry	400500	Chemistry	Prof	07/01/96	5	$64,521	$85,737	75.3%
	CHE Chemistry	400500	Chemistry	Prof	09/16/86	15	$79,461	$85,737	92.7%
	CHE Chemistry	400500	Chemistry	Assc	08/01/01	-	$58,005	$58,349	99.4%
	CHE Chemistry	400500	Chemistry	Assc	09/16/96	5	$54,675	$58,349	93.7%
	CHE Chemistry	400500	Chemistry	Assc	09/16/98	3	$49,941	$58,349	85.6%
	CHE Chemistry	400500	Chemistry	Asst	08/22/97	4	$46,827	$48,596	96.4%
	CHE Chemistry	400500	Chemistry	Asst	09/16/98	3	$45,243	$48,596	93.1%
	ECN Economics	450600	Economics	Prof	09/16/94	7	$67,878	$93,499	72.6%
	ECN Economics	450600	Economics	Prof	07/01/92	9	$68,067	$93,499	72.8%
	ECN Economics	450600	Economics	Prof	09/16/78	23	$77,031	$93,499	82.4%
	ECN Economics	450600	Economics	Asst	09/16/97	4	$50,085	$58,205	86.0%
	ECN Economics	450600	Economics	Asst	09/01/01	-	$47,502	$58,205	81.6%
	ECN Economics	450600	Economics	Asst	09/16/98	3	$47,835	$58,205	82.2%

Source: CUPA-HR and Portland State University Budget Office

- number of contested procurements or vendor complaints; and

- some quantification of the savings achieved by aggregating purchases or otherwise obtaining vendor discounts each year.

TREASURY SERVICES

This function accepts and invests all cash received by the institution. Investments are managed either directly by internal staff or through contracted investment management firms. Evaluation and reporting criteria for this function include:

- average rates of return on invested funds;

- total investment income and losses;

- total cash inflows and outflows; and

- comparison reporting of internally and externally managed funds.

(continued on page 71)

EXHIBIT 5.27: EMPLOYEE HEALTH AND DENTAL INSURANCE COSTS BY INSTITUTION

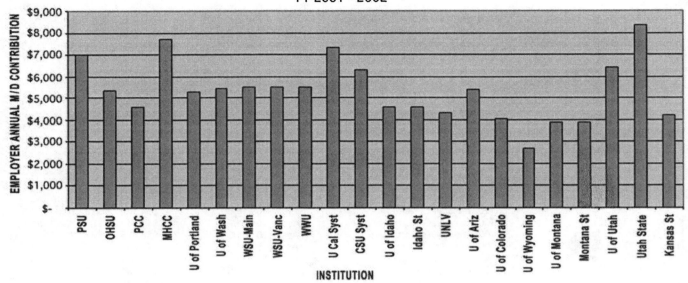

Comparison of Medical/Dental Contributions - Employee and Family Coverage
Excluding Subsidy at Portland State University
FY 2001 - 2002

Source: Portland State University Budget Office

EXHIBIT 5.28: EMPLOYEE RETIREMENT COSTS BY INSTITUTION

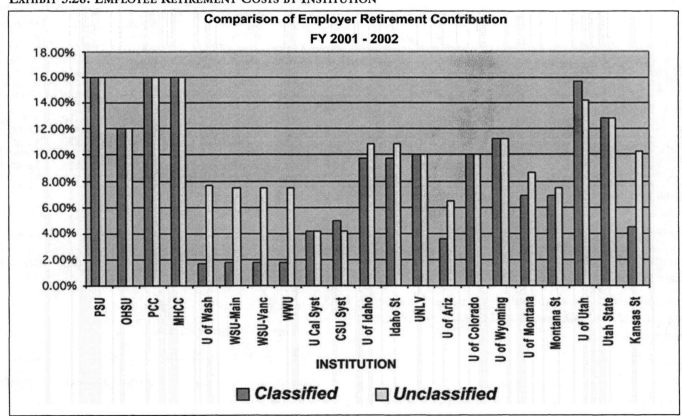

Comparison of Employer Retirement Contribution
FY 2001 - 2002

Source: Portland State University Budget Office

EXHIBIT 5.29: CRIME STATISTICS – 1996

CRIME STATISTICS 1996			
Federal Campus Crime Awareness and Campus Security Act 1990			
REPORTS	**1994**	**1995**	**1996**
Homicide	0	0	0
Rape	0	0	0
Sex Offenses			
Forcible	2	1	1
Non-Forcible	0	15	0
Aggravated Assault	3	7	9
Burglary	24	1	15
Robbery	1	1	2
Theft	299	253	255
Unauthorized Use of Motor Vehicle	14	5	1
Bias Crime	0	1	0
ARRESTS			
Liquor Law Violations	0	4	0
Drug-related Violations	1	3	4
Weapon Violation	0	1	0

Source: Portland State University Campus Public Safety Office

(continued from page 69)

AUXILIARY ENTERPRISES AND INTERNAL SERVICE ACTIVITIES

Auxiliary enterprise and internal service operations support the instruction, research, and public service missions of the institution. These activities are intended to be self-sustaining, in that total revenues from operations should cover total costs. Because this is not always the case, subsidies from student fees or other institutional resources should be tracked and reported on a regular basis. Typical auxiliary enterprise and internal service operations include athletics, student housing, bookstores, food services, parking, vending, print shops, telecommunications services, and other activities. Some institutions distinguish service operations from auxiliary enterprise operations based on the level or number of services offered to internal (departmental) vs. external (student and the general public) users. Typically, internal service operations offer services predominately to internal users, while auxiliaries offer services to a more diverse clientele, including internal and external users. Nevertheless, the self-sustaining principle applies to both types of operations.

Since both auxiliary enterprises and service departments are self-sustaining entities within an institution, they must manage their operations as a business enterprise. These operations can be self-operated or contracted to either an unrelated commercial provider or to an affiliated cooperative corporation or other nonprofit provider. When analyzing auxiliary and service department operations, attention should be paid to pricing policies, especially as it relates to average mark-ups for various types of goods, and to the level of institutional subsidization or assessment. Some institutions use auxiliary enterprises as a money-making activity for the institution, transferring excess funds to the general fund or other fund groups. Other institutions keep prices low to maintain access and low cost services to students.

ATHLETICS

Evaluating the effectiveness of athletics operations can be done in many ways, including (1) win-loss records, (2) athlete graduation rates, and (3) budget prowess—i.e., making revenue expectations and staying within expense budgets. When analyzing athletics' finances, attention should be paid to the amount of self-generated revenues (from gate receipts, advertising, conference revenues, fundraising activities, etc.); institutional subsidies of both direct and indirect costs; and student fee appropriations. Similarly, monitoring athletic department expenses can be very revealing, especially in regard to scholarships, salaries, travel, and administrative expenditures. Many institutions compare themselves to other institutions in the athletic conference to determine relative proportions in the sources of revenues and in the level and composition of expenditures. Exhibit 5.30 *(page 72)* is an example of a report that compares athletic budgets from various institutions within an athletic conference.

(continued on page 72)

EXHIBIT 5.30: ANALYSIS OF ATHLETIC BUDGETS

Analysis of Athletic Conference Institutions
Athletic Budgets
For the 1998-99 Fiscal Year

	Inst. #1	Inst. #2	Inst. #3	Inst. #4	Inst. #5	Inst. #6	PSU	Conf. Average	% of Average
Revenues:									
Unearned Revenues:									
Institutional Support:									
Institutional General Funds	$2,335,026	$2,899,537	$1,487,000	$2,800,000	$1,756,031	$1,856,168	$1,650,000	$1,876,252	87.94%
Tuition Waivers	$1,064,882	$50,000	$713,400	$120,000	$0	$0	$0	$278,326	0.00%
Other Institutional Support	$0	$1,216,000	$265,445	$500,000	$100,000	$208,599	$0	$327,149	0.00%
Total Institutional Support	$3,399,908	$4,165,537	$2,465,845	$3,420,000	$1,856,031	$2,064,767	$1,650,000	$2,481,727	66.49%
Student Fees	$567,000	$1,627,500	$1,322,475	$0	$2,094,717	$625,500	$1,628,510	$891,027	182.77%
Other Unearned Revenues	$0	$0	$22,000	$5,000	$0	$247,000	$245,000	$39,143	625.91%
Total Unearned Revenues	$3,966,908	$5,793,037	$3,810,320	$3,425,000	$3,950,748	$2,937,267	$3,523,510	$3,411,897	103.27%
Earned Revenues:									
Gate Receipts	$652,000	$63,974	$385,630	$219,800	$226,800	$203,000	$329,000	$250,172	131.51%
Advert., Guar., TV/Radio, etc.	$612,000	$386,897	$399,000	$473,500	$358,500	$252,000	$510,000	$354,557	143.84%
Gifts/Fund Raising	$390,947	$413,000	$358,540	$885,000	$368,300	$243,400	$275,000	$379,884	72.39%
Camps/Clinics	$235,000	$40,000	$0	$15,000	$0	$10,000	$30,000	$42,857	70.00%
All Other Earned Revenues	$401,766	$302,139	$206,000	$260,000	$277,539	$105,000	$76,000	$221,778	34.27%
Total Earned Revenues	$2,291,713	$1,206,010	$1,349,170	$1,853,300	$1,231,139	$813,400	$1,220,000	$1,249,247	97.66%
Total Revenues	$6,258,621	$6,999,047	$5,159,490	$5,278,300	$5,181,887	$3,750,667	$4,743,510	$4,661,145	101.77%
Expenses:									
Salaries	$2,156,714	$3,007,660	$1,991,190	$2,368,000	$2,429,259	$1,624,801	$2,013,481	$1,939,661	103.81%
Grants-in-Aid	$1,734,851	$1,619,033	$1,697,602	$2,110,000	$1,402,925	$1,233,998	$1,193,432	$1,399,773	85.26%
Operations	$1,984,781	$2,622,768	$1,773,895	$1,875,300	$2,237,349	$1,005,600	$1,427,995	$1,642,813	86.92%
Other/Debt	$585,000	$0	$0	$0	$0	$0	$0	$83,571	0.00%
Total Expenses	$6,461,346	$7,249,461	$5,462,687	$6,353,300	$6,069,533	$3,864,399	$4,634,908	$5,065,818	91.49%

Source: Portland State University Athletic Department

(continued from page 71)

BOOKSTORES

Bookstores can be self-operated or are contracted out to commercial or other operators. The following factors should be monitored and reported:

- Total and mix of revenues

- Satisfaction with book ordering processes, including the numbers of late arriving orders

- Pricing policies

- Net income/loss

- Levels of inventory, including losses from spoilage or theft

- Customer satisfaction

- Capital expenditures—if any

- Operating expenses

FOOD SERVICES

When analyzing food service operations, attention should be paid to pricing policies, especially as it relates to average mark-ups for various types of foodstuffs. Food services differ in regard to retail operations and board operations associated with dormitory operations. Many contracted operations come with institutional commissions based on gross or net revenues from operations. Officials should monitor quality (as judged by customer surveys) and the efficiency and level of financial return from operations. The following factors should be monitored and reported:

- Total and mix of revenues

- Pricing policies

- Net income/loss

EXHIBIT 5.31: OCCUPANCY OF STUDENT RESIDENTIAL BUILDINGS: 1995–2000

FALL SEMESTERS	1995	1996	1997	1998	1999 ***	2000 ***
Conventional Residence Hall						
Women	3,725	3,798	3,982	3,988	3,928	3,913
Men	3,104	2,995	2,914	2,924	2,977	3,013
Total	6,829	6,793	6,896	6,912	6,905	6,926
Family and Single Graduate Student Occupancy						
Family Student Residents*	1,082	1,082	1,082	1,082	820	961
Spouses and Children in Family Units*	1,346	1,346	1,346	1,346	1,184	1,133
Single Students in Schucht Village**	145	145	0	0	0	0
Single Graduate Students in Village Housing	0	0	0	0	251	363
Total	2,573	2,573	2,428	2,428	2,255	2,457
TOTAL STUDENTS IN NON-GREEK UF HOUSING	8,056	8,020	7,978	7,994	7,976	8,020
TOTAL RESIDENTS IN NON-GREEK UF HOUSING	9,402	9,366	9,324	9,340	9,160	9,020
UF Sororities	733	740	740	745	747	747
UF Fraternities	793	880	880	880	785	825
TOTAL STUDENTS IN ALL UF HOUSING	9,582	9,640	9,598	9,619	9,508	9,592
TOTAL RESIDENTS IN ALL UF HOUSING	10,928	10,986	10,944	10,965	10,692	10,955
Family and Single Graduate Students Units (Apartments)						
Number of Family Units	980	980	980	980	980	961
Number of Schucht Village Single Graduate Student Units**	104	104	0	0	0	0
Total	1,084	1,084	980	980	980	961

* 1992-1998 totals are estimated based on 1992 census data.
** Schucht Village was closed Fall 1994 for renovations and was transferred to Shands Hospital in 1997.
*** For 1999 and 2000 only, the totals are based on real numbers, not census data.
N/A – Not Available

Source: University of Florida Web site

• Debt to equity and debt to revenues ratios

• Customer satisfaction

• Capital Expenditures—if any

• Operating Expenses

HOUSING OPERATIONS

When analyzing housing operations, pay attention to pricing policies, especially as they relate to average mark-ups for various types of housing units. Remember that there are both operating and capital issues to consider. Maintaining an adequate inventory of housing units necessary to meet the needs of undergraduates, graduates, married, and other special interest groups requires paying attention to demand indicators coming through the admissions office and other areas on campus. In addition, units must be renovated and upgraded periodically to remain attractive to prospective tenants.

The following can be used to evaluate the financial viability of a housing operation:

• Vacancy factors

• Total and mix of revenues

• Pricing policies

• Net income/loss

• Debt to equity and debt to revenues ratios

• Customer satisfaction

• Capital Expenditures—if any

• Operating Expenses

• Capacity and need analysis—number and mix of types of units, other services (Internet/institutional network connections, cable TV, telecommunications, etc.)

Exhibit 5.31 *(page 73)* is an example of the occupancy of various university housing units over the past six years.

PARKING

The parking office is responsible for managing all activities relating to campus parking permits, arranging parking accommodations for special events, alternative transportation programs, and managing parking lots and garages. Institutional parking services can be self-operated or contracted to a commercial provider. When analyzing parking operations, pay attention to pricing policies, especially as they relate to average mark-ups for various types of parking available. When evaluating parking operations, remember that there are both operating and capital issues to consider. Maintaining an adequate inventory of parking lots necessary to meet the needs of student, faculty, staff, and visitors requires that attention be paid to demand indicators coming through the parking office and other areas on campus. Evaluation and reporting criteria for this function include:

• revenue mix (permit sales, fines, other);

• user satisfaction with parking services;

• pricing history and policy—overhead;

• levels of deferred maintenance in parking structures;

• institutional revenue expectations or full-costing of overhead; and

• space usage, including numbers of turns per day, etc.

• number of tickets issued

• number of vehicles towed

STUDENT HEALTH SERVICES

This function is responsible for providing health care services and health education to students while on campus. This includes outpatient services, referrals to other health providers, nutrition counseling, disease prevention, and health education activities. Evaluation and reporting criteria for this function include:

• number (both duplicated and unduplicated) of students using health services each year;

• number and quality of health education and outreach programs and community partnerships each year; and

• user satisfaction with health services.

STUDENT UNION OPERATIONS

This function is responsible for operating and maintaining the student union on campus. This activity schedules rooms, sets up for events, and otherwise manages the operations of the student union complex. Many times, this includes both operations and facility management considerations. Evaluation and reporting criteria for this activity include:

• number and types of events accommodated;

• pricing policies and history;

• revenue mix from room rentals, game room operations, store operations, student fees, etc.;

• cost analyses;

• levels of deferred maintenance and obsolescence; and

• user satisfaction with union operations.

SUMMARY

This chapter discussed the evaluation and reporting criteria for noninstructional units, including coverage of academic support functions, student services, plant operation and maintenance, institutional support and development activities, and auxiliary and internal service activities. The next chapter will focus on blending financial and performance data and will offer a synthesis and conclusion regarding financial management reporting issues for colleges and universities.

CHAPTER 6
SYNTHESIS AND CONCLUSIONS

BLENDING FINANCIAL AND PERFORMANCE INFORMATION

The usefulness of academic and nonacademic financial and managerial information becomes richer if financial and performance information is blended in a way that facilitates unit cost or cost-benefit analyses. This is another area in which comparisons with peer or comparator institutions can help determine both the efficiency and effectiveness of current operations. Common examples of areas in which performance and financial information are blended are:

- cost per credit hour/student full-time-equivalency,
- student headcount (by major) per faculty FTE,
- research funding per faculty FTE,
- credit hours generated per faculty FTE,
- course sections taught per faculty FTE, and
- many other measures.

Exhibit 6.1 illustrates both financial and performance data for the department of computer science. This report displays the instructional budget, FTE employees, sponsored research, student credit hours, credit sections, and degrees produced during the time period 1994–2001. In addition, the report shows certain ratios of average cost per employee, cost per credit hour, etc. This type of report is useful in analyzing unit costs and other average costs over time. This report also provides a good example of interdependencies that exist between the functions performed by faculty. For example, note how increases in credit hours per faculty are offset by reductions in research funding generated per faculty FTE; one sign that more emphasis on teaching comes at the expense of research—a trend that is counter to most faculty preferences. The report shows that this trend appears to be reversing in the last year. This type of report is useful in comparing one university against another, although care must be taken when making these types of inter-institutional comparisons to ensure that the data are truly comparable.

(continued on page 77)

EXHIBIT 6.1: DEPARTMENTAL STATISTICS

Department of Computer Science

Base E&G Instructional Budget	1994-95	1995-96	1996-97	1997-98	1998-99	1999-2000	2000-01
Unclassified (Faculty) Salaries	$722,046	$791,586	$797,961	$784,146	$916,761	$952,632	$1,018,658
Unclassified Pay	$0	$16,779	$0	$0	$0	$0	$0
Classified (Staff) Salaries	$57,252	$59,136	$61,296	$60,275	$62,724	$59,700	$69,408
Classified Pay	$0	$0	$0	$0	$0	$0	$0
Student Pay	$19,376	$19,376	$19,376	$19,376	$19,376	$19,376	$19,764
Graduate Assistant Salaries	$22,806	$23,499	$24,192	$24,696	$24,696	$25,190	$25,693
Other Payroll Expenses	$267,292	$291,900	$276,370	$273,839	$305,980	$0	$0
Services and Supplies	$80,625	$80,625	$80,625	$80,625	$80,625	$322,797	$340,096
Capital Outlay	$70,000	$70,000	$70,000	$70,000	$0	$82,238	$83,883
Internal Sales Reimbursements	($28,634)	($28,634)	($28,634)	($28,634)	($28,634)	($30,066)	($30,667)
Total E&G Instructional Budget	$1,210,763	$1,324,267	$1,301,186	$1,284,323	$1,381,528	$1,431,867	$1,526,835
Full-Time Equivalent Employees							
Unclassified	12.00	13.00	13.00	12.50	13.50	13.50	13.50
Classified	3.00	3.00	3.00	2.75	2.75	2.75	2.75
Graduate Assistant	1.05	1.05	1.05	1.05	1.05	1.05	1.05
Total FTE Employees	16.05	17.05	17.05	16.30	17.30	17.30	17.30

(table continued on page 76)

EXHIBIT 6.1: DEPARTMENTAL STATISTICS *(continued from page 75)*

Average Unclassified Salary/Unclass. FTE	$60,170.50	$60,891.23	$61,381.62	$62,731.68	$67,908.22	$70,565.33	$75,456.15
Average Classified Salary/Class. FTE	$19,084.00	$19,712.00	$20,432.00	$21,918.18	$22,808.73	$21,709.09	$25,239.27
Average Graduate Assist. Salary/GA FTE	$21,720.00	$22,380.00	$23,040.00	$23,520.00	$23,520.00	$23,990.48	$24,469.52
Total Budget/Unclass. FTE	$100,896.92	$101,866.69	$100,091.23	$102,745.84	$102,335.41	$106,064.22	$113,098.89
Total Budget/Total FTE	$75,436.95	$77,669.62	$76,315.89	$78,792.82	$79,857.11	$82,766.88	$88,256.36
Funded Research Exp.	$308,610	$537,565	$594,104	$344,148	$228,967	$172,484	$641,729
Average Research Expense/FTE Faculty	$25,718	$41,351	$45,700	$27,532	$16,961	$12,777	$47,535
Credit Hours Generated							
Undergraduate	8,704	8,756	7,851	8,757	9,528	9,957	12,321
Graduate	1,314	1,588	2,178	2,382	2,838	3,053	3,767
Ph.D.	63	56	63	107	104	59	161
Total Credit Hours Generated	10,081	10,400	10,092	11,246	12,470	13,069	16,249
Average Credit Hours/FTE Faculty	840.08	800.00	776.31	899.68	923.70	968.07	1203.63
Average Credit Hours/FTE Faculty+GTA	772.49	740.21	718.29	829.96	857.04	898.21	1116.77
Total Budget/Credit Hours	$120.10	$127.33	$128.93	$114.20	$110.79	$109.56	$93.96
FTE Students by Department							
Lower Division	143	146	138	156	179	195	237
Upper Division	60	61	59	67	67	69	79
Graduate	29	34	41	42	49	44	68
Total FTE Students	232	241	238	265	295	308	384
FTE Students/FTE Faculty	19.33	18.54	18.31	21.20	21.85	22.81	28.44
Total Budget/FTE Students	$5,219	$5,495	$5,467	$4,847	$4,683	$4,649	$3,976
Credit Sections Offered	117	103	97	102	105	129	142
Average Credit Hours/Credit Sections	86.16	100.97	104.04	110.25	118.76	101.31	114.43
Total Student FTE/Credit Sections	1.98	2.34	2.45	2.60	2.81	2.39	2.70
Credit Sections/Faculty FTE	9.75	7.92	7.46	8.16	7.78	9.56	10.52
Degrees Conferred							
Bachelor's	40	38	33	54	39	39	36
Master's	7	13	15	19	20	23	28
Doctoral	0	0	0	0	0	0	0
Total Degrees Conferred	47	51	48	73	59	62	64
Total Budget/Degrees Conferred	$25,760.91	$25,966.02	$27,108.04	$17,593.47	$23,415.73	$23,094.63	$23,856.80
Degrees/FTE Faculty	3.92	3.92	3.69	5.84	4.37	4.59	4.74

Source: Portland State University–Offices of Institutional Research and Planning and Budget

(continued from page 75)

Exhibit 6.2 shows another example of library reporting. This exhibit contrasts library performance and financial indicators, and discloses a great deal of information about the library, including its processing statistics, holdings, staffing, expenditures, users, circulation, and other services.

Reports that blend financial and performance data can provide illustrative insights into organization costs. This information becomes even more useful when used to compare similar organizations in comparable institutions. A great deal of information for use in this kind of analysis is available on the Internet, including sites maintained by the Integrated Postsecondary Education Data System (IPEDS) (http://nces.ed.gov/ipeds/) and University of Delaware, both of which contain extensive information. Some of these organizations charge a membership fee and require passwords or other login criteria. In addition, many colleges and universities maintain Web sites that also contain information useful in making comparisons.

SOURCES AND USES OF PEER INFORMATION

Many colleges and universities use peer institutions to make comparisons, especially for comparisons for academic purposes. Non-academic units are more similar to support units that exist in business and industry, and as such can be benchmarked against similar processes that exist in industry as well as against other universities or colleges. However, some caution is necessary depending on the data being used in making such comparisons. At the highest level of aggregation of information found in published general purpose financial reports, valid comparisons can be made among institutions if the information being compared follows standard formats and generally accepted accounting principles. However, the use of other forms of information, including data at lower levels of detail, is likely to produce results that are potentially invalid and noncomparable. Care must be taken to ensure that the information being used is appropriate and will result in valid

(continued on page 79)

EXHIBIT 6.2: COMPREHENSIVE LIBRARY STATISTICS

	1995-96	1996-97	1997-98	1998-99	1999-2000
Library Holdings					
Processing Statistics					
Volumes Added (Gross)	102,531	81,863	97,160	90,570	123,358
New Serial Titles Added (Gross)	6,225	2,924	3,349	3,176	2,880
Catalog Items in LUIS Data Base to Date	2,678,795	2,879,574	2,973,600	3,091,516	3,229,270
Library Holdings					
Architecture/Fine Arts Libraries [1]	114,743	118,637	123,256	127,948	130,831
Education Library	129,887	132,333	135,667	138,136	141,361
Health Sciences Center Library	272,173	314,181	315,721	314,744	322,488
Humanities and Social Sciences Library [2]	1,397,659	1,403,958	1,468,034	1,528,942	1,223,478
Legal Information Center	326,752	328,572	333,189	324,453	321,391
Science Library (Marston)*	576,363	588,194	602,235	614,339	634,052
Special and Distinctive Collections [3]	576,198	584,086	599,204	621,856	633,742
Storage General**	0	0	0	0	320,552
Total	3,393,775	3,469,961	3,577,306	3,670,418	3,727,895
Other Library Materials					
Government Documents	1,194,892	1,224,621	1,244,681	1,267,632	1,272,807
Microforms	6,026,299	6,208,462	6,340,498	6,514,862	6,701,512
Maps	445,244	453,214	459,070	464,562	727,220
Aerial Photographs	239,274	240,624	245,005	248,708	257,635
Audio Materials [4]	19,231	20,620	21,242	23,366	24,557
Slides	14,485	17,125	17,250	17,726	893
Film/Videos**	0	0	0	0	11,521
Graphic Matherials**	0	0	0	0	289,608
Computer Files***	0	0	0	0	18,593
Manuscripts (In Linear Feet) [5]	7,576	8,056	8,123	8,165	8,185
Serial Subscriptions	26,775	24,788	25,213	28,082	31,203

[1] Includes AFA and Music.
[2] The humanities and social science reference and research collections in Library West serving Business, Health and Human Performance, Journalism, and Liberal Arts, excluding the sciences.
[3] Includes Archives, Baldwin, Belknap, Florida History, Judaica, Latin American and Rare Book collection.
[4] Includes tapes, cassettes, CD's, records, etc.
[5] Includes Archives, Baldwin, Belknap, Florida History, Judaica, and Rare Book Collections.

(table continued on page 78)

EXHIBIT 6.2: COMPREHENSIVE LIBRARY STATISTICS *(continued from page 77)*

	1995-96	1996-97	1997-98	1998-99	1999-2000
Library Fiscal and Human Resources					
Staff[6]					
Librarians FTE	108	109	110	110	103
Administrative and Professional Staff FTE	19	22	23	28	27
USPS Staff FTE	185	180	185	196	183
Hourly Employees FTE	78	89	94	97	92
Total	390	400	412	431	404
Expenditures[7]					
Salaries and Wages	$8,389,078	$8,887,291	$9,402,546	$9,703,854	$10,158,774
Library Materials	$5,851,417	$6,376,309	$8,288,925	$8,306,034	$9,258,002
Binding/Preservation	$268,058	$281,866	$305,468	$292,126	$402,137
Equipment/Furnishings	$436,468	$610,111	$802,567	$544,171	$1,035,296
Equipment/Computing	$481,488	$648,573	$376,004	$481,728	$563,884
Reference/Database Services	$106,407	$147,651	$123,816	$234,452	$95,542
Contracted Computing Services	$434,021	$445,713	$379,902	$184,886	$200,704
Interlibrary Loan	$35,076	$70,183	$68,797	$58,190	$50,818
Other Expenditures	$838,585	$1,007,697	$1,043,034	$1,626,906	$1,525,755
Total	$16,840,598	$18,475,394	$20,791,059	$21,432,347	$23,290,912
Library Output					
Availability of Service					
Number of Service Locations[8]	28	29	32	27	31
Total Hours of Library Service in Typical Week	1,276	1,393			1,318
Average Hours Per Week in Five Larger Libraries[9]	107	110	108	108	100.6
Annual Users Count (Door Counts)	2,787,542	2,665,860	2,860,468	3,117,701	2,798,973
Use of Book and Journals					
Number of Materials Circulated[10]	1,863,776	1,866,886	1,897,310	1,632,755	1,419,508
In-House Use of Library Materials[11]	915,385	888,914	929,682	705,070	614,448
Materials Reshelved	2,779,161	2,755,800	2,826,992	2,337,825	2,033,956
Information/Reference Assistance					
Informational Questions Answered (estimated)	117,365	160,623	125,351	119,191	163,567
Reference Questions Answered:					
In-Person	224,088	214,250	211,621	110,404	133,779
Telephone	24,054	22,335	17,049	15,375	18,864
Mail/On-line	935	2,621	2,404	3,444	6,570
Total	249,077	239,206	231,074	129,223	159,213
Lengthy Database Searches Performed	1,620	1,101	733	383	223
Ready Reference Searches (estimated)[12]	30,000	3,054	911	2,737	121,370
Total	398,062	403,984	358,069	251,534	444,373
Instruction in Use of Libraries, Databases, Bibliography[13]					
Number of Presentations Given to Classes, etc.	600	684	651	533	724
Number of Students/Faculty/Staff Trained	9,929	11,464	11,818	9,302	15,022
Inter-Library Loans					
Loans of UF Materials to Other Libraries	9,765	10,930	11,496	12,931	12,922
Copies of UF Materials to Other Libraries	34,993	34,349	35,606	32,361	31,660
Borrows of Library Materials from Other Libraries	5,268	5,228	5,888	6,134	6,002
Borrows of Copies from Other Libraries	7,348	10,824	13,683	16,090	14,353

[6]Includes all UF libraries: Architecture/Fine Arts; Education; Health Science, Humanities and Social Sciences (Library West and Smathers); Legal Information Center; Marston Science Library; and Music.

[7]Statistics are included for all UF libraries listed in (6) above.

[8]Includes all service desks (circulation, reference, periodicals, etc.) in libraries listed in (6) above.

[9]Includes Library West, Smathers, Marston, Legal Information Center, and Health Science Center Library.

[10]These are books checked out to faculty, students, and other library borrowers.

[11]These are books and journals used in the libraries and retrieved from tables/carrels for reshelving.

[12]When the appropriate manner of response to a question is to search electronic resources, it is the common practice to access a variety of databases.

[13]Librarians teach research methods courses through joint appointments with academic departments, provide instruction sessions tailored to the needs of specific courses at the request of faculty, and offer open enrollment sessions for students to learn database searching and/or internet techniques, as well as bibliographic skills.

*As of 1999-00, includes volume count for books and bound volumes in Map Library.
**Began reporting in 1999-00.
***Began reporting in 1999-00. Includes electronic databases, CD's, web resources, etc.

(table continued on page 79)

EXHIBIT 6.2: COMPREHENSIVE LIBRARY STATISTICS *(continued from page 78)*

	1995-96	1996-97	1997-98	1998-99	1999-2000
Library Output (continued)					
Annual Collection Additions					
Library Materials Acquired[14]	64,868	59,481	83,498	73,412	123,314
Journal Issues Checked In[15]	71,330	83,772	84,488	105,042	80,423
Microforms Checked In	98,837	70,480	97,528	84,092	54,017
Access to Collections					
Titles Cataloged[16]	54,497	47,343	54,165	51,981	55,472
Titles Updated and Converted[17]	1,350	2,248	785	478	639
Titles Reclassed[18]	197	242	693	482	291
Transfers/Withdrawals/Reinstates[19]	66	2,697	9,796	8,959	2,948
Total	56,110	52,530	65,439	61,900	59,350
Physical Preservation/Conservation					
Periodicals/Soft Cover Books Bound	39,824	20,298	18,991	42,435	6,543
Library Materials Photocopied	3,272	6,716	2,888	3,272	1,903
Volumes Microfilmed	1,114	798	2,474	2,454	3,390
Volumes Receiving Preservation Treatment	5,922	20,124	23,010	12,029	5,652
Other Materials Receiving Preservation Treatment	323	0	859	723	1,849
Library Materials Digitized**	0	0	0	292	488

[14]Includes books, maps, electronic, audio and video formats, manuscripts and archives. Does not include journals, newspapers, or microforms.

[15]Annually, the library checks in approximately 100,000 journal issues, which are subsequently bound and become volumes in the library collections.

[16]Includes books, journals, newspapers, microformats, maps, electronic, audio and video formats, manuscripts, archives, and kits.

[17]Recataloging of older materials previously accessible only through the card catalog and entering the records in LUIS, providing easier access by faculty and students.

[18]These materials have been reclassified to the Library of Congress (LC) system from the S Decimal system to provide easier access by faculty and students.

[19]These materials have been transferred internally to another library location, lost and withdrawn from the collection, or found and returned to the collection.

Source: University of Florida Web site, Office of the Director of University Libraries

(continued from page 77)

and accurate comparisons. Disclose any assumptions or other potential issues with the data being presented to guard against presenting misleading comparisons or results.

Common sources of information for use in making comparative analyses include:

- American Association of Collegiate Registrars and Admissions Officers
- American Association of Community Colleges
- American Association of State Colleges and Universities
- APPA: The Association of Higher Education Facilities Officers
- Association for Institutional Research
- Association of American Colleges and Universities
- Association of College and University Telecommunications Administrators
- Association of Research Libraries
- College and University Professional Association for Human Resources
- Council for the Advancement and Support of Higher Education
- Council of Graduate Schools
- Council of Higher Education Management Associations
- Council of Independent Colleges
- EDUCAUSE
- ERIC (Educational Resources Information Center)
- Government Finance Officers Association
- Higher Education Data Sharing Consortium
- International Association of Campus Law Enforcement Administrators
- Internet Resources for Institutional Research
- Integrated Postsecondary Education Data System (IPEDS)
- John Minter and Associates
- National Association of Campus Card Users
- NAFSA: Association of International Educators

- National Association of College and University Attorneys
- National Association of College and University Business Officers (NACUBO) and related regional associations in the east, central, south, and west (EACUBO, CACUBO, SACUBO, and WACUBO)
- National Association of College and University Food Services
- National Association of College Auxiliary Services
- National Association of College Stores
- National Association of Education Buyers
- National Association of State Universities and Land-Grant Colleges
- National Association of Student Financial Aid Administrators
- National Association of Student Personnel Administrators
- National Center for Education Statistics (NCES)
- National Center for Postsecondary Improvement
- National Collegiate Athletic Association
- National Consortium for Continuous Improvement in Higher Education
- National Council of University Research Administrators
- Oklahoma State University Salary Surveys
- Office of Postsecondary Education Campus Security Statistics Web site
- Society for College and University Planning
- Society for Human Resource Management
- University Continuing Education Association
- University of Delaware: National Study of Instructional Costs and Productivity by Discipline
- University Risk Management and Insurance Association
- State oversight organizations and other administrative associations
- Other informal institutional affiliations and interactions

COMPARATIVE FINANCIAL INFORMATION

The Integrated Postsecondary Educational Data System (IPEDS) is an integrated system of surveys conducted by the National Center for Education Statistics. These surveys represent a system designed to collect information on two items: (1) postsecondary institutions regarding student and financial information, and (2) the characteristics of degree recipients. This system is useful in comparing financial information from various institutions. When making comparisons, analyze proportions of revenues and expense and compare this over time using trend analysis techniques. Differences and changes over time should be acknowledged and explanations offered as to the types of changes occurring and why.

Exhibit 6.3 *(pages 81–82)* illustrates the sources of revenue in 1999–2000 from a group of comparator institutions using IPEDS data.

Similarly, peer institutions can compare expenditures using this same IPEDS database. Exhibit 6.4 *(pages 82–86)* shows the expenditures by functional classifications for the same set of peer institutions as was used in exhibit 6.3.

UNDERSTANDING INSTITUTIONAL REVENUE AND COST STRUCTURES

Many costs incurred by colleges and universities are fixed—tenure equates to lifetime employment; and because tenure is a core value in many institutions, it permeates the culture. As a service industry, higher education is extremely dependent on people to deliver its services. Many institutions have cost bases that comprise more than 60 percent to 80 percent personnel costs (salaries, wages, and other payroll expenses—FICA, health benefits, retirement, and worker's compensation and other taxes/assessments). This cost base is somewhat inflexible due to lifetime employment, frequent presence of unions, and institutional cultures that resist changes.

Because there is such a large investment in people, productivity, or lack thereof, can be a significant factor that affects institutional finances. As a result, it is crucial that higher education administrators understand faculty workloads, paying attention to areas where there is the capacity to do more, as well as those areas that are overtaxed. This information can be used to set performance goals and monitor results against established benchmarks. This is an extremely contentious issue for most colleges and universities, however, especially when being addressed by financial administrators. Nevertheless, significant cost savings and/or efficiencies can be attained if productivity is managed effectively.

Understanding cost and revenue structures can be of great value in managing the financial affairs of higher education institutions. Many recommend trying to maintain as much flexibility as possible in these revenue and cost bases to facilitate adjustments in operations and costs when changes occur. This is a partial reason why more institutions are hiring fixed-term and part-time faculty in increasing numbers, a controversial practice that it is being closely monitored by the American Association of University Professors (AAUP) and other faculty advocacy groups. Many associate the use of part-time faculty with degraded quality. But despite these feelings, the use of part-time faculty can

(continued on page 86)

EXHIBIT 6.3: IPEDS REVENUES BY SOURCE BY PEER INSTITUTIONS (Part 1 of 3)

1999-2000 IPEDS Revenues by Source by PSU Comparator

	Tuition and fees	Federal appropriations	State appropriations	Federal grants & contracts	State grants & contracts	Local grants & contracts	Private gifts, grants & contracts	Endowment income	Sales & services of educational activities	Auxiliary enterprises	Hospital revenues	Other sources	Independent operations	Total current funds revenues
PORTLAND STATE UNIVERSITY	$63,706,466	$0	$61,125,151	$28,950,142	$3,159,028	$933,787	$5,007,355	$7,282	$4,943,719	$21,051,971	$0	$996,620	$0	$189,881,781
UNIVERSITY OF ILLINOIS AT CHICAGO	$116,278,929	$0	$278,650,269	$158,595,952	$24,364,788		$56,052,944	$843,375	$60,115,701	$65,747,789	$292,199,623	$112,868,152	$5,471,896	$1,171,189,418
INDIANA UNIVERSITY-PURDUE UNIVERSITY-INDIANAPOLIS	$105,759,278	$24,928,344	$194,280,697	$72,899,907	$8,963,151		$51,190,432	$277,680	$22,631,833	$123,193,898		$106,240,545		$710,365,765
UNIVERSITY OF TOLEDO	$103,914,217		$87,705,988	$18,160,158	$9,443,292	$667,843	$8,557,506	$1,536,929	$2,379,217	$38,594,024	$0	$3,484,423	$0	$274,443,597
UNIVERSITY OF MEMPHIS	$64,325,044	$0	$97,265,862	$26,263,848	$2,600,949	$1,589,299	$11,602,097	$1,554,232	$12,388,244	$12,975,775	$0	$2,709,935	$0	$233,275,285
THE UNIVERSITY OF TEXAS AT ARLINGTON	$67,511,795	$0	$87,447,828	$19,364,409	$4,260,525	$263,665	$5,446,247	$1,335,064	$6,120,419	$9,393,113	$0	$4,773,075	$0	$205,916,140
GEORGE MASON UNIVERSITY	$73,212,616		$99,490,181	$26,440,731	$9,160,183	$536,172	$17,790,756	$1,377,844	$329,963	$58,072,216	$0	$4,027,412	$0	$290,438,074
WESTERN MICHIGAN UNIVERSITY	$105,282,969	$0	$116,517,837	$15,943,585	$1,093,867	$1,882,184	$12,985,020	$2,689,634	$14,692,707	$79,620,951	$0	$3,022,007	$0	$353,710,761
UNIVERSITY OF WISCONSIN-MILWAUKEE	$80,659,138		$121,456,336	$26,767,587	$542,949	$193,608	$7,750,092	$37,820	$18,217,428	$22,935,197	$0	$17,329,341	$0	$295,889,496
SAN DIEGO STATE UNIVERSITY	$92,247,472	$0	$170,955,170	$86,085,344	$18,358,058	$0	$49,697,115	$1,876,506	$20,597,829	$70,324,953	$0	$17,733,128	$0	$527,875,575
Average	$87,289,792	$2,492,834	$131,489,532	$47,947,166	$8,194,705	$606,656	$22,605,956	$1,153,637	$16,241,706	$50,190,989	$29,219,962	$27,318,464	$547,190	$425,298,589
Maximum	$116,278,929	$24,928,344	$278,650,269	$158,595,952	$24,364,788	$1,882,184	$56,052,944	$2,689,634	$60,115,701	$123,193,898	$292,199,623	$112,868,152	$5,471,896	$1,171,189,418
Minimum	$63,706,466	$0	$61,125,151	$15,943,585	$542,949	$0	$5,007,355	$7,282	$329,963	$9,393,113	$0	$996,620	$0	$189,881,781

EXHIBIT 6.3: IPEDS REVENUES BY SOURCE BY PEER INSTITUTIONS (Part 2 of 3)

1999-2000 IPEDS Revenues by Source by PSU Comparator

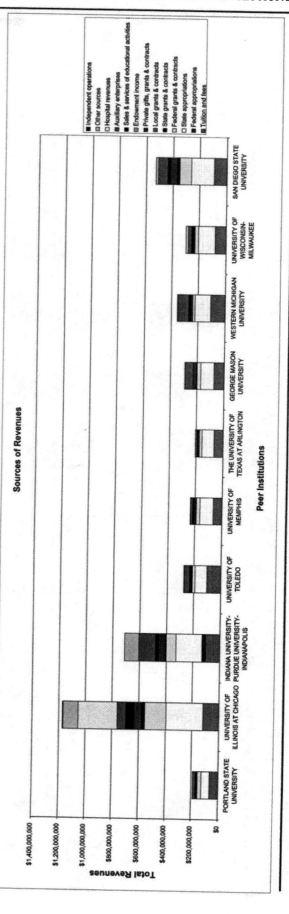

Sources of Revenues

Legend: Independent operations; Other sources; Hospital revenues; Auxiliary enterprises; Sales & services of educational activities; Endowment income; Private gifts, grants & contracts; Local grants & contracts; State grants & contracts; Federal grants & contracts; State appropriations; Federal appropriations; Tuition and fees

Vertical axis (Total Revenues): $0, $200,000,000, $400,000,000, $600,000,000, $800,000,000, $1,000,000,000, $1,200,000,000, $1,400,000,000

Horizontal axis (Peer Institutions): PORTLAND STATE UNIVERSITY, UNIVERSITY OF ILLINOIS AT CHICAGO, INDIANA UNIVERSITY-PURDUE UNIVERSITY-INDIANAPOLIS, UNIVERSITY OF TOLEDO, UNIVERSITY OF MEMPHIS, THE UNIVERSITY OF TEXAS AT ARLINGTON, GEORGE MASON UNIVERSITY, WESTERN MICHIGAN UNIVERSITY, UNIVERSITY OF WISCONSIN-MILWAUKEE, SAN DIEGO STATE UNIVERSITY

EXHIBIT 6.3: IPEDS REVENUES BY SOURCE BY PEER INSTITUTIONS *(Part 3 of 3)*

1999-2000 IPEDS Revenues by Source by PSU Comparator

EXHIBIT 6.4: IPEDS EXPENDITURES BY FUNCTION BY PEER INSTITUTIONS *(Part 1 of 5)*

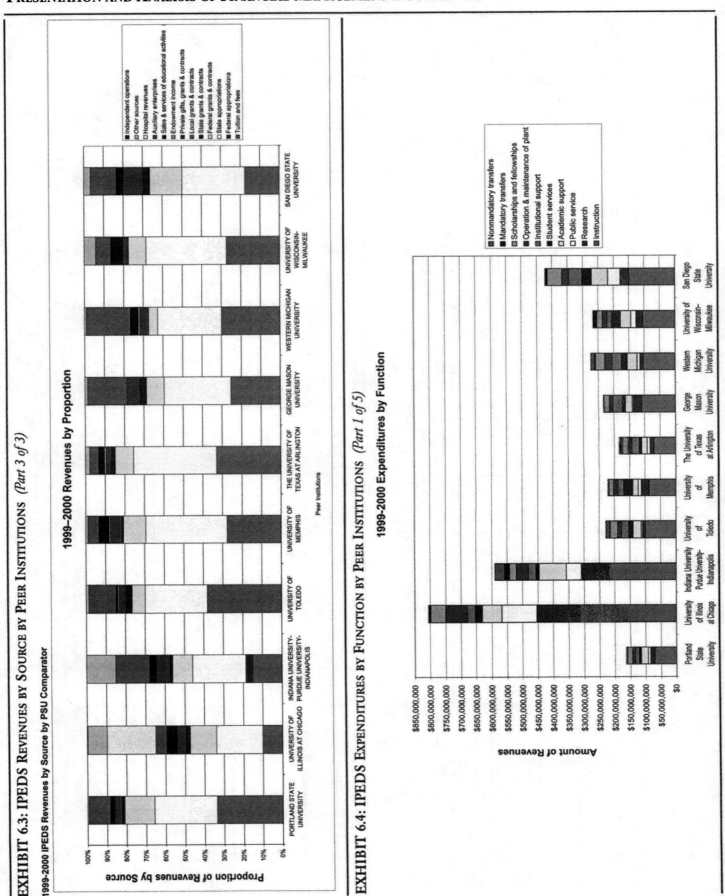

EXHIBIT 6.4: IPEDS EXPENDITURES BY FUNCTION BY PEER INSTITUTIONS   *(Part 2 of 5)*

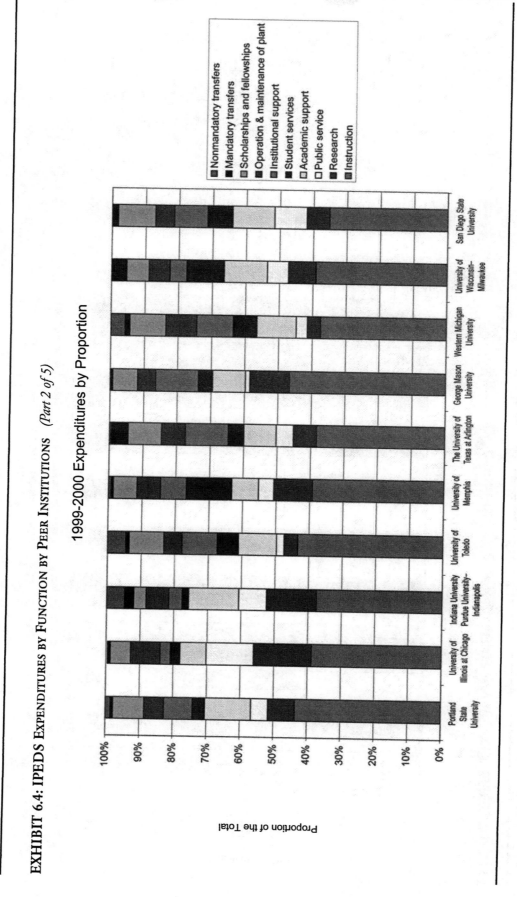

1999-2000 Expenditures by Proportion

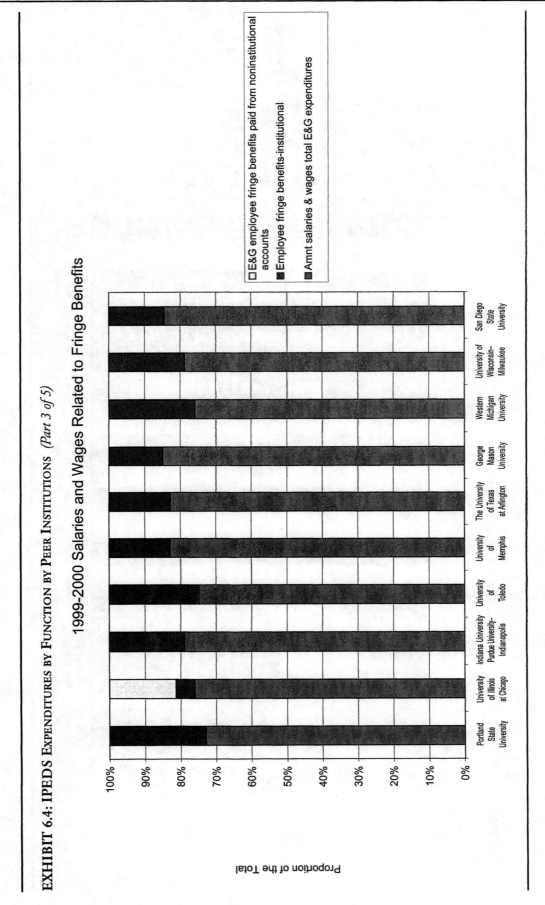

EXHIBIT 6.4: IPEDS EXPENDITURES BY FUNCTION BY PEER INSTITUTIONS *(Part 3 of 5)*

1999-2000 Salaries and Wages Related to Fringe Benefits

Legend:
- ☐ E&G employee fringe benefits paid from noninstitutional accounts
- ■ Employee fringe benefits-institutional
- ▨ Amnt salaries & wages total E&G expenditures

Proportion of the Total

EXHIBIT 6.4: IPEDS EXPENDITURES BY FUNCTION BY PEER INSTITUTIONS *(Part 4 of 5)*

1999-2000 Salaries and Wages Related to Fringe Benefits

1999-2000 IPEDS Comparator Expenditures by Portland State University Peer

	Instruction	Research	Public service	Academic support	Student services	Institutional support	Operation & maintenance of plant	Scholarships and fellowships	Mandatory transfers	Nonmandatory transfers	Total educational & general expenditures
PORTLAND STATE UNIVERSITY	$70,998,455	$13,018,891	$8,292,817	$22,393,276	$5,934,505	$13,828,978	$9,675,276	$14,961,200	$1,381,376	$2,296,000	$162,780,774
UNIVERSITY OF ILLINOIS AT CHICAGO	$314,101,141	$139,266,394	$114,547,908	$62,471,805	$23,844,599	$24,161,327	$71,528,565	$48,441,215	$7,136,081	($3,519,422)	$801,979,613
INDIANA UNIVERSITY-PURDUE UNIVERSITY-INDIANAPOLIS	$220,314,152	$88,347,970	$48,738,112	$88,270,843	$10,761,016	$23,921,187	$39,684,380	$21,768,071	$16,519,504	$30,620,872	$588,946,107
UNIVERSITY OF TOLEDO	$98,514,711	$9,529,882	$4,902,578	$25,789,122	$14,542,874	$23,795,907	$12,480,819	$23,467,315	$2,318,264	$12,293,066	$227,634,538
UNIVERSITY OF MEMPHIS	$86,608,785	$25,643,564	$9,990,717	$17,689,775	$30,085,890	$16,885,781	$15,633,813	$15,491,074	$1,505,153	$1,691,137	$221,225,689
THE UNIVERSITY OF TEXAS AT ARLINGTON	$69,849,280	$12,682,484	$9,509,427	$17,551,737	$8,636,602	$23,293,138	$13,035,979	$18,158,172	$9,380,483	$804,201	$182,901,503
GEORGE MASON UNIVERSITY	$108,696,628	$27,513,380	$3,325,785	$22,796,421	$9,894,080	$29,578,439	$12,723,380	$17,248,367	$1,720,532	$0	$233,497,012
WESTERN MICHIGAN UNIVERSITY	$102,749,291	$10,769,265	$9,171,571	$32,109,273	$19,444,721	$29,735,739	$25,153,750	$29,223,899	$4,133,170	$11,389,739	$273,880,418
UNIVERSITY OF WISCONSIN-MILWAUKEE	$104,074,588	$21,968,227	$16,702,243	$34,001,934	$29,865,446	$13,222,287	$16,783,202	$17,481,988	$12,091,170	($55,895)	$266,135,190
SAN DIEGO STATE UNIVERSITY	$148,331,557	$28,642,678	$40,730,685	$52,601,760	$31,953,140	$41,213,848	$24,070,837	$46,876,187	$7,425,176	($42,863)	$421,803,005
Average	$132,423,859	$37,738,274	$26,591,184	$37,567,595	$18,496,287	$23,963,663	$24,077,000	$25,311,749	$6,361,091	$5,547,684	$338,078,385
Maximum	$314,101,141	$139,266,394	$114,547,908	$88,270,843	$31,953,140	$41,213,848	$71,528,565	$48,441,215	$16,519,504	$30,620,872	$801,979,613
Minimum	$69,849,280	$9,529,882	$3,325,785	$17,551,737	$5,934,505	$13,222,287	$9,675,276	$14,961,200	$1,381,376	($3,519,422)	$162,780,774

(table continued below)

	Auxiliary enterprises	Auxiliary enterprises (nonmandatory)	Hospital expenditures	Hospitals (nonmandatory)	Independent operations	Independent operations (nonmandatory)	Other current funds expenditure	Total current funds expenditures and transfers
PORTLAND STATE UNIVERSITY	$22,721,795	($286,464)	$0	$0	$0	$0	$0	$185,502,569
UNIVERSITY OF ILLINOIS AT CHICAGO	$61,946,508	$3,435,793	$284,921,294	$8,661,162	$4,986,409	$0	$0	$1,153,833,824
INDIANA UNIVERSITY-PURDUE UNIVERSITY-INDIANAPOLIS	$122,572,308	$0	$0	$0	$0	$0	$0	$711,518,415
UNIVERSITY OF TOLEDO	$38,835,998	$11,638,655	$0	$0	$0	$0	$0	$266,470,536
UNIVERSITY OF MEMPHIS	$11,618,744	$1,367,317	$0	$0	$0	$0	$0	$232,844,433
THE UNIVERSITY OF TEXAS AT ARLINGTON	$18,225,254	$295,518	$0	$0	$0	$0	$0	$201,126,757
GEORGE MASON UNIVERSITY	$60,139,498	$0	$0	$0	$0	$0	$0	$293,636,510
WESTERN MICHIGAN UNIVERSITY	$85,462,488	$4,674,992	$0	$0	$0	$0	$0	$359,342,906
UNIVERSITY OF WISCONSIN-MILWAUKEE	$24,696,002	$533,664	$0	$0	$0	$0	$0	$290,831,192
SAN DIEGO STATE UNIVERSITY	$70,093,376	$0	$0	$0	$0	$0	$0	$491,896,381
Average	$51,631,197	$2,165,948	$28,492,129	$866,116	$498,641	$0	$0	$418,700,352
Maximum	$122,572,308	$11,638,655	$284,921,294	$8,661,162	$4,986,409	$0	$0	$1,153,833,824
Minimum	$11,618,744	($286,464)	$0	$0	$0	$0	$0	$185,502,569

EXHIBIT 6.4: IPEDS EXPENDITURES BY FUNCTION BY PEER INSTITUTIONS *(Part 5 of 5)*

1999-2000 IPEDS Comparator Salaries and Fringe Expenditures by PSU Peer

	Amnt salaries & wages total E&G expenditures	Employee fringe benefits-institutional	E&G employee fringe benefits paid from noninstitutional accounts	Total E&G employee compensation	Fringe as a percentage of Compensation
PORTLAND STATE UNIVERSITY	$79,119,567	$29,513,367	$0	$108,632,934	37.30%
UNIVERSITY OF ILLINOIS AT CHICAGO	$434,820,204	$30,592,703	$107,114,732	$572,527,639	31.67%
INDIANA UNIVERSITY-PURDUE UNIVERSITY-INDIANAPOLIS	$281,471,370	$75,521,785	$0	$356,993,155	26.83%
UNIVERSITY OF TOLEDO	$116,240,560	$39,537,194	$0	$155,777,754	34.01%
UNIVERSITY OF MEMPHIS	$118,309,126	$24,489,982	$0	$142,799,108	20.70%
THE UNIVERSITY OF TEXAS AT ARLINGTON	$97,811,729	$20,254,085	$0	$118,065,814	20.71%
GEORGE MASON UNIVERSITY	$139,199,058	$24,712,603	$0	$163,911,661	17.75%
WESTERN MICHIGAN UNIVERSITY	$132,194,631	$42,231,803	$0	$174,426,434	31.95%
UNIVERSITY OF WISCONSIN-MILWAUKEE	$139,377,683	$37,940,220	$0	$177,317,903	27.22%
SAN DIEGO STATE UNIVERSITY	$216,853,079	$39,850,364	$0	$256,703,443	18.38%

(continued from page 80)

be very cost effective; it can add real-world flavor to the classroom (as many part-time faculty are practitioners); and it adds great workforce flexibility, allowing the institution to expand or contract its operations as market demand changes.

CATEGORIES OF REVENUE AND COST BASES

As noted, revenue and cost structures play an important role in the analyzing and reporting of financial management information. The following discussion addresses nine revenue and cost structures and concepts common in higher education institutions.

INDIRECT REVENUES AND COSTS

Indirect revenues or costs are defined as the benefits and costs that cannot be traced to a specific activity or objective without some form of allocation. Direct costs include items such as salaries, wages, and other payroll expenses; needed supplies; and services and travel typically associated with, and charged directly to, the activity being reviewed (no allocations should be necessary). Indirect costs, on the other hand, are typically considered to be overhead, and are not directly charged to the project or activity being analyzed. Typically, indirect costs include general and administrative expenses—expenses for administrative oversight, space in most cases, and the utilities (heat, light, and power) and other forms of support required by the activity being analyzed. These items are generally thought of as "overhead," and require some form of allocation to

attribute the revenues or costs to a specific activity. The federal government requires most colleges and universities to calculate and negotiate an indirect cost overhead rate on federally sponsored research and service projects. The negotiation part of this process is required, since differences of opinion exist on allocation technique or basis utilized.

UNRESTRICTED, RESTRICTED, AND TEMPORARILY RESTRICTED FUNDS

Unrestricted funds are also thought of as education and general funds, operating funds, or other current fund unrestricted accounts, such as service departments, auxiliary enterprise, and designated operating accounts. These funds can be used for any lawful purpose of the organization, and these types of funds have the greatest flexibility in terms of use; as such, they are important to the financial viability of the institution.

According to NACUBO's Financial Accounting and Reporting Manual for Higher Education, "institutions often receive public and private contributions, grants, and appropriations that have restrictions imposed on their use by law, the donor, the grantor, or other external third parties. These moneys may be restricted to use for a particular program, function, or activity or they may be required to be held for a period of time or in perpetuity and invested, with only the income to be used for general or specified purposes" (Section 209). But only external entities can create restrictions, and once accepted by the recipient institution, they are binding in nature, and the institution is legally obligated to comply with their terms and conditions. Some restrictions can be temporary, meaning that they are restricted until a specified date or event, at which time they become unrestricted funds. Restricted resources must be segregated in the accounting records, from resources designated by an internal source (governing board or management) for a specified purpose.

DESIGNATED AND UNDESIGNATED FUNDS

NACUBO's Financial Accounting and Reporting Manual for Higher Education defines internal designations as "limitations made by the institution's governing board or management and can be modified at any time. These designations do not carry the same legal force as restrictions placed by external sources (assuming such authority has been delegated by the board)" (Section 215). For accounting purposes, designated funds should be recorded in the unrestricted net asset class; however, these designations should be reflected in the institution's financial statements or notes.

HARD AND SOFT REVENUES AND EXPENSES

A distinction should be made between recurring, or "hard," revenues (such as tuition or appropriations funding) and nonrecurring, or "soft," revenues (such as grants and contracts). If the institution relies heavily on soft money to fund long-term commitments (such as tenured faculty positions), its funding strategy is relatively risky, since these funds are not necessarily guaranteed to recur.

Hard and soft match is also a term used to describe different types of funds (matching funds) provided in order to obtain or fulfill matching requirements of certain types of grants or contracts. Hard match typically requires an out-of-pocket disbursement of incremental funds, whereas soft match is typically only an earmark, or shifting, of pre-existing costs to meet matching obligations. A common example of soft match is the certification of time and effort expended on an externally sponsored project, even though the salary was charged to an unrestricted budget.

FIXED AND VARIABLE REVENUES AND COSTS

Revenues and costs that are unaffected by changes in activity levels are referred to as fixed. In the short run, fixed revenues and costs will remain the same. Fixed revenues and costs per unit vary inversely with changes in activity levels. Buildings are typically viewed as a fixed cost, since they remain more or less constant in the short-run despite changes (positive or negative) in activity levels.

Conversely, variable revenues and costs are those whose total dollar amount changes in direct proportion to changes in the total volume of activity. Variable revenues and costs per unit are constant with changes in volume. An example of variable costs is the use of part-time, or adjunct

faculty, as their use will be directly proportionate to enrollments. A variable revenue source is tuition as it fluctuates with enrollment levels.

BUDGETED AND UNBUDGETED REVENUES AND COSTS

Most institutions adopt a budget in anticipation of certain revenues and costs associated with institutional operations. Thus, most revenues and costs are budgeted or accounted for in this anticipated financial plan. However, some revenues or costs typically are unbudgeted due to unexpected activities, one-time activities, or unpredictable events. As discussed in chapter 3, care must be taken not to become reliant on the use of one-time revenues, since they tend to be an unexpected source of funds. Similarly, reserves should be maintained to guard against unexpected costs that may be associated with unanticipated losses, repairs, penalties, or other assessments.

HISTORICAL AND FAIR/CURRENT MARKET VALUES AND COSTS

Historical costs or benefits are recorded in the accounting system on an after-the-fact basis. They are also referred to as the actual costs or benefits. Alternatively, fair or current market value represents the current value (garnered via appraisal or other means) as of the date being reported, such as the date of donation or date of the financial statement.

CONTROLLABLE AND NON-CONTROLLABLE COSTS

Controllable revenues and costs are those that can be controlled by management decisions. Alternatively, uncontrollable revenues and costs are unaffected by the decisions of a specific manager. The price of utilities is an example of an uncontrollable cost, given that prices are typically set by a monopoly provider in the short-run. In the longer run, however, utility costs can become controllable as new sources or providers can be developed and other efficiencies achieved.

OPPORTUNITY AND SUNK COSTS

Opportunity costs represent the net benefits foregone when one alternative is chosen in favor of other alternatives. Opportunity cost can also be described as the net benefit foregone between the most likely alternative and the next best available alternative. A sunk cost, on the other hand, is a cost for which the expenditure of cash has already been made and no current cash expenditure is required.

It is useful to consider the institution's mix of revenues and costs by breaking down the education and general fund revenues and costs using these categorizations. This information can be helpful in assisting management in understanding, forecasting, and controlling revenues and costs.

DIFFERENT VIEWS OF INSTITUTIONAL REVENUES AND EXPENSES

In addition to the revenue and cost categorizations discussed above, it is also useful to monitor revenues and expenses by fund, organization, program, object, activity, and location. Most financial management information systems use these distinctions as part of their chart of accounts or similar functionality. At a minimum, the following distinctions should be maintained:

By Fund:

Current Funds–Unrestricted

Education and General Funds

Designated Operations, Service Departments, and Auxiliary Enterprises

Current Funds–Restricted

Gifts, Grants, and Contracts

Loan Funds

Endowment, Annuity, and Life Income Funds

Plant Funds

Unexpended Plant Funds

Funds for Renewal and Replacement

Funds for Retirement of Indebtedness

Investment in Plant Funds

By Organization:

President's Office

Academic Affairs

Finance and Administration

University Relations

Other

Exhibit 6.5 illustrates Portland State University's Education and General Fund budget by organization.

By Program or Function:

Instruction

Research–IDC rebates, GA's, Equipment, Facilities

Public Service

Academic Support

Student Services

Student Financial Aid

Plant Operations and Maintenance

(continued on page 90)

EXHIBIT 6.5: BUDGET BY ORGANIZATION

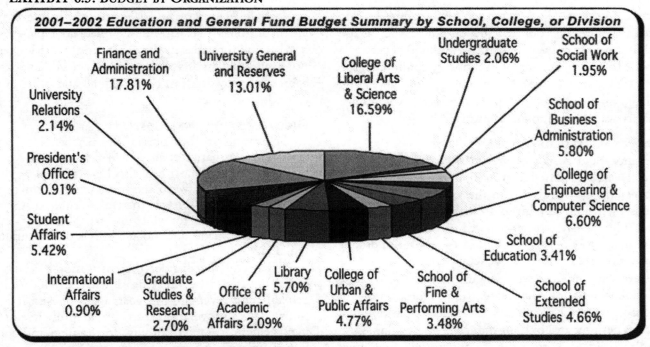

2001–2002 Education and General Fund Budget Summary by School, College, or Division

Finance and Administration 17.81%

University General and Reserves 13.01%

College of Liberal Arts & Science 16.59%

Undergraduate Studies 2.06%

School of Social Work 1.95%

University Relations 2.14%

School of Business Administration 5.80%

President's Office 0.91%

College of Engineering & Computer Science 6.60%

Student Affairs 5.42%

School of Education 3.41%

International Affairs 0.90%

Graduate Studies & Research 2.70%

Office of Academic Affairs 2.09%

Library 5.70%

College of Urban & Public Affairs 4.77%

School of Fine & Performing Arts 3.48%

School of Extended Studies 4.66%

Source: Portland State University Budget Office

EXHIBIT 6.6: BUDGET BY PROGRAM (FUNCTION)

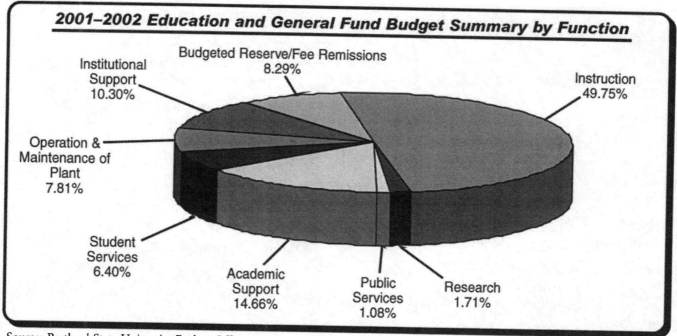

2001–2002 Education and General Fund Budget Summary by Function

- Budgeted Reserve/Fee Remissions 8.29%
- Institutional Support 10.30%
- Instruction 49.75%
- Operation & Maintenance of Plant 7.81%
- Student Services 6.40%
- Academic Support 14.66%
- Public Services 1.08%
- Research 1.71%

Source: Portland State University Budget Office

EXHIBIT 6.7: BUDGET BY OBJECT OF REVENUE

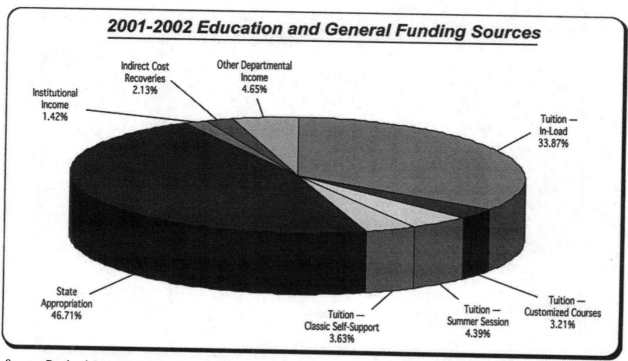

2001-2002 Education and General Funding Sources

- Indirect Cost Recoveries 2.13%
- Other Departmental Income 4.65%
- Institutional Income 1.42%
- Tuition — In-Load 33.87%
- State Appropriation 46.71%
- Tuition — Classic Self-Support 3.63%
- Tuition — Summer Session 4.39%
- Tuition — Customized Courses 3.21%

Source: Portland State University Budget Office

(continued from page 88)

Institutional Support

Budgeted Reserves

Exhibit 6.6 *(page 89)* illustrates Portland State University's Education and General Fund budget by program, also called function.

By Object Code:

Revenues (by source)

Exhibit 6.7 *(page 89)* illustrates Portland State University's Education and General Fund budget by object of revenue source.

Expense:

Personnel (salaries, wages, and OPE by type of employee)

Services

Supplies

Travel

Merchandise for resale

Depreciation

Student Aid

Exhibit 6.8 illustrates Portland State University's Education and General Fund budget by object of expenditure.

By Activity

Attributes revenues and expenses by activity

By Location

Main Campus

Branch Campuses

Other Centers or Satellite Locations

ANALYZING TRENDS IN FINANCIAL MANAGEMENT INDICATORS

To become meaningful, data must be compared against pre-established benchmarks (like budgets or other goals), compared against similar data from peer institutions, or analyzed over time (trends). Trend analyses also help one learn about the factors being analyzed, including whether

EXHIBIT 6.8: BUDGET BY OBJECT OF EXPENDITURE

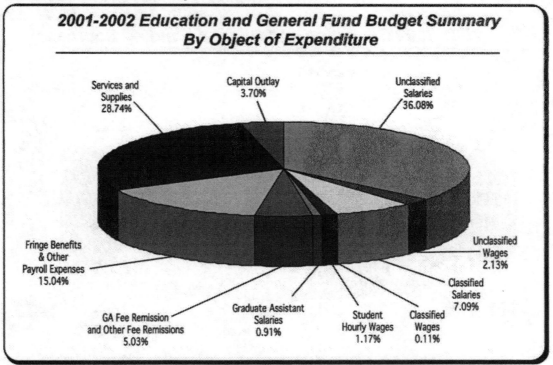

2001-2002 Education and General Fund Budget Summary By Object of Expenditure

- Services and Supplies 28.74%
- Capital Outlay 3.70%
- Unclassified Salaries 36.08%
- Unclassified Wages 2.13%
- Classified Salaries 7.09%
- Classified Wages 0.11%
- Student Hourly Wages 1.17%
- Graduate Assistant Salaries 0.91%
- GA Fee Remission and Other Fee Remissions 5.03%
- Fringe Benefits & Other Payroll Expenses 15.04%

Source: Portland State University Budget Office

they are increasing or decreasing and if they have changed in proportion to other related factors. Trend analysis produces richer information and descriptions of the influence and inter-relationships that other issues have on the factor being analyzed, such as the relationship between enrollment and income or expense.

It is very important to develop an understanding of the relationships that exist between changes in these trends and changes in the environment. This is where much can be learned about the cause and effect relationships that exist between certain factors. This information can then be used in formulating future plans, thereby increasing the validity of such plans. This is an important element in financial management, since higher education is increasing reliant on its relationship with, and the support derived from, the external environment. There are many terms used to describe this process, including futures research, organizational learning, and environmental scanning to name a few. Failure to recognize and use this type of information can make the institution vulnerable to changes occurring in the external environment. The following trends should be monitored:

• Income trends

• Expense trends

• Ratio trends

• Enrollment trends

PROSPECTIVE FINANCIAL MANAGEMENT

From a financial management perspective, it is important to make *pro forma* projections of future revenues, expenses, and other commitments that will be required as the institution evolves. One of the most important indicators of financial security is the level of unrestricted net assets or fund balance that is available. Items affecting fund balance include major revenues streams like tuition, state or federal tax revenues, property tax revenues, endowment returns, and the availability of financial aid. They should be closely monitored. Increased expenses or other commitments should be noted as one-time or recurring obligations with the effects being extrapolated in a financial *pro forma* projection that would include revenue from growth or new sources as well as expense projections. Know and understand your "burn rate," meaning your spending rate expressed in terms of "x" dollars per day, week, month, or year. In addition, revisit past budgets to pick up any one-time funding that will no longer be needed and can there-

fore become a resource for use in future periods. Many administrators look at changes, both positive and negative, from a base year budget so they can keep changes in the current context.

Planning and forecasting is analogous to looking into a crystal ball in hope of seeing into the future. Some crystal balls, however, are clearer and more accurate than others. Thus, when making financial projections, be conservative when projecting revenues and liberal when projecting expenses. It is always easier to come back with better news if revenues were higher or expenses lower than projected. The saying, "plan for the worst, hope for the best," applies in this situation. The key point: The more lead time you have, the more options you will have for dealing with problems or capitalizing on opportunities.

LOOKING FORWARD WITH PROJECTIONS

K. Patricia Cross writes, "No education, no matter how brilliantly designed and delivered, will last a lifetime in an era in which entire industries are created and wiped out in a single decade" (1989, p. 10). Internal and external changes to the institution must be monitored and compensating adjustments will frequently be required. Monitoring revenues and expenses against approved budgets is one way to detect needed changes. However, projections can be a valuable means of looking ahead to the end of the year, or even further, to guard against financial surprises.

Quarterly projections of revenues and expenses can be made using simple extrapolation calculations, through which you compare current year-to-date information against same time last year-to-date information in relation to the end of the year last year. For example, assume that you are looking at revenue and expense information at December 31, 2001, and you are curious as to what these amounts will be at June 30, 2002. One easy way to do this is to take the proportion of the same revenue or expense items at December 31, 2000, as a proportion of the June 30, 2001, totals. Once the percentage earned or spent at the same time last year has been calculated, divide the current year totals by the percentage to estimate the balance at June 30, 2002. This is a simple approach that assumes the same revenue and expense activities patterns will continue from year to year. Exhibit 6.9 *(page 92)* illustrates this forecasting approach.

EXHIBIT 6.9: REVENUE FORECASTING MODEL

Revenue Projection:	Col. 1	Col. 2	Col. 3	Col. 4	Col. 5	Col. 6	Col. 7
			Derived Col. 1/Col.2			Derived Col. 5/Col. 3	Derived Col. 6-Col. 4
Education and General Fund Tuition Income	YTD 12-31-00	YTD 6-30-01	12/31/2000 % of Total	2001-02 Budget	YTD 12-31-01	Projected YTD 6-30-02	Projected Variance
Resident Undergraduate	$11,453,240	$19,347,210	59.20%	$21,223,930	$12,742,081	$21,524,365	$300,435
Non-Resident Undergraduate	$4,761,652	$7,852,848	60.64%	$8,614,591	$5,387,650	$8,885,235	$270,644
Part-time Undergraduate	$2,921,009	$4,833,423	60.43%	$4,153,224	$2,583,420	$4,274,811	$121,587
Western Undergraduate Exchange	$243,214	$425,428	57.17%	$466,676	$271,685	$475,229	$8,553
Faculty/Staff Fees	$79,368	$129,310	61.38%	$141,851	$87,561	$142,658	$807
Resident Graduate	$5,046,089	$8,564,784	58.92%	$9,395,057	$5,558,826	$9,435,058	$40,001
Non-Resident Graduate	$1,195,618	$1,895,334	63.08%	$2,079,466	$1,331,666	$2,111,002	$31,536
Part-time Graduate	$3,396,627	$5,876,572	57.80%	$4,695,614	$2,765,825	$4,785,209	$89,595
Total	$29,096,817	$48,924,909	59.47%	$50,770,409	$30,707,721	$51,633,568	$863,159

Source: Portland State University Budget Office

SETTING GOALS AND MONITORING OUTCOMES

One lesson learned by Elton Mayo in the Hawthorne studies conducted years ago in the Western Electric factory is expressed in the following statement: that which is monitored will normally perform very well. Similarly, performance that is tracked and monitored will generally exhibit positive attributes. Thus, setting goals and monitoring performance against these preconceived standards will generally enable an institution to accomplish its goals. Goals are an important part of any planning effort, and can be very useful in budgeting and financial analysis and performance. Goals also are an important source of information useful in drawing attention to areas that need improvement.

It is important to involve faculty and academic administrators in the establishment of goals regarding academic performance. Goals should be set high enough to encourage creativity and productivity while, at the same time, being attainable. Goals can be an important factor in maintaining morale and in otherwise planning for both academic and non-academic programs and support services. As a result, they have utility that extends far beyond the realm of fiscal management.

PROVIDING MEANINGFUL FINANCIAL INFORMATION FOR MANAGEMENT DECISION-MAKING

It is important to guard against information overload when analyzing and presenting financial management information reports. It is easy to produce multiple analyses that may be interesting but may not measure the most important or strategic information for either the institution or its strategic initiatives. Reporting too much or non-important information can be distracting and misleading.

The National Center for Higher Education Management Systems (NCHEMS) recommends that institutions monitor and report on certain key attributes to ensure that institutional assets are managed strategically. These attributes are included in Appendix E. In addition, some of the key factors to consider in analyzing and reporting strategic financial information follows.

Key Indicators:

1. Net assets should be monitored. Are net assets projected to increase or decrease? Why or why not? If you can answer these questions, you have a very good start in managing the institution's finances. Ask yourself if annual revenues exceed annual expenses or vice versa. The unrestricted net assets balance is the most flexible reserve, and as such is the most important item to monitor.

2. Cash balances and activities should be controlled. Using the information contained in the statement of cash flows, cash balances can be measured and trends analyzed. This information can also be used to project future cash activities for decision making. For example, are cash balances sufficient to meet obligations in the short run? How do inflows relate to outflows in

terms of timing and amounts? Do you have excessive cash balances, thereby limiting investment earnings? Are cash balances insufficient, thereby necessitating borrowing?

3. For most institutions, enrollment is a key driver of both revenues and expenses. Therefore, set goals and monitor performance and, if possible, reward performance. Understand fee remission, tuition discounting, and enrollment incentive programs, if any, in terms of the full costs and full benefit gained. Involve others in goal setting and make expectations clear and reasonable.

4. Understand and monitor key cost drivers for the institution. In today's environment, these costs include faculty salaries, specialized staff salaries (such as information technology support positions), health care benefits, utility costs (electricity and natural gas), pension funding, and marketing/recruiting costs. Plan for changes well in advance by setting goals to fund cost increases before considering new initiatives.

5. Monitor and report on your affiliated foundation's finances. Most public institutions have affiliated foundations that are private 501(c)(3) entities. A foundation's fiscal problems can affect the institution, since there are typically many transfers from the foundation to the university to fund scholarships, endowed professorships, etc. If the foundation is unable to make these transfers, the institution must fund the difference. This is why the GASB now requires that material affiliated foundation finances be reported in institutional financial statements. Affiliated foundations typically exist for the following reasons:

- To enlist private support of an institution both in terms of fund raising and setting institutional direction and priorities.

- As a convenient means of attracting, accommodating, and aggregating interested and related institutional affiliates and associations.

- As a more flexible corporate form with less rigid investment and expenditure policies. An affiliated foundation can have a significant impact on the financial viability of the institution. Know this, and maintain lines of communication to ensure that foundation problems do not adversely affect the institution.

6. Know and understand who owes you money, and to whom you are indebted, and why. Monitor accounts receivable and accounts payable balances. Also, analyze and understand accrued receivables and liabilities, since this is an easy place to mask financial problems. Monitor amounts reported as accrued revenues and expenses, and understand your obligation to fully disclose amounts of exposure due to compensated absence balances, risk management, and active litigation (both real and potential).

7. Monitor levels of sponsored projects. For many higher education institutions, the number and level of sponsored projects are a qualitative indicator that lends itself to the stature of the institution. It also can generate significant unrestricted funds via indirect cost recoveries, and can act as a key factor in recruiting and retaining quality faculty, students, and other forms of support for the institution.

8. Know which organizations and departments are revenue or cost centers. If possible, analyze and report transfer payments from profit to cost centers. In this context, transfer payments represent the invisible transfers that result from differential cost and revenue structures within the institution. In other words, certain activities make money and others lose money. Transfer payments represent the transfer (either realized or unrealized) of profits from revenue centers (organizations or activities) to cost centers that operate at a loss. The old saying that we make money on undergraduates and use this to fund graduate education and research presents another good example of transfer payments. Typically, undergraduate classes have both more students and a lower instructional costs (lower paid faculty members—a junior member of the department, part-time/adjuncts, and graduate assistants), whereas graduate classes have both fewer students and higher instructional costs (higher paid faculty members who are typically senior members of the department). Similarly, most research requires specialized facilities and equipment and other costs that typically are greater than the amounts recovered from externally sponsored grants and contracts.

9. Understand the environment in which your institution operates and its relationship to your financial affairs. Ask yourself whether the national, regional, and state economies are strong or are vulnerable to significant fluctuation in the short-run. Determine the effect these economies could have on enrollment, donations, government support, and other revenues or costs in the institution. Are there new institutions entering your marketplace? If so, what effect will this competition have on the demand for your programs?

THE COSTS AND THE BENEFITS OF INFORMATION

"Analysis paralysis" is a term used to describe both information overload and reticence to make a decision for want of added information. There are limits to the amount of information needed to make decisions. At some point, there is diminishing marginal utility in analyzing and reporting esoteric financial management information. Constantly monitor the amount of information being analyzed, and weigh the costs of this analysis against the benefits needed to sustain the operations of the institution. In many cases, it is difficult to quantify with sufficient specificity either the cost or the benefits derived from information, so use judgment in determining a proper balance. Remember that information must be useful, timely, cogent, and concise.

Also, the analysis and presentation of financial management information constitutes an important form of communication. Limit the number of messages being sent to ensure that they are meaningful and important. Faculty have multiple obligations, many times to numerous entities, and are, on average, very busy. It is best to limit monitoring and reporting activities to the two or three most important factors for campus-wide reporting. Production of student credit hours, externally funded sponsored projects, and budgets with comparisons to actual revenues and costs are typical factors that are monitored and reported at most campuses. These factors form the basis for a successfully managed institution.

Analyzing and reporting financial management information can help ensure that the institution remains a sustainable entity. This discussion has been offered in the context that much of the success of a higher education institution lies in its ability to attract and retain faculty, students, financial resources, and political support. The foregoing discussion provides the background and a review of the key issues needed to be successful in this regard.

BIBLIOGRAPHY

American Institute of Certified Public Accountants "Accounting Research and Terminology Bulletins," *Accounting Terminology Bulletin No. 1.*, Final Ed., 1941, 9.

Anthony, Robert N. and Herzlinger, Regina. *Management Control in Nonprofit Organizations.* Homewood, IL: Richard D. Irwin, 1975.

Austin, Ann E. and Gameson, Zelda, F. *Academic Workplace: New Demands, Heightened Tensions.* ASHE–ERIC Higher Education Research Report No. 10. Washington, D.C.: Association for the Study of Higher Education, 1983.

Baldwin, Roger G. and Krotseng, Marsha V. "Incentives in the Academy: Issues and Options." In R. Baldwin (Ed.), *Incentives for Faculty Vitality.* New Directions in Higher Education, 51, San Francisco: Jossey-Bass, 1985.

Becher, T. *Academic Tribes and Territories: Intellectual Enquiry and the Cultures of Disciplines.* Philadelphia: Open University Press, 1989.

Becher, T. and Kogan, M. *Process and Structure in Higher Education.* London, England: Routledge Publishers, 1992.

Benne, Kenneth D. and Birnbaum, Max. "Principles of Changing." In *The Planning of Change.* Warren Bennis and Robert Chin (Eds.), Chicago, IL: Holt, Rinehart and Winston, Inc., 1969.

Biglan, A. "The Relationship Between Subject Matter Characteristics and the Structure and Output of University Departments." *Journal of Applied Psychology,* 57, 1973, 204–213.

Blackburn, Robert T., Lawrence, Janet H., and Trautvetter, Lois. "Administrators' career backgrounds and their congruence with faculty beliefs and behaviors." Paper presented at the annual meeting of the American Education Research Association, San Francisco, 1989.

Blackburn, Robert T., Lawrence, Janet H., and Associates. *Same Institution, Different Perceptions: Faculty and Administrators Report on the Work Environment.* Publication of the National Center for Research to Improve Postsecondary Teaching and Learning. Ann Arbor, MI: The University of Michigan, 1990.

Blazek, Jody. *Financial Planning for Nonprofit Organizations.* New York: John Wiley and Sons, 1996.

Bossert, Phillip J. *Operational Planning and Budgeting for Colleges.* Washington, D.C.: National Association of College and University Business Officers, 1988.

Bowen, Howard R. and Schuster, Jack H. *American Professors: A National Resource Imperiled.* New York: Oxford University Press, 1986.

Carnegie Commission on Higher Education, *The Purposes and Performance of Higher Education in the United States: Approaching the Year 2000.* New York: McGraw-Hill, 1973.

Clark, B.R. *The Academic Life: Small Worlds, Different Worlds.* Princeton, N.J.: Carnegie Foundation for the Advancement of Teaching, 1987.

Cross, K. Patricia. *International Journal of University Adult Education,* Volume 28, Number 1, April 1989, 1–14.

Donald, Janet. "Disciplinary Differences in Knowledge Validation." In N. Hativa and M. Marincovich (eds), *Disciplinary Differences in Teaching and Learning: Implications for Practice.* New Directions for Teaching and Learning, no. 64. San Francisco: Jossey-Bass, 1995.

Eimers, Mardy T. "Working with Faculty from Different Disciplines." *About Campus,* March–April 1999, 18–24.

Financial Accounting Standards Board Web site, www.fasb.org.

Government Finance Officers Association (GFOA) Web site, www.GFOA.org.

Governmental Accounting Standards Board Web site, www.gasb.org.

Gray, Peter and Diamond, Robert. "Defining Faculty Work." *New Directions in Institutional Research,* 84. San Francisco: Jossey-Bass Publishers, 1994.

Harvard Management Update. "Fast-Cycle Benchmarking," April 1999, Volume 4, Number 4.

Hatry, Harry P.; Sullivan, Jonathan; Fountain, James R.; and Kremer, Lorraine. *Service Efforts and Accomplishments Reporting: Its Time Has Come: An Overview*. Governmental Accounting Standards Board: Library of Congress, 1990.

Henke, Emerson O. *Introduction to Nonprofit Organization Accounting*. Boston: Kent Publishing Company, 1978.

Hyatt, James A. *Presentation and Analysis of Financial Management Information*. National Association of College and University Business Officers, 1989.

Institute for Higher Education Policy, *Reaping the Benefits: Defining the Public and Private Value of Going to College*, March 1998.

KPMG Peat Marwick and L.F. Rothschild, Unterberg and Towbin. *Ratio Analysis in Higher Education*. 2nd Edition. KPMG Peat Marwick: 1991.

KPMG LLP and Prager, McCarthy and Sealy, LLC. *Ratio Analysis in Higher Education: Measuring Past Performance to Chart Future Direction, Fourth Edition for Independent Institutions*, 1999.

Leslie, Larry L.; Brinkman, Paul T. "Student Price Response in Higher Education: The Student Demand Studies," *Journal of Higher Education*, Volume 58, Number 2, p.181–204, March–April 1987.

McLaughlin, Thomas A. *Streetsmart Financial Basics for Nonprofit Managers*. New York: John Wiley and Sons, 1995.

Massey, William F., et al. *Resource Allocation in Higher Education*. Ann Arbor, MI: University of Michigan Press, 1996.

National Advisory Council on State and Local Budgeting (NACSLB) Web site, www.gfoa.org/services/nacslb.

National Association of College and University Business Officers. *College and University Business Administration*, fifth edition, 1994.

National Association of College and University Business Officers. *Financial Accounting and Reporting Manual for Higher Education*, 2002.

National Center for Higher Education Management Systems (NCHEMS), 1994.

National Commission on the Cost of Higher Education; "Straight Talk About College Costs & Prices," January, 1998.

Neumann, Anna. Defining "good faculty leadership": Interpretations of professors and presidents. Paper presented at the annual meeting of the Association for the Study of Higher Education, Baltimore, MD, 1987.

Palm, Thomas, et al. Unpublished work on Faculty Productivity, 1994.

Peterson, Marvin W. and White, Theodore. "Faculty and Administrator Perceptions of Their Environments: Different Views, or Different Models of Organization? *Research in Higher Education*, 33, 1992.

Reed, B.J. and Swain, John W. *Public Finance Administration*. Englewood Cliffs, N.J.: Prentice Hall, 1990.

Rice, Eugene, and Austin, Ann E. "High Faculty Morale: What Exemplary Colleges Do Right." *Change*, 20, 1988, 50–58.

Ruppel, Warren. *GAAP for Governments: Interpretation and Application of Generally Accepted Accounting Principles for State and Local Governments 1998*. New York: John Wiley and Sons, 1998.

Schon, Donald. *Beyond the Stable State*. New York: Random House Publishers, 1971.

United Way of America. *Accounting and Financial Reporting, A Guide for United Ways and Not-for-Profit Human Service Organizations*, revised 2nd ed., 1989, 9.

University of Florida Web site, www.ufl.edu.

Weisbord, Marvin R. *Productive Workplaces: Organizing and Managing for Dignity, Meaning and Community*. San Francisco: Jossey-Bass Publishers, 1987.

White, Theodore. (1990) "Differences in Faculty and Administrator Perceptions of Their Institutions: Implications for Institutional Performance." Unpublished doctoral preliminary examination. Ann Arbor, MI: University of Michigan, 1990.

APPENDIX A

OREGON UNIVERSITY SYSTEM
FINANCIAL STATEMENTS

Oregon University System
BALANCE SHEET
June 30, 2001

	CURRENT FUNDS		Loan Funds	Endowment Funds	PLANT FUNDS				Agency Funds	June 30, 2001	June 30, 2000
	Unrestricted	Restricted			Unexpended	Renewal and Replacement	Retirement of Indebtedness	Investment In Plant			
ASSETS											
Cash	$123,591,596	26,847,758	8,825,253	923,776	68,105,975	33,410,747	45,674,173	-	1,847,121	309,226,399	311,367,024
Securities Lending Cash Collateral	5,050,583	14,838,601	360,645	1,083,851	2,783,157	1,365,333	1,866,480	-	-	27,348,650	54,345,765
Investments	-	13,218,480	-	61,923,140	3,821,199	1,006,250	2,279,624	-	-	82,248,693	102,788,542
Accounts Receivable (Net of $6,422,904 Allowance)	54,934,630	38,742,051	-	-	1,684,726	10,625	299,673	-	317,420	95,989,125	81,211,129
Notes Receivable (Net of $3,601,340 Allowance)	-	-	73,861,186	-	-	-	-	53,987,820	-	127,849,006	127,272,659
Inventories	5,788,485	-	-	-	-	-	-	-	-	5,788,485	5,923,938
Prepaid Expenses and Deferred Charges	7,027,247	39,131	47,186	-	-	969	4,153,338	-	2,055	11,269,926	11,487,999
Due from Other Funds	22,818,278	-	-	-	-	957,855	-	-	-	23,776,133	24,432,937
Land	-	-	-	-	-	-	-	39,238,657	-	39,238,657	36,840,523
Buildings	-	-	-	-	-	-	-	993,537,982	-	993,537,982	952,467,326
Equipment	-	-	-	-	-	-	-	491,091,086	-	491,091,086	456,505,443
Improvements Other than Buildings	-	-	-	-	-	-	-	83,157,641	-	83,157,641	72,645,083
Museum Collections	-	-	-	-	-	-	-	30,584,258	-	30,584,258	30,444,276
Total Assets	$219,210,819	93,686,021	83,094,270	63,930,767	76,395,057	36,751,779	54,273,288	1,691,597,444	2,166,596	2,321,106,041	2,267,732,644
LIABILITIES AND FUND BALANCE											
Certificates of Participation Payable					-	-	(40,060)	12,970,000	-	12,929,940	16,928,605
Accounts Payable and Accrued Expenses	37,087,252	3,311,021	6,762	-	3,946,980	192,869	7,449,169	-	172,735	52,166,788	50,864,725
Obligations Under Securities Lending	5,050,583	14,838,601	360,645	1,083,851	2,783,157	1,365,333	1,866,480	-	-	27,348,650	54,345,765
Salaries and Wages Payable	6,706,175	-	-	-	-	-	-	-	-	6,706,175	6,802,223
Notes Payable	-	-	-	-	57,348	-	-	16,401,218	-	16,458,566	15,645,357
Bonds Payable	-	-	-	-	57,484,857	-	53,472,086	363,464,070	-	474,421,013	485,874,834
Liability for Compensated Absences	29,541,052	-	-	-	-	-	-	-	-	29,541,052	28,384,798
Deposits	788,910	-	-	-	-	-	-	-	1,910,966	2,699,876	2,323,967
Deferred Revenue	39,978,671	3,877,759	9,922	-	254	91,010	713,710	-	82,895	44,754,221	40,077,007
Due to Other Funds	3,012,781	20,763,352	-	-	-	-	-	-	-	23,776,133	24,432,937
Fund Balances:											
Unrestricted - General	62,236,331	-	-	-	-	-	-	-	-	62,236,331	45,482,225
Unrestricted - Designated	34,809,064	-	-	-	-	-	-	-	-	34,809,064	28,760,970
Institutional Loan Funds - Restricted	-	-	10,214,788	-	-	-	-	-	-	10,214,788	9,467,489
Governmental Loan Funds - Restricted	-	-	72,502,153	-	-	-	-	-	-	72,502,153	71,320,912
Endowment	-	-	-	29,386,397	-	-	-	-	-	29,386,397	32,588,623
Quasi-Endowment - Unrestricted	-	-	-	7,200,217	-	-	-	-	-	7,200,217	7,335,370
Quasi-Endowment - Restricted	-	-	-	26,260,302	-	-	-	-	-	26,260,302	30,652,090
Net Investment in Plant	-	-	-	-	-	-	-	1,298,762,156	-	1,298,762,156	1,223,323,737
Fund Balance (Deficit)	-	50,895,288	-	-	12,122,461	35,102,567	(9,188,097)	-	-	88,932,219	93,121,010
Total Liabilities and Fund Balance	$219,210,819	93,686,021	83,094,270	63,930,767	76,395,057	36,751,779	54,273,288	1,691,597,444	2,166,596	2,321,106,041	2,267,732,644

See Accompanying Notes to the Financial Statements

Oregon University System
STATEMENT OF CHANGES IN FUND BALANCE
Year Ended June 30, 2001

	CURRENT FUNDS		Loan Funds	Endowment Funds	PLANT FUNDS				June 30, 2001	June 30, 2000
	Unrestricted	Restricted			Unexpended	Renewal and Replacement	Retirement of Indebtedness	Investment In Plant		
REVENUES AND OTHER ADDITIONS										
Revenues	$362,434,907	-	-	-	-			-	362,434,907	335,374,030
Gifts, Grants & Contracts	3,679,502	463,657,196	-	414,976	21,132,700	-	2,931,924	-	491,816,298	462,029,420
Student Building Fees & Other Resources							4,950,430	-	4,950,430	4,788,142
State Appropriations	362,825,899	4,874,988	-			-	8,549,175	-	376,250,062	378,609,323
Sale of Building Bonds & C.O.P.'S	-	-			2,691,253	-			2,691,253	92,700,655
Contribution to Loan Principal	-	-	637,865						637,865	722,636
Property, Plant, and Equipment	-	-				-		88,706,973	88,706,973	84,662,884
Interest, Investments & Other Additions	3,022,806	18,153,113	2,967,344	(6,674,526)	1,026,816	3,938,819	6,668,556	-	29,102,928	39,810,384
Auxiliary Enterprises	192,059,456	-	-	-	-	-	-	-	192,059,456	178,558,840
Indirect Cost Recovery	33,347,400	-	-	-	-	3,068,985	-	-	36,416,385	34,271,638
Total Revenues and Other Additions	957,369,970	486,685,297	3,605,209	(6,259,550)	24,850,769	7,007,804	23,100,085	88,706,973	1,585,066,557	1,611,527,952
EXPENDITURES AND OTHER DEDUCTIONS										
Expenditures	738,825,732	479,248,711	25,659	126,154	70,773,500	6,311,966	1,138,720	-	1,296,450,442	1,202,967,855
Retirement of Bonds	-	-	-	-	-	-	18,875,074	-	18,875,074	19,752,182
Retirement of C.O.P.'s	-	-	-	-	-	-	6,709,775	-	6,709,775	6,965,697
Bond & C.O.P. Interest	-	-	-	-	-	-	26,517,071	-	26,517,071	25,287,415
Change in Bonds and Notes Payable	-	-	-	-	-	-	-	(22,359,920)	(22,359,920)	94,984,781
Administrative Fees	-	-	374,189	-	-	-	-	-	374,189	391,544
Notes Issued, Charged Off and Cancelled	-	-	986,037	-	-	-	-	-	986,037	845,309
Auxiliary Enterprise Funds	169,046,160	-							169,046,160	156,117,862
Total Expenditures and Other Deductions	907,871,892	479,248,711	1,385,885	126,154	70,773,500	6,311,966	53,240,640	(22,359,920)	1,496,598,828	1,507,312,645
TRANSFERS AND OTHER ADDITIONS (DEDUCTIONS)										
Mandatory Transfers - Debt Service	(22,907,872)	(4,471)	-		(79,211)	(250,535)	23,242,089		-	-
Nonmandatory Transfers	(3,788,006)	48,905	(290,784)	(1,343,463)	41,041,377	11,418	(50,973)	(35,628,474)	-	-
Refunds to Grantors	-	(216,528)							(216,528)	(138,169)
Total Transfers and Other Additions (Deductions)	(26,695,878)	(172,094)	(290,784)	(1,343,463)	40,962,166	(239,117)	23,191,116	(35,628,474)	(216,528)	(138,169)
Net Increase (Decrease) in Fund Balance	22,802,200	7,264,492	1,928,540	(7,729,167)	(4,960,565)	456,721	(6,949,439)	75,438,419	88,251,201	104,077,138
Fund Balance (Deficit) at Beginning of Year	74,243,195	43,630,796	80,788,401	70,576,083	17,083,026	34,645,846	(2,238,658)	1,223,323,737	1,542,052,426	1,437,975,288
Fund Balance (Deficit) at End of Year	$97,045,395	50,895,288	82,716,941	62,846,916	12,122,461	35,102,567	(9,188,097)	1,298,762,156	1,630,303,627	1,542,052,426

See Accompanying Notes to the Financial Statements

Oregon University System

STATEMENT OF CURRENT FUNDS REVENUES, EXPENDITURES, AND OTHER CHANGES

Year Ended June 30, 2001

	CURRENT FUNDS		June 30, 2001	June 30, 2000
	Unrestricted	Restricted		
REVENUES				
Student Tuition and Fees	$302,146,516	-	302,146,516	282,568,565
Government Appropriations	378,036,298	4,874,988	382,911,286	364,622,629
Gifts, Grants and Contracts	3,679,502	456,026,611	459,706,113	421,623,540
Sales and Services of Educational Departments	33,628,337	-	33,628,337	33,095,864
Auxiliary Enterprises	192,059,456	-	192,059,456	178,558,840
Other Revenue	14,472,461	18,347,112	32,819,573	28,362,236
Indirect Cost Recovery	33,347,400	-	33,347,400	31,411,020
Total Current Revenues	957,369,970	479,248,711	1,436,618,681	1,340,242,694
EXPENDITURES				
Instruction	321,168,136	35,063,421	356,231,557	328,861,776
Public Service	50,170,531	36,649,837	86,820,368	78,913,990
Research	53,881,629	131,940,674	185,822,303	171,549,048
Academic Support	92,996,146	4,429,328	97,425,474	91,326,545
Student Services	40,794,133	1,437,978	42,232,111	39,453,122
Operation and Maintenance of Physical Plant	54,594,953	208,070	54,803,023	51,444,234
Capital Improvements	1,319,733	-	1,319,733	619,068
Institutional Support	92,569,735	2,595,081	95,164,816	91,647,224
Student Aid	20,608,848	257,545,053	278,153,901	254,942,680
Service Departments	4,555,100	-	4,555,100	4,020,442
Auxiliary Program Expenditures	172,709,117	7,600,284	180,309,401	166,650,430
Other Expenditures	2,503,831	1,778,985	4,282,816	9,653,595
Total Current Expenditures	907,871,892	479,248,711	1,387,120,603	1,289,082,154
TRANSFERS				
Mandatory Transfers - Debt Service	(22,907,872)	(4,471)	(22,912,343)	(21,100,858)
Nonmandatory Transfers	(3,788,006)	48,905	(3,739,101)	(10,716,261)
Total Transfers	(26,695,878)	44,434	(26,651,444)	(31,817,119)
Excess of Revenues Over Expenditures and Transfers Before Other Additions (Deductions)	22,802,200	44,434	22,846,634	19,343,421
OTHER ADDITIONS (DEDUCTIONS)				
Refunds to Grantors		(216,528)	(216,528)	(138,169)
Excess of Restricted Receipts over Revenues Applied	-	7,436,586	7,436,586	8,762,241
Net Change in Fund Balance	22,802,200	7,264,492	30,066,692	27,967,493
Fund Balance at Beginning of Year	74,243,195	43,630,796	117,873,991	89,906,498
Fund Balance at End of Year	$97,045,395	50,895,288	147,940,683	117,873,991

See Accompanying Notes to the Financial Statements

Appendix A — Notes to Financial Reports
Oregon University System Year Ended June 30, 2001

1. Organization

The Oregon University System (the System) consists of the six public universities in the State of Oregon and the Oregon Institute of Technology. The System is governed by the Oregon State Board of Higher Education (the Board). Since the System is a component unit of the State of Oregon, it is accounted for within college and university funds in the *State of Oregon Comprehensive Annual Financial Report*.

2. Summary of Significant Accounting Policies

The significant accounting policies, as summarized below, and the financial statements for the System are in accordance with generally accepted accounting principles as prescribed by the American Institute of Certified Public Accountants in *Audits of Colleges and Universities* and applicable pronouncements of the Governmental Accounting Standards Board (GASB).

GASB Statement No. 28, *Accounting and Financial Reporting for Securities Lending Transactions*, establishes accounting and financial reporting standards for securities lending transactions and requires that the balance sheet include cash and certain securities received as collateral under securities lending transactions as assets and liabilities. Revenues from and costs of securities lending transactions, such as borrower rebates and agent fees, are reported as investment income and expenditures, respectively, in the statement of changes in fund balance. The System does not directly engage in securities lending transactions; such transactions, involving the System's investment securities and short-term securities, are handled by and are under the control of the Oregon State Treasury. Short-term securities arise from the System's cash balances held on deposit at the Oregon State Treasury and invested in the Oregon State Treasury Short-Term Fund. Amounts presented in the accompanying financial statements reflect the portion of the State's securities lending attributable to the System.

Basis of Accounting

Basis of accounting refers to the timing of when revenues, expenditures, assets, and liabilities are recognized in the accounts and reported in the financial statements. The System's financial statements have been prepared on the accrual basis of accounting except as follows:

- Depreciation is not recorded as an expense nor as a reduction of buildings and equipment.

- Summer session tuition and fees received before year-end are recorded as deferred revenue as of June 30 with the revenue being reported in the fiscal year in which the program is predominantly conducted. Summer session expenditures through June 30 are recorded as prepaid expenses.

- Interest income is not recorded until received in the Loan Funds. Most outstanding loans will not accrue interest until after the student leaves school.

- Current Restricted Fund revenues are recognized only to the extent expended.

- There are no known material pledges receivable.

Investments

Investments are recorded at fair value. All investment income, including changes in the fair value of investments, is reported as revenue.

Inventories

Inventories are recorded at the lower of average cost or market and consist primarily of supplies in organized storerooms and physical plant stores.

Investment in Plant

Investment in plant assets is recorded at cost or, if donated, at the estimated fair market value at the date received. Equipment acquired with lease-purchase agreements is recorded at a value based on the purchase price at the time of acquisition excluding executory costs. The corresponding liability is also recorded. Disposals of library holdings are recorded at an annually revised average cost per volume. Amounts due from Oregon Health Sciences University under its debt service agreement with the System are recorded as a note receivable in the Investment in Plant Fund.

Income Taxes

The System is a tax-exempt organization under the provisions of Section 115 of the Internal Revenue Code and is exempt from Federal income taxes, except for unrelated business income for which no provision is considered necessary.

2000 Comparative Totals

The amounts shown for 2000 in the accompanying financial statements are presented to provide a basis for comparison with 2001 and are not intended to present all information necessary for a fair presentation in accordance with generally accepted accounting principles.

Use of Estimates

The preparation of financial statements in conformity with generally accepted accounting principles requires management to make estimates and assumptions that affect the reported amounts of assets and liabilities and disclosure of contingent assets and liabilities at the date of the financial statements and revenues and expenditures during the year. Actual results could differ from those estimates.

Fund Accounting

All financial transactions have been recorded and reported by activities or objectives within fund groups in order to ensure observance of limitations and restrictions placed on the use of the resources available to the institutions. Each fund is an independent fiscal and accounting entity with a self-balancing set of accounts.

These fund groups are:

Current Funds

Unrestricted—This fund accounts for the unrestricted economic resources which are expendable for the primary mission of the institutions—instruction, research, and public service. Other operations include auxiliary enterprises which provide goods and services to students, faculty, and staff.

Restricted—This fund accounts for operating funds restricted by external donors or other agencies for specific operating purposes. Examples include restricted gifts and grants and contracts from federal and/or private sources.

Loan Funds

The resources available for student loans are recorded in this fund group. Loan sources include gifts, grants, endowment income, interest earned on loans, and repayment of loan principal.

Endowment Funds

This fund group consists of endowment and quasi-endowment funds. Endowment funds are subject to the restrictions of donor gift instruments requiring that the principal be invested in perpetuity and the income only be utilized for restricted or general purposes. Quasi-endowment funds have been established by Board policy for the same purpose as endowment funds; any portion of the quasi-endowment funds may be expended with Board approval.

Plant Funds

Unexpended—This fund accounts for those resources specified for acquisition and construction of long lasting plant assets. The resources consist of appropriations from the State of Oregon, proceeds from bond sales, gifts, grants, and other allocations made by the Board.

Renewal and Replacement—This fund accounts for auxiliary enterprises building repair and equipment replacement for auxiliary enterprises and service departments. Funds for building repair and equipment replacement are set aside from operating revenues of auxiliary enterprises and service departments.

Retirement of Indebtedness—These moneys are used for the retirement of bonded debt. Resources include appropriations, student fees, and earnings from specific auxiliary enterprises.

Investment in Plant—These accounts reflect investment in land, buildings, improvements, equipment, and museum collections. They also include bonded debt or other liabilities associated with the assets.

Agency Funds

These accounts record assets held by the System as custodian or fiscal agent for others. Balances represent liabilities to the individuals or organizations owning the assets.

The statement of current funds revenues, expenditures, and other changes is a statement of financial activities of current funds related to the current reporting period. It does not purport to present the results of operations or net income or loss for the period as would a statement of income or a statement of revenues and expenses.

The System has not completed the process of evaluating the impact that will result from adopting Statement No. 34 of the Governmental Accounting Standards Board, *Basic Financial Statements—and Management's Discussion and Analysis—*

for State and Local Governments, Statement No. 35, *Basic Financial Statements–and Management's Discussion and Analysis for Public Colleges and Universities–an amendment of GASB Statement No. 34*, Statement No. 37, *Basic Financial Statements-and Management's Discussion and Analysis-for State and Local Governments: Omnibus*, and Statement No. 38, *Certain Financial Statements and Note Disclosures* (collectively, the "Statements"). The System is therefore unable to disclose the impact that adopting the Statements–as required when the Statements become effective for periods beginning after June 15, 2001–will have on its financial position and results of operations.

3. CASH

The System maintains its cash balances on deposit with the State Treasurer. The State Treasurer maintains these and other State funds on a pooled basis. All deposits are fully insured by federal depository insurance or secured by the statewide collateral pool which secures public deposits pursuant to Oregon Revised Statutes.

4. INVESTMENTS

The State Treasurer is the investment officer for the System's funds. The System's investment policies are governed by statute, the Oregon Investment Council, and the Board. In order to manage the overall risk of the State investment pool, of which the System is a participant, the State Treasurer may invest in "derivative" financial instruments. These instruments are held by a commercial bank and are required to be fully collateralized by U.S. Treasury Securities.

The System records investments at fair value. Values are provided by the applicable investment trustee. The System's investments are classified in three categories of credit risk to give an indication of the level of risk assumed by the System as of year-end. The three categories of credit risk are (1) investments that are insured or registered or for which the securities are held by the System or its agent in the System's name; (2) uninsured or unregistered investments for which the securities are held by the counterparty's trust department or agent in the System's name; and (3) uninsured or unregistered investments for which the securities are held by the counterparty or by its trust department or agent but not in the System's name. Categorized investments include debt instruments with a maturity of less than 90 days; such investments may reflect a reported value based on cost rather than fair value. The following schedule presents the reported value and fair value of the System's investments as of June 30, 2001:

CATEGORY OF CREDIT RISK					
Investment Type:	1	2	3	Reported Value	Fair Value
Investments Categorized:					
Cash and Cash Equivalents	$ -	-	556,259	556,259	556,259
U.S. Government and Agency Securities	2,268,872	3,275,692	-	5,544,564	5,544,564
Total	$2,268,872	3,275,692	556,259	6,100,823	6,100,823
Investments Not Categorized:					
Investments held by broker-dealers under securities loans with cash collateral: U.S. Government and Agency Securities				26,224,255	26,224,255
Securities lending short-term collateral investment				27,348,650	27,485,001
Real Estate				3,513,279	3,513,279
Pooled Investments				58,311,435	58,311,435
Other Investments				98,926	98,926
Subtotal				121,597,368	121,733,719
Less Amounts Recorded as Cash				(39,348,675)	(39,485,026)
Total Investments				$82,248,693	82,248,693

5. SECURITIES LENDING

In accordance with the State investment policies, the System, through transactions handled by and under the control of the Oregon State Treasury (OST), participates in securities lending transactions. A portion of that securities lending activity relates to investment securities owned by the System; the remainder of the activity relates to securities purchased by OST with System funds deposited into the Oregon State Treasury Short-Term Fund (OSTSTF).

Securities Owned by the System

The OST has, through a Securities Lending Agreement, authorized its custodian to lend the System's securities to broker-dealers and banks pursuant to a form of loan agreement. Both OST and the borrowers maintain the right to terminate all securities lending transactions on demand. There have been no significant violations of the provisions of securities lending agreements.

During the year, the custodian lent the System's fixed income securities and received as collateral U.S. dollar-denominated cash. Borrowers were required to deliver cash collateral for each loan equal to at least 102 percent of the fair value of the security on loan. The OST did not impose any restrictions during the year on the amount of loans of the System's fixed income securities. The OST is fully indemnified by the custodian against losses due to borrower default; there were no losses during the year from the failure of borrowers to return securities on loan.

The custodian is authorized by the Securities Lending Agreement to invest cash collateral received for securities loans in the Oregon Short-Term Investment Fund (Fund) held by the custodian. At June 30, 2001, the Fund had an average weighted maturity of 347 days. Since the securities loans are callable on demand by either the lender or borrower, the life of the loans at June 30, 2001 is effectively one day and consequently does not generally match the life of the investments in the Fund. The fair value of collateral held was $14,861,292 (reported value of $14,787,566); the fair value of the System's securities on loan at June 30, 2001 was $14,224,230. Thus, the System had no credit risk exposure to borrowers. The collateral is reflected as securities lending cash collateral and the resulting obligation is included in obligations under securities lending in the System's financial statements.

System Deposits in Oregon State Treasury Short-Term Fund

The System deposits funds into the OSTSTF, which participates in a securities lending program. In accordance with State investment and accounting policies, the System is allocated a portion of the State's transactions in securities lending activities. The OST has, through a Securities Lending Agreement, authorized its custodian to lend the OST securities to broker-dealers and banks pursuant to a form of loan agreement. Both OST and the borrowers maintain the right to terminate all securities lending transactions on demand. There have been no significant violations of the provisions of securities lending agreements.

During the year, the custodian lent OST's securities and received as collateral U.S. dollar-denominated cash or securities issued or guaranteed by the United States government, or foreign sovereign debt securities of Organisation for Economic Co-operation and Development (OECD) countries. Borrowers were required to deliver collateral for each loan equal to not less than 102 percent of the market value of the loaned security, or 105 percent in the case of international securities. The custodians did not have the ability to pledge or sell collateral securities absent a borrower default and the OST did not impose any restrictions during the fiscal year on the amount of the loans the custodian made on its behalf. The OST is fully indemnified by the custodian against losses due to borrower default; there were no losses during the year from the failure of borrowers to return securities on loan.

The cash collateral was invested by the OST into U.S. Government and Agency Securities, repurchase agreements, and commercial paper. The maturities of these investments made during the year generally did not match the maturities of their securities loans, because the loans were terminable at will. The System's cash deposits invested in the OSTSTF are commingled with the cash deposits of other State agencies. As of June 30, 2001, the total cash collateral received for securities on loan was $296,392,500; the fair value of all investments made with the cash collateral held by the OSTSTF was $297,870,212, of which $12,623,709 (reported value of $12,561,084) was allocated to the System. The fair value of securities on loan by the OSTSTF as of June 30, 2001 was $283,153,705, of which $12,000,025 was allocated to the System. At June 31, 2001, the OST had no credit risk exposure to borrowers. The collateral is reflected as securities lending cash collateral and the resulting obligation is included in obligations under securities lending in the System's financial statements.

6. ENDOWMENT FUNDS

Investments of endowment funds are carried at fair value. Endowment fund assets are pooled except for endowments having a fair value of $3,611,701 and quasi-endowments having a fair value of $7 representing bequests with investment restrictions or maturing securities. Each fund subscribes to or disposes of units on the basis of the market value per unit as of the end of the preceding month in which the transaction occurred. Gains, losses, and adjustments on investment transactions of the State Treasurer are reflected in the financial statements. Trust funds in which the System has a remainder interest have been individually recorded at a $1 nominal value in the investment accounts. Pooled investments are managed through Barclays Global Investors, Batterymarch, The Commonfund and T. Rowe Price. Endowment funds by institution at June 30, 2001 are as follows:

| Institution: | POOLED | | SEPARATELY INVESTED | | |
	Endowment Funds	Quasi-Endowment Funds	Endowment Funds	Quasi-Endowment Funds	Totals
Eastern Oregon University	$ 888,212	326,343	-	-	1,214,555
Oregon Institute of Technology	-	230,468	-	-	230,468
Oregon State University	1,924,016	26,233,399	3,513,283	2	31,670,700
Portland State University	1,466,137	592,043	1	-	2,058,181
Southern Oregon University	154,643	248,048	-	-	402,691
University of Oregon	19,315,791	5,747,650	98,417	5	25,161,863
Western Oregon University	8,072	52,045	-	-	60,117
Chancellor's Office	2,017,825	30,516	-	-	2,048,341
Total at Fair Value	$25,774,696	33,460,512	3,611,701	7	62,846,916

7. COMPENSATED ABSENCES

Vacation pay for classified employees is earned at 8 to 16 hours per month depending on length of service with a maximum accrual of 250 hours per employee. Unclassified employees and 12-month academic employees are granted 15 hours per month with a maximum accrual of 260 hours per employee.

Sick leave is recorded as an expenditure when paid. Sick leave for academic, unclassified, and classified employees is earned at the rate of eight hours per month with no restrictions on maximum accruals. No liability exists for terminated employees.

8. RETIREMENT PLANS

The System offers various retirement plans to qualified employees as described below.

• Oregon Public Employees Retirement Plan

The State of Oregon Public Employees Retirement System (PERS) is a cost-sharing multi-employer defined benefit plan administered by the Public Employees Retirement Board (Retirement Board) under the guide-

lines of Oregon Revised Statutes. An employee is considered vested and eligible for retirement benefits if he or she has had a contribution in each of five calendar years or has reached at least 50 years of age before ceasing employment. The 1995 Oregon Legislature enacted a law creating two tiers of PERS benefits. Employees hired into an eligible position prior to January 1, 1996 are enrolled in Tier One, while employees hired into an eligible position on or after January 1, 1996 are enrolled in Tier Two.

Tier One members are eligible for retirement with unreduced benefits at age 58 or at any age with 30 or more years of service. Employees may retire after reaching age 55; however, benefits are reduced if retirement occurs prior to age 58 with less than 30 years of service. Tier One members may elect a guaranteed interest rate which is tied to the actuarial valuations; currently, this rate is 8 percent.

Tier Two members are eligible for retirement with unreduced benefits at age 60 or at any age with 30 or more years of service. Employees may retire after reaching age 55; however, benefits are reduced if retirement occurs prior to age 60 with less than 30 years of service. The statutes prohibit offering Tier Two members the option of a guaranteed interest rate.

PERS contribution requirements are established by Oregon Revised Statutes and may be amended by an act of the Oregon Legislature. PERS collects contributions from both employers and employees for the purpose of funding retirement benefits. Beginning July 1, 1979, the employee's contribution has been assumed and paid by the employer at the 6 percent rate set by law. The employer contribution rate through June 30, 2001 was 9.73 percent. The System's employer contributions to PERS for the years ending June 30, 1999, 2000, and 2001 were $26,887,334, $33,193,516, and $35,124,419 respectively, equal to the required contributions for each year. An actuarial valuation of PERS is performed every two years to determine the level of employer contributions. The most recently completed valuation was performed as of December 31, 1999. Of the actuarial assumptions used in the valuation, projected salary increases were 4.25 percent in the 1999.

The pension benefit obligation is a standardized disclosure measure of the present value of pension benefits. It is adjusted for the effects of projected salary increases estimated to be payable in the future as a result of employee service to date. The pension benefit obligation at December 31, 1999, for PERS as a whole, determined through an actuarial valuation performed as of that date, was $14,065.5 million. PERS' net assets available for benefits on that date (valued at market) were $14,082.9 million. Information for the System as a stand-alone entity is not available. The ten-year historical trend information showing progress made in accumulating sufficient assets to pay benefits when due is presented in the separately issued PERS Component Unit Financial Report for the fiscal year ended June 30, 2001. The PERS financial report is publicly available and may be obtained by writing to PERS, P.O. Box 23700, Tigard, OR, 97281-3700 or by calling 1-503-598-7377.

• *Optional Retirement Plan*

The 1995 Oregon Legislature enacted legislation which authorized the System to offer a defined contribution retirement plan as an alternative to PERS. The System's Board appointed a Retirement Plan Committee to administer the Optional Retirement Plan (ORP) and established trustees to manage plan assets placed with mutual funds.

Beginning April 1, 1996, the ORP was made available to the System's unclassified faculty and staff who are eligible for PERS membership. Employees choosing the ORP may invest the employee and employer contributions in one of four different investment companies. As with PERS, the ORP consists of two tiers. Membership under ORP Tier One and Tier Two is determined using the same criteria as PERS. Under the ORP Tier One and Tier Two, the employee's contribution rate is 6 percent and is paid by the employer. The employer contribution rate, through June 30, 2001, for the ORP Tier One and Tier Two was 9.73 percent and 7.33 percent, respectively.

• *Teacher's Insurance and Annuity Association/College Retirement Equities Fund*

Eligible unclassified faculty may participate in the Teacher's Insurance and Annuity Association and College Retirement Equities Fund (TIAA-CREF) retirement program, a defined contribution plan, on all salary in excess of $4,800 per calendar year. Employee contributions are directed to PERS on the first $4,800. The employer contribution to TIAA-CREF is an amount sufficient to provide an annuity pension equal to the employee's contributions. To participate in this retirement option, employees must have been hired on or before September 9, 1995.

• *Federal Civil Service Retirement*

Some Extension Service employees at Oregon State University hold Federal appointments. Prior to December 31, 1986, Federal appointees were required to participate in the Federal Civil Service Retirement System (CSRS), a defined benefit plan. CSRS employees are subject to the Hospital Insurance portion of FICA, CSRS employee deduction of 7.0 percent, and employer contribution of 8.51 percent, and are also eligible for optional membership in PERS.

The Federal Employees Retirement System (FERS) was created beginning January 1, 1987. Employees hired after December 31, 1983 were automatically converted to FERS. Other Federal employees not covered by FERS had a one-time option to transfer to FERS up to December 31, 1987. New FERS employees contribute 0.8 percent with an employer contribution rate of 10.7 percent. FERS employees are not eligible for membership in PERS and they contribute at the full FICA rate. They also participate in a Thrift Savings Plan with an automatic employer contribution of 1 percent. Employees may also contribute to this plan at variable rates up to 10 percent, in which case the employer contributes at a variable rate up to 5 percent. CSRS employees are also eligible for participation in the Thrift Savings Plan but without employer contributions.

The System's total payroll for the year ended June 30, 2001 was $571.2 million, of which $491.7 million was subject to retirement benefits. The following schedule lists payments to pension plans made by the System for the fiscal year:

	Employer Contribution	As a Percentage of Covered Payroll	Employee[1] Contribution	As a Percentage of Covered Payroll
PERS	$35,124,419	7.14%	$20,441,259	4.16%
ORP	9,355,366	1.90%	6,214,213	1.26%
TIAA-CREF	264,181	.05%	250,922	.05%
Federal	832,891	.17%	394,947	.08%
FERS	181,869	.04%	353,936	.07%
Total	$45,758,72		$27,655,277	

(1) Of the employee's share, the employer paid $20,346,609 of PERS, $6,207,158 of ORP, and $250,922 of TIAA-CREF. The Federal contributions of $394,947 represent FERS and CSRS employees, and the $353,936 represents employee contributions to the Thrift Savings Plan for FERS employees which were matched 1 to 5 percent by the employer.

9. EARLY RETIREMENT PLANS

During 1994, 1996, and 1997, the System offered early retirement incentives to eligible faculty and staff.

The 1994 incentives were offered to unclassified staff with at least ten years of service who were eligible to retire under PERS. Employees electing this plan had to sign up by April 15, 1994 and agree to retire not later than December 31, 1994. The plan provided a health insurance premium subsidy of up to $400 per month for seven years from the effective date of retirement. A total of 64 employees participated in this plan; the System has a recorded a liability of $110,842 for benefits to be paid in 2002.

The 1996 incentives were offered to all unclassified, management service, and classified unrepresented employees who had at least five years of service to the System and 30 years of public service or who would reach age 55 prior to June 30, 1997. Employees electing the 1996 plan had to sign up prior to June 15, 1996 and agree to retire not later than June 30, 1997. Benefits generally included a lump-sum payment of one-half the employee's annual salary in the month following termination of regular employment and a health insurance subsidy of up to $403 per month for seven years. A total of 330 employees participated in this plan;

the System has recorded a liability of $3,572,528 for benefits to be paid in future years.

The 1997 incentives were offered to all Oregon Public Employees Union (OPEU) represented employees who had at least five years of service to the System and 30 years of public service or who would reach age 55 prior to June 30, 1997. Employees electing this plan had to sign up between April 1, 1997 and May 31, 1997 and agree to retire not later than June 30, 1997. Benefits included a health insurance subsidy of up to $386 per month for seven years. Part-time employment after retirement may also be offered on a case-by-case basis. A total of 247 employees participated in this plan; the System has recorded a liability of $2,400,797 for benefits to be paid in future years.

10. BONDS AND COPs PAYABLE, SMALL SCALE ENERGY LOAN PROGRAM (SELP) LOANS, LEASE OBLIGATIONS, AND OTHER LOAN PAYABLE

• XI-F(1) Bonds

Article XI-F(1) of the Oregon Constitution authorizes the System to issue State of Oregon General Obligation Bonds to finance the construction of self-liquidating and self-supporting projects. General Obligation Bonds have been sold to finance the construction of dormitories, cafeterias, parking facilities, apartments for married students, student unions, student health service facilities, and other student activity buildings and facilities. The Board's Administrative Rules require sinking fund reserve balances based on a percentage of annual debt service as follows: 200 percent for bonds issued prior to July 1, 1986 and 100 percent for bonds issued after June 30, 1986. These reserves are recorded in the Retirement of Indebtedness Fund. The liability for XI-F(1) bonds is recorded in the Unexpended Plant Fund, the Retirement of Indebtedness Fund, and the Investment in Plant Fund. Article XI-F(1) bonds, with effective yields ranging from 3.6 percent to 7.5 percent, are due serially through 2030. The total outstanding XI-F(1) bonded indebtedness for the System was $331,669,237 at June 30, 2001.

- *XI-G Bonds*

Article XI-G of the Oregon Constitution authorizes the System to issue State of Oregon General Obligation Bonds, with debt service funded by Legislative appropriation, to finance designated educational buildings and facilities. The liability for XI-G bonds is recorded in the Unexpended Plant Fund, the Retirement of Indebtedness Fund, and the Investment in Plant Fund. Article XI-G bonds, with effective yields ranging from 3.6 percent to 7.5 percent, are due serially through 2030. The total outstanding XI-G bonded indebtedness for the System was $89,279,690 at June 30, 2001.

- *Bond Payment Schedule*

Future bond principal requirements are summarized as follows:

2001-02	$19,457,284
2002-03	20,306,597
2003-04	21,552,276
2004-05	19,600,063
2005-06	18,859,974
Thereafter	321,172,733
Subtotal	420,948,927
Add: Accreted Interest	56,318,023
Less: Unamortized Bond Discounts	(2,845,937)
Total	**$474,421,013**

- *Certificates of Participation*

The System has issued Certificates of Participation (COPs) to finance lease/purchase agreements for certain equipment and computer software. The System makes monthly lease payments (principal and interest) to a trustee in accordance with the lease/purchase agreements. The trustee, in turn, makes the debt service payments to COPs holders. The liability for COPs is recorded in the Investment in Plant Fund and is secured by the related equipment and computer software. COPs, with effective yields ranging from 3.5 percent to 5.1 percent, are due through fiscal year 2005-06. The total outstanding COPs indebtedness for the System was $12,970,000 at June 30, 2001.

2001-02	$5,430,000
2002-03	3,205,000
2003-04	2,890,000
2004-05	865,000
2005-06	580,000
Subtotal	12,970,000
Less: Unamortized COPs Discounts	(40,060)
Total	**$12,929,940**

COPs Payment Schedule

Future COPs principal requirements are summarized as follows:

- *Oregon Department of Energy Loans*

The System has entered into Department of Energy Small Scale Energy Loan Program (SELP) loan agreements for energy conservation projects at System institutions. The System makes monthly loan payments (principal and interest) to the Department of Energy in accordance with the loan agreements. The liability for SELP loans is recorded as notes payable in the Investment in Plant Fund. SELP loans, with interest rates ranging from 5.6 percent to 8.0 percent, are due through 2019. The total outstanding indebtedness for SELP loans was $15,089,354 at June 30, 2001.

SELP Loan Payment Schedule

Future SELP loan principal requirements are summarized as follows:

2001-02	$1,017,085
2002-03	969,622
2003-04	1,095,187
2004-05	1,172,806
2005-06	1,188,001
Thereafter	9,646,653
Total	**$15,089,354**

• *Capital Leases and Operating Leases*

The System is the lessee of equipment under capital leases expiring through fiscal year 2006-07. The assets under capital leases are recorded at the lower of the present value of the minimum lease payments or the fair market value of the asset at acquisition. Interest rates on capitalized leases vary from 4.9 percent to 22.5 percent.

Minimum future lease payments under capital leases are:

2001-02	$570,588
2002-03	387,224
2003-04	293,347
2004-05	176,480
2005-06	84,823
Thereafter	62,106
Total Minimum Lease Payments	**1,574,568**
Less: Amount representing interest	(262,704)
Present Value of Minimum Lease Payments	**$1,311,864**

Minimum future rental payments on operating leases are:

2001-02	$1,217,531
2002-03	913,794
2003-04	575,467
2004-05	495,122
2005-06	417,675
Thereafter	372,075
Total Future Rental Payments	**$3,991,664**

• *Other Loan Payable*

The System entered into a loan agreement for the purchase of land. Quarterly loan payments (principal and interest) of $4,117 are made in accordance with the loan agreement. The liability for the loan is recorded as a note payable in the Investment in Plant Fund. The loan bears interest at 6 percent and the final payment is due June 30, 2005. The total outstanding indebtedness for the loan was $57,348 at June 30, 2001.

• *Debt Related to Oregon Health Sciences University*

Prior to 1996, Oregon Health Sciences University (OHSU) was part of the System. Pursuant to an act of the Oregon Legislature (the 1995 Act), OHSU became an independent public corporation. In connection with this change in status, responsibility for governing OHSU was transferred from the Board to a newly formed Board of Directors of OHSU. Consequently, OHSU is no longer included in the System's financial statements.

The new public corporation was given ownership of all personal property related to OHSU; was granted exclusive care, custody, and control of the real property related to OHSU; and assumed liability for all outstanding indebtedness of the System incurred for the benefit of OHSU. Oregon Revised Statutes require the System to maintain title to all real property acquired prior to OHSU's change in status. OHSU is leasing certain real property from the System for a nominal amount; such real property has been transferred to OHSU and is excluded from the accompanying financial statements. A receivable from OHSU has been recorded in the Investment in Plant Fund for System debt that was incurred for the benefit of OHSU. At June 30, 2001, long-term debt of the System that relates to OHSU is $54,100,177.

• *Defeased Debt*

In prior years, the System and OHSU defeased various bond issues. The proceeds were used to purchase U.S. Government Securities that were placed in an irrevocable trust. The investments and fixed earnings from the investments are sufficient to fully service the defeased debt until the debt is called or matures. For financial reporting purposes, the debt has been considered defeased and therefore removed as a liability from the Investment in Plant Fund. At June 30, 2001, the amount of the defeased debt outstanding but removed from the Investment in Plant Fund amounted to $93,685,456, of which $27,680,457 relates to OHSU.

11. BUILDING REPAIR AND EQUIPMENT REPLACEMENT RESERVES

Building repair reserves have been established for self-sustaining auxiliary enterprise activities such as housing and dining, parking, and student unions. The reserve requirement is 1.5 percent of the replacement value of the auxiliary enterprise building. The reserve is designed to fund major or unusual building repairs such as re-roofing and major renovations and repairs to land improvements such as driveways and sidewalks. These reserves are carried in the Renewal and Replacement Plant Fund.

Equipment replacement reserves have been established to provide equipment replacement funds for all self-sustaining service departments and auxiliary enterprise activities. These reserves are also carried in the Renewal and Replacement Plant Fund.

12. FOUNDATIONS (UNAUDITED)

Affiliated, but separately incorporated, non-profit foundations exist at each institution in the System. The primary purpose of these foundations is to raise money for research, scientific, or educational programs. Financial data for the foundations are not included in the System's financial statements and records. The unaudited net worth of each foundation at June 30, 2001 is summarized as follows:

	Net Worth
Eastern Oregon University Foundation	$ 1,816,032
Oregon Institute of Technology Development Foundation	13,090,710
Oregon State University Foundation	366,168,902
OSU Agricultural Research Foundation	9,665,589
Portland State University Foundation	26,477,709
Southern Oregon University Foundation	14,073,000
JPR Foundation (Southern Oregon University-Jefferson Public Radio)	158,848
University of Oregon Foundation	335,574,010
Western Oregon University Foundation	5,502,248
Total	**$772,527,048**

13. FUNDS HELD IN TRUST BY OTHERS (UNAUDITED)

Funds held in trust by others, for which the System is an income beneficiary, are not recorded in the financial records. The approximate value of such trust funds at June 30, 2001 is $6,603,399.

14. COMMITMENTS AND CONTINGENCIES

The System purchases various commercial insurance policies (for students) directly from insurance agents and participates in a State risk pool. The State risk pool covers exposure to various risks of loss related to: torts; theft, damage, and destruction of assets; errors and omissions; injuries to employees; and natural disasters.

Unemployment compensation claims are administered by the Oregon Employment Division pursuant to Oregon Revised Statutes. Actual benefits paid are reimbursed to the State's Unemployment Compensation Trust Fund by the System. Each year resources are budgeted to pay current charges. The amount of future benefit payments to claimants and the resulting liability to the System cannot be reasonably determined at June 30, 2001.

An encumbrance system is used by the System to record outstanding purchase orders and other commitments. These are not recorded as expenditures or liabilities but are used only for budget control purposes. Accounting entries have not been made to formally reserve a portion of the Current Fund Unrestricted fund balance for outstanding encumbrances at June 30, 2001. Oregon Revised Statutes and Department of Administrative Services regulations require the cancellation of general funds year-end encumbrances if not paid in a specified period of time or if certain circumstances are not met. Reversions of funds are not expected to be material.

Outstanding commitments on partially completed construction contracts total approximately $187.3 million at June 30, 2001. These commitments will be primarily funded from gifts and grants, bond proceeds, and other System funds.

The System is contingently liable in connection with certain other claims and contracts, including those currently in litigation, arising in the normal course of its activities. Management and general counsel are of the opinion that the outcome of such matters will not have a material effect on the financial statements.

APPENDIX B

GRAND VALLEY STATE UNIVERSITY
ANNUAL REPORT

Grand Valley State University

Annual Report

2001

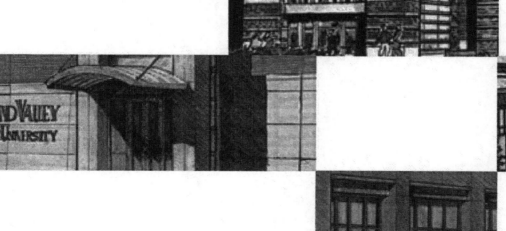

Grand Valley State University

**Financial Report
with Additional Information
June 30, 2001**

Grand Valley State University

Contents

Independent Auditor's Report

Board of Trustees
Grand Valley State University

We have audited the accompanying basic financial statements of Grand Valley State University as of June 30, 2001 and for the year then ended, as listed in the table of contents. These basic financial statements are the responsibility of the University's management. Our responsibility is to express an opinion of these basic financial statements based on our audit.

We conducted our audit in accordance with auditing standards generally accepted in the United States of America and the standards applicable to financial audits contained in *Government Auditing Standards* issued by the Comptroller General of the United States. Those standards require that we plan and perform the audit to obtain reasonable assurance that the statements are free of material misstatement. An audit includes examining, on a test basis, evidence supporting amounts and disclosures in the financial statements. An audit also includes assessing the accounting principles used and significant estimates made by management, as well as evaluating the overall financial statement presentation. We believe that our audit provides a reasonable basis for our opinion.

In our opinion, the basic financial statements referred to above present fairly, in all material respects, the financial position of Grand Valley State University at June 30, 2001, and the results of its operations and cash flows for the year then ended, in conformity with accounting principles generally accepted in the United States of America.

As described in Note 1 to the financial statements, the University adopted the provisions of Governmental Accounting Standards Board Statement Nos. 34, *Basic Financial Statements – and Management's Discussion and Analysis – for State and Local Governments*, and 35, *Basic Financial Statements – and Management's Discussion and Analysis – for Public Colleges and Universities* as of July 1, 2000.

In accordance with *Government Auditing Standards*, we have also issued our report dated August 29, 2001, on our consideration of University's internal controls over financial reporting and our tests of its compliance with certain provisions of laws, regulations, contracts and grants. That report is an integral part of an audit performed in accordance with *Government Auditing Standards* and should be read in conjunction with this report in considering the results of our audit.

The Management's Discussion and Analysis presented on pages 2 through 12 is not a required part of the basic financial statements but is supplemental information required by the Governmental Accounting Standards Board. We have applied certain limited procedures, which consisted principally of inquiries of management regarding the methods of measurement and presentation of the supplemental information. However, we did not audit the information and express no opinion on it.

Plante & Moran, LLP

August 29, 2001

Grand Valley State University
Administrative Officers as of July 1, 2001

Board of Trustees

Dorothy A. Johnson	Chairperson
Paul Hillegonds	Vice Chairperson
Daniel Aronoff	
Donna K. Brooks	
Jessie Dalman	
Donnalee Holton	
José Infante	
Karen Henry Stokes	
Paul A. Johnson	(Honorary)
Arnold C. Ott	(Honorary)
L. William Seidman	(Honorary)

Executive and Board Officers

Mark A. Murray	President
John Gracki	Acting Provost and Vice President for Academic Affairs
Timothy O. Schad	Vice President for Finance and Administration Treasurer, Board of Trustees
Matthew E. McLogan	Vice President for University Relations
Maribeth Wardrop	Vice President for Development
Jean Enright	Executive Assistant to the President Secretary, Board of Trustees
Patricia Oldt	Special Assistant to the President for Campus Equity and Planning
James Bachmeier	Assistant Vice President, Business and Finance Assistant Treasurer, Board of Trustees

New Accounting Standards

In June 1999, the Governmental Accounting Standard's Board (GASB) released Statement No. 34, "Basic Financial Statements and Management's Discussion and Analysis for State and Local Governments," which established a new reporting format for annual financial statements. In November 1999, GASB released Statement No. 35, "Basic Financial Statements and Management's Discussion and Analysis for Public Colleges and Universities," which applies the new reporting standards to public colleges and universities. The State of Michigan has elected to adopt these new standards in fiscal year 2001 and, as a component unit of the state government, Grand Valley State University (the "University") has adopted the new standards as well.

The following discussion and analysis provides an overview of the University's financial activities. Since this is a transition year for the new format, only one year of information is presented in the audited financial statements. For management's discussion and analysis we have restated the previous year's financial information in order to provide a comparison.

The new accounting standards resulted in a prior period adjustment of $9 million to the beginning fund balance. The components of this adjustment are included in the footnotes to the financial statements and primarily include net revenue for spring classes, pledges receivable and pension assets.

As required by the newly adopted accounting principles, the annual report consists of three basic financial statements that provide information on the University as a whole: the Statement of Net Assets; the Statement of Revenues, Expenses and Changes in Net Assets; and the Statement of Cash Flows. Each one of these statements will be discussed.

Grand Valley State University

Financial and Enrollment Highlights

- Net assets increased 13% due to continuing investment in capital assets and reserves for repairs, maintenance and future debt service.

- The downturn in the equity market affected the market value of endowment and retirement investments.

- Capital campaigns and capital appropriations from the State of Michigan supported several construction projects.

- In October 2000, the University issued $36 million in debt to finance additional student housing in Allendale and renovations for the student activities center.

- Operating revenue increased 14% as a result of increased enrollment, tuition rates, housing capacity and grant activity.

Historical Enrollment

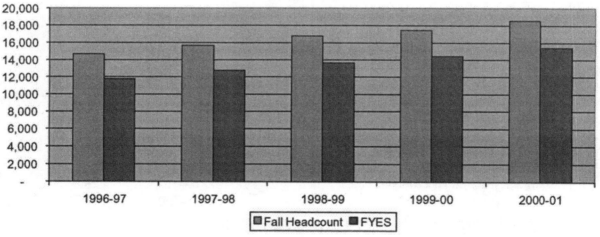

- Enrollment increased by 7.2% based on FYES (fiscal year equated students). Headcount for the fall semester increased by 6.5%.

- State appropriations for operations increased 11%.

PLANTE & MORAN, LLP

Statement of Net Assets

The Statement of Net Assets includes all assets and liabilities using the accrual basis of accounting, which is similar to the accounting used by most private-sector institutions. Net assets – the difference between assets and liabilities – are one way to measure the financial health of the University.

	(in thousands) 2001	2000 (unaudited)	Change
Current assets:			
Cash and short-term investments	$ 50,674	$ 33,047	53%
Receivables	35,647	32,363	10%
Inventory, prepaid expenses and other	2,933	2,397	22%
Total current assets	89,254	67,807	32%
Non-current assets			
Long-term investments	56,547	50,274	12%
Long-term receivables	18,923	12,812	48%
Capital assets, net of depreciation	288,882	239,609	21%
Other	1,253	739	70%
Total non-current assets	365,605	303,434	17%
Total assets	$ 454,859	$ 371,241	23%
Current liabilities:			
Accounts payable and accrued liabilities	$ 33,616	$ 24,868	35%
Deferred revenue	7,798	5,728	36%
Long-term liabilities - current portion	4,670	3,355	39%
Total current liabilities	46,084	33,951	36%
Non-current liabilities:			
Long-term liabilities	81,457	48,579	68%
Total liabilities	127,541	82,530	55%
Net assets			
Invested in physical properties	208,352	188,013	11%
Restricted	58,581	51,561	14%
Unrestricted	60,385	49,137	23%
Total net assets	$ 327,318	$ 288,711	13%

PLANTE & MORAN, LLP

The cash and short-term investment increase consists primarily of the unspent bond proceeds from the October 2000 bond issue. These unspent bond proceeds are classified as restricted because the tax-exempt bonds require the proceeds to be spent on capital projects. Operating cash also increased as reflected in the Statement of Cash Flows.

Receivables include grants, state appropriations, pledges, student notes and various operating receivables. Grants receivable increased because the University received certain new federal grants such as the Michigan Small Business Development Center. State appropriation receivables include the general operating appropriation, public school academy funds and capital appropriations. Increases in both the general operating receivable and the public school academy receivable were offset by a $5 million decrease in the receivable for capital appropriation. Pledges receivable have been recorded according to the new accounting standards. Current pledges are those expected to be collected within a year. Increases are a result of the Health Professions Building capital campaign.

Long-term investments include both unrestricted cash and endowment. The endowment investments stayed the same – market losses and spending distributions offset gifts. Other changes in unrestricted long-term investments are a result of operating activity and investment policy. Long-term pledges receivable increased because of the capital campaign for the Health Professions Building. These long-term pledges were discounted to net present value for financial statement purposes.

Capital assets have increased by $58 million due to new construction. Buildings that were completed included the Richard M. DeVos Center, Secchia Hall apartments, Grand Valley Apartments, a remodeled Robinson Living Center, the Fred M. Keller Engineering Laboratories, the Alumni House and Visitor Center, and the Lake Michigan Center. The University also began several other capital projects including a new Health Professions Building, new student housing and several additions to buildings on the Allendale campus. These additions, net of depreciation and some disposals, are summarized in Note 3 of the footnotes to the financial statements.

Accounts payable increased because of the additional construction projects and overall increases in the accrual for public school academy distributions. Increased enrollment in the summer session of 2001 resulted in $855,000 additional deferred tuition revenue. Increases in the volume as well as the amounts of grants and contracts resulted in $1.2 million of additional deferred revenue. Of that increase, $955,000 is due to an autism grant received from the State of Michigan.

Long-term debt increased in October 2000 when the University issued $36,475,000 in General Revenue bonds to fund capital additions for housing and student activities. The University's bond rating continues to be A+, as rated by Standard & Poors. More detailed information about the University's long-term debt is presented in the footnotes to the financial statements.

Many of the University's unrestricted net assets have been designated or reserved for specific purposes such as: insurance reserves, repairs and replacement of equipment, future debt service, quasi-endowments, capital projects, and student loans. The following graph shows the allocations:

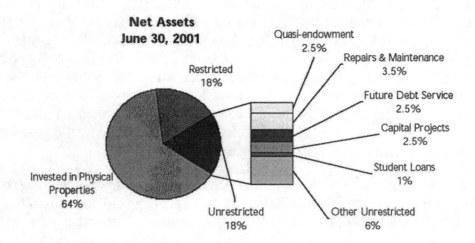

Net Assets June 30, 2001

- Restricted 18%
- Invested in Physical Properties 64%
- Unrestricted 18%
- Quasi-endowment 2.5%
- Repairs & Maintenance 3.5%
- Future Debt Service 2.5%
- Capital Projects 2.5%
- Student Loans 1%
- Other Unrestricted 6%

The increase in the University's net assets of 13% reflects the expansion that occurred in this past year. The University's physical assets have grown because of the generous support from the community and the State of Michigan. The increase in restricted net assets reflects pledges from capital campaigns that have been accrued as gift revenue but the related construction expenses have not yet been incurred. Unrestricted net assets primarily increased due to funds set aside for repairs and maintenance, debt service, capital projects and investment income on pooled cash. These increases were offset by unrealized investment losses in quasi-endowment.

Grand Valley State University

Statement of Revenues, Expenses and Changes in Net Assets

The Statement of Revenues, Expenses and Changes in Net Assets presents the operating results of the University, as well as the non-operating revenues and expenses. Annual state appropriations, while budgeted for operations, are considered non-operating revenues according to generally accepted accounting principles.

	(in thousands)		
	2001	2000	Change
		(unaudited)	
Operating revenue:			
Net tuition and fees	$69,456	$61,881	12%
Auxiliary	23,730	20,179	18%
Grant and contracts	14,692	11,863	24%
Other	8,871	8,212	8%
Total	116,749	102,135	14%
Operating expenses	169,411	145,764	16%
Net operating expenses	(52,662)	(43,629)	21%
Non-operating revenues:			
State appropriations	60,688	54,706	11%
Gifts (including endowment and capital)	26,183	9,466	177%
Capital appropriations	5,298	21,757	-76%
Investment income	2,152	5,754	-63%
Other income and expense	(3,052)	(1,668)	83%
Total	91,269	90,015	1%
Increase in net assets	38,607	46,386	-17%
Net assets - Beginning of year	288,711	242,325	19%
Net assets - End of year	$ 327,318	$ 288,711	13%

Tuition and fees, net of scholarship allowances, increased by 12% to $69 million in 2001. The increase was caused by tuition rate increases of 4.5% and enrollment increases of 7.2% FYES (fiscal year equated students). Scholarship allowances increased by 12.7% overall primarily due to an additional $4.8 million from the State of Michigan's MEAP program.

PLANTE & MORAN, LLP

Auxiliary revenue consists of housing, bookstores, vending, golf course, health center fees and telephone charges. The 18% increase is primarily related to housing rate increases of 3.8% and additional housing capacity of 13%. In the fall the University opened 153 beds in Secchia Hall and 284 beds through the acquisition of Grand Valley Apartments.

Grants and contracts revenue increased by $2.8 million as a result of increased student financial aid and increased activity in grants. For example, new grants received include the Michigan Small Business Development Center and an autism grant from the State of Michigan.

Gifts to the University reflect community support for the mission and goals of the University. After a GASB 35 adjustment to record pledges, gifts to the University more than doubled. Capital campaigns included gifts for the Health Professions Building, the Richard M. DeVos Center, the Fred M. Keller Engineering Laboratories, the Alumni House & Visitors Center and the Lake Michigan Center. Gifts to the endowment of the University totaled $3.5 million compared to $2 million last year. Planned giving, a new program of the University's Development Office, contributed $865,000 of gift revenue through charitable gift annuities.

Interest, dividends and realized gains of $6.1 million were offset by unrealized losses of $3.6 million and expenses of $300,000. The income on operating cash and unspent bond proceeds was offset by unrealized losses on long-term investments in the endowment.

Capital appropriations for 2000 and 2001 represent the State of Michigan's support for the construction of the Richard M. DeVos Center in downtown Grand Rapids. This building was funded 75% by the State of Michigan and 25% by gifts from the community. The University celebrated the opening of this building in August 2000.

Grand Valley State University

**Total Revenue
June 30, 2001**

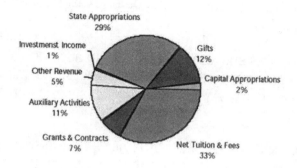

Tuition and fees, net of scholarship allowances, makes the largest contribution (33%) to the total revenue of the University. State appropriation is the next largest at 29%. These two sources, along with grants and contracts, provide for the majority of the operating expenses. Gifts and capital appropriations support the continued investments in endowments and capital assets while auxiliary activities are considered self-supporting enterprises.

Operating Expenses (by functional classification and in thousands)

	2001	2000 (unaudited)	Change	Percent
Instruction	$ 69,767	$ 60,884	$ 8,883	15%
Research	1,795	1,608	187	12%
Public service	9,063	8,253	810	10%
Academic support	17,054	13,967	3,087	22%
Student services	14,044	12,870	1,174	9%
Institutional support	10,277	8,093	2,184	27%
Operation and maintenance of facilities	14,123	10,741	3,382	31%
Depreciation	9,340	7,464	1,876	25%
Scholarships and related expenses	5,183	5,185	(2)	0%
Auxiliary activities	18,475	16,282	2,193	13%
Other expenditures	290	417	(127)	-30%
	$ 169,411	$ 145,764	$ 23,647	16%

PLANTE & MORAN, LLP

Expenses for instruction, research, and public service continue to grow at a steady rate. Instruction as a percent of total expenses remained constant at 41%. Salaries, wages, and benefits for instruction increased $8 million, which included 38 new positions for faculty, additional staff and annual pay increases. Supplies and other expenses increased by $1 million.

Academic support expenses increased $3.1 million overall with $1.9 million for salaries and benefits and $1.2 million for supplies and other expenses. In addition to annual pay increases, the increased expenses are a result of the new Steelcase Library, academic support for the Pew Campus, additional administration expenses for various dean offices and the establishment of an office for grants and graduate studies.

Institutional support, operation, and maintenance of facilities have grown by an unusually large amount due to the opening of new buildings. While the largest impact has been the opening of the Richard M. DeVos Center, the Alumni & Visitors Center and Fred M. Keller Engineering Laboratories have increased operating expenses as well.

Institutional support also reflects expansion of the development office into planned giving and cost related to changes in the executive office. Increases in public safety expenses relate to the opening and operation of the Pew Campus.

The increase in the operation and maintenance of facilities expenses again reflects the opening of the new facilities. Utility increases, annual salary increases, inflationary increases, and special maintenance projects are also reflected in this category.

Scholarships and related expenses include work-study programs as well as the portion of financial aid that is not considered a scholarship allowance. Increases in federal awards, stability in university-funded awards and increases in third-party awards are all factors that offset each other and result in the same level of expense.

Increases in expense for auxiliary activities reflect the additional housing on both the Pew Campus and in Allendale.

PLANTE & MORAN, LL

Grand Valley State University

Operating Expenses (by natural classification and in thousands)

	2001	2000	Change	Percent
		(unaudited)		
Salaries and benefits	$ 103,567	$ 90,439	$ 13,128	15%
Scholarships and awards	4,419	4,195	224	5%
Utilities	5,200	4,516	684	15%
Supplies and other	46,885	39,150	7,735	20%
Depreciation	9,340	7,464	1,876	25%
	$ 169,411	$ 145,764	$ 23,647	16%

Salaries and benefit expenses, which clearly represent the largest operating expense, increased due to additional positions and annual pay increases throughout every functional category. Both salaries and supplies expenses reflect the opening of the Richard M. DeVos Center, the Fred M. Keller Engineering Laboratories and the Alumni & Visitors Center. Scholarships and awards represent financial aid expense less scholarship allowance and work-study wage. The increase from fiscal year 2000 reflects and increases in non-work-study awards. Utilities expense increased due to market prices. Depreciation on buildings increased with the completion and opening of several new buildings.

Statement of Cash Flows

The Statement of Cash Flows provides information about cash receipts and cash payments during the year. This statement also helps users assess the University's ability to generate net cash flows, its ability to meet its obligations as they come due, and its need for external financing.

	(in thousands)	
	2001	2000
		(unaudited)
Cash Provided By (Used In) :		
Operating activities	$ (35,609)	$ (29,048)
Non-capital financing activities	64,961	56,665
Capital and related financing activities	(7,498)	(20,313)
Investing activities	(11,388)	(9,353)
Net increase (decrease) in cash	10,466	(2,050)
Cash - Beginning of year	3,221	5,271
Cash - End of year	$ 13,687	$ 3,221

PLANTE & MORAN, LLP

Grand Valley State University

The primary cash receipts from operating activities consist of tuition and housing revenues. Cash outlays include payment of wages, benefits, supplies, utilities and scholarships. Overall, net cash used by operations increased, reflecting the growth in the University.

State appropriation is the primary source of non-capital financing. The new accounting standards require that we reflect this source of revenue as non-operating even though the University's budget depends on this to continue the current level of operations. Appropriations increased by 11% from fiscal year 2000. Other non-capital financing activity includes gifts received for endowment and charitable gift annuities.

The main financing activities include the October 2000 bond issue of $36 million, state appropriations received for the Richard M. DeVos Center, and gifts received from several capital campaigns that were conducted. Financing income is offset by capital expenditures of $58 million that represent several construction projects undertaken during the year.

Economic Factors That Will Affect the Future

The economic position of Grand Valley is closely tied to that of the State of Michigan. State appropriation comprises 29% of total revenues and, after tuition revenue, is the second largest source of funding. The appropriation for the upcoming fiscal year has not been finalized. Since the state economy has slowed down, payrolls at major manufacturing concerns have been reduced, causing state revenues to decrease. This will most likely result in smaller increases in state appropriation for higher education. The specific impact on the University is uncertain.

Grand Valley State University

Assets

Current assets:		
Cash & cash equivalents (Note 2)	$	12,670,760
Restricted cash & cash equivalents (Note 2)		1,016,245
Short-term investments (Note 2)		23,707,181
Restricted short-term investments (Note 2)		13,279,961
Accounts receivable		6,202,298
State appropriation receivable		21,822,389
Pledges receivable		5,319,067
Inventory		1,795,231
Prepaid expenses & other		1,138,157
Student notes receivable - current portion		2,303,000
Total current assets		89,254,289
Noncurrent assets:		
Endowment investments (Note 2)		39,735,741
Other long-term investments (Note 2)		16,811,243
Pledges receivable		10,878,556
Student notes receivable, net of allowance of $570,000		8,043,530
Capital assets, net (Note 3)		288,882,469
Other assets		1,252,509
Total noncurrent assets		365,604,048
Total assets	$	**454,858,337**

Liabilities and Net Assets

Current liabilities:		
Accounts payable and accrued liabilities	$	33,615,927
Deferred revenue		7,798,417
Long-term liabilities - current portion (Note 5)		4,669,830
Total current liabilities		46,084,174
Noncurrent liabilities:		
Long-term liabilities (Note 5)		81,456,504
Total noncurrent liabilities		81,456,504
Total Liabilities		127,540,678
Net assets:		
Invested in capital assets, net of related debt		208,351,923
Restricted for:		
Nonexpendable -		
Scholarships & academic support		15,342,683
Expendable -		
Scholarships & academic support		16,034,683
Capital projects		16,405,221
Loans		10,797,539
Unrestricted		60,385,610
Total net assets		327,317,659
Total liabilities and net assets	$	**454,858,337**

PLANTE & MORAN, LLP

Grand Valley State University

Statement of Revenues, Expenses, and Changes in Net Assets
Year Ended June 30, 2001

Revenues:	
Operating revenues:	
Student tuition and fees (net of scholarship allowances of $8,146,147)	$ 69,456,040
Government grants and contracts	14,414,080
Nongovernmental grants	277,682
Sales and services of educational activities	3,737,481
Auxiliary activities:	
Residential life (net of scholarship allowances of $1,658,533)	14,782,435
Bookstores	6,641,530
Other	2,305,672
Other operating revenues	5,133,584
Total operating revenue	116,748,504
Expenses:	
Operating expenses:	
Education and general:	
Instruction	69,767,112
Research	1,794,503
Public service	9,063,014
Academic support	17,054,226
Student services	14,043,915
Institutional support	10,277,381
Operation and maintenance - Plant	14,123,470
Depreciation expense	9,340,062
Scholarships and related expenses	5,182,992
Auxiliary activities	18,475,126
Loan administrative fees and collection costs	289,669
Total operating expenses	169,411,470
Operating loss	(52,662,966)
Nonoperating revenues (expenses):	
State appropriations	60,688,422
Gifts	4,666,959
Investment income (net of investment expense of $239,193)	2,152,407
Interest on capital asset - Related debt	(3,923,062)
Net non-operating revenues	63,584,726
Income before other revenues, expenses, gains or losses	10,921,760
Capital appropriations	5,298,182
Capital grants and gifts	19,079,213
Additions to permanent endowments	2,436,702
Gain on disposal of plant assets	871,026
Total other revenue	27,685,123
Increase in net assets	38,606,883
Net Assets - Beginning of year as restated (Note 1)	288,710,776
Net Assets - End of year	**$ 327,317,659**

Grand Valley State University

Statement of Cash Flows
Year Ended June 30, 2001

Cash Flows from Operating Activities

Tuition and fees	$ 70,252,353
Grants and contracts	13,014,446
Payments to suppliers	(42,975,054)
Payments for utilities	(5,244,151)
Payments to employees	(81,353,053)
Payments for benefits	(20,519,694)
Payments for scholarships and fellowships	(4,418,546)
Loans issued to students	(10,901,362)
Collection of loans from students	11,022,203
Auxiliary enterprise charges:	
Residence halls	14,892,974
Bookstore	6,491,733
Other	2,050,525
Sales and service of educational activities	4,293,735
Other receipts	7,785,394
Net cash used in operating activities	**(35,608,497)**

Cash Flows from Noncapital Financing Activities

State appropriations	57,141,710
Gifts and grants for other than capital purposes	3,802,250
Private gifts for endowment purposes	2,436,702
Charitable annuities receipts, net of payments	1,535,724
Federal direct loan receipts	42,680,945
Federal direct loan lending disbursements	(42,636,345)
Net cash provided by noncapital financing activities	**64,960,986**

Cash Flows from Capital and Related Financing Activities

Proceeds from capital debt	36,475,000
Capital appropriations	10,959,667
Capital grants and gifts received	10,083,302
Proceeds from sale of capital assets	955,806
Purchases of capital assets and construction	(58,698,119)
Principal paid on capital debt	(3,355,000)
Interest paid on capital debt	(3,365,408)
Bond issue costs paid on new debt issue	(553,675)
Net cash used in capital and related financing activities	**(7,498,427)**

Cash Flows from Investing Activities

Proceeds from sales and maturities of investments	69,000,425
Investment income	2,044,992
Purchase of investments	(82,433,705)
Net cash used in investing activities	**(11,388,288)**
Net Increase in cash	10,465,774
Cash and Cash Equivalents - Beginning of the year	3,221,231
Cash and Cash Equivalents - End of the year	**$ 13,687,005**

15

PLANTE & MORAN, LLP

Grand Valley State University

Reconciliation of Net Operating Loss To Net Cash Used in Operating Activities

Operating loss	$ (52,662,996)
Adjustments to reconcile operating loss to net cash used in operating activites:	
Depreciation expense	9,340,062
Change in assets and liabilities:	
Receivables (net)	(2,464,643)
Inventories	(64,718)
Other assets	(455,971)
Accounts payable	8,911,325
Deferred revenue	2,070,461
Deposits held for others	(282,017)
Net cash used in operating activities	$ (35,608,497)

PLANTE & MORAN, LLP

Grand Valley State University

Assets:

Cash and investments	$ 15,991,810
Accrued interest receivable	649
Total assets	$ **15,992,459**
Net Assets - Held in trust for pension benefits	$ **15,992,459**

PLANTE & MORAN, LLP

Grand Valley State University

Additions

Investment income:	
Interest and dividends	$ 528,636
Net depreciation in fair value of investments	(2,667,166)
Total investment income	(2,138,530)
Employer contributions	690,831
Total additions	(1,447,699)

Deductions

Benefit payments	596,929
Administrative expense	67,103
Total deductions	664,032

Net Decrease   (2,111,731)

Net Assets Held in Trust for Pension Benefits

Beginning of year	18,104,190
End of year	$ 15,992,459

PLANTE & MORAN, LLP

Grand Valley State University

Note 1 – Summary of Significant Accounting Policies

Reporting Entity - Grand Valley State University (the "University") is an institution of higher education created by the Michigan Constitution of 1963 and is considered to be a component unit of the State of Michigan (the "State"). Its Board of Trustees is appointed by the Governor of the State. Accordingly, the University is included in the State's financial statements as a discrete component unit. Transactions with the State relate primarily to appropriations for operations and capital improvements and grants from various state agencies.

No component units are required to be reported in the University's financial statements. The financial statements of all organizations which are affiliated with but not controlled by the University, such as the Grand Valley University Foundation, Inc. and University Properties, Inc., are not included in the University's financial statements. The net assets of these organizations are immaterial to the financial statements and accordingly have not been separately disclosed.

Basis of Presentation - The financial statements have been prepared in accordance with generally accepted accounting principles as prescribed by the Governmental Accounting Standards Board (GASB), including Statement No. 34, *Basic Financial Statements - and Management's Discussion and Analysis - for State and Local Governments,* and Statement No. 35, *Basic Financial Statements and Management's Discussion and Analysis of Public College and Universities,* issued in June and November, 1999. While these Statements are scheduled for a phased implementation according to the size of the governmental unit, the University is required to adopt the Statement in the year that the State adopts it, and the State has elected adoption for the year ended September 30, 2001. The University now follows the "business-type activities" reporting requirements of GASB Statement No. 34 that provides a comprehensive one-line look at the University's financial activities.

Basis of Accounting - The financial statements of the University have been prepared on the accrual basis whereby all revenues are recorded when earned and all expenses are recorded when they have been reduced to a legal or contractual obligation to pay.

Investments - In accordance with GASB Statement No. 31, *Accounting and Financial Reporting for Certain Investments and for External Investment Pools,* investments are reported at fair value. Investments for which there are no quoted market prices are not material.

Inventories - Inventories, consisting principally of bookstore merchandise, golf equipment and apparel and computer equipment, are determined on first-in, first out (FIFO) method and stated at the lower of cost or market. The cost is recorded as an expense as the inventory is consumed.

Grand Valley State University

Note 1 – Summary of Significant Accounting Policies (Continued)

Physical Properties - Capital assets with a unit cost of over $2,000, and all library books, are recorded at cost at the date of acquisition, or, if donated, at fair market value at the date of donation. Infrastructure assets are included in the financial statements and are depreciated. Depreciation is computed using the straight-line method over the estimated useful life of the asset and is not allocated to the functional expenditure categories. Expenditures for construction in progress are capitalized as incurred. Interest expense relating to construction is capitalized net of interest income earned on resources set aside for this purpose. Certain maintenance and replacement reserves have been established to fund costs relating to residences and other auxiliary activity facilities.

Deferred Tuition and Fee Revenue - Tuition and fee revenues received and related to the period after June 30, 2001 have been deferred.

Provision for Unemployment Compensation - The University has elected to establish a provision for unemployment compensation under the terms of the Michigan Employment Security Act. Under this provision, the State of Michigan is reimbursed by the University for claims paid to former employees.

Compensated Absences - Compensated absence costs are accrued when earned by employees.

Operating Revenues - All revenues from programmatic sources are considered to be operating revenues. Included in non-operating revenues are state appropriations, investment income, and gifts. Gifts (pledges) that are received on an installment basis are recorded at net present value.

Scholarship Allowances and Student Aid - Financial aid to students is reported in the financial statements under the alternative method as prescribed by the National Association of College and University Business Officers (NACUBO). Certain aid such as loans, funds provided to students as awarded by third parties, and Federal Direct Lending is accounted for as a third party payment (credited to the student's account as if the student made the payment). All other aid is reflected in the financial statements as operating expenses, or scholarship allowances, which reduce revenues. The amount reported as operating expense represents the portion of aid that was provided to the student in the form of cash. Scholarship allowances represent the portion of aid provided to the student in the form of reduced tuition. Under the alternative method, these amounts are computed on a university basis by allocating the cash payments to students, excluding payments for services, on the ratio of total aid to the aid not considered to be third party aid.

Note 1 – Summary of Significant Accounting Policies (Continued)

Federal Financial Assistance Programs - The University participates in federally funded Pell Grants, SEOG Grants, Federal Work-Study, Federal Direct Lending, and Perkins Loans programs. Federal programs are audited in accordance with the Single Audit Act Amendments of 1996, the U.S. Office of Management and Budget Revised Circular A-133, *Audit of States, Local Governments and Non-Profit Organizations*, and the Compliance Supplement.

During 2000-2001, the University distributed $42,636,345 for direct lending through the U.S. Department of Education, which is not included as revenues and expenditures on the accompanying financial statements.

Encumbrances - The University maintains an encumbrance system for tracking outstanding purchase orders and other commitments for materials or services not received during the year. At year-end, encumbrances totaled $56,559,100, which represents the estimated amount of expenses ultimately to result if unperformed contracts in process at June 30, 2001 are completed. Approximately $55,009,000 of the total is committed for capital projects, including $32,544,100 for the new Health Professions building, $16,574,200 for new student housing projects, and $5,120,100 for the addition to the student activities building and new classroom additions.

Encumbrances outstanding at June 30, 2001 do not constitute expenses or liabilities and are not reflected in the financial statements

Net Assets - GASB Statement No. 34 reports equity as "Net Assets" rather than "fund balance." Net assets are classified according to external donor restrictions or availability of assets for satisfaction of University obligations. Nonexpendable restricted net assets are gifts that have been received for endowment purposes, the corpus of which cannot be expended. Expendable restricted net assets represent funds that have been gifted for specific purposes and funds held in federal loan programs.

The unrestricted net asset balance of $60,385,610 at June 30, 2001 includes $1,132,367 in reserves held for insurance purposes, $8,765,586 in quasi-endowment, $8,835,374 reserved for future debt service, $2,854,597 held for student loans, $8,231,411 reserved for future capital projects, and $11,820,480 reserved for repairs and maintenance, with $18,745,795 remaining for other purposes. Expenditures of quasi-endowment funds require approval by the Board of Trustees.

Note 1 – Summary of Significant Accounting Policies (Continued)

Restatement of Beginning Net Assets - In connection with the implementation of GASB Statements No. 34 and No. 35, the following adjustments have been made to reflect the cumulative effect of this accounting change:

Accrual of spring tuition revenue, net of associated teaching expenses	$	2,019,327
Accrual of unrecorded pledges receivable at present value		7,201,712
Accrual of interest earned on student loans		205,692
Capitalization of infrastructure, net of accumulated depreciation		275,500
Capitalization of historical treasures		204,507
Fiduciary classification of defined benefit plans		(18,104,190)
Recording contract advances as deferred revenue		(1,146,822)
Total adjustments		(9,344,274)
Fund balances reported at June 30, 2000		298,055,050
Net asset balance at July 1, 2000	$	288,710,776

Note 2 – Cash and Investments

Policies:

Cash and Short-term Investments: Investment policies for cash and short-term investments as set forth by the Board of Trustees authorize the University to invest in interest-bearing time deposits, short-term cash funds, money market funds, intermediate cash funds, U.S. Government-backed obligations, managed equity mutual funds, and commercial paper. All investments must be held by financial institutions organized under Federal or State law.

Note 2 – Cash and Investments (Continued)

Investments: Investment policies as set forth by the Board of Trustees also authorize the University to invest in equity securities, bonds, or other securities and real estate investments for production of rental income. The Board of Trustees has authorized the treasurer or assistant treasurer of the Board of Trustees to make the University's investment decisions with the members of the appropriate board committee. In accordance with policies set forth by the Board of Trustees, complete discretion in selecting individual investments of endowment assets is assigned to two or more money managers who are chosen at the discretion of the Board of Trustees. The University's treasurer and the appropriate board committee monitor the money managers' performance.

In accordance with the GASB Statement No. 3, deposits and investments are classified into three categories of custodial credit risk:

	Cash	**Investments**
Category 1	Deposits that are either insured or collateralized with securities held by the University or by its agent in the University's name.	Investments that are insured or registered, or securities held by the University or by its agent in the University's name.
Category 2	Deposits collateralized with securities held by the pledging financial institution's trust department or agent in the University's name.	Investments that are uninsured and unregistered, with securities held by the counterparty's trust department or agent in the University's name.
Category 3	Deposits that are uncollateralized (including any bank balance that is collateralized with securities held by pledging financial institution, or by its trust department or agent, but not in the University's name).	Investments that are uninsured and unregistered, with securities held by the counterparty's trust department or agent but not held in the University's name.
Not Categorized		Investments in mutual funds, money markets and investment management funds are not categorized because they are not evidenced by securities that exist in physical or book entry form.

Note 2 – Cash and Investments (Continued)

Investments are reported at fair value (market) and reported on the Statement of Net Assets as follows:

	Business Type Activities	Fiduciary Activities
Cash and cash equivalents	$ 13,687,005	$ -
Short-term investments	36,987,142	-
Endowment investments	39,735,741	-
Other investments	16,811,243	15,991,810
Total	$ 107,221,131	$ 15,991,810

For purposes of the Statement of Cash Flows, the University considers all highly liquid investments with an original maturity of three months or less to be cash equivalents. Cash equivalents representing assets of the University's endowment are included in non-current investments.

The following tables summarize the categorization of investments at June 30, 2001:

	Category 1	Category 2	Category 3	Not Categorized	Total Per Bank
Cash and short-term investments:					
Cash	$ 164,304	$ -	$ 679,654	$ -	$ 843,958
Certificates of deposits	400,000	-	5,875,798	-	6,275,798
Repurchase agreements	-	2,633,234	-	-	2,633,234
Money markets	-	-	-	1,502,673	1,502,673
Commercial paper	12,135,000	-	-	-	12,135,000
Investment management funds	-	-	-	22,745,036	22,745,036
Total cash and short-term investments	12,699,304	2,633,234	6,555,452	24,247,709	46,135,699
Investments:					
Governement securities	20,426,576	-	-	-	20,426,576
Equity securities	-	161,639	-	-	161,639
Real estate	-	86,126	-	-	86,126
Money market funds	-	-	-	1,116,382	1,116,382
Mutual funds	-	-	-	4,384,569	4,384,569
Investment management funds	-	-	-	39,549,477	39,549,477
Total investments	20,426,576	247,765	-	45,050,428	65,724,769
Total cash and investments	$ 33,125,880	$ 2,880,999	$ 6,555,452	$ 69,298,137	$ 111,860,468

Note 3 – Capital Assets

Capital asset activity for the year ended June 30, 2001 was as follows:

	Beginning Balance	Additions	Reductions	Ending Balance
Land	$ 14,247,416	$ 458,014	$ 9,608	$ 14,695,822
Non-depreciable artwork and historical treasures	2,296,326	1,064,565	-	3,360,891
Non-depreciable land improvements	1,722,820	-	-	1,722,820
Construction in progress (net)	56,620,885	(20,121,449)	-	36,499,436
Total cost of nondepreciable capital assets	74,887,447	(18,598,870)	9,608	56,278,969
Land improvements and infrastructure	17,146,803	5,952,647	-	23,099,450
Buildings	176,684,167	64,037,650	-	240,721,817
Equipment	32,681,164	4,566,960	387,738	36,860,386
Library books	10,094,920	2,739,732	224,430	12,610,222
Total cost of depreciable capital assets	236,607,054	77,296,989	612,168	313,291,875
Total cost of capital assets	311,494,501	58,698,119	621,776	369,570,844
Less accumulated depreciation for:				
Land improvements and infrastructure	4,795,713	988,454	-	5,784,167
Buildings	38,242,608	4,624,509	-	42,867,117
Equipment	23,690,189	2,593,258	312,565	25,970,882
Library books	5,156,798	1,133,841	224,430	6,066,209
Total accumulated depreciation	71,885,308	$ 9,340,062	$ 536,995	80,688,375
Capital assets - Net	$ 239,609,193			$ 288,882,469

The following estimated useful lives are used to compute depreciation:

Buildings	50 years
Library books	10 years
Land improvements and infrastructure	20 years
Equipment	7-15 years

Grand Valley State University

Note 4 – Endowments and Similar Funds

The Board of Trustees has established an investment policy with the objectives of protecting the principal of these funds and maximizing total investment return without assuming extraordinary risks. It is the goal of the University to provide spendable income levels that are reasonably stable and sufficient to meet budgetary requirements and to maintain a spending rate, currently established at 5%, which insures a proper balance between the preservation of corpus and enhancement of the purchasing power of investment earnings.

Note 5 – Long-term Liabilities

Long-term liabilities of the University consist of bonds payable, interest accrued on capital appreciation bonds, and charitable gift annuities payable. The changes in long-term liabilities are as show below:

	Beginning Balance	Additions	Reductions	Ending Balance	Due Within One Year
General Revenue Bonds, Series 1989	$ 10,000	$ -	$ 5,000	$ 5,000	$ 5,000
General Revenue and Refunding Bonds, Series 1994	5,450,000	-	900,000	4,550,000	367,090
General Revenue and Refunding Bonds, Series 1997	21,060,000	-	1,780,000	19,280,000	1,855,000
General Revenue Bonds, Series 1998	14,745,000	-	335,000	14,410,000	345,000
General Revenue Bonds, Series 1999	9,030,000	-	335,000	8,695,000	350,000
General Revenue Bonds, Series 2000	-	36,475,000	-	36,475,000	1,465,000
Total bonds payable	50,295,000	36,475,000	3,355,000	83,415,000	4,387,090
Accrued interest –					
Capital appreciation bonds	1,639,060	401,259	-	2,040,319	168,047
Charitable gift annuities payable	-	698,240	27,225	671,015	114,693
Total	$ 51,934,060	$ 37,574,499	$ 3,382,225	86,126,334	$ 4,669,830
Due within one year				4,669,830	
Total long-term liabilities				$ 81,456,504	

Note 5 – Long-term Liabilities (Continued)

The General Revenue Bonds, Series 1989, were issued in May 1989 by the Board of Trustees to provide funds for an addition to an existing classroom and office building and for the redevelopment of an open campus area.

The General Revenue Refunding Bonds, Series 1994, were issued in January 1994 by the Board of Trustees for the advance refunding of $6,680,000 of Series 1988 bonds and $1,130,000 of Series 1989 bonds. The University has covenanted to maintain revenues available for debt service and certain other revenues at or beyond specified minimum levels. The advance refunding of the callable portions of the Series 1988 and Series 1989 bonds resulted in an in-substance defeasance. Appropriate portions of the proceeds of the Series 1994 bonds were placed in an irrevocable trust and were used to purchase United States Treasury securities. Accordingly, both the Treasury securities and the refunded bonds have been excluded from the statement of net assets.

The General Revenue and Refunding Bonds, Series 1997, were issued in June 1997 by the Board of Trustees to provide funds for construction of residential facilities, an addition to an existing classroom and office building, and refunding a 5.85% bank note payable.

The General Revenue Bonds, Series 1998, were issued in January 1998 by the Board of Trustees to provide funds for construction of additional residential facilities.

The General Revenue Bonds, Series 1999, were issued in July 1999 by the Board of Trustees for an advance bond refunding of $1,775,000 and $7,325,000 to fund a portion of the cost of constructing student housing in downtown Grand Rapids.

The General Revenue Bonds, Series 2000, were issued in October 2000 by the Board of Trustees to fund new construction and remodeling on the Allendale campus.

As of June 30, 2001, the aggregate amount of outstanding principal on all bonds which have been refinanced is $955,000.

The University has issuance costs as well as bond premiums and discounts in connection with all of the bond issues. These items are accrued and are being amortized over the life of the bonds using the straight-line method. The net amount of unamortized bond issuance costs, discounts and premiums at June 30, 2001 totaled $1,010,012.

PLANTE & MORAN, LLP

Grand Valley State University

Note 5 – Long-term Liabilities (Continued)

Principal and interest on all of the outstanding bonds are payable from, and secured by, the University's general revenues. The Bonds, consisting of both serial, term and capital appreciation serial bonds, bear interest primarily from 4.0% to 7.1% and mature in varying amounts through 2025. Interest payments on the capital appreciation bonds begin in 2002.

In October 2000, the Board of Trustees authorized the implementation of a charitable gift annuity program. Assets received from these gift arrangements belong to the university, subject to a liability for future payments due to annuitants. The estimated present value of annuities payable at June 30, 2001 was $671,015.

Scheduled maturities of long-term liabilities are as follows:

Fiscal Year	Revenue Bonds and Accrued Interest	Annuities Payable	Total
2002	$ 4,555,137	$ 114,693	$ 4,669,830
2003	4,975,057	114,693	5,089,750
2004	5,259,664	114,693	5,374,357
2005	3,869,216	114,693	3,983,909
2006	4,109,995	114,693	4,224,688
Thereafter	62,686,250	97,550	62,783,800
Totals	$ 85,455,319	$ 671,015	$ 86,126,334

Note 6 – Retirement Benefits

The University has established retirement plans for substantially all permanent employees. Total payroll at June 30, 2001 was approximately $82,690,000 for the University, of which $60,225,000 was payroll covered by the various University retirement plans.

The executive, administrative, and professional staff and faculty are covered under a defined contribution retirement plan through the TIAA-CREF (Teachers Insurance and Annuity Association of America - College Retirement Equities Fund) or Fidelity Investments. Employees may contribute an amount not to exceed the Internal Revenue Service designated maximum. Participants become fully vested upon completion of two years of employment. During 2001, the University made contributions equal to 12% of the participants' base salary.

PLANTE & MORAN, LLP

Note 6 – Retirement Benefits (Continued)

No contributions were required from participants. The total expense under this plan was $5,765,500 for year ended June 30, 2001. Total payroll covered under this plan was $47,640,000 in 2001.

Clerical, office, technical, maintenance, grounds and service staff and public safety officers not entitled to participate in the TIAA-CREF retirement plans are covered under two non-contributory defined benefit plans sponsored by the University that are designed to provide monthly sources of retirement income at future dates. The University maintains an unaudited stand alone financial report of its pension plans that is available at its Human Resource Office.

The University's funding policy is to match the current annual required contribution. The University contributed 5.5% of payroll during the fiscal year ended June 30, 2001.

For the year ended June 30, 2001, the University's annual pension cost totaled $490,014. The annual required contribution was determined as part of an actuarial valuation at June 30, 2000, using the aggregate actuarial cost method. This method does not identify or separately amortize unfunded actuarial liabilities. Significant assumptions include (a) an 8 percent investment rate of return, (b) projected salary increases of 4 percent per year, (c) no cost of living adjustment.

Three year trend information:

	2001	2000	1999
Annual pension cost	$ 490,014	$ 652,456	$ 492,877
Percentage of annual pension cost contributed	141%	108%	108%
Net pension obligation	-	-	-

Note 6 – Retirement Benefits (Continued)

The University also provides certain health care benefits for retired faculty and staff. Substantially all of the University's employees may become eligible for those benefits if they reach retirement age while working for the University, are vested in a University sponsored retirement plan, and their years of University service and age total a minimum of 75. The University recognizes the cost of providing these benefits by expensing them on a current basis. The number of retirees who received benefits under this program and the related costs are as follows:

	2001	2000	1999
Retirees receiving benefits	146	150	134
Total costs	$ 159,200	$ 156,900	$ 137,500

Note 7 – Commitments

The University has an arrangement with the State of Michigan and State Building Authority (the "SBA") to finance a large portion of the Life Science Complex located on the Allendale Campus and the Graduate School of Business and Graduate Library Building located on the Pew Campus in downtown Grand Rapids. The arrangement is based upon a lease agreement that is signed by the University. It stipulates that the SBA will hold title to the buildings and the State will make all lease payments to the SBA on behalf of the University, and the University will pay all operating and maintenance costs. At the expiration of the lease, the SBA has agreed to sell each building to the University for $1.

The University has also committed $3,000,000 for the purchase of property adjacent to its downtown campus.

Note 8 – Contingencies

The University is self-funded for coverage under portions of its hospital/medical benefits and for all workers' compensation. The University also offers two HMO plans to employees. Stop loss coverage has been purchased by the University for the self-funded hospital/medical benefits and workers' compensation claims. The stop loss insurance limits the claims for hospital/medical benefits to $125,000 per individual up to $1 million in aggregate. Individual claims in excess of the $1 million limit are funded by the University with an aggregate annual stop loss of $3.7 million in 2001. The workers' compensation stop loss insurance limits its liability for claims paid to $300,000 per individual in 2001.

Note 8 – Contingencies (Continued)

Effective July 1, 1987, the University entered into an arrangement with several other Michigan public universities to form a separate corporation that provides comprehensive general liability, errors and omissions, property and vehicle liability coverages. The corporation provides coverage for claims in excess of agreed upon deductibles.

Reserves for insurance activities have been internally funded and are included in Unrestricted Net Assets.

In the normal course of its activities, the University has been a party in various legal actions. Historically, the University has not experienced significant losses from such actions. After taking into consideration legal counsel's evaluation of pending actions, the University is of the opinion that the outcome thereof will not have a material effect on its financial statements.

Note 9 – Subsequent Events

In July 2001, General Revenue bonds totaling $31,375,000 were issued by the Board of Trustees to fund the cost of constructing new student housing, classroom additions, and an athletic facility addition on the Allendale campus. This issue consists of serial bonds totaling $10,100,000 that bear interest in the range of 3.25% to 4.1% and mature in varying amounts through 2008. The remainder of $21,275,000 consists of variable rate term bonds that mature through 2027.

Note 10 – Related Organizations

Pursuant to the State of Michigan Public Act 362 of 1993, the University has authorized thirty public school academies. Twenty-eight of these public school academies operate schools funded by the State School Aid Act. The University, as fiscal agent, provides guidance in and review of compliance with state requirements and forwards the state payment to the public school academy. Public funding is provided by the State of Michigan on a per pupil basis. Funding of $62,465,951 was appropriated by the State in 2001 to be allocated to the public school academies, net of a 3% administrative fee retained by the University. At June 30, 2001, $11,081,125 is outstanding from the State, of which $10,753,832 will be subsequently forwarded to the public school academics. This activity is treated as an agency transaction.

To the Board of Trustees
Grand Valley State University

We have audited the basic financial statements of Grand Valley State University for the year ended June 30, 2001. Our audit was made for the purpose of forming an opinion on the basic financial statements taken as a whole. The additional information listed in the table of contents is presented for purposes of additional analysis and is not a required part of the basic financial statements of Grand Valley State University. This information has been subjected to the procedures applied in the audit of the basic financial statements and, in our opinion, is fairly stated in all material respects in relation to the basic financial statements taken as a whole.

Plante & Moran, LLP

August 29, 2001

Additional Information

Grand Valley State University

Schedule of Endowment and Similar Funds
June 30, 2001

	Balance July 1, 2000	Gifts and Additions	Investment Income and Deductions	Distribution Beneficiary Funds	Intra Fund Distribution	Balance June 30, 2001	Retained Investment Income	Principal Balance 06/30/01
Endowment Funds								
Alumni Heritage Scholarship Fund	$ 166,754	$ 8,472	$ (10,619)	$ 8,508	$ 100	$ 156,199	$ 20,156	$ 136,043
Joseph E. Appelt P.E. Engineering Scholarship Fund	34,261	2,869	(2,292)	1,845	-	32,993	3,597	29,396
APICS Scholarship Fund	34,862	200	(2,191)	-	200	33,071	28,071	5,000
Ara Cary Lectureship Fund	13,105	977	(865)	-	591	13,808	4,009	9,799
Art & Design Endowment	12,775	1,670	(865)	-	1,412	14,992	802	14,190
Baker-Hall Physics Fund	46,706	1,276	(2,954)	2,364	-	42,664	14,222	28,442
Fred A. Bell Business Scholarship Fund	40,447	-	(2,521)	2,022	-	35,904	5,663	30,241
William C. Baum Endowment	35,621	8,171	(2,420)	1,926	2,926	42,372	(561)	42,933
David Alan Bergsma Scholarship Fund	58,112	-	(3,641)	2,906	-	51,565	40,930	10,635
Hyman H. & Greta M. Berkowitz Scholarship Fund	434,241	50	(27,122)	21,714	50	385,505	122,325	263,180
Blodgett Music Scholarship	55,514	836	(3,489)	2,799	200	50,262	21,297	28,965
Biology Department Science Equipment Fund	59,105	1,659	(3,769)	3,009	1,284	55,270	16,860	38,410
The Biomedical/Health Science Fund	1,369	591	(103)	-	502	2,359	(9)	2,368
Joan Boand Athletic Scholarship Fund	35,845	1,729	(2,292)	1,842	435	33,875	6,560	27,315
William J. & Margaret G. Branstrom Fund	119,362	-	(7,461)	5,968	-	105,933	57,347	48,586
The Donna K. Brooks Presidential Scholarship	-	250,000	(7,563)	6,046	6,046	242,437	(7,563)	250,000
The Brooks Family Minority Scholarship	-	250,000	(7,563)	6,048	6,048	242,437	(7,563)	250,000
Johnny C. Burton Memorial Scholarship	78,008	200	(4,889)	3,906	-	69,413	15,798	53,615
Greg Cadaret Baseball Fund	69,958	115	(4,380)	3,500	50	62,243	23,978	38,265
Bernard & Camile Cebelak Scholarship Fund	45,042	10,000	(2,801)	2,252	-	49,989	4,989	45,000

Grand Valley State University

Schedule of Endowment and Similar Funds (Continued)
June 30, 2001

	Balance July 1, 2000	Gifts and Additions	Investment Income and Deductions	Distribution Beneficiary Funds	Intra Fund Distribution	Balance June 30, 2001	Retained Investment Income	Principal Balance 06/30/01
Endowment Funds (Continued)								
Robert L. Chamberlain Scholarship Fund	54,538	961	(3,464)	2,763	358	49,630	21,227	28,403
Hong Chen Memorial Endowment Fund	22,330	25	(1,401)	1,117	99	19,936	-	19,936
School of Communications Scholarship Fund	28,072	1,677	(1,809)	1,455	465	26,950	2,686	24,264
Computer Science and Information Systems Endowment	70,526	2,423	(4,482)	3,595	414	65,286	20,707	44,579
The COT Association Scholarship Endowment Fund	50,949	3,840	(3,362)	2,683	3,594	52,338	2,267	50,071
David Daniels Memorial Scholarship Fund	52,693	1,448	(3,337)	2,669	616	48,751	20,180	28,571
Gilbert and Patricia Davis Endowed Merit Scholarship	70,040	2,048	(4,457)	3,566	377	64,442	17,840	46,602
Greta & Arthur Delong Perpetual Scholarship Fund	66,685	100	(4,176)	3,337	-	59,272	16,549	42,723
Mary Jane Dockeray Scholarship Fund	45,854	4,174	(3,031)	2,430	-	44,567	16,335	28,232
L. V. Eberhard Scholarship Fund	596,118	2,739	(37,334)	29,875	-	531,648	267,993	263,655
Etzen Voice Scholarship Fund	93,475	1,959	(5,908)	4,724	769	85,571	32,085	53,486
School of Engineering Fund	107,513	4,693	(6,850)	-	2,589	107,945	40,285	67,660
Enrichment Fund	593,696	500	(37,079)	29,688	-	527,429	257,804	269,625
Faculty Teaching and Learning Center Endowment	2,079,625	160	(129,903)	103,987	59,425	1,905,320	-	1,905,320
Film and Video Scholarship	-	2,005	(51)	-	652	2,606	(51)	2,657
Richard E. Flanders Scholarship Fund	128,463	1,301	(8,073)	6,459	432	115,664	40,925	74,739
Geology Development Fund	114,881	691	(7,208)	5,760	130	102,734	44,407	58,327
Geology Student Field Endowment	12,831	2,443	(891)	-	1,085	15,468	1,163	14,305
Charlotte A. Gierst & Salome C. Egeler Trust Fund	72,457	300	(4,532)	3,637	300	64,888	22,808	42,080
Richard Giles Memorial Scholarship Fund	350,925	1,204	(21,978)	17,582	154	312,723	162,447	150,276

Grand Valley State University

Schedule of Endowment and Similar Funds (Continued)
June 30, 2001

	Balance July 1, 2000	Gifts and Additions	Investment Income and Deductions	Distribution Beneficiary Funds	Intra Fund Distribution	Balance June 30, 2001	Retained Investment Income	Principal Balance 06/30/01
Endowment Funds (Continued)								
The Graduate Teacher Certification Scholarship	-	28,807	(1,146)	-	1,375	29,036	(1,146)	30,182
Grand Valley Grand Forum Endowment	88,986	12,442	(5,908)	-	220	95,740	7,349	88,391
Grand Valley State University Athletic Fund	143,697	7,228	(9,015)	7,226	361	135,045	33,537	101,508
GVSU Women's Scholarship Endowment	14,044	5,534	(1,146)	-	5,033	23,465	(26)	23,491
Grand Valley State University Fund	4,356,531	135,725	(274,374)	30,257	(100,000)	4,087,625	2,276,051	1,811,574
Earl Harper Scholarship Fund	63,739	670	(3,999)	3,208	177	57,379	21,573	35,806
Joyce Hecht Distinguished Scholarship in Philanthropy	-	92,169	(2,725)	2,175	11,038	98,307	(2,725)	101,032
William Hegarty Endowment Fund	27,917	-	(1,732)	1,396	-	24,789	1,019	23,770
Arthur C. Hills Music Scholarship Fund	71,065	1,782	(4,507)	3,601	101	64,840	28,394	36,446
Hispanic Scholarship Fund	52,688	1,641	(3,362)	2,691	1,482	49,758	13,696	36,062
W. G. Jackson Fund	221,534	3,530	(13,955)	11,171	182	200,120	52,455	147,665
Dr. Thomas & Mrs. Joann Jackson Scholarship Endowment	5,140	473	(357)	-	577	5,833	(16)	5,849
Dorothy A. Johnson Center for Philanthropy Endowment	529,241	8,000	(33,209)	26,579	26,579	504,032	(11,193)	515,225
Lynne Kraemer Memorial Scholarship Fund	38,236	-	(2,395)	1,912	-	33,929	16,335	17,594
Kirkhof School of Nursing Endowment	82,659	3,037	(5,272)	4,226	1,832	78,030	17,931	60,099
Don Klein Endowment	37,585	21,855	(3,056)	-	1,018	57,402	690	56,712
Walton Boston Koch Memorial Scholarship	32,472	704	(2,064)	1,642	227	29,697	12,360	17,337
Koeze Art Scholarship	-	10,082	(485)	-	100	9,697	(485)	10,182
Loutit Foundation Fund	213,684	50	(7,971)	-	8,022	213,785	-	213,785
Lubbers Presidential Scholarship	-	132,520	(560)	-	-	131,960	(560)	132,520

Grand Valley State University

Schedule of Endowment and Similar Funds (Continued)
June 30, 2001

	Balance July 1, 2000	Gifts and Additions	Investment Income and Deductions	Distribution Beneficiary Funds	Intra Fund Distribution	Balance June 30, 2001	Retained Investment Income	Principal Balance 06/30/01
Endowment Funds (Continued)								
Faite R-P. Mack Scholarship Fund	59,909	1,294	(3,795)	3,043	1,300	55,665	17,606	38,059
Mathematics and Statistics Endowment	160,678	4,957	(10,237)	8,190	3,705	150,913	40,365	110,548
Corky Meinecke Scholarship Endowment Fund	21,864	5,733	(1,502)	1,208	596	25,483	-	25,483
Paul C. Miller Scholarship Fund	112,231	-	(7,003)	5,612	-	99,616	49,404	50,212
Minority Scholarship Endowment Fund	712,601	48,613	(46,247)	37,019	2,261	680,209	39,219	640,990
Mithilesh & Jitendra Mishra								
Foreign Student/Faculty Scholarship	31,991	38	(2,012)	1,601	-	28,416	5,586	22,830
Jacob B. Mol Family Scholarship Fund	85,964	-	(5,374)	4,299	50	76,341	28,478	47,863
Niemeyer Endowment Fund	69,518	4,076	(4,507)	-	3,452	72,539	16,965	55,574
Nursing Nontraditional Student Scholarship	13,000	(5,496)	(713)	-	4,183	10,974	(713)	11,687
Arnold C. Ott Lectureship in Chemistry	-	500,000	(13,013)	10,417	10,417	486,987	(13,013)	500,000
Barbara Padnos Scholarship Fund	205,380	200,000	(19,074)	15,269	15,269	386,306	(13,969)	400,275
Seymour and Esther Padnos Engineering Scholarship	-	500,000	(13,013)	10,417	10,417	486,987	(13,013)	500,000
Peace & Justice Award Fund	45,839	530	(2,877)	2,308	335	41,519	17,257	24,262
Physical Therapy Department Fund	30,453	1,453	(1,961)	1,567	905	29,283	9,847	19,436
William F. Pickard Fund	73,502	50	(4,583)	-	50	69,019	38,283	30,736
Positive Black Woman Endowment Fund	26,494	2,446	(1,758)	1,414	2,193	27,961	3,264	24,697
Berthold Price Scholarship Fund	138,943	2,019	(8,760)	7,010	1,118	126,310	48,152	78,158
Plant Service Personnel Descendants Scholarship Fund	254,908	16,779	(16,553)	13,254	9,824	251,704	44,246	207,458
Reister Family Scholarship	-	10,030	(51)	-	-	9,979	(51)	10,030
Warren Reynolds Endowment	3,541	5,486	(509)	-	665	9,183	(363)	9,546

Grand Valley State University

Schedule of Endowment and Similar Funds (Continued)
June 30, 2001

	Balance July 1, 2000	Gifts and Additions	Investment Income and Deductions	Distribution Beneficiary Funds	Intra Fund Distribution	Balance June 30, 2001	Retained Investment Income	Principal Balance 06/30/01
Endowment Funds (Continued)								
Science Math Development Fund	69,308	1,319	(4,380)	3,503	275	63,019	36,197	26,822
Science Equipment Fund	2,123,506	852	(132,679)	106,209	312	1,885,782	916,601	969,181
School of Public and Nonprofit Administration Endowment	11,430	936	(765)	-	1,035	12,636	2,019	10,617
Mary & Wilhelm Seeger Scholarship Fund	117,576	3,683	(7,486)	5,999	2,560	110,334	37,810	72,524
Esther L. Seidman Chair in Management Fund	358,232	-	(22,384)	17,912	-	317,936	142,536	175,400
Seidman Endowment Fund	1,289,572	11,829	(80,982)	64,819	4,804	1,160,404	547,672	612,732
Marilyn and B. P. Sherwood III Scholarship Fund	25,505	200	(1,604)	1,279	-	22,822	7,371	15,451
The Social Work Minority Scholarship	-	1,677	(51)	-	1,052	2,678	(51)	2,729
Social Work Scholarship Fund	23,117	1,278	(1,502)	-	1,190	24,083	5,495	18,588
Joseph Stevens Freedom Fund	104,050	1,632	(6,571)	5,255	364	94,220	29,460	64,760
Ryan Short Memorial Scholarship Fund	51,453	1,912	(3,285)	2,640	1,798	49,238	7,695	41,543
Esther Rehm Stotz Scholarship Fund	145,090	-	(9,066)	7,255	-	128,769	60,470	68,299
Tax Program Fund	125,913	525	(7,869)	6,309	-	112,260	49,377	62,883
The Telephone Pioneers of America, Great Lakes Chapter #90 Scholarship Fund	69,513	113	(4,355)	3,480	50	61,841	20,395	41,446
Edward Tremba Geology Scholarship Fund	70,856	385	(4,431)	3,556	338	63,592	27,303	36,289
A Trust for Science Education Endowment	113,937	2,107	(7,208)	-	2,290	111,126	1,279	109,847
University Library Fund	187,491	3,969	(11,867)	-	1,606	181,199	65,340	115,859
VanSteeland Arboretum Fund	96,792	1,950	(6,087)	-	831	93,486	40,262	53,224
Kenneth Venderbush Endowment Fund	1,646	1,800	(103)	-	100	3,443	43	3,400
The Donald and Barbara Vanderjagt Mathematics and Athletic Scholarship	-	10,100	(51)	-	-	10,049	(51)	10,100

Grand Valley State University

Schedule of Endowment and Similar Funds (Continued)
June 30, 2001

	Balance July 1, 2000	Gifts and Additions	Investment Income and Deductions	Distribution Beneficiary Funds	Intra Fund Distribution	Balance June 30, 2001	Retained Investment Income	Principal Balance 06/30/01
Endowment Funds (Continued)								
Florence Cowan Ward Scholarship for Nursing	68,389	15,096	(4,558)	3,654	3,706	78,979	(10)	78,989
WRI Equipment Fund	2,318,848	1,000	(144,878)	115,967	-	2,059,003	902,419	1,156,584
Margaret Ward Music Scholarship	20,000	5,161	(1,401)	1,127	1,177	23,810	(1,401)	25,211
WGVU-TV Scholarship Fund	304,209	4,669	(19,150)	15,329	312	274,711	102,005	172,706
Margaret F. Ward Art and Design Scholarship	20,000	5,000	(1,401)	1,125	1,125	23,599	(1,401)	25,000
Weldon Memorial Chemistry Fund	92,278	18,658	(6,444)	-	5,785	110,277	29,213	81,064
Westerman Nursing Scholarship Fund	151,375	22	(9,447)	7,570	-	134,380	33,142	101,238
William James Fund	32,998	295	(2,064)	1,659	150	29,720	14,717	15,003
Shelia Williams Student Leadership Development Fund	119,700	1,331	(7,511)	6,021	354	107,853	52,998	54,855
Doug and Linda Woods Athletic Training Scholarship	31,807	1,440	(2,064)	1,644	1,436	30,975	1,754	29,221
Felix V. & Gladys A. Zukaitis Athletic Trust	211,981	-	(13,243)	10,598	-	188,140	62,990	125,150
Felix V. & Gladys A. Zukaitis Scholarship Trust	211,799	-	(13,243)	10,591	-	187,965	62,965	125,000
Subtotal	22,547,163	2,436,702	(1,468,036)	924,195	149,017	22,740,651	7,397,968	15,342,683

Grand Valley State University

Schedule of Endowment and Similar Funds (Continued)
June 30, 2001

	Balance July 1, 2000	Gifts and Additions	Investment Income and Deductions	Distribution Beneficiary Funds	Intra Fund Distribution	Balance June 30, 2001	Retained Investment Income	Principal Balance 06/30/01
Funds Functioning as Endowments								
Accounting Scholarship Fund	331,771	10,060	(21,035)	16,843	1,272	305,225	118,703	186,522
Alumni Scholarship Fund	732,784	7,939	(45,992)	36,807	542	658,466	240,809	417,657
Angus Fund	1,499,300	4,644	(93,767)	75,046	294	1,335,425	509,356	826,069
Owen F. Bieber Scholarship Trust	647,026	-	(40,415)	32,351	-	574,260	260,850	313,410
Business & Engineering Internship Fund	1,266,706	150	(79,125)		-	1,187,731	646,499	541,232
Entrepeneurial Center Endowment	1,290,630	200,000	(91,016)	72,865	-	1,326,749	106,399	1,220,350
Grand Rapids Continuing Education	864,518	-	(54,015)		-	810,503	436,521	373,982
Leon W. Hall Trust Fund	732,996	-	(45,788)	36,650	-	650,558	316,146	334,412
Charles & Florence Irwin Scholarship Endowment Fund	159,531	17,195	(10,492)	8,406	1,012	158,840	47,168	111,672
Russel H. Kirkhof Fund	2,398,830	-	(139,995)	119,756	-	2,139,079	1,131,780	1,007,299
Seymour & Esther Padnos School of Engineering Endowment	2,441,555	344	(152,517)	122,088	104	2,167,398	666,002	1,501,396
Padnos Fund	1,626,969	-	(101,636)	81,348	-	1,443,985	443,960	1,000,025
Joe E. Reid Memorial Scholarship Fund	78,975	765	(4,941)	3,957	200	71,042	25,739	45,303
SPX Corporation Engineering Scholarship Fund	136,112	-	(8,506)	6,806	-	120,800	70,690	50,110
Robert C. Trotter Scholarship Fund	455,035	-	(28,421)	22,752	-	403,862	255,995	147,867
Undistributed Income Fund	1,549,826	-	(81,837)		(152,689)	1,315,300	1,315,300	-
VanderMey Endowment	161,283	-	(10,084)	8,064	-	143,135	28,708	114,427
R.B. Annis WRI Endowment	869,806	3,726	(54,396)		248	819,384	257,620	561,764
Subtotal	17,243,653	244,823	(1,063,978)	643,739	(149,017)	15,631,742	6,878,245	8,753,497
Life Income and Annuity Funds								
Ross W. Perry Charitable Remainder Unitrust	278,907	-	(16,553)	27,743	-	234,611	27,772	206,839
Ralph and Grace Hauenstein Charitable Gift Annuity	-	229,748	(1,137)	-	-	228,611	(1,137)	229,748
Harvey E. Lemmen Charitable Gift Annuities	-	617,992	(23,725)	-	-	594,267	(23,725)	617,992
Dr. Dorothy Merrill Charitable Gift Annuity	-	16,969	(1,903)	-	-	15,066	(1,903)	16,969
Subtotal	278,907	864,709	(43,318)	27,743	-	1,072,555	1,007	1,071,548
Total	$40,069,723	$3,546,234	$(2,575,332)	$1,595,677	$ -	$39,444,948	$14,277,220	$25,167,728

APPENDIX C

STANFORD UNIVERSITY
ANNUAL REPORT

Building a
University
That Lasts

2001 Annual Report

STANFORD UNIVERSITY

CONTENTS:

STANFORD FACTS:

Enrollment (2001): **14,173**

Undergraduate Students: **6,637**

Graduate Students: **7,536**

Degrees Awarded (2000–2001):

Bachelor's: **1,676**

Master's: **2,086**

Doctoral: **850**

The Stanford Professoriate: **1,701**

Nobel Laureates: **17**

Pulitzer Prize Winners: **4**

MacArthur Fellows: **23**

National Medal of Science Recipients: **21**

National Medal of Technology Recipients: **3**

American Academy of Arts and Sciences Members: **219**

National Academy of Sciences Members: **124**

National Academy of Engineering Members: **82**

American Philosophical Society Members: **41**

National Academy of Education Members: **24**

Wolf Foundation Prize Winners: **6**

Koret Foundation Prize Winners: **6**

Presidential Medal of Freedom Recipients: **2**

ON THE COVER The Frances C. Arrillaga Alumni
Center opened fall 2001. The 116,000-square-
foot center on Galvez Street features a two-story
"great hall" and other areas for visiting alumni.
Funded through the generosity of the Arrillaga
family and several other alumni donors, it honors
the memory of alumna Frances Arrillaga, who
worked tirelessly on behalf of Stanford until her
death in 1995. (Photograph by Linda A. Cicero)

Building a University That Lasts

John L. Hennessy

This first year of the millennium has been a time of extraordinary change and challenge—for Stanford University, for the nation, and for the world. California's energy crisis led to rolling blackouts; the global economy began a steady decline; and the dot-com juggernaut returned to earth. And on Tuesday, September 11, the world was shocked by unprecedented acts of terror against thousands of people going about their daily lives.

Some years offer more stability than others, but the future always holds the potential for uncertainty, whether natural or man-made. Certainly, this past year has been challenging. Challenges, however, also provide an opportunity for examining our goals and priorities and assessing how those challenges should affect our course. In the face of both long-term evolutionary changes and the more rapid revolutionary changes of the past year, the same question remains: How do we build a university that lasts and continues to excel?

Stanford has always been clear in its priorities and bold in its thinking. In October 2000, we launched a campaign to raise $1 billion for undergraduate education. This campaign, believed to be the largest ever devoted exclusively to undergraduate education at any college or university, is a clear statement of our priorities and the plan that we have been pursuing for nearly a decade. Given the revolutionary changes of this year, we might well ask ourselves: What does it mean to go forward with a campaign at this time, and can we achieve our goals?

The work that we are doing has never been more important. Stanford, from the time of its founding, has been about building futures. Just as our predecessors educated generations of leaders, researchers, doctors, and teachers, the students we are educating today will play an important role in building a better world for the generations to come. This campaign will ensure those generations are given every opportunity to do so.

From its earliest days, Stanford has countered adversity with perseverance. When Jane and Leland Stanford's only child died, they transformed their grief into something positive by founding a university in his name. Soon after the University opened its doors, Leland Stanford died. This event generated great economic uncertainty and strain for the new University. Jane Stanford demonstrated remarkable strength of will: Not only did she keep the doors open, she continued to envision a better and stronger future. In July 1904, in her last address to the Board of Trustees, she exhorted:

> "Let us not be afraid to outgrow old thoughts and ways, and dare to think on new lines as to the future of the work under our care. Let us not be poor copies of other universities. Let us be progressive."

Throughout its history, this University has met enormous challenges, including two major earthquakes, and thrived. Today, Stanford is a leader throughout the world in teaching and research. Among the more than 1,700 faculty members, there are 17 Nobel laureates, four Pulitzer Prize winners, and 21 recipients of the National Medal of Science. Their research initiatives have advanced the frontiers of knowledge in fields ranging from history to economics, from biomedical research to information technology. Our innovations in undergraduate education have generated both admirers and imitators. New initiatives, like the Stanford Graduate Fellowships and the Bio-X collaboration, have inspired others to create similar programs.

Resolute in our commitment to excellence, we recognize that such advances do not come from standing still. The Campaign for Undergraduate Education supports programs that offer the world's brightest students access to the best teachers and scholars, particularly through small classes and personal mentoring relationships. Given the challenges facing all of us, the innovations we have made—and continue to make—in our undergraduate curriculum have never been more important. Our commitment to provide an extraordinary education to our students, who will go on to become future leaders of our country and the world, is more critical than ever.

For more than a century, our mission has been constant: to educate "cultured and useful citizens" for the benefit of humankind. In his last letter to President Jordan, Leland Stanford wrote: "The imagination needs to be cultivated and developed to assure success in life. A man will never construct anything he cannot conceive."

If we are to educate the leaders of tomorrow, we must cultivate intellectual curiosity. The Campaign for Undergraduate Education is an investment in cultivating the imagination and creativity of the extraordinary undergraduates who come to Stanford.

We have already begun to see the dividends from our investments in programs like Freshman and Sophomore Seminars, Overseas Studies, and Undergraduate Research Programs. Our return on that investment comes from the students whose lives we change—students like Sulggi Lee. Ms. Lee, a member of the Class of 1998, majored in Human Biology and minored in Latin American Studies. Research during overseas study in Santiago, Chile, led to an Undergraduate Research Opportunities grant and her Honors Research Thesis on the respiratory effects of particulate air contamination. But more important, Ms. Lee noted:

> "I learned to see academics as a gift, ... I learned to study just for the sake of learning and understanding. ... Most of all, I learned a lot about myself and gained the kind of self-confidence that propels me forward to this day."

Jane and Leland Stanford transformed their grief into a living gift that nurtures students like Sulggi Lee more than a hundred years later. It is now our responsibility to pass this gift on to future generations. We cannot predict what discoveries will come from our investments, nor what roles our students will play after they graduate. Nonetheless, just as Jane and Leland Stanford would be incredibly proud of the return on their investment, I am confident that we can and will be proud of the results from our investments in Stanford and from our steadfast commitment to building a university that will endure the test of time.

JOHN L. HENNESSY
President

SUPPORTING
STANFORD'S
HIGHEST PRIORITIES

When President John Hennessy was inaugurated in October of 2000, he announced the five-year, $1 billion Campaign for Undergraduate Education, known as CUE. CUE, believed to be the largest fundraising campaign devoted to undergraduate education ever undertaken by a college or university, is a bold statement about Stanford's commitment to undergraduates.

Most capital campaigns include buildings, but CUE is focused on people, programs, and ideas—the very essence of Stanford. CUE is designed to ensure that Stanford continues to provide its exceptional under-graduate students with unrivaled access to faculty and with an important role in its research mission.

CUE'S OBJECTIVES ARE:

✦ $300 million to create the Stanford Endowment for Undergraduate Education. Among the targeted programs is Stanford Introductory Studies, which

includes Freshman and Sophomore Seminars and other small-group learning experiences.

✦ $300 million for endowed scholarships, including $250 million to ensure that Stanford can continue to admit students without regard for their ability to pay—a process called "need-blind" admission. Stanford is one of only a handful of private U.S. colleges and universities that provide this guarantee.

✦ $300 million to support the full range of opportunities available to undergraduates, including new and enhanced programs in the schools of Humanities and Sciences, Engineering, and Earth Sciences, as well as in the libraries, athletics, the Haas Center for Public Service, Overseas Studies, and Stanford in Washington.

✦ $100 million for The Stanford Fund for Undergraduate Education, which provides need-based scholarships and seed funding for ongoing curriculum and teaching innovations.

January 2001 ›

THE YEAR IN REVIEW

A LOOK BACK AT SELECTED STANFORD EVENTS DURING THE CALENDAR YEAR 2001

F.W. DE KLERK, FORMER PRESIDENT OF SOUTH AFRICA AND A NOBEL PRIZE WINNER, SPEAKS ABOUT SOUTH AFRICA'S PAST AND FUTURE TO A PACKED KRESGE AUDITORIUM AUDIENCE.

WILLIAM HEWLETT, AN ALUMNUS WHOSE VISION HELPED BUILD STANFORD INTO ONE OF THE WORLD'S PREEMINENT RESEARCH UNIVERSITIES, DIES JAN. 12.

MARY PRATT, PROFESSOR OF SPANISH AND PORTUGUESE, IS ELECTED SECOND VICE PRESIDENT OF THE MODERN LANGUAGE ASSOCIATION, A POSITION THAT WILL LEAD TO THE PRESIDENCY.

DEBRA ZUMWALT, A STANFORD ALUMNA AND PARTNER AT PILLSBURY WINTHROP LLP, IS NAMED GENERAL COUNSEL.

GENERAL MOTORS FUNDS A $3 MILLION RESEARCH LAB IN THE SCHOOL OF ENGINEERING FOR THREE YEARS TO STUDY "WORK SYSTEMS"– THE WAY PEO-PLE USE MATERIALS AND INFORMATION TO CREATE PRODUCTS AND SERVICES.

Clockwise from the top:

Among the students featured on the Campaign for Undergraduate Education (CUE) Web pages is Jason Walker, Class of 2003. Says Walker, "When I was in high school, one of my teachers warned me that college professors wouldn't care whether or not I came to class, and they wouldn't care if I passed or failed. So, that is what I was expecting when I got here. But, it's not anything like that at Stanford." ✦ The William and Flora Hewlett Foundation's record-breaking $400 million gift, which supports the School of Humanities and Sciences and CUE, was announced during a noon-time gathering in the Main Quadrangle. ✦ Walter Hewlett, chairman of the Hewlett Foundation, said the gift honors his late father's devotion to Stanford.

HEWLETT GIFT MAKES HISTORY

The stunning news was delivered to the campus community at a hastily scheduled noontime gathering May 2 in the Main Quadrangle. Upon being introduced by President John Hennessy, Walter B. Hewlett, chairman of the William and Flora Hewlett Foundation, said simply: "The board of directors of the William and Flora Hewlett Foundation [has] unanimously approved a gift to Stanford University of $400 million."

The crowd of several hundred faculty and students—alerted to the event by an e-mail promising an "unprecedented historical announcement"—initially gasped in awe and then broke out in applause.

When Hewlett went on to say that $300 million of the gift was for the School of Humanities and Sciences (H&S) and $100 million for the Campaign for Undergraduate Education, the gasps and applause turned into sustained cheers. At that time, it was the largest single gift to an American college or university.

"This gift honors my father, who passed away in January, and honors his lifetime of philanthropy, his lifelong devotion to Stanford, and his passionate belief in the value of a liberal arts education," Walter Hewlett said, referring to his late father, the engineering pioneer

William R. Hewlett, who established the foundation in 1966.

Although it is the largest of Stanford's seven schools, H&S has strained its resources in recent years to remain competitive with the schools of liberal arts at comparable institutions. The school offers 90 percent of the University's undergraduate instruction, awards nearly half of the doctoral degrees, and represents 41 percent of tenure-line faculty. The foundation's gift includes support for unrestricted endowment and matching funds for designated priorities, including professorships and graduate fellowships.

CUE builds on the renaissance in undergraduate programs at Stanford during the past decade. Most of these programs, including Stanford Introductory Studies, were funded through University seed money or expendable gifts. From 1994 to 2001, the University increased its budget for these initiatives from $4 million to $17 million. CUE seeks gifts to the endowment to make these enhancements permanent parts of the Stanford undergraduate program.

When Stanford announced the campaign, $429 million in gifts and pledges already had been committed. Six months later, CUE passed the halfway mark. At the end of the 2000-2001 fiscal year, CUE totaled $639 million. Among the gifts accelerating the campaign's progress was a $100 million gift—part of a larger $400 million gift—from the Hewlett Foundation (see accompanying story).

The campaign builds on the work of the Commission on Undergraduate Education, appointed in 1993 by President Gerhard Casper. The commission's report led to the creation of the programs that CUE is designed to support.

In the fall, Stanford began offering CUE-related events—called "Think Again"—in cities throughout the country to bring the current undergraduate experience to life for alumni, parents, and friends.

MEET THE STUDENTS

The Campaign for Undergraduate Education Web pages (http://cue.stanford.edu) have provided alumni and others with opportunities to meet, read the online journals of, and exchange e-mail messages with the students their gifts benefit. Below are comments from two featured students.

KATE PEDATELLA, CLASS OF 2003
"It's such an amazing feeling to be taught by someone who wrote the textbook," Pedatella says of her Freshman Seminar, "Saints: The Rhetoric of Religious Perfection," taught by French Professor Brigitte Cazelles. "I'll never get over that! What made the class so rewarding was that Professor Cazelles always seemed to value our opinions so much. Obviously she's a world-renowned scholar in her field, but she sought our thoughts about what she'd written. She made us feel that, despite our age, we knew something or had the potential to know something."

TONY SUNG, CLASS OF 2004
"One of the best parts of Sophomore College was the opportunity to spend so much time with a respected faculty member in nontraditional settings. Professor [Richard] Zare would often share our meals, eating every lunch with us and twice inviting us to his home for dinner. His office door is open even on weekends, and conversations are not limited to science. I feel privileged to be at Stanford, where professors like Richard Zare are the rule rather than the exception and gifts of learning are freely passed on to later generations."

February 2001 >

RANDALL LIVINGSTON, A STANFORD ALUMNUS AND EXECUTIVE VICE PRESIDENT, CHIEF FINANCIAL OFFICER, AND DIRECTOR OF OPEN TV, IS NAMED VICE PRESIDENT FOR BUSINESS AFFAIRS AND CHIEF FINANCIAL OFFICER.

LADORIS CORDELL, A STANFORD ALUMNA AND SANTA CLARA COUNTY JUDGE, IS NAMED VICE PROVOST AND SPECIAL COUNSELOR TO THE PRESIDENT FOR CAMPUS RELATIONS.

A STUDY OF LAKE TITICACA, CO-AUTHORED BY GEOLOGY PROFESSOR ROBERT DUNBAR IN THE JOURNAL *SCIENCE*, DEMONSTRATES HOW NATURE CAN PRODUCE SUDDEN, UNEXPECTED CLIMATE CHANGES THAT AFFECT THE ENTIRE PLANET.

PRESIDENT HENNESSY AND EIGHT OTHER RESEARCH UNIVERSITY PRESIDENTS AGREE TO WORK TOWARD GENDER EQUALITY FOR WOMEN FACULTY IN SCIENCE AND ENGINEERING.

ALUMNA LINDA MEIER RECEIVES THE "DEGREE OF UNCOMMON WOMAN," THE UNIVERSITY'S HIGHEST HONOR, FOR EXTRAORDINARY SERVICE.

PSYCHOLOGY PROFESSOR JOHN GABRIELI AUTHORS A STUDY IN *NEUROREPORT* THAT SHOWS CHILDREN SUFFERING FROM DYSLEXIA HAVE A BIOLOGICAL DISRUPTION IN HOW THEIR BRAINS ARE WIRED FOR LANGUAGE AND READING.

CONTINUING
THE RENAISSANCE

Undergraduate education at Stanford has been virtually transformed since the Commission on Undergraduate Education concluded its comprehensive review in 1994. During the past several years, under the purview of the new office of the vice provost for undergraduate education, Stanford has intensified small-group learning experiences for freshmen and sophomores through such programs as:

✦ Freshman and Sophomore Seminars, limited to 16 students, which are taught by tenure-line professors, including those from Stanford's law, business, and medical schools;

✦ Sophomore Dialogues, which enroll no more than five students in an intensive course of directed reading;

✦ Sophomore College, which is a two-week residential academic program for returning sophomores held just prior to the start of the school year and featuring an intensive learning experience in a class with just 12 students;

✦ Freshman-Sophomore College, which brings together 180 freshmen and sophomores in one living area for a two-year

program combining courses offered in the residence with special programs led by faculty and advising staff; and

✦ Introduction to the Humanities, which builds a foundation during the freshman year for the study of human thought, values, and culture.

In addition, resources have been committed to enhancing writing education through the creation of a new writing center and expansion of the writing requirement to include rhetoric and oral communication.

With many of these initiatives successfully underway, Stanford's attention has turned to the experience of juniors and seniors. Research opportunities have been augmented and major fields of studies strengthened.

In January, Vice Provost for Undergraduate Education John Bravman announced new faculty grants for independent study and research designed to enhance research opportunities for undergraduates. The grants fall under a new organization called Undergraduate Research Programs that places all such programs—including the highly successful Undergraduate Research Opportunities

JOHN CIOFFI, ALICE GAST, AND AMOS NUR ARE ELECTED TO THE NATIONAL ACADEMY OF ENGINEERING, ONE OF THE HIGHEST PROFESSIONAL DISTINCTIONS ACCORDED ENGINEERS.

March 2001 ›

THE BOARD OF TRUSTEES SETS RATES FOR UNDERGRADUATE TUITION, ROOM, AND BOARD FOR 2001- 2002 REFLECTING A 5.4 PERCENT INCREASE OF PREVIOUS RATES. THE BOARD ALSO IMPROVES THE UNIVERSITY'S FINANCIAL AID PROGRAM FOR THE FOURTH YEAR IN A ROW.

BIOCOMPUTATION, WHICH USES POWERFUL COMPUTERS TO SOLVE COMPLEX PROBLEMS IN THE BIOSCIENCES, TAKES A GIANT LEAP FORWARD WITH THE INSTALLATION AT THE GATES BUILDING OF AN SGI ORIGIN 3800 SUPERCOMPUTER.

THE REV. SCOTTY McLENNAN IS INSTALLED AS THE NEW DEAN FOR RELIGIOUS LIFE.

ECONOMICS PROFESSOR JOHN B. TAYLOR IS NOMINATED BY PRESIDENT GEORGE W. BUSH TO BE UNDERSECRETARY OF THE TREASURY FOR INTERNATIONAL AFFAIRS.

GEOLOGIST MARK ZOBACK THEORIZES IN THE JOURNAL GEOLOGY THAT THE CONTINUING REBOUNDING OF PAST GLACIERS CONTRIBUTES TO EARTHQUAKES TODAY.

PEHONG CHEN, FOUNDER AND CEO OF BROADVISION, AND HIS WIFE, ADELE, DONATE $15 MILLION TO ESTABLISH A NEW INSTITUTE FOR THE STUDY OF PARTICLE ASTROPHYSICS AND COSMOLOGY.

Clockwise from the top:

Jo Boaler, associate professor of education, is among the faculty members whose research group welcomes undergraduates, including Hermione Giffard, Sean Whalen, and Lisa Yiu. ✦ Jamie Hui and Terence Chia were among the students pursuing research during the Summer Research College. Hui is sequencing genes that may be involved in basal cell carcinoma, while Chia studied a fluorescence catheter that detects plaque in arteries or cancer cells in intestines. Chia calls the Summer Research College a "very horizon-broadening experience. During the day, you go to the lab and do research. You come back and talk to people who have diverse interests and are very passionate about them."

THE POWER OF UNDERGRADUATE RESEARCH

One of the first new faculty grants for Stanford undergraduate research, announced recently by Vice Provost John Bravman, was awarded to Jo Boaler, associate professor of education (see photo above top). She worked with three undergraduates to evaluate the effectiveness of mathematics teaching at three area high schools.

"They were fantastic," says Boaler of her undergraduate assistants. As a member of a graduate faculty, Boaler doesn't interact as much as she would like with undergraduates. Her research project, which also includes doctoral research assistants, follows about 1,000 students over four years of high school, examining qualitative and quantitative

data as the students go through different mathematics programs.

"I was really impressed with the undergraduates' insights," she says. "I didn't necessarily expect them to be as good as they were."

The admiration was mutual, according to sophomores Sean Whalen and Hermione Giffard.

"It was the first research project I'd ever been on, so it was interesting to be in a situation where you don't know the outcome of your experiment," says Whalen. "In most situations in school, for example, all the problems presented are ones that have definite solutions that someone has already calculated. Working with Professor Boaler was very different."

He adds, "I really liked working in a small group. I liked how much responsibility they gave us. I wasn't expecting to be so integral to the group, but they really got us involved in directing the path of the study."

Says Giffard, "The best thing that I've gotten from this project is an enticing view into issues affecting teaching and learning—how best to do each and how the two affect one another. It broadened my worldview and changed many of my preconceptions."

SUMMER RESEARCH COLLEGE EXPANDS

Now in its second year, Stanford's Summer Research College (SRC) gives undergraduates pursuing research an opportunity to build a community among students with similar interests.

Linking the many department-based research programs for undergraduates, the SRC makes summer research feasible through housing subsidies. The eight- to 10-week program follows the models of Honors College and Sophomore College, both of which have combined residential and academic life.

In addition to performing their research duties, students meet each week to give short presentations about their work, exposing each other to subjects as diverse as infant language processing, beliefs about illness in Ghana, and proteins that protect the heart.

"The goal is to allow students to experience research over a concentrated period of time," says Susan Brubaker-Cole, director of undergraduate research programs in the Office of the Vice Provost for Undergraduate Education. "They learn what kinds of questions researchers ask and what counts as legitimate evidence." A few co-author papers with faculty members.

Psychology Professor Russell Fernald mentored four students through the SRC. He lauds the energy undergraduates bring to the lab. "They have a willingness to work hard, to ask questions, and they don't have preconceptions. And, they see how slow it is to find new knowledge—it gives them another perspective."

John Bravman

program—under one umbrella. During the 2000-01 academic year, the office gave $1.47 million for programs involving 795 students.

"This ties students more into the central mission of scholarship of the University in a way that many faculty and students find extremely rewarding," Bravman says. "The non-classroom component of a Stanford education can be as important as anything done in a classroom."

AMONG THE INITIATIVE'S NEW PROGRAMS ARE:

- grants that allow undergraduates to work individually with faculty mentors, providing a bridge between introductory course work and more advanced independent study during the junior and senior years;

- expansion of a similar program that makes funding available for department-based undergraduate research offerings; and

- Summer Research College, which expanded from 70 students in its pilot year last year to 165 students in 2001. The college allows students who have secured summer research positions to live together in a dorm with a significant portion of their room and board costs subsidized. Social activities provide a scholarly community for the students.

In addition, to strengthen the major, the Faculty Senate approved guidelines for comprehensive reviews of all undergraduate degree-granting programs every six to eight years.

April 2001 >

May 2001 >

ASSOCIATE PROFESSOR OF CHEMISTRY CHRISTOPHER CHIDSEY REPORTS IN *SCIENCE* THAT HE AND HIS STUDENTS HAVE SYNTHESIZED A MATERIAL THAT WILL BE IMPORTANT IN FUTURE APPLICATIONS OF NANOTECHNOLOGY.

THE UNIVERSITY MAKES OFFERS OF ADMISSION TO 2,406 FOR THE 1,600-STUDENT CLASS OF 2005—A CLASS THAT WILL BE AMONG STANFORD'S MOST DIVERSE.

HOWARD WOLF IS APPOINTED PRESIDENT OF THE STANFORD ALUMNI ASSOCIATION.

JUNIOR DONALD MATSUDA IS AMONG 80 STUDENTS NATIONWIDE AWARDED TRUMAN SCHOLARSHIPS.

SHARON LONG IS APPOINTED THE VERNON R. & LYSBETH WARREN ANDERSON DEAN OF THE SCHOOL OF HUMANITIES AND SCIENCES.

THE HEWLETT FOUNDATION PLEDGES STANFORD $400 MILLION IN UNRESTRICTED ENDOWMENT FUNDS. AT THAT TIME, IT IS THE LARGEST PLEDGE TO A UNIVERSITY.

RELENTLESSLY
PURSUING
NEW KNOWLEDGE

As one of the nation's leading research universities, Stanford has been at the forefront of discovery and innovation, participating, for instance, in the creation and application of the information technology and biotechnology revolutions.

Stanford scholars and researchers have been credited with creating the process for recombinant DNA cloning, performing the first heart transplant in North America, producing the discoveries that have led to magnetic resonance imaging, and inventing new laser technology, music synthesizers, and the global positioning system.

Following are some of the ongoing efforts through which Stanford researchers and their graduate and undergraduate students are contributing to scholarship and society today.

Enhancing biomedical research Biomedical research is being strengthened with the construction of the James H. Clark Center for Biomedical Engineering and Sciences. The Clark Center is at the core of an initiative—known as Bio-X—that brings together the biosciences, physical sciences, medicine, and engineering to focus on interdisciplinary biomedical research.

Unlocking the human genome Stanford teams involved in the International Human Genome Sequencing Consortium joined colleagues this year to announce the analysis of the human genome sequence—the 3 billion DNA letters that comprise the complete set of human genes. The teams were headed by geneticists Richard Myers and Ronald Davis.

Creating engineering marvels The School of Engineering has a widespread reputation for innovation. Among its most recent contributions are a microphone array necklace that increases speech discernment for the hearing impaired, an innovative camera that uses a single chip and pixel-level processing to render enhanced images, and a low-cost magnetic resonance imaging scanner that provides better contrast in soft tissue compared to other imaging techniques. Stanford faculty are also among the most widely

PHYSICIST CHARLES PRESCOTT AND BIOLOGIST CHRISTOPHER FIELD ARE ELECTED TO THE NATIONAL ACADEMY OF SCIENCES.

W.S. DI PIERO, PROFESSOR OF ENGLISH, ROELAND NUSSE, PROFESSOR OF DEVELOPMENTAL BIOLOGY, AND W.E. MOERNER, PROFESSOR OF CHEMISTRY, ARE ELECTED FELLOWS OF THE AMERICAN ACADEMY OF ARTS AND SCIENCES.

THE RENOVATED THOMAS WELTON STANFORD ART GALLERY REOPENS WITH THE 2001 MASTER OF FINE ARTS EXHIBITION.

FOR THE FIRST TIME IN THE NATION, HUMAN CELLS COAXED IN THE LABORATORY TO BECOME NEURONS ARE IMPLANTED INTO THE BRAIN OF A STROKE-IMPAIRED MAN UNDER A TRIAL DIRECTED BY NEUROSURGEON GARY STEINBERG.

PROFESSORS DAVID M. KENNEDY, JAMES SHEEHAN, AND JAMES MARCH ARE NAMED TO THE AMERICAN PHILOSOPHICAL SOCIETY.

NOVELIST DOROTHY ALLISON SPEAKS AS PART OF THE 2001 TANNER LECTURES IN HUMAN VALUES.

THE CAMPUS SAYS GOOD-BYE IN WHITE PLAZA TO JAMES MONTOYA, OUTGOING VICE PROVOST FOR STUDENT AFFAIRS.

CHYBA AWARDED MacARTHUR FELLOWSHIP

Christopher Chyba, a prominent astro-biologist, former White House security adviser and co-director of the Stanford Center for International Security and Cooperation (CISAC), was one of 23 people awarded a 2001 fellowship from the John D. and Catherine T. MacArthur Foundation.

Chyba, an associate professor (research) of geological and environmental sciences, becomes the 23rd Stanford winner of the so-called "genius award." In granting the fellowship, the foundation cited Chyba's "passion for understanding life on Earth and for protecting human civilization from self-destruction," as well as his recent work focusing on "the relationship between preparing for biological terrorism and improving public health."

The unrestricted fellowships are given to talented individuals who have demonstrated extraordinary originality. Each recipient receives a $500,000 "no-strings-attached" stipend.

During the Clinton administration, Chyba served as director for environmental affairs for the National Security Council and as energy liaison for the White House Office of Science and Technology. In February 2000, he became co-director of CISAC—part of Stanford's Institute for International Studies—which brings together scholars, policymakers, and other experts to focus on international security questions.

Christopher Chyba

June 2001 ›

recognized pioneers in nanotechnology, particularly in such areas as microscopy, microsensors, and nanomaterials.

Understanding the importance of sleep Stanford faculty such as William Dement have long been at the forefront of the study of sleep. Emmanuel Mignot, director of the Center for Narcolepsy, recently identified the gene that causes narcolepsy. Other researchers are now working to make sense of a link between apnea, a common sleep disorder, and Alzheimer's disease.

Rethinking American history Stanford's American historians are among the most recognized, including Pulitzer Prize winners David Kennedy and Jack Rakove. Kennedy's *Freedom from Fear* is a comprehensive history of the Great Depression, the New Deal, and World War II. Rakove's *Original Meanings: Politics and Ideas in the Making of the Constitution* challenges 'originalism' as a method of interpreting the framers' intentions.

Probing the universe Stanford researchers are among scientists worldwide seeking a better understanding of the fundamental particles of matter and the nature of the universe. The international BaBar Collaboration at the Stanford Linear Accelerator Center released initial results on the behavior of subatomic particles known as B mesons. Their experiments provide clues about why our universe contains more matter than antimatter. At the Hansen Experimental Physics Laboratory, physicists involved in Gravity Probe B are preparing to launch into space an experiment testing Einstein's theory of relativity in 2002.

Pushing the humanities envelope Scholarship in the humanities is expanding because of the Stanford Humanities Laboratory (SHL). SHL provides seed money to collaborative,

HOPKINS MARINE STATION OPENS THE STATE-OF-THE-ART MAZIA MICROSCOPY CENTER.

THE UNIVERSITY CELEBRATES THE 20TH ANNIVERSARY OF THE NATION'S FIRST PROGRAM IN FEMINIST STUDIES.

ATHLETICS DIRECTOR TED LELAND ACCEPTS STANFORD'S SEVENTH SEARS DIRECTORS CUP AS THE NATION'S TOP DIVISION I COLLEGE SPORTS PROGRAM.

STANFORD ALUMNA CARLY FIORINA, CEO OF HEWLETT-PACKARD, ADDRESSES 29,000 PEOPLE AT THE 110TH COMMENCEMENT CEREMONIES.

ECONOMICS PROFESSOR ANNE KRUEGER IS APPOINTED FIRST DEPUTY MANAGING DIRECTOR OF THE INTERNATIONAL MONETARY FUND.

ALONG WITH THE PRESIDENTS OF 27 OTHER INSTITUTIONS, PRESIDENT HENNESSY ENDORSES PRINCIPLES AIMED AT ENSURING FINANCIAL AID IS DISTRIBUTED FAIRLY TO STUDENTS BASED ON THEIR LEVEL OF NEED.

Clockwise from the upper left-hand corner:

Psychology professor Brian Wandell and Electrical Engineering faculty member Abbas El-Gamal and their students have developed a camera-on-a-chip that captures images at 10,000 frames per second, processes one billion pixels per second, and sets a record for continuous imaging. ✦ A. Michael Spence, the Philip H. Knight Professor Emeritus and former dean of the Graduate School of Business, shared the 2001 Nobel Memorial Prize in Economic Sciences for his work in information economics (see story below). ✦ The work of biologist Barbara Block of the Hopkins Marine Station is influencing international marine conservation efforts.

A NOBEL PRIZE FOR SPENCE AND STIGLITZ

A. Michael Spence (photo top right), the Philip H. Knight Professor Emeritus and the former dean of the Graduate School of Business, and Joseph Stiglitz, a professor emeritus of economics now at Columbia, were awarded the 2001 Nobel Memorial Prize in Economic Sciences. They shared the $1 million prize with George Akerlof of the University of California at Berkeley. Stanford is now home to 17 living Nobel laureates.

The Royal Swedish Academy of Sciences awarded the prize for the trio's work in information economics. In the 1970s, the laureates laid the groundwork for a theory about markets with so-called "asymmetric" information. Their work explained how agents with differing amounts of information affect many kinds of markets. In its announcement, the Royal Swedish Academy of Sciences said that

the winners' contributions "form the core of modern information economics."

Their work has led to real-world applications in areas ranging from agricultural markets to modern financial markets, according to the academy.

Biomedical research is being strengthened with the construction of the James H. Clark Center for Biomedical Engineering and Sciences.

interdisciplinary projects whose results are considered non-traditional. For instance, dpResearch: A Digital Performance Journal, is exploring and expanding the notion of perform-ance. The project will result in a Website that is a cross between an online journal and exhibition space.

Studying disease at a cellular level Molecular and genetic medicine are among the specialties of Stanford researchers who search for the root causes of disease. Among them is biochemist Patrick Brown, a researcher at the Howard Hughes Medical Institute, whose work with DNA microarrays was singled out by the National Cancer Institute as representing the best hope for cancer diagnosis and treatment.

Conserving the ocean's resources Stanford's Hopkins Marine Station is the oldest marine laboratory on the American Pacific Coast. Among the researchers seeking a better understanding of the marine world is biologist Barbara Block, who works with the Tuna Research and Conservation Center, a joint project of Hopkins and the Monterey Bay Aquarium. Her research could affect interna-tional efforts to conserve the bluefin tuna, whose numbers have sharply declined.

Leading in digital-age law Scholars at the School of Law have made a major effort to be the leaders in technology-related law research and teaching through the Law, Science & Technology Program and the new Center for Internet and Society. Among them is Lawrence Lessig, whose book, *Code and Other Laws of Cyberspace*, stirred debate through its exploration of how the architecture of computer net-works affects basic liberties. Another scholar, John Barton, is heading an international commission investigating how intellectual property rules affect developing nations.

Focusing on writing Stanford has long been recognized for its writing programs, partly because of the Creative Writing Program founded by Wallace Stegner more than 50 years ago. Two new gifts to the endowment support a visiting prose writer and visiting poet every year.

Highlighting environmental research Stanford has launched the Environmental Initiative to bring together the work of some 56 faculty working in 15 areas related to the environment. Stanford is particularly strong in environ-mental law, population studies, geochemistry, climate change, agricultural sustainability, energy policy, biodiver-sity, and world health.

Exploring the worlds of music For all their stylistic differ-ences, the composition faculty in the Department of Music share international recognition. Last year's performances of Stanford composers covered cities around the globe. Melissa Hui's soundtrack for the Oscar-nominated National Film Board of Canada documentary *Sunrise Over Tiananmen Square* was heard worldwide at film festivals.

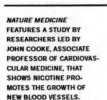

July 2001 ›

August 2001 ›

CONSTRUCTION WORKERS AT BUILDING 160– THE WALLENBERG GLOBAL LEARNING CENTER– DISCOVER A FORGOTTEN TIME CAPSULE BURIED BY JANE STANFORD MORE THAN A CENTURY AGO.

NATURE MEDICINE FEATURES A STUDY BY RESEARCHERS LED BY JOHN COOKE, ASSOCIATE PROFESSOR OF CARDIOVAS-CULAR MEDICINE, THAT SHOWS NICOTINE PRO-MOTES THE GROWTH OF NEW BLOOD VESSELS.

ANTHROPOLOGIST JOHN RICK AND HIS STUDENTS UNEARTH 3,000-YEAR-OLD STROMBUS SHELLS AT THE ANCIENT PERUVIAN CENTER CHAVIN DE HUANTAR.

SCIENTISTS FROM STANFORD AND SEVEN EUROPEAN AND CANADIAN INSTITUTIONS ANNOUNCE IN *SCIENCE* THE DECOD-ING OF THE GENOME OF A MICROBE PROVIDING AN ESSENTIAL SOURCE OF NITROGEN.

GENE AWAKUNI, VICE PRESIDENT FOR STUDENT SERVICES AT COLUMBIA UNIVERSITY, IS NAMED VICE PROVOST FOR STUDENT AFFAIRS.

TO PROTEST PRESIDENT GEORGE W. BUSH'S POLICY ON STEM-CELL RESEARCH, ENTREPRENEUR JIM CLARK SUSPENDS PAYMENT OF $60 MILLION OF HIS $150 MILLION PLEDGE FOR STANFORD'S NEW PROGRAM, BIO-X.

INVESTING
IN COMMUNITY

In March 2001 President John Hennessy invited faculty, staff, and students to "Taking Stock: Five Successes—and Five Continuing Challenges," a presentation before the Academic Council.

Among the successes the president cited was the negotiation with Santa Clara County of a new General Use Permit and Community Plan overseeing land use on campus for the next decade.

The General Use Permit allows Stanford to add 2 million additional square feet of academic facilities and up to 3,000 new housing units on campus, while preserving more than 2,000 acres of the campus foothills for 25 years. The agreement involved a complex set of understandings in areas as diverse as open space, traffic, financial support for schools, and land for community services.

In the aftermath of the General Use Permit approval, the president identified one of Stanford's challenges as bolstering relationships with neighbors in the surrounding communities.

"This will require us to do a better job of listening and responding to the community concerns about our plans as we communicate the challenges and opportunities that Stanford faces," he said.

Among the steps he announced to improve community relations was the creation of a group to review the public access policy for the conservation area in the Stanford foothills. Also, local residents have been invited to celebrate Community Day at Stanford in spring 2002, a new event underscoring the University's many assets and contributions to the quality of life within the region.

Such moves will augment many existing programs and contributions to local communities. For instance, 128 acres of Stanford's lands are used by five public schools. About 40 percent of the students in the Palo Alto school district at any one time attend school in one of the four Palo Alto schools on Stanford lands. In addition, Stanford gave $10 million to the Palo Alto

September 2001 ›

THE CAMPUS JOINS THE NATION IN MOURNING THE TRAGIC TERRORIST EVENTS OF SEPT. 11. MOST CAMPUS EVENTS ARE CANCELED OR RESCHEDULED.

October 2001 ›

GROUND IS BROKEN FOR THE NEW CENTER FOR CANCER TREATMENT, WHICH IS SCHEDULED TO BE COMPLETED IN THE SUMMER OF 2003.

COIT "CHIP" BLACKER, DEPUTY DIRECTOR OF THE INSTITUTE FOR INTERNATIONAL STUDIES, IS AWARDED THE LAURANCE AND NAOMI CARPENTER HOAGLAND PRIZE FOR UNDERGRADUATE TEACHING.

THE TAUBE FAMILY FOUNDATION COMMITS $2.5 MILLION TO ENDOW THE TAUBE CENTER FOR JEWISH STUDIES. THE CENTER WILL GIVE THE PROGRAM IN JEWISH STUDIES MORE OPPORTUNITY TO EXPAND ITS CURRICULUM, ORGANIZE CONFERENCES, AND FUND RESEARCH.

AN ENVIRONMENTAL INITIATIVE IS ANNOUNCED TO UNDERSCORE THE UNIVERSITY'S LEADERSHIP IN ENVIRONMENTAL RESEARCH AND EDUCATION.

REUNION DRAWS A RECORD-BREAKING 6,700 PARTICIPANTS.

FORMER PAKISTANI LEADER BENAZIR BHUTTO BACKS U.S. MILITARY EFFORTS IN AFGHANISTAN BEFORE A CAPACITY CROWD IN MEMORIAL AUDITORIUM.

Clockwise from the upper left:

Nadinne Cruz, director of the Haas Center for Public Service, estimates there are at least 319 community-related groups across the University. ✦ The East Palo Alto Tennis and Tutoring Program, housed at the Taube Family Tennis Stadium, involves some 150 volunteers and 13 staff who provide one-on-one tutoring and tennis lessons to about 100 K-12 students. ✦ In recognition of area traffic challenges and the requirements of the new General Use Permit and Community Plan, Stanford will be increasing efforts such as "Bike-to-Work Day" to decrease single-occupant automobile trips to campus.

FOCUSING ON TRANSPORTATION

Transportation and traffic are issues of intense concern among those living and working on the Peninsula. Stanford is expanding its already widely recognized transportation programs to contribute to regional solutions.

Stanford's Marguerite bus system, for instance, is believed to be the largest free, privately run, open-to-the-public transit system anywhere. The Marguerite runs throughout campus, to Caltrain stations serving Stanford, and to major commercial areas on campus and in Palo Alto and Menlo Park.

The University's Transportation Demand Management (TDM) programs—the most extensive in Santa Clara County—also include a vanpool and carpool incentive program, a Guaranteed Ride Home Program, a Clean Air Cash Rewards Program, and a Bicycle Support Program (see photo above). Among the organizations recognizing the University's TDM programs have been the American Lung Association, the Peninsula Corridor Joint Powers Board, and the Peninsula Conservation Center Foundation.

The new General Use Permit negotiated with Santa Clara County requires that future development create no net new commute trips for Stanford. As a result, Stanford will continue to focus new construction in the core campus and near transit corridors to reduce traffic congestion. Students, faculty, and staff are encouraged to walk or bike, on-campus housing is being increased, and investments are being made in additional alternative transportation programs.

APPLYING EDUCATIONAL THEORY

The Ravenswood City School District had been without a public high school for 25 years. But, thanks to collaboration among Stanford's School of Education, a Bay Area nonprofit organization, and the district, a new school opened in September. The collaboration is just one among many projects through which Stanford reaches out to area school districts.

Stanford Professor of Education Linda Darling-Hammond, along with a half-dozen other faculty, helped design the charter school, the first in the area since Ravenswood High School closed in 1976.

Plans for creating a new community school took root last year, when Aspire Public Schools, a nonprofit organization dedicated to creating small schools, and Stanford School of Education professors began working with the Ravenswood City School District. They received funding from the state of California, the Bill and Melinda Gates Foundation, and Hewlett-Packard.

Stanford is providing curriculum development and support and school design assistance. The University also helped recruit staff and fundraise for the school. The School of Education plans to take advantage of the chance to give teachers in training practical experience—the Stanford Teacher Education Program will send student teachers to work with experienced teachers at the school.

schools to support construction of a new middle school and offered land to the city of Palo Alto for a new city community center.

Stanford's volunteer efforts in the surrounding communities may not be widely known, according to Nadinne Cruz, director of the Haas Center for Public Service, who gave a presentation this year to the Faculty Senate called "Stanford in the Community: The Untold Story." Cruz is documenting the many Stanford organizations with outreach to the area communities. Stanford has at least 319 such organized service efforts across 20 major programs and departments, Cruz reports.

"I discovered so many deep and true tales that I have come to be a believer in the individuals I have met and the programs that have been evident all across Stanford. And I'm very proud of what those individuals do," she said.

"There are costs to not telling this story," she adds. Cruz suspects a lack of knowledge of the efforts of members of the University community can lead to misperceptions in the surrounding cities.

AMONG THE UNIVERSITY'S MANY OUTREACH PROGRAMS ARE:

+ the East Palo Alto Law Project, in which volunteer law students work on special projects, counseling as many as 225 people annually;

+ the Tom Ford Community Outreach Program, which supports Stanford athletes in participating in visits to hospitals and holiday food drives;

Among the steps the president announced to improve community relations was the appointment of a group to review the public access policy for the conservation area in the Stanford foothills.

+ the Ravenswood Reads program, which provides more than 150 student tutors;

+ the East Palo Alto Tennis and Tutoring Program, in which 150 volunteers and 13 staff provide one-on-one tutoring and tennis lessons to about 100 K-12 students;

+ the Arbor Free Clinic, in which medical students, undergraduates, and physicians provide free medical care to some 1,000 uninsured and underinsured patients; and

+ Barrio Assistance, the oldest community service program on campus, through which El Centro Chicano students tutor and mentor Latino grade school students in East Palo Alto and East Menlo Park.

In addition, many University academic departments work collaboratively with community groups. For instance, in 2001, the Stanford Division of Child and Adolescent Psychiatry, with the Division of General Pediatrics and the Children's Health Council, received a grant aimed at building self-esteem and reducing high-risk behaviors among East Palo Alto middle school students.

November 2001 >

December 2001 >

ASTROBIOLOGIST CHRISTOPHER CHYBA, CO-DIRECTOR OF THE CENTER FOR INTERNATIONAL SECURITY AND COOPERATION, IS AWARDED A 2001 FELLOWSHIP BY THE JOHN D. AND CATHERINE T. MacARTHUR FOUNDATION.

EMERITI A. MICHAEL SPENCE AND JOSEPH STIGLITZ SHARE THE NOBEL PRIZE IN ECONOMICS, WHILE TWO OF THE THREE WINNERS OF THE NOBEL PRIZE IN PHYSICS EARNED DEGREES AT STANFORD.

THE AMERICAN ASSOCIATION FOR THE ADVANCEMENT OF SCIENCE ANNOUNCES ITS NEW FELLOWS, INCLUDING STANFORD'S ROBERT SIEMANN, CAROL BOGGS, ERIC KOOL, DAVID McKAY, JAMES SPUDICH, LUCY TOMPKINS, AND PAUL WENDER.

A $100 MILLION GRANT FROM THE DAVID AND LUCILE PACKARD FOUNDATION LAUNCHES THE $500 MILLION CAMPAIGN BY THE LUCILE PACKARD FOUNDATION FOR CHILDREN'S HEALTH ON BEHALF OF LUCILE PACKARD CHILDREN'S HOSPITAL AND PEDIATRIC RESEARCH AND TRAINING AT THE SCHOOL OF MEDICINE.

THE "THINK AGAIN" TOUR, CELEBRATING THE CAMPAIGN FOR UNDERGRADUATE EDUCATION, KICKS OFF IN PORTLAND, ORE.

A STANFORD LINEAR ACCELERATOR CENTER SYMPOSIUM MARKS THE 10TH ANNIVERSARY OF PAUL KUNZ'S CREATION OF THE FIRST U.S. WEBSITE.

Putting Stanford in Perspective

Isaac Stein

The 1990s were a time of unparalleled growth in the U.S. economy. Until last year, Stanford, like many universities, saw its endowment earnings soar. Some people may have wondered why Stanford did not use more of those extraordinary gains to meet operating expenses. And why would we launch the $1 billion Campaign for Undergraduate Education (CUE) if the University could simply spend more of its endowment to cover new undergraduate programs?

A year like fiscal 2000-2001 answers that question. Just as the U.S. and international economies declined, so too did the value of Stanford's endowment, which decreased by approximately seven percent, or more than $600 million. Clearly the University cannot count on soaring returns every year, nor can our programs fluctuate whenever the markets do. Stanford is committed to its students and faculty in perpetuity, and the University's financial plan must be similarly long-term.

At times like this, the prudence of Stanford's endowment "payout" policy becomes clear. Like most universities, Stanford spends only about five percent of its endowment each year, even if its actual income is higher. This payout is calculated taking into account several years of past performance in order to smooth the impact of market fluctuations. It is also calculated to ensure that the endowment grows with inflation, so that the amount of payout we can count on increases gradually over the years.

Because Stanford drew on the endowment carefully in the past, the University was able to meet its obligations last year despite the economic decline. We are also confident that, over the long term, Stanford's endowment performance will continue to compare very favorably with

that of other universities and with the markets in general. Stanford's endowment is an excellent investment.

But even with superb professional management, Stanford's current endowment goes only so far. And that, to return to the previous question, is the reason for the Campaign for Undergraduate Education.

In fiscal year 2001, payout from the endowment supported just 18.1 percent of the University's operating expenses, far less than some of our peer institutions. This payout is needed to preserve the new undergraduate programs, as well as the scope and quality of the entire Stanford enterprise. But it still left a tremendous financial challenge to maintain these programs, a challenge that Stanford must face each year.

This is why we need efforts such as CUE, which seeks further investment in Stanford's endowment, as well as an increase in the "living endowment" of annual giving. In undergraduate education, in graduate studies, and in law, business, and medicine, Stanford must not only preserve existing programs but also innovate continually. The flow of Stanford's intellectual endowment must never depend on the financial markets.

A university is an unusual organization, both conservative and progressive. Stanford represents both the value of stability and the spirit of innovation. If we continue to invest in this rare combination, whatever the future holds, our most important "investments" will grow.

Isaac Stein

ISAAC STEIN
Chair, Stanford University Board of Trustees

STANFORD UNIVERSITY

2001 Financial Review

CONTENTS:

Discussion of Financial Results

During the 2000-2001 fiscal year (FY01), Stanford benefited from the strong financial resources built over the past several years and the continued generous support of its alumni and friends. These factors enabled Stanford to successfully pursue its teaching and research missions despite a significantly weakened investment environment, a volatile health care market, and the continuing high costs of living in the Bay Area.

Highlights of the year included:

Initial success of the five-year, $1 billion Campaign for Undergraduate Education (CUE) ‣ This campaign is one of the largest ever devoted to undergraduate education at any university and will allow Stanford to continue implementing innovations in undergraduate education. When it was announced in October 2000, the campaign had already generated $429 million in gifts and pledges. At the end of the fiscal year, the campaign total was up to $639 million.

Receipt of the largest pledge in University history and one of the largest ever to any college or university ‣ On May 2, the William and Flora Hewlett Foundation announced a $400 million pledge to Stanford, benefiting the School of Humanities and Sciences and the Campaign for Undergraduate Education. In addition to being the largest pledge in Stanford history, at the time of the announcement, it was the largest pledge ever made to any college or university. The gift honors the late William Hewlett, a Stanford alumnus whose vision helped position the University as a world leader in innovation. Of the total $400 million Hewlett Foundation pledge, $300 million is earmarked to increase the endowment of the School of Humanities and Sciences and to create endowed professorships and student fellowships in the school. The remaining $100 million of the pledge is to the Campaign for Undergraduate Education. Half of the Humanities and Sciences pledge and the total CUE pledge are to match gifts from other donors.

One of the most successful overall development programs among universities nationwide ‣ Total cash gifts in FY01 were $469 million from 66,420 donors. Nearly 40 percent of undergraduate alumni gave gifts to the University. This was the second most successful year in Stanford's fundraising history.

Improved financial performance of Stanford Hospital and Clinics (SHC) and Lucile Packard Children's Hospital (LPCH) ‣ A strategic plan is in place that continues to move the Hospitals on the path to financial stability, despite the ongoing challenges of reductions in federal reimbursements for academic medical centers. (See further discussion in the inset beginning on page 20.)

Continued capital improvement ‣ Construction commenced on the James H. Clark Center for Biomedical Engineering and Sciences. The construction was unaffected by Mr. Clark's decision to protest President George W. Bush's stem-cell policies by suspending $60 million of his $150 million pledge. Work also continues on the new Wallenberg Global Learning Center, and ground was broken for the Center for Cancer Treatment and Prevention/Ambulatory Care Pavilion.

Following is a review of the FY01 financial activities of the University, excluding the results of the Hospitals and Clinics (the Hospitals), which are discussed separately on page 21. The financial activities of the Hospitals are consolidated with the University and reported in a separate column of the financial statements. The UCSF Stanford Health Care joint venture is reported on the equity method and is also presented in the "Hospitals" column.

Statement of Activities

The Statement of Activities details operating revenues and expenses and other non-operating changes during the year and reports a total decline in the University's net assets of $571 million in FY01 compared to the $3.3 billion increase in the 1999-2000 fiscal year (FY00). The decrease in net assets is directly attributable to the decline in public and private equity market valuations. Total investment losses of $497 million were recognized in FY01, as compared to the total investment return of $2.8 billion in FY00. See the "Report from the Stanford Management Company" on page 25 for further discussion of investment performance. Additionally, gifts and pledges recorded in the financial statements—although still at high levels—were down from $848 million in FY00 to $460 million in FY01.

Unrestricted Net Assets

Results of Operations Operating activities include all revenues and expenses that are used to support current-year teaching and research efforts and other University priorities. Compared to FY00, total University revenues increased 1.4% to more than $2.0 billion, and total expenses increased 11.1% to approximately $2.0 billion. Operations resulted in an excess of revenues over expenses of $59 million in FY01, compared to $227 million in FY00.

HOSPITALS

Since April 1, 2000, after the operating activities of UCSF Stanford Health Care were terminated, the financial results and financial position of Stanford Hospital and Clinics (SHC) and Lucile Salter Packard Children's Hospital (LPCH) have been consolidated in the University's financial statements under the "Hospitals" column. The University's investment in UCSF Stanford Health Care and its share of the joint venture's results are recorded on the equity method and are also included in the "Hospitals" column.

SHC and LPCH recorded a $13 million operating loss for FY01, including a realized gain on investments of $25 million. This is an improvement compared to a loss of $48 million for the five months ended August 31, 2000, following the termination of UCSF Stanford Health Care (see page 21). Operational improvements, including cost reductions, program closures, and increased volume in key areas, accounted for the reduction in losses. SHC and LPCH, like other academic medical centers around the nation, continue to be negatively affected by the reductions in federal reimbursement. Labor costs continue to increase due to shortages in skilled positions.

Both management teams continue to implement operational improvements on their path toward achieving financial stability and break-even operating results. SHC and LPCH continue to strive to provide excellent health care services in addition to furthering their missions in education and innovative research.

Effective September 1, 2001, the University became the sole corporate member of LPCH, replacing SHC. This enables both institutions to focus on institution-specific objectives, while remaining committed to working together on common issues. Several services are shared between the two facilities, including

Highlights of the University's operating activities are summarized below:

+ Student income increased 7.1% to $300 million in FY01. Contributing to this increase were the undergraduate tuition rate increase of 6% and the room and board rate increase of 1.9%. Additionally, room and board fees were affected by an increase in off-campus housing stock and new on-campus residences such as the Escondido Village housing for graduate students, which opened in September 2000. Offsetting tuition and room and board revenues is need-based and merit-based aid for undergraduate and graduate students, which increased during FY01 by 2.9% to a total of $92 million.

+ In total, sponsored research support increased by $53 million, or 7.9%, to $727 million in FY01. The University's direct cost reimbursement was up $21 million due largely to higher levels of research activity in the School of Medicine. SLAC's direct cost reimbursements were up $26 million due to two major projects (GLAST and Spear-3), upgrades to the B Factory, construction on the Research Administration Building, and general operating expenses to support the increased activity level. Indirect cost recovery was up 5.4% due to increased research volume. The indirect cost rate for FY01 was comparable to the prior year's rate.

+ Expendable gifts in support of operations increased $12 million from FY00 to $125 million. These gifts are immediately expendable for the purpose set forth by the donor.

+ Endowment income and gains distributed for operations covered 18.1% of total operating expenses for FY01, up from 17.9% for FY00. To protect the value of the endowment, the University has a policy governing distributions that was established by the Board of Trustees. Despite the 7.2% decline in the endowment in FY01, amounts distributed for operations were up 12.4% in FY01 at $354 million, compared to $315 million in FY00. The increase in the payout

laboratory, general services, information technology, patient financial services, payroll, and accounts payable. SHC and LPCH continue to be co-obligated on outstanding bonds and certificates.

On November 15, 2001, the Lucile Packard Foundation for Children's Health announced the five-year Campaign for Lucile Packard Children's Hospital. This campaign will benefit LPCH and the University School of Medicine by supporting efforts to improve children's health. To date, this initiative has received an inaugural grant of $100 million from the David and Lucile Packard Foundation, a promise of $200 million in matching funds also from the David and Lucile Packard Foundation, and additional pledges of $105 million.

UCSF Stanford Health Care ‣ As of August 31, 2000, the University's investment in UCSF Stanford Health Care was $20 million. The joint venture continued to wind down its operations, transferring $17 million in net assets to Stanford Hospital and Clinics during FY01. As of August 31, 2001, the University's investment in UCSF Stanford Health Care has been reduced to $5 million. Final dissolution of the joint venture depends upon, among other things, a decision by the Internal Revenue Service and the Department of Labor regarding the distribution of the plan assets and obligations of the defined benefit plan. Net ongoing operating costs continue to be borne by the University and the University of California.

for FY01 was due to the growth in the market value of the endowment over the past several years and continued strong donor support. The market downturn contributed to the decline in other investment income, including the Expendable Funds Pool (EFP). The payout to operations from the EFP was approximately $55 million in FY01 as compared to $91 million in FY00. In FY00, other investment income included $78 million in realized and unrealized gains on an expendable investment fund that was transferred to endowment in FY01.

◆ Special program fees and other income increased $11 million, or 5.1%, to $232 million in FY01. This classification includes the external revenues generated by auxiliary enterprises and service centers and special programs, including technology licensing, Executive Education programs, and corporate affiliates programs. The increase in special program fees and other income is attributable primarily to activities of Highwire Press, a division of the libraries that provides enhanced online access to published scientific journals, to rental revenues from Stanford West Apartments, which started leasing apartments primarily to faculty and staff in October 2000, and to increased conference and catering services.

◆ Total expenses increased $196 million, or 11.1%, to $2.0 billion in FY01. The 10% increase in salaries and benefits was due in part to a budgeted 6% salary increase for faculty and staff. This was part of an initiative implemented during FY01 to make Stanford's salary program more competitive in Silicon Valley, where the University must compete for staff employees. Salary expense increased also because the University filled positions that had remained open in FY00 due to the tight labor market and strong competition for talented candidates. As a result of the recession in Silicon Valley, the University was better able to fill open positions with qualified candidates. Other operating expenses increased 20.5% due to higher costs related to utilities, interest, student stipends, and other one-time expenses. Such one-time expenses include, among other things, costs written off in connection with a canceled construction project and capitalized costs written off in connection with certain debt that was refinanced during the year. In addition, operating expenses for FY01 increased as a result of launching the Campaign for Undergraduate Education, implementing Web-integrated classes, increasing travel study and other alumni relations expenses, and increasing sponsored research activities. Partially offsetting the other operating expense increases was a decrease in depreciation expense, which was considerably higher in FY00 due to a one-time charge of approximately $40 million for the adoption of a revised set of useful lives and a change in method of computing depreciation for buildings.

Other Changes in Unrestricted Net Assets In total, unrestricted net assets of the University decreased by $787 million, including the excess of revenues over expenses of $59 million resulting from operations. The majority of other changes in unrestricted net assets were decreases in the value of investments of $869 million.

The University's endowment investment strategy and results are summarized in the Report from the Stanford Management Company on page 25. Stanford's investment strategy utilizes dividends, interest, rental income, and previously reinvested gains on the endowment to fund the payout to operations. In years of average or better market performance, the University's market gains exceed the amount of the predetermined payout, and the excess is reinvested in the endowment. For example, in FY00, the endowment's total return of $2.5 billion more than covered the $315 million of income and gains distributed to operations. In FY01, the University utilized endowment income of $216 million and withdrew previously reinvested gains of $138 million to meet the $354 million payout to operations.

Temporarily Restricted Net Assets

Temporarily restricted net assets increased by $19 million, or 4.0%, to $497 million in FY01. The University received $142 million of new gifts and pledges. During the year, $96 million of temporarily restricted net assets were released from their restrictions and utilized to fund operations and capital expenditures.

Permanently Restricted Net Assets

Permanently restricted net assets increased by $197 million, or 7.7%, to $2.7 billion during FY01. The increase was due primarily to the receipt of $187 million in new gifts and pledges for the endowment.

Financial Position

The University's Statement of Financial Position remains strong despite the impact of negative investment returns and increased debt. In FY01, total University assets declined $362 million to $13.6 billion, while total University liabilities increased $209 million to $2.5 billion.

+ Total investments, primarily consisting of endowment assets and the EFP, decreased by $663 million, or 6.3%, to $9.9 billion. As discussed in the Report from the Stanford Management Company on pages 25 through 29, the endowment was affected by the global economic move toward recession and the related negative impact on equity values.

+ Net pledges receivable increased approximately $38 million to $519 million for FY01. The gross increase in pledges was approximately $400 million, primarily attributable to the Hewlett Foundation pledge. However, only $150 million was recorded in FY01 because the remainder ($250 million) of the pledge is conditional upon matching gifts and may only be recorded when the conditions are satisfied.

+ Plant facilities, net of accumulated depreciation, grew 8.5% to $2.1 billion. New additions to plant facilities in FY01 totaled $317 million, bringing total plant facilities before accumulated depreciation to $3.3 billion. This increase reflects the significant construction activity associated with the University's renewal of its physical infrastructure and efforts to meet faculty, student, and staff housing needs. Major projects completed during FY01 include the first phase of the Stanford West apartment project, which is primarily for faculty and staff housing, the Escondido Village apartments for graduate student housing, and the Frances C. Arrillaga Alumni Center.

+ Notes and bonds payable were $1.2 billion at August 31, 2001, an increase of 7.2% from FY00. The continuing favorable interest rate environment has allowed the University to issue new debt to support the capital plan and to refinance existing debt at favorable interest rates. The University's debt ratios are within the guidelines of the internal debt policy approved by the Board of Trustees. The debt policy monitors the amount and type of debt Stanford may incur. It is intended to preserve the University's long-term debt capacity, financial flexibility, and access to capital markets at competitive rates.

◆ The endowment represents approximately 74% of the University's net assets. Net assets of the endowment decreased $636 million in FY01, or 7.2%, to $8.2 billion. The endowment recognized investment losses of $518 million, distributed $354 million to operations, and received new gifts of $158 million and transfers of $84 million of expendable funds.

Conclusion

As a result of its strong financial base and the generosity of its many friends and alumni, the University was able to meet the challenges of the year despite negative investment returns. With the continued support of the faculty, staff, students, trustees, alumni, and other friends, our strong financial base will ensure that the University's resources will be available to future generations of students. Stanford remains committed to ensuring its excellence in teaching and research.

RANDALL S. LIVINGSTON
Vice President for Business Affairs
and Chief Financial Officer

M. SUZANNE CALANDRA
Controller

Report from the Stanford Management Company

The test of any long-term strategic plan is its performance in the face of a difficult environment. Fiscal year 2000-2001 provided Stanford Management Company (SMC) the opportunity to test our diversified allocation policy. Following a decade of tremendous gains in the U.S. economy and capital markets, growth slowed significantly and the global economy moved toward recession, causing a substantial decline in broad public market stock indices. This environment presented a challenge to endowments. After a decade of outstanding returns, 16 of the largest 20 university endowments showed negative returns for the period ended June 30, 2001. Stanford ranked eighth among this group of 20, reporting a -2.1% return. A difficult market environment in July and August caused further deterioration in Stanford's results, and the return for the fiscal year ended August 31, 2001, was -7.2%. Although Stanford's 2001 returns are disappointing when compared to recent historical results, our diversified portfolio substantially outperformed broad market indices such as the S&P 500, which declined approximately 25% for the year ended August 31, 2001.

Given the perpetual nature of the University, Stanford's strategic investment horizon must be long-term. Our objective is to develop and execute an investment strategy that generates optimal total return (income plus price appreciation) relative to the risk taken. To meet this goal, SMC was established in 1991 to manage Stanford's financial and real estate investment assets. SMC is a division of the University with oversight by a Board of Directors appointed by the University Board of Trustees. The SMC board consists of at least three trustees, several investment and real estate professionals, and University representatives. SMC directs in excess of $10 billion of endowment and trust assets, working capital, temporarily invested expendable funds, and commercial real estate investments including the Stanford Research Park.

SMC's primary endowment management responsibilities involve establishing asset allocation policy and implementing that policy through manager selection. Performance is measured relative to real return objectives, as well as market benchmarks.

Endowment Asset Allocation > Most of Stanford's $8.2 billion of endowment assets are invested in a diversified portfolio, referred to as the Merged Endowment Pool (MEP). Results discussed in this report reflect the performance of this $7.8 billion portfolio. During fiscal year 2000-01, asset allocation targets shifted significantly from the prior year. Fifteen percent of MEP assets were moved from domestic and international public stocks to alternatives in private equity, absolute return, and real estate. SMC also redefined the category of Alternative Investments into its component sectors—Private Equity, Absolute Return, and Natural Resources—to illustrate their relative weights and different risk/return characteristics.

The asset classes of the Merged Endowment Pool and their target allocations as of August 31, 2001 follow:

Asset Class	Strategic Allocation
Domestic Stocks	15%
International Stocks	17%
Private Equity	17%
Absolute Return	12%
Natural Resources	7%
Real Estate	20%
Domestic Fixed Income	12%
	100%

Endowment Performance Compared to Inflation ▹ The table below illustrates annualized returns for various periods ending August 31, 2001 and shows the performance of Stanford's multi-asset strategy in a long-term context. Stanford's objective is to return a minimum of 6.25% over the rate of inflation. If this real return target is achieved over time, the value of the endowment will be maintained net of annual payouts to support endowed activities. Over the past three-, five-, and 10-year periods, Stanford's annualized real return has substantially exceeded the 6.25% target.

	One Year	Three Years	Five Years	Ten Years
Nominal Endowment Return	- 7.3%	20.5%	17.0%	15.3%
GDP Deflator [1]	2.3%	2.0%	1.9%	2.0%
Real Endowment Return	- 9.6%	18.5%	15.1%	13.3%

[1] The Gross Domestic Price (GDP) deflator, a measure of inflation, is through the quarter ended June 30, 2001.

Endowment Performance Compared to Benchmarks ⟩ SMC evaluates the performance of investment managers by comparing their returns to benchmarks that are appropriate for each individual asset class. For example, the benchmark for the Domestic Stocks asset class is the Russell 3000 Index. SMC evaluates overall portfolio performance by comparison to a composite benchmark, which represents a blending of the benchmark returns for each asset class weighted by the strategic allocations above. Actual performance, net of management fees, is compared to the composite benchmark for periods ended August 31, 2001:

ENDOWMENT VS. BENCHMARK ■ Endowment Total Return ▧ Composite Benchmark

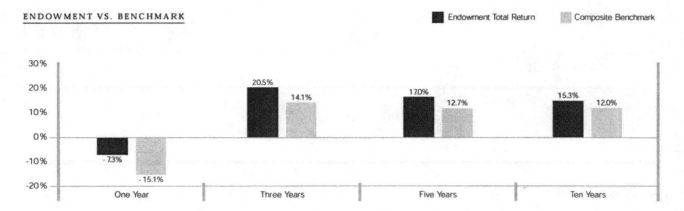

SMC's effectiveness in implementing the multi-asset class approach, through superior manager selection, has resulted in a consistent and long-term performance advantage over the composite benchmark.

The cumulative return chart below compares the growth of $100 in Stanford's endowment with that of the composite benchmark over the past 10 years:

STANFORD MERGED ENDOWMENT POOL VS. STANFORD POLICY BENCHMARK ── Endowment ┈┈ Composite Benchmark

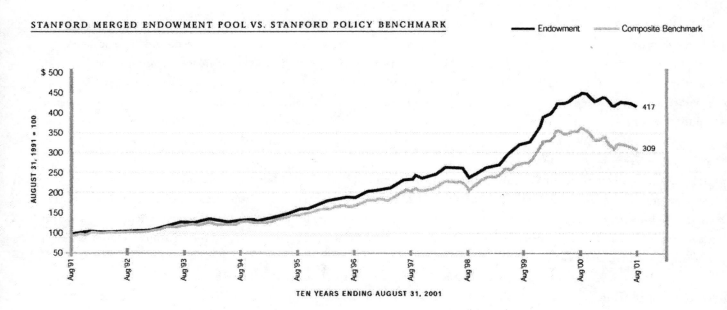

TEN YEARS ENDING AUGUST 31, 2001

The performance advantage during this 10-year period relative to benchmark returns has added in excess of $1 billion to the value of the endowment.

Individual Asset Class Performance › The performance of the individual asset classes for the year ended August 31, 2001 gives more insight into the difficult environment and illustrates the benefits of diversification. The graph below shows individual class returns relative to each benchmark:

INDIVIDUAL ASSET CLASS PERFORMANCE

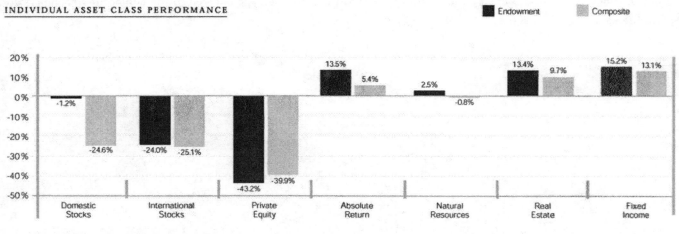

One year ended August 31, 2001

Stanford's Domestic Stock portfolio has been deliberately over-weighted in value stocks to offset the growth stock-oriented characteristics of venture capital partnerships held in Private Equity. This value orientation in Domestic Stocks resulted in a year of strong performance relative to benchmark as value stocks significantly outperformed the broader market. International equity, while slightly outperforming the benchmark, suffered a market correction similar to that of the broad domestic stock market in an environment of global economic uncertainty.

Private Equity represented the most challenging asset sector for SMC, when measured on a one-year return basis. Negative returns in this asset sector are due substantially to reversal of unrealized gains reported in prior periods. Despite this recent reversal, Private Equity has been a very successful asset class when evaluated long term, with investment gains that have added more than $2 billion to the value of the endowment over the last five years.

The Absolute Return portfolio is constructed to provide returns that are substantially uncorrelated to the broader equity markets. Absolute Return results for the last 12 months demonstrated successful execution of this strategy. The portfolio provided robust returns in several hedge fund categories including distressed debt, fixed income relative value, and multi-strategy arbitrage funds.

Stanford's endowment has a substantially larger commitment to Real Estate than peer institutions. The strategy of over-weighting real estate investments is based on SMC's extensive experience in real estate development and management of University lands. SMC's core competency in these areas provides a significant advantage when evaluating real estate investments. The Real Estate portfolio performed well in fiscal 2001, contributing returns through asset appreciation and high current cash yield.

Fixed Income was the highest returning asset class over the last 12 months as a result of open market actions by the Federal Reserve designed to reduce interest rates and investors' flight to U.S. Government securities during a time of global uncertainty. Fixed Income demonstrated a negative correlation to the equity markets, illustrating the advantage of a broadly diversified portfolio of assets.

Over a 10-year period, the total endowment return of 15.3% outperformed the benchmark's 12.0% as a result of individual asset class returns as outlined:

TEN-YEAR ASSET CLASS RETURNS VS. BENCHMARK

■ Endowment   ▨ Composite

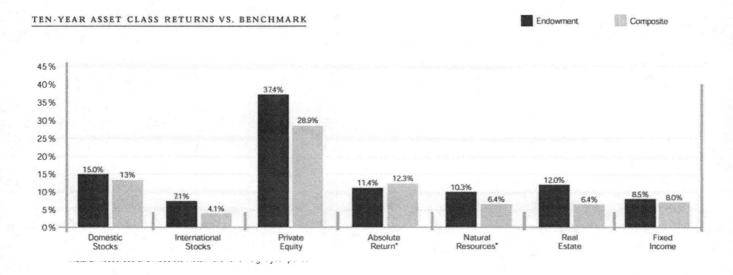

During the last few years, investment returns have been impacted by extreme volatility in global financial markets, substantial variability in U.S. economic growth, and ongoing change to U.S. Federal Reserve policy. SMC expects this challenging investment environment to continue. We are confident that our long-term investment strategy and manager selection process will preserve endowment capital and provide excellent returns during this uncertain period.

MICHAEL G. McCAFFERY
CEO, Stanford Management Company

Decade in Review

Years ended August 31

(in thousands of dollars)	2001	1996	1991
FINANCIAL:			
PRINCIPAL SOURCES OF REVENUES:			
Student tuition and fees (B)	$ 391,372	$ 308,828	$ 221,001
Sponsored research support	727,483	577,723	450,027
Patient care (A)	1,004,928	–	–
Expendable gifts in support of operations	125,284	93,169	76,650
Endowment income in support of operations	354,441	161,340	99,310
PRINCIPAL PURPOSES OF EXPENDITURES:			
Instruction and departmental research	667,991	408,104	309,988
Organized research (direct costs)	623,113	434,369	378,833
Health care services (A)	934,680	–	–
Libraries	107,001	62,001	52,740
Student financial aid (B)	91,671	65,113	57,157
Administration, development, and general	210,907	142,587	114,335
FINANCIAL POSITION HIGHLIGHTS:			
Investments at fair value	10,140,812	5,016,616	2,827,914
Plant facilities, net of accumulated depreciation	2,353,731	1,139,193	843,268
Equity investment in related health care entities (A)	5,443	319,471	240,353
Notes and bonds payable	1,445,491	729,481	458,175
Total net assets	11,533,849	5,797,708	3,735,339

	2001	1996	1991
STUDENTS:			
ENROLLMENT: (C)			
Undergraduate	6,637	6,550	6,527
Graduate	7,536	7,261	7,022
DEGREES CONFERRED:			
Bachelor's degrees	1,676	1,744	1,633
Advanced degrees	2,936	2,900	2,455
FACULTY:			
Members of the Academic Council	1,384	1,291	1,361
ANNUAL UNDERGRADUATE TUITION RATE	$ 24,441	$ 19,695	$ 14,280

(A) Beginning in fiscal year 2000, health care activities have been reported on a consolidated basis. Prior to that, they were reported on an equity basis.

(B) Financial aid is reported as a reduction of student income in the statement of activities.

(C) Enrollment for fall quarter immediately following fiscal year end.

At August 31, 2001 and 2000
(in thousands of dollars)

	UNIVERSITY	2001 HOSPITALS	CONSOLIDATED	2000 CONSOLIDATED
ASSETS				
Cash and cash equivalents	$ 701,453	$ 115,890	$ 817,343	$ 533,666
Accounts receivable, net	158,725	175,146	333,871	565,738
Receivables (payables) from SHC and LPCH, net	14,499	(14,499)	–	–
Inventories, prepaid expenses, and other assets	45,424	35,536	80,960	74,926
Pledges receivable, net	519,379	7,905	527,284	481,497
Student loans receivable, net	74,185	–	74,185	74,693
Faculty and staff mortgages and other loans receivable, net	211,358	–	211,358	173,147
Investments at fair value, including securities pledged or on loan of $389,936 and $184,424 for 2001 and 2000, respectively	9,871,498	269,314	10,140,812	10,784,236
Investment in UCSF Stanford Health Care	–	5,443	5,443	20,063
Plant facilities, net of accumulated depreciation	2,053,188	300,543	2,353,731	2,203,846
Collections of works of art	–	–	–	–
Total assets	**$ 13,649,709**	**$ 895,278**	**$ 14,544,987**	**$ 14,911,812**
LIABILITIES AND NET ASSETS				
LIABILITIES:				
Accounts payable and accrued expenses	$ 451,713	$ 281,125	$ 732,838	$ 750,803
Liabilities under security agreements	511,507	–	511,507	358,441
Income beneficiary share of living trust investments	271,046	–	271,046	258,100
Notes and bonds payable	1,217,656	227,835	1,445,491	1,370,377
U.S. Government refundable loan funds	50,256	–	50,256	49,311
Total liabilities	**2,502,178**	**508,960**	**3,011,138**	**2,787,032**
NET ASSETS:				
Unrestricted:				
Designated for operations	1,000,173	218,335	1,218,508	1,335,931
Investment in plant facilities	1,152,108	64,458	1,216,566	1,146,307
Endowment gains and funds functioning as endowment	5,750,040	–	5,750,040	6,511,772
Investment in UCSF Stanford Health Care	–	5,443	5,443	20,063
Unrestricted	7,902,321	288,236	8,190,557	9,014,073
Temporarily restricted	497,215	28,681	525,896	503,824
Permanently restricted	2,747,995	69,401	2,817,396	2,606,883
Total net assets	**11,147,531**	**386,318**	**11,533,849**	**12,124,780**
Total liabilities and net assets	**$ 13,649,709**	**$ 895,278**	**$ 14,544,987**	**$ 14,911,812**

The accompanying notes are an integral part of these consolidated financial statements.

Consolidated Statements of Activities

Years ended August 31, 2001 and 2000
(in thousands of dollars)

	UNIVERSITY	2001 HOSPITALS	CONSOLIDATED	2000 CONSOLIDATED
UNRESTRICTED NET ASSETS ACTIVITY				
REVENUES:				
Student income:				
Undergraduate programs	$ 161,164	$ –	$ 161,164	$ 154,153
Graduate programs	157,241	–	157,241	149,013
Room and board	72,967	–	72,967	65,890
Student financial aid	(91,671)	–	(91,671)	(89,117)
Total student income	**299,701**	**–**	**299,701**	**279,939**
Sponsored research support (primarily federal):				
Direct costs—University	400,344	–	400,344	379,070
Direct costs—Stanford Linear Accelerator Center	205,480	–	205,480	179,892
Indirect costs	121,659	–	121,659	115,446
Total sponsored research support	**727,483**	**–**	**727,483**	**674,408**
Health care services:				
Patient care, net	–	1,004,928	1,004,928	361,891
Physicians' services and support—SHC and LPCH, net	158,100	(158,100)	–	–
Physicians' services and support—UCSF Stanford Health Care and other facilities, net	5,215	–	5,215	102,178
Total health care services	**163,315**	**846,828**	**1,010,143**	**464,069**
Expendable gifts in support of operations	125,284	–	125,284	113,187
Investment income distributed for operations:				
Endowment	354,441	–	354,441	315,002
Expendable funds pool and other investment income	65,390	25,023	90,413	199,215
Total investment income distributed for operations	**419,831**	**25,023**	**444,854**	**514,217**
Special program fees and other income	**231,979**	**36,188**	**268,167**	**236,001**
Net assets released from restrictions	**50,974**	**13,288**	**64,262**	**57,491**
Total revenues	**2,018,567**	**921,327**	**2,939,894**	**2,339,312**
EXPENSES:				
Salaries and benefits	981,389	487,236	1,468,625	1,082,964
Depreciation	143,836	48,658	192,494	194,278
Stanford Linear Accelerator Center	205,480	–	205,480	179,892
Other operating expenses	628,516	398,786	1,027,302	703,343
Total expenses	**1,959,221**	**934,680**	**2,893,901**	**2,160,477**
Excess (deficit) of revenues over expenses	**$ 59,346**	**$ (13,353)**	**$ 45,993**	**$ 178,835**

The accompanying notes are an integral part of these consolidated financial statements.

Years ended August 31, 2001 and 2000
(in thousands of dollars)

	UNIVERSITY	2001 HOSPITALS	CONSOLIDATED	2000 CONSOLIDATED
UNRESTRICTED NET ASSETS ACTIVITY (continued)				
Excess (deficit) of revenues over expenses	$ 59,346	$ (13,353)	$ 45,993	$ 178,835
Other changes in unrestricted net assets:				
Expendable gifts invested in the endowment	5,884	—	5,884	17,742
Increase (decrease) in reinvested endowment gains	(868,919)	—	(868,919)	1,966,599
Change in equity investment in UCSF Stanford Health Care	—	(14,620)	(14,620)	(51,994)
Capital and other gifts released from restrictions	44,607	5,837	50,444	88,931
Reclassification of SHC and LPCH net assets	—	—	—	(52,838)
Income (withdrawn from) invested in the endowment	(19,407)	—	(19,407)	155,744
Other investment gains (losses)	(16,118)	(25,783)	(41,901)	566
Other	7,318	11,692	19,010	(9,347)
Net change in unrestricted net assets	(787,289)	(36,227)	(823,516)	2,294,238
TEMPORARILY RESTRICTED NET ASSETS ACTIVITY				
Gifts and pledges, net	141,813	25,503	167,316	332,651
Investment income (loss)	(18,516)	(589)	(19,105)	24,926
Living trust investment income (loss) and actuarial adjustment	(5,744)	—	(5,744)	13,757
Net assets released to operations	(50,974)	(13,288)	(64,262)	(57,491)
Capital and other gifts released to unrestricted net assets	(44,607)	(5,837)	(50,444)	(88,931)
Reclassification of SHC and LPCH net assets	—	—	—	16,186
Other	(2,916)	(2,773)	(5,689)	(26,286)
Net change in temporarily restricted net assets	19,056	3,016	22,072	214,812
PERMANENTLY RESTRICTED NET ASSETS ACTIVITY				
Gifts and pledges, net	187,169	13,655	200,824	406,836
Investment income (loss)	(33,772)	(2,117)	(35,889)	189,829
Living trust investment income and actuarial adjustment	18,599	—	18,599	10,845
Reclassification of SHC and LPCH net assets	—	—	—	36,652
Other	25,300	1,679	26,979	33,904
Net change in permanently restricted net assets	197,296	13,217	210,513	678,066
Net change in total net assets	(570,937)	(19,994)	(590,931)	3,187,116
Total net assets, beginning of year	11,718,468	406,312	12,124,780	8,937,664
Total net assets, end of year	$ 11,147,531	$ 386,318	$ 11,533,849	$ 12,124,780

The accompanying notes are an integral part of these consolidated financial statements.

Consolidated Statements of Cash Flows

Years ended August 31, 2001 and 2000
(in thousands of dollars)

	UNIVERSITY	2001 HOSPITALS	CONSOLIDATED	2000 CONSOLIDATED
CASH FLOW FROM OPERATING ACTIVITIES				
Change in net assets	$ (570,937)	$ (19,994)	$ (590,931)	$ 3,187,116
Adjustments to reconcile change in net assets to net cash provided by (used for) operating activities:				
Depreciation, amortization, and loss on disposal of fixed assets	156,589	48,658	205,247	197,383
Net realized and unrealized (gains) losses on investments and security agreements	774,839	10,746	785,585	(2,589,434)
Net realized and unrealized losses on derivatives	4,200	5,115	9,315	–
Actuarial change on living trust obligations	(733)	–	(733)	(12,947)
Equity in UCSF Stanford Health Care	–	(2,124)	(2,124)	51,994
Permanently restricted investment income	(2,339)	(260)	(2,599)	(4,344)
Gifts restricted for long-term investments	(192,814)	(28,757)	(221,571)	(356,413)
Net (increase) decrease in accounts receivable, pledges receivable, and receivables from SHC and LPCH	1,802	(13,874)	(12,072)	(431,472)
Increase in U.S. Government refundable loan funds	945	–	945	894
(Increase) decrease in inventories, prepaid expenses, and other assets	(8,556)	1,406	(7,150)	3,337
Increase (decrease) in accounts payable and accrued expenses	(42,358)	13,785	(28,573)	326,263
Net cash provided by operating activities	120,638	14,701	135,339	372,377
CASH FLOW FROM INVESTING ACTIVITIES				
Purchases of land, building, and equipment	(316,341)	(37,238)	(353,579)	(361,765)
Student, faculty, and other loans:				
New loans made	(81,131)	–	(81,131)	(76,739)
Principal collected	43,428	–	43,428	30,527
Purchases of investments	(3,681,299)	(161,293)	(3,842,592)	(4,944,294)
Sales and maturities of investments	3,621,677	131,028	3,752,705	4,599,967
Liabilities under security agreements	214,145	–	214,145	(35,222)
Cash transferred from UCSF Stanford Health Care	–	41,130	41,130	60,127
Net cash used for investing activities	(199,521)	(26,373)	(225,894)	(727,399)
CASH FLOW FROM FINANCING ACTIVITIES				
Gifts and reinvested income of endowment, capital projects, and other restricted purposes	206,056	28,757	234,813	377,317
Increase in investment income for restricted purposes	2,339	260	2,599	4,344
Proceeds from borrowing	307,224	–	307,224	95,596
Repayment of notes and bonds payable	(166,703)	(3,701)	(170,404)	(77,501)
Net cash provided by financing activities	348,916	25,316	374,232	399,756
Increase in cash and cash equivalents	270,033	13,644	283,677	44,734
Cash and cash equivalents, beginning of year	431,420	102,246	533,666	488,932
Cash and cash equivalents, end of year	$ 701,453	$ 115,890	$ 817,343	$ 533,666
SUPPLEMENTAL DATA:				
Gifts of equipment	$ 437	$ 1,116	$ 1,553	$ 127
Interest paid during the year	65,163	13,851	79,014	74,203
Reduction in debt related to real estate partnerships	60,412	–	60,412	–

The accompanying notes are an integral part of these consolidated financial statements.

1.   Basis of Presentation and Significant Accounting Policies

Basis of Presentation ›   The consolidated financial statements include the accounts of Stanford University (the University), Stanford Hospital and Clinics (SHC) and Lucile Salter Packard Children's Hospital at Stanford (LPCH), and other majority-owned entities. All significant inter-entity transactions and balances have been eliminated upon consolidation.

University   The University is a private, not-for-profit educational institution, founded in 1885 by Senator Leland and Mrs. Jane Stanford in memory of their son, Leland Stanford, Jr. It is organized into seven schools with approximately 1,700 faculty and more than 14,000 graduate and undergraduate students. The University category presented in the financial statements comprises all the accounts of the University, including the Stanford Alumni Association (SAA), the Hoover Institution and other institutes and research centers, and Stanford Linear Accelerator Center (SLAC).

The University manages and operates SLAC for the Department of Energy (DOE) under a management and operating contract; therefore, the revenues and expenditures of SLAC are included in the statement of activities. As SLAC is a federally funded research and development center, the assets and liabilities of SLAC are owned by the DOE and, accordingly, are not included in the statement of financial position.

Hospitals   The Hospitals category presented in the financial statements includes SHC, LPCH, and the University's investment in UCSF Stanford Health Care, a nonprofit corporation controlled jointly by the University and the Regents of the University of California (UC), which operated the clinical facilities of Stanford Health Services (SHS), LPCH, and the University of California, San Francisco Medical Center (UCSF) from November 1, 1997, through March 31, 2000.

The University's investment in UCSF Stanford Health Care is reported in these financial statements using the equity method of accounting. Effective March 31, 2000, the operating activities of UCSF Stanford Health Care were terminated. On April 1, 2000, UCSF Stanford Health Care transferred the operations of its clinical facilities to SHC, LPCH, and UC. The health care activities of SHC and LPCH, including revenues, expenses, assets, and liabilities, are consolidated in these financial statements. Accordingly, for fiscal year 2000, seven months of health care activities are presented under the equity method and five months are presented on a consolidated basis. For fiscal year 2001, all health care activities are presented on a consolidated basis. The organization, financial information, and agreements among the University and the aforementioned health care entities are discussed in Note 2.

Basis of Accounting ›   The financial statements are prepared in accordance with generally accepted accounting principles. These principles require management to make estimates that affect the reported amounts of assets and liabilities, the disclosure of contingent assets and liabilities at the date of the financial statements, and the reported amounts of revenues and expenses during the reporting period. Actual results could differ from those estimates.

For financial reporting purposes, net assets and revenues, expenses, gains, and losses are classified into one of three categories—unrestricted, temporarily restricted, or permanently restricted—in accordance with generally accepted accounting principles.

Unrestricted Net Assets   Unrestricted net assets are expendable resources used to support either the University's core activities of teaching and research or the Hospitals' patient care, teaching, and research missions. These net assets may be designated by the University or the Hospitals for specific purposes under internal operating and administrative arrangements or be subject to contractual agreements with external parties. Donor-restricted contributions, which relate to the University's or the Hospitals' core activities, that are received and expended, or deemed expended due to the nature of their restriction, are classified as unrestricted. Donor-restricted resources intended for capital projects are released from their temporary restrictions and reclassified as unrestricted support when spent. All expenses are recorded as a reduction of unrestricted net assets.

Unrestricted net assets include funds designated for operations, plant facilities, endowment gains and funds functioning as endowment, and the University's investment in UCSF Stanford Health Care. Unrestricted net assets were $8,190,557,000 and $9,014,073,000 at August 31, 2001 and 2000, respectively.

Temporarily Restricted Net Assets Temporarily restricted net assets include investments and pledges that are subject to donor-imposed restrictions that expire upon the passage of time, upon the pledge payment, or upon specific actions undertaken by the University or the Hospitals, at which time they are released and reclassified to unrestricted support. Temporarily restricted net assets consist of the following balances at August 31, 2001 and 2000, in thousands of dollars:

	UNIVERSITY	2001 HOSPITALS	CONSOLIDATED	2000 CONSOLIDATED
TEMPORARILY RESTRICTED NET ASSETS				
Support for capital projects	$ 206,148	$ —	$ 206,148	$ 198,794
Term endowments	56,469	—	56,469	66,259
Funds subject to living trust agreements	51,014	—	51,014	61,643
Other gifts and income for instruction, research, and University support	183,584	—	183,584	151,463
SHC and LPCH indigent care, plant, and other funds	—	28,681	28,681	25,665
Temporarily restricted net assets	$ 497,215	$ 28,681	$ 525,896	$ 503,824

Permanently Restricted Net Assets   Permanently restricted net assets are subject to donor-imposed restrictions requiring that the principal be invested in perpetuity. Permanently restricted net assets consist of the following balances at August 31, 2001 and 2000, in thousands of dollars:

	UNIVERSITY	2001 HOSPITALS	CONSOLIDATED	2000 CONSOLIDATED
PERMANENTLY RESTRICTED NET ASSETS				
Endowment funds	$ 2,481,019	$ 69,401	$ 2,550,420	$ 2,378,452
Funds subject to living trust agreements	209,432	–	209,432	174,787
Student loans	57,544	–	57,544	53,644
Permanently restricted net assets	$ 2,747,995	$ 69,401	$ 2,817,396	$ 2,606,883

Management considers all revenues and expenses to be related to operations except reinvested endowment gains, changes in equity of UCSF Stanford Health Care, capital gifts, expendable gifts invested in the endowment, and certain other non-operating changes.

Cash and Cash Equivalents › Cash and cash equivalents including U.S. Treasury bills, bankers' acceptances, commercial paper, certificates of deposit, money market funds, and other short-term investments with remaining maturities of 90 days or less at the time of purchase, are carried at cost, which approximates market. Cash and cash equivalent amounts held in the endowment, as well as certain cash restricted in its use by the Hospitals, are classified as investments.

Student Loans Receivable › Student loans receivable are carried at cost, less an allowance for doubtful accounts. Determination of the fair value of student loans receivable is considered impractical due to donor-restricted and federally sponsored student loans with mandated interest rates and repayment terms subject to significant restrictions as to their transfer and disposition.

Investments › Investments are generally recorded at fair value based upon quoted market prices, when available, or estimates of fair value. Donated assets are recorded at fair value at the date of donation. Those investments for which fair value is not readily determinable are carried at cost, fair value at date of donation, or at a nominal value. Developed real estate is generally valued based on discounted cash flows of existing leases. Non-developed land is reported at cost. Securities transactions are reported on a trade-date basis.

Derivatives › Derivative financial instruments are recorded at fair value with the resulting gain or loss recognized in the consolidated statement of activities. See Note 5.

Plant Facilities › Plant facilities are recorded at cost or fair value at date of donation. Interest for construction financing is capitalized as a cost of construction. Depreciation is computed using the straight-line method over the estimated useful lives of the plant assets.

As described in Note 7, beginning in fiscal year 2000, the University adopted a revised set of useful lives for its equipment and buildings to reflect current information and to conform with those used for federal cost reimbursement accounting purposes. The useful lives used in calculating depreciation for fiscal years 2001 and 2000 are as follows:

	UNIVERSITY	HOSPITALS
Buildings	20–40 years	10–40 years
Land and building improvements	10–40 years	5–40 years
Equipment and books	3–10 years	3–20 years

The method of computing depreciation on academic buildings was also changed in fiscal year 2000. Academic buildings placed in service before September 1, 1999, are depreciated based upon the estimated useful life of the building. Academic buildings placed in service after September 1, 1999, are depreciated based on individual component lives.

Collections of Works of Art ▸ Art objects and collections are not capitalized, as the University uses the proceeds from any sales of such items to acquire other art or collection pieces.

Self-insurance ▸ The University self-insures for unemployment, disability, property losses, and general and professional liability losses. The Hospitals self-insure for workers' compensation and medical malpractice losses. Reinsurance is purchased to cover liabilities above specific per-claim exposures. Estimates of retained exposures are accrued.

Student Financial Aid ▸ Financial assistance in the form of scholarship and fellowship grants that cover a portion of tuition, living, and other costs is reflected as a reduction in student income.

Health Care Services ▸ The Hospitals derive a majority of patient care revenue from contractual agreements with Medicare, Medi-Cal, and certain other contracted rate payors. Payments under these agreements and programs are based on a percentage of charges, per diem, per discharge, per service, a fee schedule, a cost reimbursement, or capitation methodology.

Unsponsored Community Benefit Expense ▸ SHC's and LPCH's commitment to community service is evidenced by services provided to persons who cannot afford to pay and benefits provided to the broader community. The amount of charity care services, which are not recorded as revenue (quantified at customary charges), was $4,821,000 for fiscal year 2001, and $2,172,000 for the five months ended August 31, 2000. The total quantifiable community benefits provided by SHC and LPCH for the year ended August 31, 2001, and the five months ended August 31, 2000, were $70,139,000 and $22,018,000, respectively.

Tax Status ▸ The University, SHC, and LPCH are exempt from federal income tax to the extent provided by Section 501(c)(3) of the Internal Revenue Code.

Separate Hospital Financial Statements ‣ The Hospitals prepare separate, stand-alone consolidated financial statements in conformity with generally accepted accounting principles. For purposes of presentation of the Hospitals' balance sheets, statements of operations, statements of changes in net assets, and statements of cash flows in these consolidated financial statements, conforming reclassifications have been made to the Hospitals' revenue and expenses and inter-entity receivables and payables consistent with categories in the consolidated financial statements.

Reclassifications ‣ During the year ended August 31, 2001, the University changed the method of presenting the statement of cash flows from the direct to the indirect method to conform with prevailing industry practice. The statement of cash flows for the year ended August 31, 2000, has been reclassified to conform to the current year's presentation. In addition, certain other fiscal year 2000 amounts presented for comparative purposes have been reclassified to conform to the fiscal year 2001 presentation.

2.   Related Health Care Entities

Organization and Background ‣ The University is the sole member of SHC, which was the sole member of LPCH through August 31, 2001. Effective September 1, 2001, the University became the sole member of LPCH. Effective November 1, 1997, UC and the University transferred substantially all the assets and liabilities related to the clinical operations of UCSF and SHS (now known as SHC) to UCSF Stanford Health Care, a California nonprofit public benefit corporation. UCSF Stanford Health Care was organized by the University and UC to operate the clinical facilities of SHS, LPCH, and UCSF in support of the schools of medicine of the University and UCSF. The University and UC terminated the operating activities of UCSF Stanford Health Care effective March 31, 2000. On April 1, 2000, the operations of the hospitals and professional services of the members of the medical faculties of the University and the UCSF School of Medicine were transferred back to SHC, LPCH, and UCSF.

On April 1, 2000, net assets were transferred to SHC, LPCH, and UCSF at their historical cost basis of $674,991,000. UCSF Stanford Health Care's then-remaining net assets of $40,200,000 were retained to satisfy known liabilities and pay for ongoing costs. During fiscal year 2001, UCSF Stanford Health Care transferred cash to SHC, LPCH, and UCSF in satisfaction of related party balances and to return a portion of the net assets retained on behalf of each member. In addition, during fiscal year 2001, UCSF Stanford Health Care made certain payments on behalf of SHC, LPCH, and UCSF. The University's share of UCSF Stanford Health Care's remaining net assets was $5,443,000 and $20,063,000 at August 31, 2001 and 2000, respectively.

Final dissolution of UCSF Stanford Health Care depends upon, among other things, a decision by the Internal Revenue Service and the Department of Labor regarding the distribution of the plan assets and obligations of the defined benefit plan (see Note 15). Net ongoing operating costs of UCSF Stanford Health Care subsequent to March 31, 2000, continue to be borne by the University and UC.

University's Investment in Hospitals > The following table summarizes the changes in the University's investment in UCSF Stanford Health Care and the net assets of SHC and LPCH during the years ended August 31, 2001 and 2000, in thousands of dollars:

	UCSF STANFORD HEALTH CARE	SHC AND LPCH
Investment at August 31, 1999	$ 451,613	$ 33,331
Deficit resulting from operations (seven months for UCSF Stanford Health Care, five months for SHC and LPCH)	(63,878)	(48,048)
Deficit resulting from winding-down activities	(37)	–
Other changes in net assets	11,921	21,410
Transfer of UCSF Stanford Health Care net assets	(379,556)	379,556
Investment at August 31, 2000	20,063	386,249
Deficit resulting from operations	–	(13,353)
Income resulting from winding-down activities	6,440	–
Other changes in net assets	(4,316)	(8,765)
Transfer of UCSF Stanford Health Care net assets	(16,744)	16,744
Investment at August 31, 2001	$ 5,443	$ 380,875

UCSF Stanford Health Care's net assets were $12,336,000 and $40,126,000 at August 31, 2001 and 2000, respectively.

Related-Party Transactions > The University has entered into various operating agreements with SHC and LPCH for professional services of faculty members of the Stanford University School of Medicine, telecommunications services, and other services and facility charges. Revenues and expenses related to these agreements are eliminated in consolidation. Additionally, certain investments of SHC and LPCH with a fair market value of $64,804,000 (including $17,547,000 of cash and cash equivalents) and $169,089,000 at August 31, 2001 and 2000, respectively, were managed by the University. SHC and LPCH assets with a market value of $117,718,000 on August 31, 2001 are invested in an external liquid fund managed by the University.

For the seven months ended March 31, 2000, the University recorded net revenues from UCSF Stanford Health Care of $98,193,000 for professional medical services and other facility charges and services. SHC and LPCH had receivables from UCSF Stanford Health Care of $33,167,000 as of August 31, 2000.

3.   Accounts Receivable

Accounts receivable at August 31, 2001 and 2000, in thousands of dollars, are as follows:

	2001	2000
UNIVERSITY:		
U.S. Government	$ 51,229	$ 62,103
Due from brokers	47,466	221,232
Accrued interest on investments	18,779	19,855
Non-government sponsors	14,398	14,523
Student	3,246	3,148
Other	25,607	27,867
	160,725	348,728
Less allowances for losses	2,000	2,118
	158,725	346,610
HOSPITALS:		
Hospitals' patient receivables	394,729	377,812
UCSF Stanford Health Care	–	33,167
Other	11,917	17,025
	406,646	428,004
Less allowances for losses	231,500	208,876
	175,146	219,128
Consolidated accounts receivable	$ 333,871	$ 565,738

4.   Faculty and Staff Mortgages

In a program to attract and retain excellent faculty and senior staff, the University provides home mortgage financing assistance. Notes amounting to $208,259,000 and $170,897,000 at August 31, 2001 and 2000, respectively, from University faculty and staff are included in "Faculty and staff mortgages and other loans receivable, net" in the consolidated statements of financial position and are collateralized by deeds of trust on properties concentrated in the region surrounding the University.

5. Investments

Investments held by the University and the Hospitals at August 31, 2001 and 2000, are reported as follows, in thousands of dollars:

	UNIVERSITY	2001 HOSPITALS	CONSOLIDATED	2000 CONSOLIDATED
Cash and short-term investments	$ 529,384	$ 209,191	$ 738,575	$ 767,646
Bonds and mutual funds	1,287,146	6,105	1,293,251	1,011,512
Corporate stocks and mutual funds	4,499,482	6,761	4,506,243	4,834,474
Assets held by other trustees	96,528	–	96,528	114,455
Real estate and improvements, including				
Stanford Shopping Center and Research Park	949,493	–	949,493	968,643
Limited partnership investments	2,494,535	–	2,494,535	3,022,130
Other	62,187	–	62,187	65,376
	9,918,755	222,057	10,140,812	10,784,236
SHC's and LPCH's investment in				
University's Merged Endowment Pool	(47,257)	47,257	–	–
Investments at fair value	$ 9,871,498	$ 269,314	$10,140,812	$10,784,236

The University reports endowment cash and short-term investments as investments. Assets held by other trustees are reported net of income beneficiary share in the amounts of $38,948,000 and $40,729,000 at August 31, 2001 and 2000, respectively.

Total investment return (loss) reflected in the statement of activities for the years ended August 31, 2001 and 2000, in thousands of dollars, is as follows:

	UNIVERSITY	2001 HOSPITALS	CONSOLIDATED	2000 CONSOLIDATED
Investment income	$ 277,795	$ 7,280	$ 285,075	$ 287,049
Net realized and unrealized gains (losses)	(774,839)	(10,746)	(785,585)	2,589,434
Total investment return (loss)	$ (497,044)	$ (3,466)	$ (500,510)	$ 2,876,483

For the year ended August 31, 2001, recognized investment losses and utilized prior years' gains amounted to $945,364,000. For the year ended August 31, 2000, total investment return of $2,362,266,000 was reinvested.

As indicated in the following table, as of August 31, 2001 and 2000, in thousands of dollars, the University's investments are invested in the expendable funds pool (EFP), the merged endowment pools, or in specific instruments to comply with donor requirements:

	2001	2000
UNIVERSITY:		
Expendable Funds Pool	$ 1,099,178	$ 919,665
Merged Endowment Pool	7,811,508	8,575,607
Merged Pool C	125,424	165,928
Living trusts	539,623	494,530
Other investments	960,012	1,358,270
	10,535,745	11,514,000
Less funds cross-invested in endowment pools (including SHC's and LPCH's investment of $47,257 and $159,811 in 2001 and 2000, respectively, in the University's Merged Endowment Pool)	664,247	979,559
	9,871,498	10,534,441
HOSPITALS:		
SHC's and LPCH's investments	269,314	249,795
Investments at fair value	$10,140,812	$10,784,236

The EFP is a pool of funds that is intended to provide adequate liquidity as well as an opportunity for the University to earn long-term growth on a portion of the pool. Approximately half of the EFP is invested in short-term or highly liquid securities, and the balance is cross-invested in the Merged Endowment Pool. The University Board of Trustees (the Board) has established a policy for the distribution of the investment returns of the EFP. The policy requires that an amount based upon a range of pre-set interest rates be made available to support current operations. The difference between the actual return of this pool and the required distribution amount is deposited or withdrawn from funds functioning as endowment. For the years ended August 31, 2001 and 2000, the results of the EFP, in thousands of dollars, were as follows:

	2001 UNIVERSITY	2000 UNIVERSITY
Total investment return of the EFP	$ 35,529	$ 246,514
Less income made available to fundholders	54,936	90,770
Income (withdrawn from) or invested in the endowment	$ (19,407)	$ 155,744

The University's endowment is invested with the objective of maximizing long-term total return. The University's policy governing the amounts paid annually from the endowment to support current operations is designed to protect the value of the endowment against the expected impact of inflation and to provide real growth of the endowment, while also funding a relatively constant portion of the University's current operating expenditures. The sources of the payout are earned income on the endowment assets (interest, dividends, rents, and royalties), previously reinvested income, and a portion of realized capital gains.

To meet the Board-authorized payout rate, income, gains, and previously reinvested endowment income were distributed for operations in fiscal years 2001 and 2000, as follows, in thousands of dollars:

	2001 UNIVERSITY	2000 UNIVERSITY
Endowment income	$ 215,989	$ 215,727
Realized gains and previously reinvested income	138,452	99,275
Approved payout	$ 354,441	$ 315,002

The University utilizes derivatives and other strategies to manage market risks, including interest rate and foreign currency risks, and to achieve efficient exposure to certain asset classes. The University enters into foreign currency forward contracts primarily for the purpose of minimizing the risk to the University of adverse changes in the relationship between currencies. The University uses interest rate swaps to manage the interest rate exposure of its commercial paper. See Note 8. The University generally enters into options and futures contracts for the purpose of reducing the risk level of its investments or serving as a temporary surrogate for investment in stocks and bonds.

At August 31, 2001, the University's derivative positions included foreign currency forward contracts, interest rate swaps, and options and futures contracts. The fair value of these derivatives was $14,507,000. It is not practicable to separate the gain or loss component of investment transactions associated with derivatives.

Foreign currency forward contracts, interest rate swaps, stock lending, and repurchase agreements necessarily involve counterparty credit risk. The University seeks to control this risk by entering into transactions with high quality counterparties and through counterparty credit evaluations and approvals, counterparty credit limits, and exposure monitoring. With respect to securities lending and repurchase agreements, it is the University's policy to require receipt of collateral on each contract equal to a minimum of 100% of the security loaned.

6. Pledges Receivable

Unconditional promises are included in the financial statements as pledges receivable and are classified as either temporarily restricted or permanently restricted, depending upon donor requirements. Conditional promises, which depend on the occurrence of a specified future and uncertain event, such as matching gifts from other donors, are recognized when the conditions are substantially met. Pledges are recorded at the present value of the discounted future cash flows, net of allowances. At August 31, 2001 and 2000, pledges receivable are as follows, in thousands of dollars:

	UNIVERSITY	2001 HOSPITALS	CONSOLIDATED	2000 CONSOLIDATED
One year or less	$ 71,473	$ 3,636	$ 75,109	$ 28,736
Between one year and five years	431,673	22,669	454,342	498,578
More than five years	506,610	–	506,610	90,126
	1,009,756	26,305	1,036,061	617,440
Less conditional pledges	251,630	18,400	270,030	1,448
Less discount/allowance	238,747	–	238,747	134,495
Pledges receivable	$ 519,379	$ 7,905	$ 527,284	$ 481,497

7. Plant Facilities

Plant facilities at August 31, 2001 and 2000, in thousands of dollars, are as follows:

	UNIVERSITY	2001 HOSPITALS	CONSOLIDATED	2000 CONSOLIDATED
Land and improvements	$ 142,496	$ 5,886	$ 148,382	$ 140,108
Buildings	1,968,783	420,909	2,389,692	2,136,033
Equipment and books	960,235	283,549	1,243,784	1,142,014
Construction in progress	256,457	32,001	288,458	342,500
Plant facilities	3,327,971	742,345	4,070,316	3,760,655
Less accumulated depreciation	1,274,783	441,802	1,716,585	1,556,809
Plant facilities, net of accumulated depreciation	$ 2,053,188	$ 300,543	$ 2,353,731	$ 2,203,846

In fiscal year 2000, the University revised the useful lives to reflect current useful life information and to comply with the new federal cost recovery regulations. The effect of this change in estimate was an increase in the depreciation charge for the year ended August 31, 2000 of approximately $40,000,000.

Fully depreciated assets, mainly equipment and books, that are still in use by the University amounted to approximately $567,000,000 and $539,000,000 at August 31, 2001 and 2000, respectively. During the year ended August 31, 2001, the University retired approximately $40,536,000 in fixed assets and their related accumulated depreciation.

8.   University Notes and Bonds Payable

Notes and bonds payable at August 31, 2001 and 2000, in thousands of dollars, are as follows:

	2001	2000
TAX-EXEMPT		
CALIFORNIA EDUCATIONAL FACILITIES AUTHORITY (CEFA):		
Revenue Bonds, due serially to 2032, with interest from 4.0% to 6.0%	$ 637,250	$ 558,235
Revenue Bonds, Series L with variable interest rates	99,543	83,819
Department of Education Bonds of 1959 to 1984 due serially to 2024,		
with interest from 3.0% to 3.5%	3,222	3,913
TAXABLE		
Stanford University Bonds due 2024, with fixed interest of 6.875%	150,000	150,000
Medium Term Notes ($150,000 authorized) due to 2026,		
with fixed interest from 5.85% to 7.65%	142,100	87,100
Commercial Paper, with variable interest rates	155,000	160,500
Other, with various interest rates	29,726	93,166
University notes and bonds payable before premiums (discounts)	1,216,841	1,136,733
Net unamortized premiums (discounts)	815	(1,027)
University notes and bonds payable	$ 1,217,656	$ 1,135,706

At August 31, 2001 and 2000, the fair value of these debt instruments approximated their recorded value.

The University incurred interest expense of approximately $71,352,000 and $62,958,000 for fiscal years 2001 and 2000, respectively, of which approximately $7,029,000 and $9,885,000, respectively, have been capitalized as a cost of construction.

Scheduled principal payments on notes and bonds, in thousands of dollars, are approximately:

YEAR	PRINCIPAL
2002 Commercial Paper	$ 155,000
2002 Other	18,535
2003	2,509
2004	1,057
2005	15,309
2006	965
Thereafter	1,023,466
Total	$ 1,216,841

The University has a commercial paper credit facility that provides for borrowings up to $200,000,000. The outstanding balance at August 31, 2001, was $155,000,000. The weighted average days to maturity is 82.35, and the weighted average effective interest rate is 3.7%. The University uses interest rate swaps to manage the interest rate exposure of its commercial paper program. See Note 5.

The CEFA Revenue Bonds have certain restrictive covenants, including maintenance of certain financial ratios. In October 2001, the University issued $15,490,000 in CEFA L-9 Refunding Revenue Bonds at an initial interest rate of 1.85%. During fiscal year 2001, the University legally defeased approximately $124,000,000 of CEFA J Revenue Bonds.

9.   Hospitals' Notes and Bonds Payable

Bonds and certificates at August 31, 2001 and 2000, in thousands of dollars, are as follows:

	2001	2000
Fixed Rate Revenue Bonds 1998 Series B, payable in annual amounts through 2013, with an average interest rate of 5%	$ 188,935	$ 191,475
1993 Variable Rate Certificates of Participation, payable in annual amounts through 2023, with an average interest rate of 3% in 2001	38,900	43,196
Hospitals' notes and bonds payable	$ 227,835	$ 234,671

The bonds and certificates are unsecured joint obligations of SHC and LPCH (the Obligated Group). Payments of principal and interest on the bonds and certificates are insured by municipal bond guaranty policies. The Master Trust Indenture of the Obligated Group includes, among other things, limitations on additional indebtedness, liens on property, restrictions on disposition or transfer of assets, and compliance with certain financial ratios. SHC and LPCH may redeem the bonds and certificates, in whole or in part, prior to the stated maturities. Redemption of the bonds requires a premium of up to 2%. Redemption of the certificates is without premium.

Holders of the certificates have the option to tender the certificates as of designated purchase dates. In order to ensure the availability of funds to purchase any certificates tendered that the remarketing agent is unable to remarket, LPCH has obtained bank credit agreements that expire beginning in September 2003, unless extended by mutual agreement. LPCH has the option to convert the certificates to a fixed rate.

Estimated principal payments on bonds and certificates, in thousands of dollars, are summarized below:

YEAR	PRINCIPAL
2002	$ 3,570
2003	3,800
2004	4,045
2005	4,190
2006	4,445
Thereafter	207,785
Total	$ 227,835

The fair value of these debt instruments is estimated based on the quoted market prices for the same or similar issues and on the current rates offered to SHC and LPCH for debt of the same remaining maturities. The estimated fair value of the debt instruments as of August 31, 2001 and 2000 approximated the recorded value.

At August 31, 2001, the Obligated Group had swap agreements expiring through 2023 to pay a fixed interest rate of 6.22%. The fair value of the interest rate swap is the estimated amount that the Hospitals would currently pay to terminate the swap agreement at the reporting date, taking into account current interest rates and current creditworthiness of the swap counterparties. The estimated fair value (loss) of the interest rate swap was $(8,250,000) as of August 31, 2001. The swap adjustment is net of the previously recorded fair value of the swap resulting from the purchase accounting adjustment related to the combination of SHS and LPCH in January 1997. The effect of the interest rate swap utilized to offset variable-rate funding was to increase interest expense by $1,280,000 for 2001.

The University is not an obligor or guarantor with respect to any obligations of the Obligated Group.

10. Liabilities Under Security Agreements

At August 31, 2001 and 2000, the University held $372,962,000 and $190,432,000, respectively, of short-term U.S.Government obligations and cash as collateral deposits for certain securities loaned temporarily to brokers. These amounts are included as assets and liabilities in the University's financial statements. In addition, at August 31, 2001, the University sold a security subject to an obligation to repurchase it at a future date in the amount of $28,469,000. The borrowing has been accounted for as a financing transaction and bears interest at a rate of 3.9%. The estimated market value of securities on loan and pledged under repurchase agreements at August 31, 2001 and 2000, were $389,936,000 and $184,424,000, respectively.

The University sells securities "short" in order to enhance investment returns and manage market exposure. At August 31, 2001 and 2000, the fair market value of such securities is $110,076,000 and $168,009,000, respectively.

11.   University Endowment

The University manages a substantial portion of its financial resources within its endowment. These assets include pure endowment, term endowments, funds functioning as endowment, and funds subject to living trust agreements. Depending on the nature of the donor's stipulation, these resources are recorded as permanently restricted, temporarily restricted, or unrestricted net assets.

Pure endowment funds are subject to the restrictions of the gift instruments requiring that the principal be invested in perpetuity and the income and an appropriate portion of gains only be spent as provided for under the California Uniform Management of Institutional Funds Act (CUMIFA). In the absence of further donor restrictions, the amount of gains that are to be expended in a given year is determined through the endowment payout policy discussed in Note 5. The University classifies the original endowment gift and any donor-imposed restricted gains as permanently restricted assets. The Financial Accounting Standards Board (FASB) has determined that the legal limitations imposed by CUMIFA on the amount of realized and unrealized gains on endowments that may be appropriated for current expenditure do not constitute restrictions for financial reporting purposes. Accordingly, the University reports the reinvested realized and unrealized gains as unrestricted net assets. Notwithstanding this FASB-mandated reporting, the University recognizes the limitations on expending such gains that are specified in CUMIFA.

Expendable endowment assets include term endowments and funds functioning as endowment. Term endowments are similar to other endowment funds except that upon the passage of a stated period of time or the occurrence of a particular event, all or part of the principal may be expended. These resources are classified as temporarily restricted net assets. Funds functioning as endowment are unrestricted University resources designated as endowment by the Board and are invested in the endowment for long-term appreciation and current income. However, these assets remain available and may be spent at the Board's discretion. Funds functioning as endowment are recorded as unrestricted net assets.

Funds subject to living trust agreements represent trusts with living income beneficiaries where the University has a residual interest. The investments of these funds are recorded at their fair market value. The discounted present value of any income beneficiary interest is reported as a liability on the statement of financial position in accordance with actuarial tables established by the Internal Revenue Service. Gifts subject to such agreements are recorded as revenue net of the income beneficiary share at the date of gift. Actuarial gains or losses are included in living trust investment income and actuarial adjustment. Resources that are expendable upon maturity are classified as temporarily restricted net assets; all others are classified as permanently restricted net assets.

Changes in the University's endowment, excluding pledges for the years ended August 31, 2001 and 2000, in thousands of dollars, are as follows:

	2001	2000
Endowment, beginning of year	$ 8,885,905	$ 6,226,695
INVESTMENT RETURNS:		
Earned endowment income (including $3,957 and $3,203 reinvested in endowment, as required by donor, in 2001 and 2000, respectively)	219,946	218,930
Change in net realized and unrealized appreciation of investments during the year	(737,553)	2,274,184
Total investment returns	(517,607)	2,493,114
Unrestricted income and gains distributed for operations	(354,441)	(315,002)
Endowment returns reinvested (withdrawn)	(872,048)	2,178,112
OTHER CHANGES IN ENDOWMENT:		
Gifts (net of $47,420 and $172,684 in pledges in 2001 and 2000, respectively)	158,159	242,315
Investment of funds in endowment	102,911	80,420
EFP income invested in (withdrawn from) endowment	(19,407)	155,744
Actuarial adjustment on living trusts	733	12,404
Other changes	(6,702)	(9,785)
Net increase (decrease) in endowment	(636,354)	2,659,210
Endowment, end of year	$ 8,249,551	$ 8,885,905

12. University Gifts

The University's Office of Development (OOD) reports total gifts based on contributions received in cash or property during the fiscal year. Gifts reported for financial statement purposes are recorded on the accrual basis. The following summarizes gifts and pledges received, for the years ended August 31, 2001 and 2000, per the statement of activities reconciled to the cash basis (as reported by OOD), in thousands of dollars:

	2001	2000
Expendable gifts in support of operations	$ 125,284	$ 113,187
Expendable gifts invested in the endowment	5,884	17,742
Temporarily restricted general gifts	99,120	148,750
Buildings and improvements	42,693	178,197
Permanently restricted endowment gifts	187,085	390,605
Permanently restricted student loans	84	11
Total University gifts per statement of activities	460,150	848,492
ADJUSTMENTS TO GIFT TOTAL AS REPORTED BY OOD:		
Pledges	(215,382)	(532,434)
Non-government grants, recorded as sponsored research support	48,865	37,706
Payments made on pledges	177,502	228,038
Actuarial gains on maturity of living trusts within five years of date of gift	292	265
Other	(2,461)	(1,593)
Total University gifts as reported by OOD	$ 468,966	$ 580,474

13. Functional Expenses

Expenses for each of the years ended August 31, 2001 and 2000, were categorized as follows, in thousands of dollars:

	2001	2000
UNIVERSITY:		
Instruction and departmental research	$ 667,991	$ 610,270
Organized research (direct costs)	623,113	580,566
Libraries	107,001	92,586
Student services	56,306	49,129
Administration and general	128,446	116,547
Development	82,461	66,780
SLAC construction	12,433	7,332
Auxiliary activities	281,470	239,777
	1,959,221	1,762,987
HOSPITALS:		
Health care services	934,680	397,490
Total consolidated expenses	$ 2,893,901	$ 2,160,477

Depreciation, interest, and plant operations and maintenance expenses are allocated to program and supporting activities, except for SLAC construction. Auxiliary activities include housing and dining services, intercollegiate athletics, SAA, other activities, and certain patient care provided by the School of Medicine.

14. University Pension Plans and Other Postretirement Benefits

The University provides retirement benefits, through both contributory and noncontributory pension plans, for substantially all of its employees. In addition to providing pension benefits, the University provides certain health care benefits for retired employees (other post-retirement benefits).

Pension Plans › The University's policy is to fund pension costs in accordance with the Employee Retirement Income Security Act's minimum funding requirements. Total net pension expense for the years ended August 31, 2001 and 2000, was approximately $43,594,000 and $40,613,000, respectively.

Retirement benefits for certain nonexempt employees are provided through a noncontributory defined benefit pension plan. The University recognized a credit to net pension expense related to the defined benefit pension plan of $11,016,000 and $8,805,000 for the years ended August 31, 2001 and 2000, respectively. Effective January 1, 2001, benefits for each year of service prior to 1992 are based on 1992 earnings. The amendment applies to those who were both eligible employees and participants in the plan on January 1, 2001.

The University offers a defined contribution pension plan to eligible faculty and staff. University and participant contributions are invested in annuities and mutual funds. University contributions under this plan amounted to approximately $54,496,000 and $49,404,000 for the years ended August 31, 2001 and 2000, respectively.

Other Post-Retirement Benefit Plans › The University's employees may become eligible for other post-retirement benefits upon retirement. Retiree health plans are paid for in part by retiree contributions, which are adjusted annually. Benefits are provided through various insurance companies whose charges are based either on the benefits paid during the year or annual premiums. Health benefits are provided to retirees and their covered dependents. The University recognizes the cost of post-retirement benefits over the periods that employees render service. The University recognizes the prior service obligation over 20 years.

Effective January 1, 1999, the University capped its health care benefits plan subsidy for post-65 benefits for non-Medicare+ Choice programs. The University's subsidy for post-65 benefits for non-Medicare+ Choice programs was increased effective January 1, 2001. Effective January 1, 2002, the University will remove the cap and provide a subsidy equal to the lowest cost plan for non-Medicare+ Choice programs.

The change in pension and other post-retirement plan assets and the related change in benefit obligation, in thousands of dollars as of and for the years ended August 31, 2001 and 2000, were as follows:

| | PENSION | | OTHER POST-RETIREMENT | |
	2001	2000	2001	2000
CHANGE IN PLAN ASSETS				
Fair value of plan assets at beginning of year	$ 284,642	$ 253,611	$ 28,103	$ 25,266
Actual return on plan assets	(13,022)	45,543	(2,516)	3,698
Employer contributions	–	–	6,843	3,555
Plan participants' contributions	–	–	2,575	1,588
Benefits paid	(15,695)	(14,512)	(9,418)	(6,004)
Fair value of plan assets at end of year	$ 255,925	$ 284,642	$ 25,587	$ 28,103
CHANGE IN BENEFIT OBLIGATION				
Benefit obligation at beginning of year	$ 194,559	$ 196,226	$ 103,566	$ 75,965
Service cost	4,699	4,286	3,678	2,777
Interest cost	14,961	13,760	7,551	5,352
Plan participants' contributions	–	–	2,575	1,588
Amendments	10,724	–	34,756	2,274
Actuarial (gain) loss	8,390	(5,201)	14,778	21,614
Benefits paid	(15,695)	(14,512)	(9,418)	(6,004)
Benefit obligation at end of year	$ 217,638	$ 194,559	$ 157,486	$ 103,566

The accrued benefit asset (cost), in thousands of dollars, was determined as follows at August 31, 2001 and 2000:

| | PENSION | | OTHER POST-RETIREMENT | |
	2001	2000	2001	2000
Plan assets minus benefit obligation	$ 38,287	$ 90,083	$ (131,899)	$ (75,463)
Unrecognized transition (asset) liability	(905)	(1,806)	31,080	33,391
Unrecognized prior service cost	10,980	1,493	36,818	2,274
Unrecognized net actuarial (gain) loss	(44,027)	(96,451)	31,387	11,715
Accrued benefit asset (cost) recorded in the statement of financial position	$ 4,335	$ (6,681)	$ (32,614)	$ (28,083)

The discount rate, expected rate of return on plan assets, and the projected covered payroll growth rates used in determining the previous accrued benefit costs were as follows for the years ended August 31, 2001 and 2000:

	PENSION		OTHER POST-RETIREMENT	
	2001	2000	2001	2000
Discount rate	7.00%	7.50%	7.00%	7.50%
Expected return on plan assets	8.75%	8.75%	8.75%	8.75%
Covered payroll growth rate	5.00%	5.00%	N/A	N/A

The assumed health care cost trend rate used to measure the accumulated post-retirement benefit obligation at August 31, 2001, was 10% for calendar year 2002. The rate was assumed to decrease by 1% for each of the next four calendar years, and to decrease to 5.5% for the following year and remain level thereafter.

The assumed health care cost trend rate used to measure the accumulated post-retirement benefit obligation at August 31, 2000, was 10% for calendar year 2001. The rate was assumed to decrease by 1% for each of the next four calendar years, with a 6% annual rate for calendar year 2006, and to remain at that level thereafter.

Net benefit (income) expense related to the plans for the years ended August 31, 2001 and 2000, in thousands of dollars, included the following components:

	PENSION		OTHER POST-RETIREMENT	
	2001	2000	2001	2000
Service cost	$ 4,699	$ 4,286	$ 3,678	$ 2,777
Interest cost	14,961	13,760	7,551	5,352
Expected return on plan assets	(24,353)	(21,628)	(2,459)	(2,211)
Amortization of transition (asset) liability	(901)	(901)	2,568	2,568
Amortization of prior service cost	1,237	187	212	–
Recognized net actuarial (gain) loss	(6,659)	(4,509)	81	(52)
Net periodic benefit (income) expense	$ (11,016)	$ (8,805)	$ 11,631	$ 8,434

Assumed health care cost trend rates have a significant effect on the amounts reported for the health care plans. Increasing the health care cost trend rate by 1% in each future year would increase the accumulated post-retirement benefit obligation by $25,607,000 and the aggregate service and interest cost by $1,800,000. Decreasing the health care cost trend rate by 1% in each future year would decrease the accumulated post-retirement benefit obligation by $20,639,000 and the aggregate service and interest cost by $1,411,000.

15. Hospitals' Pension Plans and Other Post-Retirement Benefits

SHC and LPCH provide retirement benefits through defined benefit and defined contribution retirement plans covering substantially all employees.

Defined Benefit Plans › Certain employees of SHC and LPCH are covered by a noncontributory, defined benefit pension plan (SHC Staff Pension Plan). Benefits of certain prior employees of LPCH are covered by a frozen defined benefit plan. Benefit obligations of the LPCH plan at August 31, 2001, were $4,675,000, offset by $4,644,000 of plan assets, and at August 31, 2000 were $4,200,000, offset by an equal amount of plan assets. Benefits are based on years of service and the employee's compensation. Contributions to the plans are based on actuarially determined amounts sufficient to meet the benefits to be paid to plan participants.

Benefits accumulated through March 31, 2000 (other than benefits under the frozen LPCH plan), are included in the benefit obligation recorded on the books of UCSF Stanford Health Care. Management of SHC, UCSF Stanford Health Care, and UC are in discussion with the IRS and Department of Labor in order to transfer those obligations and related plan assets to SHC and UC. At this time, eligible employees will be paid benefits for services provided before April 1, 2000 from UCSF Stanford Health Care, and benefits for services provided after April 1, 2000 will be paid by the SHC Staff Pension Plan. Since SHC ultimately expects UCSF Stanford Health Care to transfer certain of these obligations and all of the plan assets to SHC Staff Pension Plan, SHC and LPCH have recorded the net periodic benefit gain allocated to SHC and LPCH since March 31, 2000. SHC and LPCH also recorded service costs incurred since March 31, 2000, and other pension costs related to benefits accumulated since March 31, 2000. As a result, a net prepaid pension benefit of $1,871,000 was recorded by SHC and LPCH.

Defined Contribution Plan › Employer contributions to the defined contribution retirement plan are based on a percentage of participant annual compensation. Employer contributions to this plan totaling $19,900,000 and $6,700,000 are included in the employee benefits expense for fiscal year 2001 and the five months ended August 31, 2000, respectively.

Post-Retirement Medical Benefit Plan › SHC and LPCH currently provide health insurance coverage for employees upon retirement at age 55 with years of service as defined by certain criteria, or, for specific employees, at age 65 with at least five years of service. The health insurance coverage is the same as that provided for active employees. The obligation for these benefits has been recorded in the accompanying consolidated statement of financial position.

The plan assets and benefit obligation presented below include the portion of the UCSF Stanford Health Care pension plan related to SHC and LPCH employees, the frozen LPCH plan, and the SHC Staff Pension Plan. The net periodic pension cost and post-retirement medical benefit cost include the following components, in thousands of dollars, as of and for the year ended August 31, 2001, and as of and for the five months ended August 31, 2000:

	PENSION BENEFITS		POST-RETIREMENT MEDICAL BENEFITS	
	2001	2000	2001	2000
CHANGE IN PLAN ASSETS				
Fair value of plan assets at beginning of year	$ 129,165	$ 129,222	$ −	$ −
Actual return on plan assets	(10,952)	1,545	−	−
Employer contributions	527	208	2,727	898
Benefits paid	(5,872)	(1,810)	(2,727)	(898)
Fair value of plan assets at end of year	$ 112,868	$ 129,165	$ −	$ −
CHANGE IN BENEFIT OBLIGATION				
Benefit obligation at beginning of year	$ 99,815	$ 97,966	$ 49,812	$ 47,782
Service cost	1,764	681	1,958	751
Interest cost	7,669	3,331	3,777	1,528
Actuarial (gain) loss	10,531	(353)	12,019	649
Benefits paid	(5,872)	(1,810)	(2,727)	(898)
Benefit obligation at end of year	$ 113,907	$ 99,815	$ 64,839	$ 49,812

The accrued benefit asset (cost), in thousands of dollars, was determined as follows at August 31, 2001 and 2000:

	PENSION BENEFITS		POST-RETIREMENT MEDICAL BENEFITS	
	2001	2000	2001	2000
Plan assets minus benefit obligation	$ (1,039)	$ 29,350	$ (64,839)	$ (49,812)
Unrecognized prior service cost	−	−	3,317	2,730
Unrecognized (gain) loss	(11,436)	(43,599)	7,628	(4,721)
Accrued benefit cost recorded in the statement of financial position	(12,475)	(14,249)	(53,894)	(51,803)
Less: Accrued benefit cost at UCSF Stanford Health Care	14,998	14,998	−	−
Accrued benefit asset (cost) recorded by SHC and LPCH	$ 2,523	$ 749	$ (53,894)	$ (51,803)

Net benefit (income) expense related to the plans for the years ended August 31, 2001 and 2000, in thousands of dollars, included the following components:

| | PENSION BENEFITS | | POST-RETIREMENT MEDICAL BENEFITS | |
	2001	2000	2001	2000
Service cost	$ 1,764	$ 681	$ 1,958	$ 751
Interest cost	7,669	3,331	3,777	1,528
Expected return on plan assets	(9,422)	(4,016)	–	–
Amortization of prior service cost	–	–	(587)	(436)
Recognized net actuarial (gain)	(1,237)	(607)	(330)	(403)
Net periodic benefit (income) expense	$ (1,226)	$ (611)	$ 4,818	$ 1,440

The discount rate, expected rate of return on plan assets, and the projected covered payroll growth rates used in determining the above accrued benefit costs were as follows for the years ended August 31, 2001 and 2000:

| | PENSION | | OTHER POST-RETIREMENT | |
	2001	2000	2001	2000
Discount rate	7.25%	7.75%	7.25%	7.75%
Expected return on plan assets	8.00%	8.00%	N/A	N/A
Rate of compensation increase	5.50%	3.5–5.5%	N/A	N/A

The assumed health care cost trend rate used to measure the accumulated post-retirement benefit obligation at August 31, 2001 was 12% for the year ended August 31, 2002. The rate was assumed to decrease by 1.5% for the next five years and to remain at 4.75% thereafter.

Assumed health care cost trend rates have a significant effect on the amounts reported for the medical benefit plan. Increasing the health care cost trend rate by 1% in each future year would increase the accumulated post-retirement benefit obligation by $3,608,000 and the aggregate service and interest cost by $56,000. Decreasing the health care cost trend rate by 1% in each future year would decrease the accumulated post-retirement benefit obligation by $3,256,000 and the aggregate service and interest cost by $301,000.

16. Commitments and Contingencies

Management is of the opinion that none of the following commitments and contingencies will have a material adverse effect on the University's consolidated financial position.

Sponsored Projects › The University conducts substantial research for the federal government pursuant to contracts and grants from federal agencies and departments. The University records reimbursements of direct and indirect costs (facilities and administrative costs) from grants, contracts, and SLAC as operating revenues. The Office of Naval Research is the University's cognizant federal agency for determining indirect cost rates charged to federally sponsored agreements. It is supported by the Defense Contract Audit Agency, which has the responsibility for auditing direct and indirect charges under those agreements. Direct and indirect costs recovered by the University in support of sponsored research are subject to audit and adjustment.

Hospitals ‣ Cost reports filed under the Medicare program for services based upon cost reimbursement are subject to audit. The estimated amounts due to or from the program are reviewed and adjusted annually based upon the status of such audits and subsequent appeals.

The health care industry is subject to numerous laws and regulations of federal, state, and local governments. Compliance with these laws and regulations can be subject to future government review and interpretation, as well as regulatory actions unknown or unasserted at this time. Recently, government activity has increased with respect to investigations and allegations concerning possible violations of regulations by health care providers. These violations could result in the imposition of significant fines and penalties, as well as significant repayments for patient services previously billed. SHC and LPCH are subject to similar regulatory reviews, and while such reviews may result in repayments and/or civil remedies that could have a material effect on SHC's and LPCH's financial results of operations in a given period, management believes that such repayments and/or civil remedies would not have a material effect on the hospitals' financial position.

HIPAA ‣ The Health Insurance Portability and Accountability Act (HIPAA) was enacted August 21, 1996, to assure health insurance portability, reduce healthcare fraud and abuse, guarantee security and privacy of health information and enforce standards for health information. Organizations are required to be in compliance with certain HIPAA provisions beginning October 2002. Provisions not yet finalized are required to be implemented two years after the effective date of the regulation. Organizations are subject to significant fines and penalties if found not to be compliant with the provisions outlined in the regulations. Management is in the process of evaluating the impact of this legislation on its operations including future financial commitments that will be required to comply with the legislation.

Litigation ‣ The University and the Hospitals are defendants in a number of other legal actions. While the final outcome cannot be determined at this time, management is of the opinion that the liability, if any, resulting from these legal actions will not have a material adverse effect on the University's consolidated financial position.

Contractual Commitments ‣ At August 31, 2001, the University had contractual obligations of approximately $86,292,000 in connection with major construction projects. Remaining expenditures on construction in progress are estimated to be $531,506,000, which will be financed with certain unexpended plant funds, gifts, and debt.

At August 31, 2001, the remaining commitment on contracts for the construction and remodeling of hospital facilities was approximately $38,000,000.

The consolidated financial statements on the preceding pages have been prepared in conformity with generally accepted accounting principles. The management of Stanford University is responsible for the integrity and objectivity of these consolidated financial statements.

In accumulating and controlling its financial data, management maintains a highly developed system of internal accounting controls. Management believes that a high level of internal control is maintained by the establishment and communication of accounting and business policies, by the selection and training of qualified personnel, and by a program of internal audits to give it reasonable assurance at reasonable cost that the University's assets are protected and that transactions and events are recorded properly.

The accompanying consolidated financial statements, where indicated, have been audited by the University's independent accountants, PricewaterhouseCoopers LLP. Their report expresses an informed judgment as to whether management's consolidated financial statements considered in their entirety, present fairly, in conformity with generally accepted accounting principles, the University's financial position and changes in net assets and cash flows. The independent accountants' opinion is based on audit procedures described in their report, which include obtaining an understanding of University systems, procedures, and internal accounting controls, and performing tests and other auditing procedures to provide reasonable assurance that the financial statements are neither materially misleading nor contain material errors. While the independent accountants make extensive tests of University procedures and controls, it is neither practical nor necessary for them to scrutinize a large portion of the University's transactions.

The Board of Trustees, through its Audit Committee, composed of trustees not employed by the University, is responsible for engaging the independent accountants and meeting with management, internal auditors, and the independent accountants to ensure that each is carrying out its responsibilities and to discuss auditing, internal control, and financial reporting matters. Both the internal auditors and the independent accountants have full and free access to the Audit Committee. Both meet with the Audit Committee at least annually, with and without each other, and with and without the presence of management representatives.

RANDALL S. LIVINGSTON
Vice President for Business Affairs
and Chief Financial Officer

M. SUZANNE CALANDRA
Controller

Report of Independent Accountants

To The Board of Trustees
Stanford University
Stanford, California

In our opinion, based on our audits and the report of other auditors, the accompanying consolidated statements of financial position and the related consolidated statements of activities and cash flows, which appear on pages 31 through 58, present fairly, in all material respects, the financial position of Stanford University at August 31, 2001 and 2000, and the changes in its net assets and its cash flows for the years then ended in conformity with accounting principles generally accepted in the United States of America. These financial statements are the responsibility of the University's management; our responsibility is to express an opinion on these financial statements based on our audits. We did not audit the financial statements of Stanford Hospital and Clinics, an entity controlled by the University, which statements reflect total assets of $910 million and $924 million as of August 31, 2001 and 2000, respectively, and total unrestricted revenues of $1,059 million and $399 million for the years then ended. Those statements were audited by other auditors whose report thereon has been furnished to us, and our opinion expressed herein, insofar as it relates to the amounts included for Stanford Hospital and Clinics, is based solely on the report of the other auditors. We conducted our audits of these statements in accordance with auditing standards generally accepted in the United States of America, which require that we plan and perform the audit to obtain reasonable assurance about whether the financial statements are free of material misstatement. An audit includes examining, on a test basis, evidence supporting the amounts and disclosures in the financial statements, assessing the accounting principles used and significant estimates made by management, and evaluating the overall financial statement presentation. We believe that our audits and the report of other auditors provide a reasonable basis for our opinion.

PricewaterhouseCoopers LLP

San Francisco, California
November 21, 2001

The Stanford University Annual
Report is prepared by the Office
of the Controller and the Office of
University Communications.

DESIGN Brian Dittmar Graphic Design,
San Francisco

PHOTOGRAPHY Linda A. Cicero,
Stanford News Service; Jason Walker
photograph on page 4 by Joel Simon;
Linda Meier photograph on page 5 by
Steve Castillo; foothill photographs are
courtesy of the Stanford News Service.

Published February 2002

Appendix D

Understanding Institutions and Faculty:
Activities and Motivations

Appendix E

Data Necessary to Implement and Sustain
Strategic Institutional Management

Appendix F

Theoretical Model for Evaluating
Institutional Productivity

APPENDIX D
UNDERSTANDING INSTITUTIONS AND FACULTY: ACTIVITIES AND MOTIVATIONS

To develop an understanding of colleges and universities, one must understand the motivations and activities of its faculty. Many have said that the most important and valuable asset that a college or university has is its faculty. Indeed, some will refer to faculty as an institution's scholarly assets. However, this may be much too crass. Faculty are people; they have feelings, inspirations, motivations, egos, wants, needs, etc. When discussing faculty, it is important, however, to understand that faculty have loyalties that extend beyond the institution. These loyalties are, perhaps, first to their disciplines, secondly to their individual research interest(s), thirdly perhaps to their students and, lastly, to their institutions. They are scholars in search of the creation and dissemination of new knowledge. In fact, in many institutions, to attain tenure or advance in rank, faculty must publish or they will perish—one of the most feared means of failing after many years of intense preparation. Most tenure track appointments afford faculty only six to seven years to prove themselves as capable scholars or seek alternative employment. Therefore, expect that new faculty will concentrate on scholarly activities in their early years as they must appeal to a broader audience of their peers for acceptance of their thoughts and ideas to gain publication in refereed journals, etc. Only their peers, who are as deeply mired in the specific discipline and specialty field as they, are competent judges of the quality of their work. Few, if any, within the institution will be viewed as having the same level of mastery of their topical areas as they themselves. Thus, they do not take direction from the institutional administration beyond perhaps their departmental administrator. Understanding this simple fact will aid in developing an understanding of the rationale for much of the following text.

To take this notion one step further, one needs to understand that you simply do not attempt to manage intelligent, creative people with separate and divided loyalties with top-down bureaucratic management. Most college and university faculties do not respond well to a command and control management style. People who are compelled to think and write creatively are largely self-motivated and do not do well in rigid, limiting environments. They need the freedom to be innovative and flexible in using their time and energy. Most faculty do not create and write well in the confines of an 8:00 a.m.–5:00 p.m. work shift with rigid supervision. For these reasons, many a president/provost has lamented that managing a faculty is akin to herding cats. Each faculty member possesses unique interests, driven by different stimuli and incentives, all a bit finicky and coy in their mannerisms and attitudes. It really is quite a challenge to be an effective manager in this environment. This, combined with the protections afforded by tenure, a.k.a. life-time employment and academic freedom, gives them certain privileges and the security to speak their minds, and to defy many forms of authority.

To a person with a business orientation, the faculty, our most important assets, may appear to be (and likely are) our least managed resources. Nevertheless, attempting to overlay a rigid management structure on faculty will likely backfire, and this is perhaps the most important message the readers of this material need to understand. Given this, there is a certain amount of magic in a successful formula for the management of faculty in colleges and universities. Despite these drawbacks, many believe that faculty will respond to data-driven decision-making. They understand that data allows one to better understand the concepts and using information can produce better decisions. Furthermore, data can be used to create peer pressures that can greatly influence positive outcomes for the institution, assuming that it is done correctly.

FACULTY CULTURE AND CHANGE

According to Benne and Birnbaum (1969), both the formal and the informal organization of an institution must be considered in planning any process of change. Besides the formal structure, every social system has a network of cliques, guilds, and other informal systems that can exert strong restraining influences on changes initiated by formal authorities. These informal systems have significant power that unless harnessed in support of the change, either no enduring change is likely to occur, or the change will be less than envisioned. These informal groupings can control rates of work, that become norms which if violated by individuals invites ostracism, or other negative consequences for the offender. In an academic institution, these norms are established by departmental colleagues, people who will participate in peer review for salary increases, promotion and tenure decisions, and other important events that can have a significant influence on the ultimate success of the individual faculty member. Thus, these norms, beliefs and attitudes become very powerful in the shaping of the culture of an institution and have a profound impact on the individuals and activities that are allowed to occur within the institution.

Benne and Birnbaum (1969) also point out that the effectiveness of a planned change is often directly related to the degree to which members at all levels of an institutional hierarchy take part in the fact-finding and the diagnosis of needed changes and in the formulation and reality testing of goals and programs of change. Participation by those affected by the change increases the likelihood that new insights will be formed and that the goals of the change will be accepted. Consequently, faculty who are not involved in a change effort may feel little investment in, and commitment to, the proposed change.

Another factor that can influence the attitudes, values, and beliefs in an academic institution is the manner in which funding is allocated. According to Massey (1996), examining four assumptions implicit in traditional resource allocation can yield some interesting insights into the faculty beliefs regarding resource allocation, analysis, and reporting processes. These assumptions are very illustrative of the mindset that many faculty bring to the table when it comes to making decisions, especially when those decisions are related to financial management issues:

- The first assumption can be summed up by the phrase, "property rights." Once a unit has obtained approval for a program, that program has the right to continue unless circumstances change dramatically. Similar to tenure, most feel that programs should continue absent a declaration of financial exigency or other dramatic event. Tenure lines in program budgets involve contractual property rights, and faculty and students are viewed as deserving academic freedom. Thus their programs should be exempt from scrutiny or other capricious or malevolent judgments. Therefore, most faculty believe that no reductions can occur without due process, and that programs funded in the base budget are protected as first priority.

- Massey's second assumption is that academic units are too fragile and their work too important to be disrupted by the ebbs and flows of the marketplace. Academic time constraints as measured by the duration of faculty employment contracts and the evolutionary nature of their scholarship is simply incompatible with market

principles. Because of these issues faculty believe that the central administration should shield divisions and departments from financial fluctuations to the greatest extent possible. Revenue shortfalls or expense overruns should be covered from central reserves until the need for reduction is absolutely necessary and irrefutable.

- Massey's third assumption, related to the second, holds that the central administration should take responsibility for the financial health of the academic units. Not to maintain adequate funding for a unit is viewed as institutional failure—"a perception that can be mitigated but not eradicated by blaming external forces," according to Massey (1996, p. 30). Funding reductions are perceived as reductions in quality. Searching for productivity improvement or other operating efficiencies is not part of a faculty member's job. The institution is responsible for delivering the funding needed to maintain quality using traditional, academically acceptable methods.

- Massey's fourth assumption is that these responsibility principles are deeply embedded in the academic culture and are reaffirmed in the faculty marketplace. An institution that fails to provide the essential funding components can be subject to raiding activities of institutions in better financial condition. The concern for faculty morale and the prospect of losing one's best faculty make saying "no" difficult. Massey's conclusion is that this behavior results in a vicious circle as administrators believe that their job is to protect academic units from financial vicissitudes, which reinforces the faculty member's belief that it is indeed the institution's responsibility. This behavior serves to lower the tolerance for budget reductions among deans, department chairs, and faculty.

RESISTANCE TO CHANGE

According to Weisbord, "the urge to hold on—to old habits, familiar patterns, relationships, and structures (whether they satisfy or not)—is as old as human history" (1987, p. 268-269). Donald Schon called this concept, "dynamic conservatism" (1971, p. 32). According to Gray and Diamond, "Faculty culture, like any culture is resistant to change. The processes that have evolved in the United States to educate, select, reward, and protect faculty to be productive and creative scholars now acts as forces to limit the impact society can have on changing faculty culture. Furthermore, demographic and economic conditions over the last 10 to 15 years have led to large numbers of faculty being tenured, thereby enhancing their autonomy. Together these processes and conditions inhibit opportunity to change what faculty prefer, or have been prepared to do, and what they are expected to do. The conservative nature of faculty culture also is evident in its resistance to changes in the processes used to document what faculty actually do in their professional work and evaluate how well they do it" (1994, p. 65-66).

According to Becher and Kogan, "what is commonly seen as academic conservatism–the hostile reaction of academics, individually and collectively, to top-down pressures for root and branch reform–can also be viewed in a different light. The individuals concerned may well have invested years and much intellectual capital in the acquisition of a particular body of ideas, and the development of an associated strategy of research, scholarship, and teaching. Anything which can be seen as threatening to devalue this professional investment will naturally be resisted; its eventual acceptance will depend on overcoming the initial resistance by one strategy or another" (1992, p. 131–132).

In considering change and the resistance to change, Becher and Kogan stress that a distinction needs to be made between what is often referred to as "planned change" and change which is in a sense unplanned but inexorable. The latter embraces the type of adjustment that institutions, divisions, and individuals find themselves forced to make in the pattern of their daily activities as a result of external forces which are largely beyond their control. This type of change has only a negligible, or at most indirect and gradual, effect on individual and collective norms. There is no contesting this type of change as it is necessary for survival.

In contrast, however, are those innovations that originate in planned changes based on deliberate coercion. Becher and Kogan state that it is this type of change that is more likely to arouse conflict and contention. It is this type of coercive change, especially changes that conflict with strongly held internal norms, that are inherently unstable. Operational compliance may consist of no more than going through the motions, if not deliberate subversion. According to Massey (1996), faculty culture is such that there is a steady shift of faculty allegiance away from the goals of a given institution, toward those of an academic specialty. Massey refers to this phenomenon as "the ratchet" effect. He states that the ratchet effect can be traced to several processes that operate in academic department culture. Massey believes that together, these four processes form a potent force to resist changes posed from the external environment:

- The pursuit of faculty lines is a powerful objective of most department chairs regardless of enrollment levels. The push to hire more faculty is strong as they assist in building department prestige, teach introductory courses, or increase the intellectual capacity of the department.

- Leveraging faculty time refers to the use of graduate assistants, staff, and others to free up time for faculty to concentrate on their research and professional activities.

- De-structuring the curriculum, a process which began in the 1960s in response to student demand, has placed the burden of coordinating courses on individual faculty. This takes time and is often ignored, leaving students with a highly unstructured curriculum.

- Enactment of group norms and propagation of perceived property rights can have a significant impact in terms of obstructing change, even if the change could bring positive results during periods of cutbacks. Faculty members in all academic departments possess shared strongly held beliefs about their relationship to the external environment. On the basis of these norms, faculty develop certain property rights that they believe are inherent to their position and that they use to govern their activities. A senior faculty member may believe that he/she has the right not to teach any large introductory courses, teach a lesser number of courses/students, or other privileges.

However, when considering faculty as a group it would be a mistake to think that they are all alike. The next section will review studies of faculty culture which have found that faculty from different disciplines have differing cultural standards, values, and beliefs. Thus, any change effort, with associated analysis and reporting, needs to take these differences in faculty cultures into account as well.

UNDERSTANDING FACULTY AND INSTITUTIONAL DIFFERENCES

To more fully understand faculty cultures, it is important to have a discussion of faculty differences, from an institutional, disciplinary affiliation, and status (e.g. faculty vs. administrator) perspective. According to Eimers, "one common trap we stumble into when we think about faculty is to perceive them as a fairly homogeneous group" (1999, p. 19). Clark (1987) agrees and postulates that two characteristics, institutional and disciplinary affiliation, are the most powerful indicators useful in delineating the differences among faculty. According to Clark, the mission of an institution in many ways determines the role and autonomy that faculty enjoy. For example, according to Clark, faculty at research institutions enjoy the most autonomy and tend to dedicate more time to scholarship and graduate education than do faculty from other types of institutions. According to both Eimers (1999) and Clark (1987), institutional affiliation is probably the single most important factor in understanding differences among faculty members.

Writing about incentives and institutional differences, Baldwin and Krotseng state, "The various colleges and universities select professors with somewhat differing interests and skills. Likewise, they have different expectations of effective faculty performance. Hence the incentives various types of institutions employ and the incentives their faculty members respond to sometimes reflect special values and goals. For this reason, the incentives that will support faculty vitality in a liberal arts college are not the same incentives that will support vitality in a research university" (1985, p. 15).

Institutional affiliation, however, does little to help understand the differences among faculty from different disciplines. Thus, Clark's second characteristic, disciplinary affiliation is particularly important.

FIGURE 2: BIGLAN'S DISCIPLINARY DIMENSIONS

Dimensions	Hard	Soft
Pure	Biology	Anthropology
	Physiology	Political Science
	Astronomy	Psychology
	Chemistry	Sociology
	Geology	English
	Mathematics	History
	Physics	Philosophy
Applied	Agriculture	Education
	Chemical Engineering	Accounting
	Electrical Engineering	Finance
	Food Science and Nutrition	Economics
	Computer and Information Science	Business Administration
		Journalism
		Social Work
		Nursing
		Natural Resources

Source: Adapted from Biglan, 1973

UNDERSTANDING DISCIPLINARY DIFFERENCES:

Biglan (1973) was among the first researchers to attempt to understand the differences among faculty from different disciplines. Biglan examined the tasks performed by faculty from specific subject areas and characterized these tasks into dimensions as outlined in Figure 2.

The hard-soft dimension as used in Figure 2 refers to the level of paradigmatic development within the field of study. Biglan found that faculty in hard dimensions, as contrasted to faculty in soft dimensions, were more likely to agree on what constituted knowledge in the field and how research should be approached, and what research avenues were worthy of investigation. According to Eimers (1999), this has been proven by a Carnegie Foundation study in 1999 which found that 77 percent of faculty in physical sciences (the hard dimension) as contrasted to 39 percent of faculty in education (the soft dimension) agreed with the question, "In my discipline, most faculty agree on the standards of good scholarship."

According to Donald (1995), faculty in hard disciplines are also more likely to study a relatively narrow phenomenon that is frequently well-structured, logical, and incremental. When exploring these phenomena, scholars tend to agree on underlying theory, assumptions, and methodological approaches. In addition, replication is critical to these studies, and generally once a theory is accepted, it is often not revisited. Furthermore, according to Donald, because scholars in the field have reached consensus on many underlying premises, the likelihood of getting manuscripts published in refereed journals in their fields is much higher in hard disciplines than it is in soft disciplines.

In contrast, Donald suggests that knowledge in soft dimensions is much less cumulative and incremental. In these disciplines, scholars often revisit the same questions, and the lack of accepted parameters and premises adds to the complexity. Studies in soft disciplines frequently are difficult to replicate, hampering theory development and fragmenting the knowledge base. According to Eimers, many disciplinary societies in soft fields continue to have lively debates on: which topics in the discipline are most significant in advancing knowledge in the field; disciplinary philosophical foundations; and the virtues of different methodologies. This demonstrates why the acceptance rate for manuscripts in refereed journals is lower in soft areas.

Becher (1989) suggests that there are also cultural differences between faculty in the hard and soft dimensions. According to Becher, these cultural differences can be largely attributed to the cognitive nature and paradigmatic development in the field of study. Like Biglan (1973), Becher (1989) found that faculty members in hard disciplines tended to share the same intellectual style and mutual identity, whereas, members in soft disciplines exhibited a variety of intellectual styles and high levels of fragmentation. Thus, Becher posited that faculty in hard areas were typically in a better position to advance their own interests because they agreed on those interests. Conversely, the lack of consensus among scholars in soft fields impeded their ability to advance their interests within their own institutions.

The second dimension that Biglan introduced was the pure-applied dimension. This dimension refers to the likelihood that a faculty member investigates issues of application versus theoretical issues to advance knowledge for knowledge's sake. According to Becher, the academic culture in applied fields can be highly entrepreneurial. Faculty are eager to master the physical environment and develop new products, techniques, programs, and materials for doing things. They are interested in finding new uses for their discoveries and often will forge partnerships with external entities to this end. In addition, faculty in applied fields are influenced in significant ways by the norms and values of their affiliated professions. They are keenly interested in, and influenced by, practitioners in the field. It is not unusual to find faculty members in applied disciplines who have followed a non-traditional career path to academia. Many have served as educators, social workers, or engineers before they entered doctoral programs. This experience has socialized them to perspectives that are maintained after their doctoral training is completed. On the other hand, faculty in pure disciplines have exhibited less interest in practice. Their loyalties lie within the discipline and with other academic colleagues, and their major interests are enhancing and revising knowledge in their field.

It is not surprising then that faculty in hard disciplines tend to prefer research over teaching, spend more time in research and have department chairs who are likely to emphasize research and graduate education. Conversely, faculty in soft disciplines are more likely to prefer teaching over research and spend more time on teaching. In addition, faculty in applied areas may be much more open to providing students with opportunities for learning outside the classroom, and in particular with opportunities for direct experience in the applied profession.

In research done for my dissertation, in which survey responses from faculty and academic administrators were contrasted, I found faculty from differing disciplines to be quite different in their perceptions of financial information and programs. These differences in perceptions were most pronounced when contrasting responses from faculty that were in the pure and applied disciplines. Faculty responses received from those in the pure disciplines were much more skeptical about both the motives and outcomes of a pending budget reform. Conversely, faculty from the applied disciplines not only agreed with the motives and outcomes, but seemed excited by the prospects of the reform. The most extreme cases, in both a negative and positive sense respectively, were liberal arts and hard science disciplines contrasted to business and engineering faculty. In addition, academic administrators were also much more positive regarding the perceived effects of the reform than were faculty members generally. Knowing that these differences exist can be very useful when designing reports or presenting information to these audiences. It can also help to understand their interest or attitudes regarding financial management, which can serve as a good indicator of where monitoring, training, or other staff resources should be directed.

UNDERSTANDING DIFFERENCES BETWEEN FACULTY AND ADMINISTRATORS

According to White (1990) numerous studies have identified differences between administrator and faculty perceptions of their institutions, however, these differences have not been examined extensively and may be substantial (Peterson and White, 1992). Numerous studies of organizational phenomena in colleges and universities present differences in faculty and administrative beliefs about and perceptions of their institutions. Most of these studies are based on faculty perspectives (Austin and Gameson, 1983; Bowen and Schuster, 1986; Rice and Austin, 1988). Research on what administrators believe about faculty is less extensive (Blackburn, Pitney, Lawrence, and Trautvetter, 1989).

In a national study of college and university presidents and faculty officers, Neuman (1987) found that presidents and faculty officers disagreed on the attributes of good leaders. In a national survey of faculty, Blackburn, Lawrence and Associates (1990), found consistent differences between faculty and administrator views of the organization on several dimensions, including views of organizational climate, academic workplace, and administrative supportiveness. According to Peterson and White (1992), these studies conclude: 1) that there are faculty and administrator differences on many organizational variables, 2) that these different perspectives occur in all institutional types, 3) that there are differences by institutional type, and 4) that those differences can be counterproductive.

Thus, we see how these attitudes have been shaped over time and how they affect the culture of the academic organization. To ignore the importance of these strongly held beliefs and values in the presentation and analysis of financial management information is a serious oversight.

APPENDIX E

DATA NECESSARY TO IMPLEMENT AND SUSTAIN STRATEGIC INSTITUTIONAL MANAGEMENT

(Adapted from the National Center for Higher Education Management Systems (NCHEMS), 1994):

I. Assets

  A. Personnel

    1. Institutional

      a. Number of full-time equivalent (>.50 FTE) personnel by EEO category

      b. FTE of part-time (<.50 FTE) personnel by EEO category

      c. FTE (or an equivalent measure) of student personnel by category

      d. Array the above data over a multi-year (five years at least) period

      e. Analyses should focus on:

        –Changes (if any) in distribution of FTE personnel over time

        –Changes in dependence on part-time and student personnel

    2. Unit Level

      a. Number of full-time (>.50 FTE) personnel by EEO category

      b. FTE of part-time (<.50 FTE) personnel by EEO category

      c. FTE (or an equivalent measure) of student personnel by category

      d. Array the above data over a multi-year (five year at least) period

      e. Analyses should focus on:

        –Variations in staffing levels across academic units

        –Changes in staffing levels in administrative units

  B. Facilities

    1. Buildings

      a. Replacement value

      b. Expenditures on renewal and renovation

    2. Rooms

      a. Summary of net assignable square feet (NASF) by room type

  C. Equipment and Library Holdings

    1. Book value and holdings value

    2. Annual expenditures on equipment and library acquisitions

  D. Program Inventory

    1. Inventory as of now

    2. Additions and deletions in last 5–10 years

  E. Financial Resources

    1. Revenues by source

      a. Trends over time

      b. Compared to peer institutions

    2. Restricted revenues acquired

      a. Amount

      b. Purpose

II. Allocation/Utilization of Assets

    A. Personnel

        1. Faculty

            a. Student credit hours (SCH) produced/FTE Faculty–for instruction and for each department (trend data)

            b. Funded research per FTE faculty by department (trend data)

        2. Administrative Employees

            a. For student service and academic support functions

                – Headcount and FTE students per employee

            b. For institutional support

                – total number of employees (institution-wide) per administrative and professional (as defined by EEO category) employee

    B. Facilities

        1. Classrooms

            a. NASF/weekly student hour of classroom instruction (a ratio of 1 or less indicates full utilization)

        2. Class labs–comparison with system standards

        3. Offices–comparison with system standards

        4. Study space–comparison with system standards

        5. Other types of facilities for which state standards exist

III. Maintenance of Assets

    A. Buildings

        1. Expenditures/replacement value (should be 1.5 to 2.0%)

        2. Depreciation

    B. Equipment

        1. Annual expenditures/book value (should be in the 10–15% range)

        2. Annual expenditures for library acquisitions

    C. Program

        1. $ investment in curriculum development in the past 5 years

        2. Number of years since each major (and general education) has had a thorough curriculum review/revision

    D. Personnel

        1. $ Expenditures on professional development/total salaries (no national standards but conventional wisdom says 2-5% would be about right)

    E. Financial Resources

        1. Expenses by function

            a. Trends over time

            b. Comparisons with peer institutions

    F. Expenses by organizational unit (multiple years)

IV. Price and Fiscal Measures

    A. Average faculty salaries as compared with peer institutions–by rank

    B. Expenses on services and supplies

        1. Institutional trends (per FTE student) over time

        2. Departmental allowances (per FTE student) for most recent year

V. Outputs and Quality

A. Persistence and completion by entering cohort
   1. Fall to Fall persistence
   2. Cumulative completion rate by cohort by year
   3. Cumulative credits enrolled for and completed by term of enrollment
   4. Average time to completion in elapsed terms and in enrolled terms
   5. Each of the above broken down by program and student characteristics (including key demographics, ability levels, etc.)
   6. Calculated separately for first-time freshmen and for transfers at various levels of incoming credit

B. Outputs
   1. Distribution of credit hours by level by department and term
   2. Distribution of degree awards by level by department and program

C. "Factors of Production" in Degree Awards
   1. Number of credits at graduation by program
   2. Cross-credit matrix at graduation by program
      a. Reflecting contributions by other institutions
      b. Reflecting contributions of different disciplines and faculties
      c. Resulting direct instructional cost to produce a degree

D. Quality of Instructional Processes
   1. Percentage of lower-division students enrolling in at least one regular class of fewer than X students
   2. Reported incidence of instructional "good practices" by students and faculty
   3. Number of classes failed by discipline/level broken down by:
      a. Whether pre-requisite courses taken
      b. Whether a performance of C or better was achieved in pre-requisite courses

E. Quality of Instructional Outcomes
   1. Accreditation of accreditable programs
   2. Post-graduate placement rates in further study or employment situations
   3. Licensure pass rates where applicable
   4. Student satisfaction and self-reported knowledge gains
   5. Any direct assessments by ability by program

APPENDIX F
THEORETICAL MODEL FOR EVALUATING INSTITUTIONAL PRODUCTIVITY

The construction of a model or models for measuring the relative efficiency of various institutional units is theoretically based, and by its nature, will be an ongoing process. While this report details some of the technical problems associated with this type of effort, as widely recognized in the literature on the economics of education, the real limitations to such modeling in units within an institution, or across institutions, may prove to be in generating faculty and administrative participation and acceptance.

This appendix discusses two exploratory models that have been developed at Portland State University (Thomas Palm, Professor of Economics, et al., 1994) and while original, adapts some ideas from attempts to model productivity at other institutions. This report summarizes the concepts considered in these models and summarizes issues for further discussion.

The general intent of both models is to establish benefit/cost ratios for the units under consideration. That is, measures of output are examined relative to associated inputs. The higher the output per unit of input, the more efficient is the unit in question. The data and units in the models are hypothetical, even whimsical, but many of the data already exist or could be assembled for actual cases.

The first model has a very limited measure of input and is restricted to a single institution. It is structured, in principle, to permit comparison of the (relative) productivity of (individual) professors across different departments. The second model expands on possible measures of multiple resource inputs, and introduces the possibility of measurement, by departments, across (roughly) comparable institutions. However, the relative rankings of departments across institutions could also be used for internal comparisons at a single institution across departments.

Let us consider the two approaches in more detail. The initial model seeks, in principle, to evaluate the productivity of individual professors in any given academic department. The model could be expanded across departments. As an obvious simplification, the input within any one department is measured solely by the 9-month salary of the individual professors. That is, there is no measure of other intradepartmental labor inputs, no measure of capital costs—depreciation or (implicit) rent—and no charge for administrative overhead. The defense of the procedure is the appeal of simplicity.

PROFESSORIAL OUTPUTS ARE MEASURED BY SEVERAL DIFFERENT INDICATORS

The first output is the number of weighted credit hours produced by each professor. Two types of weights are suggested. First, credit hours are weighted by lower division, upper division, master's, or doctoral levels. Then, for each professor, we can identify the total number of thus weighted credit hours produced and the credit hours produced per dollar of salary.

The model additionally proposes a general "utility weighting" schema. That is, a function is utilized to reduce the relative importance of *marginal* (i.e., additional or incremental) units of any output, here credit hours. Practically this means that doubled output of, for example, credit hours, would be counted as something less than a doubled value. The intent of such (diminishing marginal) utility weighting is to discourage generation of mere quantity in outputs, however conceived, at the expense of quality or other considerations. In a manner otherwise analogous to that already suggested, for each professor, we can also identify the total number of credit hours produced, as weighted both by level *and utility.*

A second possible measure of output considers the number of publications, as weighted by the type of item and again, if desired, by a utility function. The latter would again show "diminishing marginal utility." The productivity measure (benefit/cost ratio) would be the number of the weighted publications per salary dollar. For each such ratio, we can construct the reciprocal (cost/benefit ratio). In this case, that would be the salary dollars per publication, again weighted by utility and type.

The contributions of individual professors to community outreach, the service output, could be measured in a similar fashion. That is, contacts with the community would be counted, but weighted differently as appropriate. The resulting "score" could again be adjusted by a utility function. The productivity measure of community outreach would then be the number of weighted contacts per salary dollar, or the reciprocal.

A summary template could report the "scores" of the individual professors in teaching, research, and service. In principle, the production of individual professors could be aggregated and compared to that of other departments. Some of the practical problems associated with constructing and using such data within and across departments are discussed after the second model is introduced immediately below.

The general intent of the second model is to broaden and aggregate the concept of inputs and to compare equivalent departments (not individual professors) across (roughly) comparable institutions. This approach *a priori* assumes that the required data would be constructed and willingly shared; in reality, institutions may choose not to use comparable definitions or weights and they may restrict outsider access.

On the input side, it is proposed that we use the sum of departmental instructional salaries as the measure of aggregate professorial input. The remaining labor inputs are measured by the other departmental salaries. Measuring the use of (physical) capital is more difficult. Most institutions do not keep departmental depreciation figures, but we do have the initial market value, i.e. original prices, for installed equipment. Thus we could use some reasonable function to generate "depreciation" values for the capital used by any one department. For example, if we assume a 10-year life span on equipment, and straight-line depreciation, the annual depreciation on capital not already fully depreciated would be 10 percent of the purchase price. The space devoted to a given department could be evaluated by implicit rent figure, as determined by the commercial rental rates on (roughly) comparable office or laboratory space in the given market. Non-departmental institution expenses (upper administration, the library etc.) could be allocated *pro rata* as a function, for example, of the department's faculty full-time-equivalents (FTE) as a percentage of institutional faculty FTE. (This approach, *de facto*, means that upper administration is not being evaluated as to its B/C ratio. Such an attempt was not mandated).

An additional possibility in the modeling of departmental inputs would be to reduce "departmental costs" to the extent of any funding brought in by the department itself (i.e. by its faculty) in the form of outside grants, endowments etc.; such money would in effect offset the public funding provided. By measuring the *net* resources provided by the institution budget, the thus reduced "net departmental costs" would serve to raise the productivity indicators for the department in the modeling.

The measures of input just discussed would be used to measure total inputs in each comparable department across different institutions. The total measures of inputs, by faculty or other input, could of course also be converted into departmental averages. Indeed, if desired, the specific, individual input expenditures that aggregate to the totals could be listed.

On the output side, the procedures are similar to those used in the first model, but additional ratios are suggested. Let us take, for example, publications as the index of research productivity. Once again, the different types of publications need to be weighted by type and possibly by a (diminishing marginal) utility function. In this second model, the measure will apply to publication output by department in each of the comparator institutions. The total weighted outputs of service contracts, credit hours produced etc., each weighted by a utility function if desired, would be constructed in the analogous fashion, *mutatis mutandis*.

A final summary comparison across "analogous departments" in comparator institutions could include, for example:

- credit hours produced, weighted by level
- credit hours produced, weighted by level and a utility function
- credit hours produced/faculty FTE
- credit hours produced/dollar of cost
- credit hours produced/dollar of net cost
- (net) dollars/credit hour
- (net) dollars/degree
- (net) dollars/(weighted) publication
- (net) dollars/(weighted) public contact
- outside dollars/faculty FTE
- outside dollars/instructional dollar, etc.

WEAKNESSES OF THE MODELS AS ISSUES FOR FURTHER DELIBERATION

The intended appeal of the first approach is its simplicity, that of the second, its inclusiveness. The second model attempts to deal with some of the weaknesses specific to the first, but it thereby encounters others. Nonetheless, most of the issues raised below apply to both modeling approaches. When they do not, the references should be obvious.

In measuring faculty input, professorial salary may be an inadequate measure, as opposed, for example, to time committed, earlier education, (quality of) degrees held, prior experience, collaboration with colleagues etc. In the first model, inputs other than professorial labor are ignored.

In determining teaching productivity, what are the "correct" measures of teaching output? Number of degrees awarded, students advised, student evaluations, colleague observations, number of preparations, level at which courses are offered, etc.? Or, as suggested in both models, credit hours? If credit hours, how should they be weighted? For example, should there be weighting for the "quality" of the teaching? Who would make these judgments, and how?

As regarding research and publications, what are the item "types"—books, articles, book reviews, papers given etc.—that are to be counted and how should they be weighted relative to each other? Is the only research to be recognized that which results in publications? How should quality differences be incorporated? Who should make these judgments, and how?

Does service consist of "community contacts?" What is a "community contact?" Are there qualitative and quantitative differences that should impact on the weights? Who would make that judgment and on what basis?

Is the rationale for the use of a utility function itself convincing? (Why should a doubled output not be counted as such?) If we do wish to use a "diminishing marginal utility function, what form should it take and what parameters should it have? Should the same utility function apply in weighting teaching, research productivity, and community service?

With reference to the first model, the members of a given academic department engage in activities that have generally agreed upon parameters as to methodology and topical content. That is, the colleagues in one department in an institution compete in doing "the same thing," albeit in the different categories of research, teaching, and service. (Quite possibly they allocate different percentages of their efforts to the three.) But what happens when we seek to make productivity comparisons across departments, when, by definition, the faculties are no longer doing the same thing? Comparability issues become all the more acute when productivity is to be measured across schools within an institution and still worse when we try to include units other than the traditional teaching department, e.g., the library or upper administration. With reference to the second model, is it really true that members of "analogous" departments, say in economics, do the "same thing" in "comparable" institutions? (This is an old philosopher's conundrum—can different things ever be the same?)

On the technical level, the problem of aggregation and comparison revolves around the search for a common "unit of account." We need a measure in terms of which the magnitudes of the different activities can be added together or compared. In the absence of market prices* (see appended note) on individual professorial activities, are there any other units that would serve as the basis for aggregation? Is there any common attribute to indicate even the relative "social merit" of individual acts of teaching, research, and community service? Regrettably, there is no consensus in the literature on the economics of education. Since multiple measures are suggested, we lack the required *single, common* unit of account.

A second technical problem has to do with identifying the origin of each productive outcome. Many departments provide services for each other; how should the productivity of department A be fully recognized if its product is manifested in department B? Analogous possibilities may apply to broader units: the College of Liberal Arts and Sciences in particular provides services to other units within the institution. Still other productive outcomes may be the result of attributes of the institution that are not "caused" by any single component in it. As an example, the division of labor/interactivity/capital intensity enabled by the sheer size of most institutions may itself contribute to overall institutional productivity. If the total productivity of the entire institution is more than the sum of the productivity of the parts then how would that increment be identified and quantified? That is, if there are economies of scale that contribute to institutional productivity, there is no one segment responsible for it.

Finally, the solutions forthcoming to the issues posed above may well depend on what uses are intended (or perceived) for the data to be produced. "Success indicators" such as those we are seeking to create will themselves, once announced, be quickly recognized as incentives. The members of the institutional community—faculty, staff, and administration, and possibly students and even the general public—will be perceptive enough to quickly prefer some measurement techniques, criteria, and weights over others, quite possibly on individual, subjective grounds. Thus it is predictable that each professor will prefer those approaches—criteria and weights—that elevate the significance of what he or she likes to do and is good at doing. Furthermore, in picking criteria and weights, the institution will not only measure what faculty are doing, it will determine the

---

*The Gross Domestic Product, GDP, roughly measures that market value of the goods and services produced annually by an economy, not the efficiency with which they are produced. Nonetheless, the concept illustrates the role of the single unit of account—market price—in aggregation. The GDP measure uses such prices as weights for the volume of goods and services generated. Although universities charge nominal fees for an extended experience to students, they do not typically "sell" units of teaching, research, and community services in the conventional sense. Prices are usually not charged per event or item. When they are, they are typically not market determined. In addition, to measure productivity, i.e., the output/input ratio, a common unit of account would have to be applied to both outputs and inputs.

direction of subsequent efforts as well. That, of course, could be the intent of productivity measurement; it will certainly be perceived as such.

While there are severe problems in any attempt at quantifying the productivity of academic units, at whatever level of aggregation and whether within institutions or across them, it must also be noted that comparisons are inevitably made in any event—for tenure, promotion, and merit decisions among others.** There is a great deal of merit in stating openly how productivity measurements are made, even if the measures are flawed. The only real question is whether we will continue to tolerate administrative subterfuge under the rubric of "academic judgment" or force explicitly stated criteria and weights, whatever the limitations to openly stated rules may be.

**Promotion, tenure, and salaries will continue to be constrained by market forces, institutional budgets, the collective bargaining agreement etc., regardless of what institutional productivity measures may determine about individual contributions.